THE CAMBRIDGE COMPANION TO
GOTHIC FICTION

Gothic as a form of fiction-making has played a major role in western culture since the late eighteenth century. Here fourteen world-class experts on the Gothic provide thorough and revealing accounts of this haunting-to-horrifying type of fiction from the 1760s (the decade of *The Castle of Otranto*, the first so-called "Gothic story") to the end of the twentieth century (an era haunted by filmed and computerized Gothic simulations). Along the way, the authors explore the connections of Gothic fictions to political and industrial revolutions, the realistic novel, the theatre, Romantic and post-Romantic poetry, nationalism and racism from Europe to America, colonized and postcolonial populations, the rise of film and other visual technologies, the struggles between "high" and "popular" culture, changing psychological attitudes toward human identity, gender and sexuality, and the obscure lines between life and death, sanity and madness. The volume also includes a chronology and guides to further reading.

JERROLD E. HOGLE is Professor of English and University Distinguished Professor at the University of Arizona. He has published widely in Romantic literature, cultural theory, and the Gothic.

CAMBRIDGE COMPANIONS TO LITERATURE

CAMBRIDGE COMPANIONS TO CULTURE

THE CAMBRIDGE
COMPANION TO
GOTHIC FICTION

EDITED BY

JERROLD E. HOGLE

CAMBRIDGE
UNIVERSITY PRESS

PUBLISHED BY THE PRESS SYNDICATE OF THE UNIVERSITY OF CAMBRIDGE
The Pitt Building, Trumpington Street, Cambridge, United Kingdom

CAMBRIDGE UNIVERSITY PRESS
The Edinburgh Building, Cambridge CB2 2RU, UK
40 West 20th Street, New York, NY 10011-4211, USA
477 Williamstown Road, Port Melbourne, VIC 3207, Australia
Ruiz de Alarcón 13, 28014 Madrid, Spain
Dock House, The Waterfront, Cape Town 8001, South Africa

http://www.cambridge.org

First published 2002

Printed in the United Kingdom at the University Press, Cambridge

Typeface Sabon 10/13 pt   *System* LATEX 2$_\varepsilon$ [TB]

A catalogue record for this book is available from the British Library

Library of Congress Cataloguing in Publication data

Cambridge companion to gothic fiction / edited by Jerrold E. Hogle.
p.   cm. – (Cambridge companions to literature)
Includes bibliographical references and index.
ISBN 0 521 79124 3 (hardback) – ISBN 0 521 79466 8 (paperback)
1. Horror tales, English – History and criticism.   2. Horror tales, American – History and
criticism.   3. Gothic revival (Literature) – United States.   4. Gothic revival (Literature) –
Great Britain.   I. Hogle, Jerrold E.   II. Series.
PR830.T3 C36   2002
823'.0872909 – dc21   2002020172

ISBN 0 521 79124 3 hardback
ISBN 0 521 79466 8 paperback

CONTENTS

FIGURES

CONTRIBUTORS

FRED BOTTING is Professor of English at Keele University in England and editor of the Macmillan New Casebook on *Frankenstein,* among other volumes. He is also the author of *Making Monstrous:* Frankenstein, *Criticism, Theory* (Manchester University Press), *Gothic* in the New Critical Idioms series (Routledge), and *Sex, Machines, and Navels: Fiction, Fantasy, and History in the Future Present* (Manchester University Press).

STEVEN BRUHM is Associate Professor of English at Mount Saint Vincent University in Halifax, Nova Scotia, a contributing guest editor for *Gothic Studies,* and the current president of the International Gothic Association. He is also the author of *Gothic Bodies: the Politics of Pain in Romantic Fiction* (University of Pennsylvania Press) and *Reflecting Narcissus: a Queer Aesthetic* (University of Minnesota Press), which includes his "The Gothic in a Culture of Narcissism."

E. J. CLERY is Senior Lecturer in English Studies at Sheffield Hallam University, where she directs the Corvey Library Project on British Women's Writing. She is also the author of *The Rise of Supernatural Fiction, 1762–1800* (Cambridge University Press) and *Women's Gothic: from Clara Reeve to Mary Shelley* (Northcote House), as well as coeditor of the collection *Gothic Documents: a Sourcebook, 1700–1820* (Manchester University Press).

JEFFREY N. COX is Professor of English and Comparative Literature at the University of Colorado, Boulder, and the editor of *Seven Gothic Dramas, 1789–1825* (Ohio University Press). He is also the author of *In the Shadows of Romance: Romantic Tragic Drama in Germany, England, and France* (Ohio University Press) and *Poetry and Politics in the Cockney School: Shelley, Keats, Hunt, and their Circle* (Cambridge University Press).

MICHAEL GAMER is Associate Professor of English at the University of Pennsylvania and has authored several articles on the Gothic's interactions with drama, poetry, and the historical novel in journals ranging from *English Language History* and *College English* to *Studies in Romanticism* and *Publications of the Modern Language Association*. His *Romanticism and the Gothic: Genre, Reception, and Canon Formation* has been published by Cambridge University Press, and his edition of Walpole's *Castle of Otranto* has recently appeared from Penguin Classics.

TERRY HALE is the British Academy Research Fellow in the Translation Performance Centre of the Department of Drama at the University of Hull. He has published numerous editions and translations of non-English Gothic texts from the eighteenth through the twentieth centuries and is the editor and cotranslator of *The Dedalus Book of French Horror: the Nineteenth Century*.

JERROLD E. HOGLE is Professor of English and University Distinguished Professor at the University of Arizona. He is also a past president of the International Gothic Association and guest editor for two issues of its new journal, *Gothic Studies*. In addition to his books on Romantic poetry – most notably *Shelley's Process* (Oxford University Press) – he has authored numerous essays on Gothic fiction from *The Castle of Otranto* to *Dracula*. His book on the whole history and cultural significance of *The Phantom of the Opera* has recently been published by St. Martin's Press/Palgrave.

KELLY HURLEY is Associate Professor of English at the University of Colorado, Boulder, and author of *The Gothic Body: Sexuality, Materialism, and Degeneration at the* Fin de Siècle (Cambridge University Press).

MISHA KAVKA is Lecturer in Film, Television, and Media Studies at the University of Aukland, New Zealand. She is the coeditor, with Elisabeth Bronfen, of *Feminist Consequences: Theory for the New Century* (Columbia University Press) and has published articles on the history of male hysteria and on gender, sexuality, and technology in Hollywood films.

ALISON MILBANK is Associate Professor of English at the University of Virginia and the editor of two novels by Ann Radcliffe for the Oxford World's Classics series. She is also the author of *Daughters of the House: Modes of Gothic in Victorian Fiction* (Macmillan) and *Dante and the Victorians* (Manchester University Press/St. Martin's).

ROBERT MILES is Professor of English Studies at the University of Stirling in Scotland, the immediate past president of the International Gothic Association, editor-in-chief of *Gothic Studies*, and the other coeditor of *Gothic Documents*. His many publications include *Gothic Writing, 1750–1820: a Genealogy* (Macmillan) and *Ann Radcliffe: the Great Enchantress* (Manchester University Press).

LIZABETH PARAVISINI-GEBERT is Professor of Caribbean Literature and Culture and the Director of Latin American Studies at Vassar College, as well as the author of *Phyllis Shand Allfrey: a Caribbean Life* (Rutgers University Press), *Jamaica Kincaid: a Critical Companion* (Greenwood Press), and cocompiler of *Caribbean Women Novelists: an Annotated Critical Bibliography* (also Greenwood Press). The many volumes which she has coedited include *Sacred Possessions: Vodou, Santeria, Obeah, and the Caribbean* (Rutgers University Press) and *Women at Sea: Travel Writing and the Margins of Caribbean Discourse* (St. Martin's/Palgrave).

DAVID PUNTER is Professor of English at the University of Bristol and editor of *A Companion to the Gothic* in the Blackwell Companions series. He is widely noted for his work on Gothic, particularly in *The Literature of Terror: a History of Gothic Fictions from 1765 to the Present Day* (Longman, revised in two volumes) and *Gothic Pathologies: the Text, the Body, and the Law* (Macmillan), as well as for *The Hidden Script: Writing and the Unconscious* (Routledge) and his two most recent books, *Postcolonial Imaginings: Fictions of a New World Order* (Edinburgh University Press) and *Writing the Passions* (Longman).

ERIC SAVOY is Associate Professor of English at the Université de Montréal in Canada and coeditor of *American Gothic: New Interventions in a National Narrative* (University of Iowa Press), which includes his important "The Face of the Tenant: a Theory of American Gothic." He has also published recently on Henry James and queer theory, Nathaniel Hawthorne and psychoanalysis, and American cinema of the 1950s.

PREFACE

This collection strives to introduce undergraduate students and other interested readers to the development and major works of the "Gothic" tradition in fiction, which in this case encompasses prose fiction, some poetry, writings for the stage, many films, and even recent videos and computer games. Inside the frame of an opening chapter that places the Gothic – while also defining it – within the larger needs and quandaries of western culture since the middle of the eighteenth century, each chapter by an expert scholar analyzes a specific historical span or type of Gothic fiction-making to explain the underlying drives and major advances in the works that are most exemplary of the Gothic at that time and in particular locations. The closing chapter then looks back at the progression made in the Gothic tradition from its earlier forms to its most recent manifestations, a stretch of nearly 250 years, thereby reassessing the cultural functions of the Gothic from the perspective of the beginning of the twenty-first century. The result, all the contributors hope, is both a history of the Gothic that is helpful in the reading or viewing of many such fictions and a revelation of the cultural functions that the Gothic was created to serve, and then the different ones it has proceeded to serve, across the three centuries that constitute the modern western world. The longings and anxieties of modern western civilization are brought out in the Gothic as in no other fictional medium, and this volume has been compiled with a view to playing a major role in helping students understand how that has happened and why it has happened differently in different periods and in the many forms taken by this most haunting of symbolic modes.

As this book has come together its editor has found himself grateful to many colleagues, most of all to each of the contributors, every one of whom has given considerable effort and extraordinary knowledge to this project. Working with them – and on this subject – has been a privilege. All the contributors further appreciate the support provided by our home institutions, as well as several of our students. We are especially beholden for extensive, helpful work to the Graduate Associates on this project, Ron Gard and Jay

Salisbury, research assistants to the editor, and to literature editors Linda Bree and Rachel de Wachter at Cambridge University Press, two incisive, wise, and considerate professional guides for this and other Companions. We also thank the initial outside readers of our book for their savvy suggestions and proudly celebrate our debts to the many authors, directors, and computer wizards who have made the Gothic the vibrant form it has been and continues to be. We hope we have returned all these favors by defining and explaining the Gothic with special precision so that its unique history and cultural value can be understood more completely than ever before.

1750   Horace Walpole, with Richard Bentley, begins redesign of
        Strawberry Hill in Twickenham, England, as part of a "Gothic
        revival" in architecture.

1757   Thomas Gray publishes *Odes*, including "The Bard," from the
        Strawberry Hill press; Edmund Burke publishes *A Philosophical
        Enquiry into the Origin of Our Ideas of the Sublime and
        Beautiful*, connecting sublimity to terror.

1759   Edward Young, author of *Night Thoughts* (1742–45) in the
        "Graveyard School" of poetry, publishes *Conjectures on
        Original Composition*.

1760   George III crowned King of England; James Macpherson's forged
        medieval *Ossian* poems begin appearing in Britain, culminating
        in the volumes of 1762 and 1763.

1762   Richard Hurd publishes *Letters on Chivalry and Romance*,
        while Thomas Warton brings out second edition of *Observations
        on the Fairie Queene*.

1763   The Seven Years' War between France and England ends; death
        of the Abbé Prévost, influential historical-adventure novelist,
        in France.

1764   *The Castle of Otranto* published in England by Walpole
        (December); reissued in 1765 with a new preface and subtitle
        A Gothic Story.

1768   Walpole composes Gothic play *The Mysterious Mother*
        (not staged; finally published in 1791 after years of private
        circulation).

1773   John and Anna Laetitia Aikin publish Gothic fragment
        "Sir Bertram" with essay "On the Pleasure Derived from Objects
        of Terror."

1775   The American War of Independence begins.

1777 Clara Reeve publishes *The Champion of Virtue*, reissued in 1778 as *The Old English Baron*.

1781 Robert Jephson's play *The Count of Narbonne*, an adaptation of *The Castle of Otranto*, produced at Covent Garden in London; Friedrich Schiller's *Die Räuber* (*The Robbers*) first staged in Germany.

1783 First volume of Sophia Lee's *The Recess* published (finished in 1785); American War of Independence ends.

1786 William Beckford publishes the "oriental Gothic" *Vathek* in Paris.

1789 Ann Radcliffe publishes *The Castles of Athlin and Dunbayne*, her first "romance," anonymously; Schiller's *Der Geisterseher* published unfinished in Germany; the fall of the Bastille in Paris; French Revolution begins.

1790 Radcliffe publishes *The Romance of the Forest*, acknowledges authorship in second edition (1792); Burke publishes *Reflections on the Revolution in France*.

1791 Hans Christian Spiess publishes his "spirit tale" *Das Petermännchen* in Germany (translated in 1792 as *The Dwarf of Westerbourg*).

1792 Mary Wollstonecraft publishes *A Vindication of the Rights of Woman*.

1793 Beheading of Louis XVI in Paris; Reign of Terror in full cry.

1794 Radcliffe publishes *The Mysteries of Udolpho*; William Godwin publishes *Things as They Are; or the Adventures of Caleb Williams*; Christiane Naubert's *Hermann von Unna* (1778) first translated, bringing the *Ritterroman* to England; James Boaden's *Fountainville Forest* (adapted from Radcliffe's *Romance*) staged at Covent Garden.

1795 Mercier de Compiègne publishes *Les Nuits de la conciergerie* in Paris; *Der Geisterseher* translated as *The Ghost-Seer*, accelerating the importation of the *Schauerroman* into Britain.

1796 M. G. Lewis publishes *The Monk* the same year he enters Parliament; Mary Robinson publishes Gothic novel *Hubert de Sevrac*; Beckford satirizes Radcliffean Gothic in *Modern Novel Writing* and *Azemia* (1797); Reveroni Saint-Cyr publishes *Pauliska* in Paris.

1797 S. T. Coleridge reviews *The Monk* and brings his *Osorio* to the stage; Radcliffe publishes *The Italian*, partly in response to Lewis; William Wordsworth's semi-Gothic play *The Borderers* first staged; Mary Wollstonecraft's *The Wrongs of Woman* published soon after her death at the birth of her daughter Mary; Walpole, now Earl of Orford, dies; Lewis's play *The Castle Spectre* debuts at London's Drury Lane.

1798   Wordsworth and Coleridge publish the first edition of *Lyrical Ballads*; Charles Brockden Brown publishes *Wieland* in Philadelphia.

1799   Godwin publishes *St. Leon: a Tale of the Sixteenth Century*; Brown publishes *Edgar Huntly*; Napoleon Bonaparte made Consul in France, marking the end of the French Revolution; Georges Leopold Cuvier founds comparative anatomy in Paris.

1800   The largest single year yet for number of Gothic novels published in England; Mary Robinson publishes *Lyrical Tales*; Joanna Baillie's play *De Montfort* staged at Drury Lane; J. B. I. P. Regnault-Warin publishes *Le Cimetière de la Madeleine* in France; second edition of *Lyrical Ballads* published, including Wordsworth's anti-Gothic "Preface"; Charlotte Smith publishes semi-Gothic "Story of Henrietta," set in Jamaica; Napoleon invades Austria, and Napoleonic Wars accelerate across Europe.

1805   Charlotte Dacre publishes *Zofloya, or The Moor*; Walter Scott publishes long poem *The Lay of the Last Minstrel*.

1807   C. R. Maturin publishes *The Fatal Revenge*; the Marquis de Sade issues "Ideas on the Novel"; slave trade (but not slave-owning) banned in the British Empire; British armies invade Egypt.

1810   P. B. Shelley publishes Gothic novels *Zastrozzi* and *St. Irvyne*.

1813   Coleridge's *Remorse* staged at Drury Lane; Lord Byron publishes *The Giaour*.

1815   Napoleon defeated at Waterloo and exiled; France bans slave trade; E. T. A. Hoffmann's "The Sandman" first appears in Germany.

1816   Maturin's play *Bertram* staged at Drury Lane; Scott publishes *The Antiquary*; the Shelleys, Dr. John Polidori, and Byron near Geneva begin "ghost story contest" that results in *Frankenstein* and Polidori's *The Vampyre* a few years later.

1817   Byron's Gothic "Dramatic Poem" *Manfred* published.

1818   Mary Wollstonecraft Shelley publishes *Frankenstein* anonymously; Thomas Love Peacock publishes satirical *Nightmare Abbey*; Jane Austen's counter-Gothic *Northanger Abbey* published after her death the previous year (though written mostly in the late 1790s); Collin de Plancy publishes the *Dictionnaire infernal* in France.

1819   P. B. Shelley's Gothic play *The Cenci* published but not staged; Scott publishes *The Bride of Lammermoor*; Polidori's *Vampyre* appears under Byron's name.

1820   Maturin publishes *Melmoth the Wanderer*; Charles Nodier coadapts Polidori's tale for the French stage, while Jean Planche's *Vampyre* is being performed at the English Opera House.

1821   Death of Napoleon; Nodier publishes *Smarra, or The Demons of the Night* in Paris, inaugurating *l'école frénétique* in French writing: Collin de Plancy publishes semi-Gothic *Anecdotes du dix-neuvième siècle*; Vicomte d'Alincourt publishes *Le Solitaire*, spawning many translations in the 1820s.

1823   Richard Brinsley Peake's *Presumption, or The Fate of Frankenstein* staged at the English Opera House (Mary Shelley attends); Victor Hugo publishes frequently Gothic *Hans d'Islande* in France.

1824   James Hogg publishes *The Private Memoirs and Confessions of a Justified Sinner* in Scotland and England.

1827   *Hamel, the Obeah Man* published anonymously, set in Jamaica, and focused on Gothicized Obeah magic and slave rebellion.

1829   Henri de Latouche publishes *Fragoletta* in Paris.

1830   G. P. R. James publishes *Darnley* in London; *Blackwood's Magazine* publishes "The Iron Shroud," later to influence Poe's "The Pit and the Pendulum" (1839).

1831   The autobiographical *History of Mary Prince* published in Barbados to begin series of Caribbean slave narratives that employ or echo Gothic conventions.

1835   Edgar Allan Poe begins a series of Gothic stories in Baltimore that come to include "Berenice," "Ligeia," and "The Fall of the House of Usher," all collected in *Tales of the Arabesque and Grotesque* (1839).

1836   Theophile Gautier publishes *La Morte amoureuse*, a vampire tale, in Paris.

1837   Charles Dickens begins serializing *Oliver Twist*; Victoria becomes Queen of England; Victor Sejour's African-American Gothic tale "The Mulatto" appears in France.

1840   W. H. Ainsworth in England begins his "Tudor novels" series with *The Tower of London*, followed by *Guy Fawkes* (1841) and *Windsor Castle* (1843); Dickens begins serializing *The Old Curiosity Shop*.

1844   Britain's W. M. Reynolds begins his Gothic-laden narrative *The Mysteries of London* (serialized until 1856), based on Eugène Sue's *Mysteries of Paris* (1842–43); the "Urban Gothic" thus fully established.

1845   Poe publishes "The Raven" and a second volume of *Tales*; dies in 1849.

1847   Charlotte Brontë publishes *Jane Eyre* and Emily Brontë publishes *Wuthering Heights*, both under male pseudonyms (Emily dies in 1848); Thomas Preskett publishes *Varney the Vampire, or The Feast of Blood*.

1848   Revolution in France brings Napoleon III to power; leads to Second Empire (through 1869).

1850   Nathaniel Hawthorne publishes *The Scarlet Letter*, including "The Custom House" (quite Gothic).

1851   Hawthorne publishes *The House of Seven Gables*.

1852   Dickens begins serializing *Bleak House*; Harriet Beecher Stowe publishes occasionally Gothic *Uncle Tom's Cabin*; Herman Melville publishes *Pierre, or The Ambiguities*, his most Gothic novel.

1853   Charlotte Brontë publishes frequently Gothic *Villette*.

1855   Dickens begins serializing *Little Dorrit*; Charlotte Brontë dies; Gérard de Nerval publishes *Aurelia* in France.

1859   Gothic story collection *The Haunted House* published in Dickens's journal *All the Year Round*; Edward Bulwer-Lytton publishes essay "The Haunted and the Haunters"; Charles Darwin publishes *The Origin of Species*.

1860–61   Dickens serializes *Great Expectations*; Wilkie Collins publishes *The Woman in White*; Hawthorne publishes *The Marble Faun*; American Civil War begins (leading to Emancipation Proclamation in 1863 and surrender of the South in 1865).

1864   J. S. Le Fanu publishes novel *Uncle Silas*.

1868   Collins publishes *The Moonstone*, shading the Gothic into the detective story and vice versa.

1870   Dickens dies, leaving the incomplete (and Gothic) *Mystery of Edwin Drood*; Third Republic launched in France.

1871   Darwin's *The Descent of Man* appears, and evolution debates accelerate.

1872   Le Fanu publishes collection *In a Glass Darkly*, including female vampire tale "Carmilla"; dies in 1873.

1881	Marcus Clarke publishes his Australian Gothic novella, *The Mystery of Major Molineux*.
1884	British and French women granted rights of divorce, raising increased concerns about the greater independence of women.
1885	The Labouchère Amendment passed in England, more strongly criminalizing homosexuality.
1886	Robert Louis Stevenson publishes *Strange Case of Dr. Jekyll and Mr. Hyde* to complete his most Gothic period (1881–86); Guy de Maupassant publishes novella *The Horla* in France; H. Rider Haggard begins publishing *She*.
1890	Arthur Machen publishes *The Great God Pan* in Britain; Rudyard Kipling publishes "The Mark of the Beast," his most Gothic story; Oscar Wilde publishes *The Picture of Dorian Gray* in *Lippincott's Magazine* (with expanded version in book form in 1891).
1891	Charlotte Perkins Gilman publishes "The Yellow Wallpaper" in the *New England Magazine*.
1895	Sigmund Freud and C. F. Breuer publish *Studies in Hysteria* in Austria, more fully establishing psychoanalyis; Wilde prosecuted and imprisoned for homosexuality in England; Machen publishes *The Three Imposters*; M. R. James begins series of Gothic stories with "Canon Alberic's Scrapbook."
1896	H. G. Wells publishes *The Island of Dr. Moreau*.
1897	Irish-born Bram Stoker publishes novel *Dracula* at Westminster; Richard Marsh publishes *The Beetle*.
1898	Henry James serializes *The Turn of the Screw* in *Collier's* magazine.
1899	Dick Donovan publishes *Tales of Terror* in Britain.
1900	Freud's *Interpretation of Dreams* first appears as *Die Traumdeutung*.
1903	Stoker publishes *The Jewel of the Seven Stars*, and Frank Aubrey publishes *King of the Dead*; Queen Victoria dies.
1907	William Hope Hodgson publishes *The Boats of the "Glen Carrig"*.
1908	Henry James publishes "The Jolly Corner" after a short return to America.
1910	Gaston Leroux publishes *Le Fantôme de l'Opéra* in Paris.
1911	Stoker publishes *The Lair of the White Worm*.
1912	Hodgson publishes *The Night Land*.
1914	First World War begins; Alice and Claude Askew publish "Alymer Vance and the Vampire."

1918   First World War ends with Treaty of Versailles; partial suffrage granted to women in Britain (and in the United States by 1919).

1919   Freud publishes "The Uncanny," followed shortly by *Beyond the Pleasure Principle* (1820), which posits a "death wish."

1922   F. W. Murnau's film *Nosferatu*, based on *Dracula*, released in Germany.

1925   Universal Studios releases silent *Phantom of the Opera* with Lon Chaney.

1929   Stock market crash begins Great Depression in the Americas and Europe; Herbert George De Lisser publishes *The White Witch of Rosehall*, a West Indian Gothic tale based on legends about plantation mistress Annie Palmer.

1931   Universal releases *Dracula* with Bela Lugosi and *Frankenstein* with Colin Clive and Boris Karloff; Paramount releases *Dr. Jekyll and Mr. Hyde*, which wins Academy Award for star Fredric March.

1932   William Faulkner publishes *Light in August*; Universal releases *The Mummy* with Boris Karloff and *Dracula's Daughter*; United Artists releases *White Zombie*, directed by Victor Halperin and set in Haiti.

1934   Karen Blixen publishes *Seven Gothic Tales* under the pen name "Isak Dinesen."

1935   Universal releases James Whale's *Bride of Frankenstein* with Boris Karloff and Colin Clive, as well as Louis Friedlander's *The Raven*.

1936   Faulkner publishes *Absalom! Absalom!*, for many his most Gothic novel.

1938   Daphne du Maurier publishes *Rebecca*, adapted for the screen in 1939–40 in Alfred Hitchcock's American directing debut (Academy Award winner for Best Picture of 1940).

1939   Second World War begins with German invasion of Poland; Universal releases *Son of Frankenstein*.

1941   Universal releases *The Wolf Man* with Lon Chaney Jr.; *Dr. Jekyll and Mr. Hyde* remade by MGM, with Spencer Tracy; Pearl Harbor bombed by Japan in December, bringing the US into the war.

1942   Jacques Tourneur's *Cat People* film released by RKO.

1943   Universal releases its sound-and-color remake of *Phantom of the Opera*; RKO releases Tourneur's *I Walked with a Zombie*.

1944   Paramount releases Lewis Allen's *The Uninvited*.

1945   Surrender of the Axis powers ends Second World War; women released from the work force in large numbers; "Baby Boom" begins; RKO makes *The Spiral Staircase* for release in 1946.

1950   Paramount releases Billy Wilder's highly Gothic *Sunset Boulevard*.

1957   Hammer Studios in England begins its Gothic film revival by releasing *The Curse of Frankenstein*.

1958   Vincent Price stars in popular William Castle film *House on Haunted Hill*, which was shown with the "Emergo" gimmick, whereby a skeleton suddenly sails out over the audience.

1959   Shirley Jackson publishes *The Haunting of Hill House*, later to become *The Haunting* on film (1963); Robert Bloch publishes the novella on which Hitchcock bases his Gothic film *Psycho* (1960).

1960   Roger Corman begins Poe film series with *The House of Usher*, again starring Vincent Price; MGM releases Wolf Rilla's *Village of the Damned*; Haitian Jacques-Stephan Alexis publishes "Chronique d'un faux amour" in Paris.

1966   Jean Rhys publishes *Wide Sargasso Sea*, a rewriting of parts of *Jane Eyre* from a Jamaican and postcolonial female perspective.

1967   Ira Levin publishes *Rosemary's Baby* (released by Paramount in 1968 as a film directed by Roman Polanski).

1971   William Peter Blatty publishes *The Exorcist* (released as a film in 1973, directed by William Friedkin).

1973   United States leaves Vietnam, ending long western presence in Southeast Asia.

1974   Stephen King starts Gothic best-seller run with *Carrie* (film version in 1976, directed by Brian de Palma).

1975   First release of *The Rocky Horror Picture Show* film, based on an earlier *Rocky Horror Show* on the London stage (itself revived in 2000). V. S. Naipaul publishes *Guerrillas*, a Caribbean recasting of *Wuthering Heights*.

1976   Anne Rice publishes *Interview with the Vampire* to begin series of Gothic novels, most often set in New Orleans and Paris (*Interview* film: 1994); David Seltzer publishes *The Omen* (released as a film the same year).

1977   Stephen King publishes *The Shining*, filmed by Stanley Kubrick in 1979–80.

1979   Peter Straub publishes *Ghost Story* (turned into film in 1984); first *Alien* film, directed by Ridley Scott, released by 20th-Century Fox; Angela Carter publishes her *Bloody Chamber* collection of stories.

1980   David Punter publishes *The Literature of Terror*, heralding
        an acceleration in the academic study of Gothic.

1982   Julia Kristeva's *Powers of Horror* (1980) translated into English;
        release of Ridley Scott's futuristic Gothic film *Blade Runner*;
        MGM and Steven Spielberg release *Poltergeist*, an epitome of the
        suburban Gothic; Joyce Carol Oates publishes *The Bloodsmoor
        Romance*; King publishes *Danse Macabre*, a nonfiction
        assessment of the cultural functions of modern Gothic horror;
        Michael Jackson produces and stars in ghoulish music video
        Thriller.

1985   Gloria Naylor publishes African-American Gothic novel
        Linden Hills.

1986   Andrew Lloyd Webber's stage musical version of *The Phantom
        of the Opera* opens in London, then moves to New York in late
        1987 as further adaptations increase; release of David Lynch's
        semi-Gothic film *Blue Velvet.*

1987   Toni Morrison publishes novel *Beloved* (Pulitzer Prize, 1988;
        film, 1998); Haitian Pierre Clitandre publishes voudo-laden
        Cathédrale du mois d'août.

1988   René Depestre publishes *Hadriana dans tous mes rêves,*
        interweaving zombification with reflections on Haitian history.

1990   Debut of Lynch's highly Gothic television series *Twin Peaks*
        on ABC.

1991   Mayra Montero begins sequence of Haitian Gothic fictions with
        "Corinne, Amiable Girl," soon to be followed by *The Red of his
        Shadow* (1992) and *In the Palm of Darkness* (1995).

1992   Release of *Bram Stoker's Dracula*, directed by Francis Ford
        Coppola.

1993   Debut of Chris Carter's frequently Gothic *The X-Files* series
        on FOX-TV.

1994   Carol Oates publishes *Haunted: Tales of the Grotesque.*

1995   Jamaica Kincaid publishes her Gothically inflected *Autobiography
        of my Mother.*

1997   Paramount releases *Event Horizon*, and 20th-Century Fox
        releases *Alien Resurrection*, the fourth film in the *Alien* series.

1998   Remake of *The House on Haunted Hill*, with Geoffrey Rush,
        released; color reworking of *The Haunting* released as well.

2000   Peter Straub publishes *Magic Terror: Seven Tales.*

2001   Full-blown Gothic reappears on film in *The Others*, with Nicole
        Kidman.

I

JERROLD E. HOGLE

Introduction: the Gothic in western culture

Gothic fiction is hardly "Gothic" at all. It is an entirely post-medieval and even post-Renaissance phenomenon. Even though several long-standing literary forms combined in its initial renderings – from ancient prose and verse romances to Shakespearean tragedy *and* comedy – the first published work to call itself "A Gothic Story" was a counterfeit medieval tale published long after the Middle Ages: Horace Walpole's *The Castle of Otranto*, printed under a pseudonym in England in 1764 and reissued in 1765 in a second edition with a new preface which openly advocated a "blend [of] the two kinds of romance, the ancient and the modern," the former "all imagination and improbability" and the latter governed by the "rules of probability" connected with "common life" (p. 9). The vogue that Walpole began was imitated only sporadically over the next few decades, both in prose fiction and theatrical drama. But it exploded in the 1790s (the decade Walpole died) throughout the British Isles, on the continent of Europe, and briefly in the new United States, particularly for a female readership, so much so that it remained a popular, if controversial, literary mode throughout what we still call the Romantic period in European literature (the 1790s through the early 1830s), now especially well known as the era of Mary Shelley's *Frankenstein* (1818).

This highly unstable genre then scattered its ingredients into various modes, among them aspects of the more realistic Victorian novel.[1] Yet it also reasserted itself across the nineteenth century in flamboyant plays and scattered operas, short stories or fantastic tales for magazines and newspapers, "sensation" novels for women and the literate working class, portions of poetry or painting, and substantial resurgences of full-fledged Gothic novels – all of which were satirized for their excesses, as they had also been in Romantic times, now that the Gothic mode had become relatively familiar.[2] Like the 1790s, the 1890s, still known today as the *fin de siècle*, then saw a concentrated resurgence of Gothic fiction, particularly in prose narrative, highlighted by such now-classic "Gothics" as Oscar Wilde's *The Picture of Dorian Gray* (1890–91), Charlotte Perkins Gilman's "The Yellow Wallpaper" (1892), Bram Stoker's original *Dracula* (1897), and Henry James's serialized novella *The Turn of the Screw* (1898). The 1900s finally saw the Gothic expand across the widest range in its history, into films, myriad ghost stories, a vast strand of women's romance novels, television shows and series, romantic and satirical musical (as well as nonmusical) plays, and computerized games and music videos, not to mention ongoing attempts at serious fiction with many Gothic elements. The late twentieth century has even seen a burgeoning in the academic *study* of Gothic fiction at college and university levels and in publications connected to them. There is now no question that the Gothic, particularly in prose or verse narrative, theatre, and film – all of which we here encompass in the phrase "Gothic fiction" – has become a long-lasting and major, albeit widely variable, symbolic realm in modern and even postmodern western culture, however archaic the Gothic label may make it seem.

Our objectives here are to explain the reasons for the persistence of the Gothic across modern history and how and why so many changes and variations have occurred in this curious mode over 250 years. One difficulty in doing so, of course, is how pliable and malleable this type of fiction-making has proven to be, stemming as it does from an uneasy conflation of genres, styles, and conflicted cultural concerns from its outset. Nevertheless, given how relatively constant some of its features are, we can specify some general parameters by which fictions can be identified as primarily or substantially Gothic.[3] Though not always as obviously as in *The Castle of Otranto* or *Dracula*, a Gothic tale usually takes place (at least some of the time) in an antiquated or seemingly antiquated space – be it a castle, a foreign palace, an abbey, a vast prison, a subterranean crypt, a graveyard, a primeval frontier or island, a large old house or theatre, an aging city or urban underworld, a decaying storehouse, factory, laboratory, public building, or some new recreation of an older venue, such as an office with old filing cabinets, an overworked spaceship, or a computer memory. Within this space, or a combination of such spaces, are hidden some secrets from the past (sometimes the recent past) that haunt the characters, psychologically, physically, or otherwise at the main time of the story.

These hauntings can take many forms, but they frequently assume the features of ghosts, specters, or monsters (mixing features from different realms of being, often life and death) that rise from within the antiquated space, or sometimes invade it from alien realms, to manifest unresolved crimes or conflicts that can no longer be successfully buried from view. It is at this level that Gothic fictions generally play with and oscillate between the earthly laws of conventional reality and the possibilities of the supernatural – at least somewhat as Walpole urged such stories to do – often siding with one of these over the other in the end, but usually raising the possibility that the boundaries between these may have been crossed, at least psychologically but also physically or both. This oscillation can range across a continuum between what have come to be called the "terror Gothic" on the one hand and the "horror Gothic" on the other.[4] The first of these holds characters and readers mostly in anxious suspense about threats to life, safety, and sanity kept largely out of sight or in shadows or suggestions from a hidden past, while the latter confronts the principal characters with the gross violence of physical or psychological dissolution, explicitly shattering the assumed norms (including the repressions) of everyday life with wildly shocking, and even revolting, consequences.

The readership or audience of all such Gothics began as and remains mostly middle-class and Anglo, though more kinds of audiences (postcolonial, African-American, American Indian, and Latin American, for example) have been drawn in over the years. Given that fact, Gothic fictions since Walpole have most often been about aspiring but middling, or sometimes upper middle-class, white people caught between the attractions or terrors of a past once controlled by overweening aristocrats or priests (or figures with such aspirations) and forces of change that would reject such a past yet still remain held by aspects of it (including desires for aristocratic or superhuman powers). This tug-of-war affects central characters and readers alike, frequently drawing them toward what is initially "unconscious" in at least two different senses. It can force them, first, to confront what is psychologically buried in individuals or groups, including their fears of the mental unconscious itself and the desires from the past now buried in that forgotten location. After all, several features of the Gothic, especially as practiced in the mid-nineteenth century by Edgar Allan Poe in America and the *romans frénétiques* (or "frenetic novels") in France,[5] eventually became a basis for Sigmund Freud's *fin de siècle* sense of the unconscious as a deep repository of very old, infantile, and repressed memories or impulses, the archaic underworld of the self.

At the same time, the conflicted positions of central Gothic characters can reveal them as haunted by a second "unconscious" of deep-seated social and historical dilemmas, often of many types at once, that become more fearsome the more characters and readers attempt to cover them up or reconcile them symbolically without resolving them fundamentally. The title character in the original *Frankenstein*, for example, finds that his sexless fabrication of an artificial creature, ultimately his "monster," from pieces of bodies in graveyards and charnel houses confronts him with two kinds of unconscious: his own preconscious dreams of reembracing, even as he recoils from the body of his dead mother (his psychic unconscious; Shelley, *Frankenstein*, p. 85), and the choices simmering at the subliminal levels of his culture (in his *political* unconscious) between the attractions of old alchemy and modern biochemistry, strictly biological and emergent mechanical reproduction, the centrality and marginality of women, and middle-class scientific aims set against the rise of a "monstrous" urban working class upon which bourgeois aspiration is increasingly dependent.[6] It is no wonder that the late twentieth-century effulgence in teaching and writing about Gothic fictions has been dominated either by psychoanalytic readings of such creations or by Marxist, new historicist, or cultural studies assessments that find many class-based, ideological, and even technological conflicts of particular historical times underlying the spectral or monstrous manifestations in Gothic works from several different eras. As this book will often show, therefore, the longevity and power of Gothic fiction unquestionably stem from the way it helps us address and disguise some of the most important desires, quandaries, and sources of anxiety, from the most internal and mental to the widely social and cultural, throughout the history of western culture since the eighteenth century.

In general, these deep fears and longings in western readers that the Gothic both symbolizes and disguises in "romantic" and exaggerated forms have been ones that so *contradict* each other, and in such intermingled ways, that only extreme fictions of this kind can seem to resolve them or even confront them. As E. J. Clery and Robert Miles recall in this volume, the early Gothic (or really fake *neo*-Gothic) for Walpole and his most immediate successors sees its characters and readers as torn between the enticing call of aristocratic wealth and sensuous Catholic splendor, beckoning back toward the Middle Ages and the Renaissance, on the one hand, and a desire to overthrow these past orders of authority in favor of a quasi-equality associated with the rising middle-class ideology of the self as self-made, on the other – but an ideology haunted by the Protestant bourgeois desire to *attain* the power of the older orders that the middle class wants to dethrone. Such a paradoxical state of longing in much of the post-Renaissance western psyche fears retribution from all the extremes it tries to encompass, especially from remnants of those very old heights of dominance which the middle class now strives to grasp and displace at the same time. As a result, in the words of Leslie Fiedler,

> the guilt which underlies [much early, Romantic, and even American] gothic and motivates its plots is the guilt of the revolutionary haunted by the (paternal) past which he has been trying to destroy; and the fear that possesses the gothic and motivates its tone is the fear that in destroying the old ego-ideals of Church

and State, the West has opened a way for the inruption of darkness: for [cultural and individual] insanity and the [consequent] disintegration of the self.

(Fiedler, "Invention of the American Gothic," p. 129)

Here is why, Fiedler and others have shown, the features of the Anglo-European-American Gothic have helped to prefigure and shape Freud's notion of Oedipal conflict in the middle-class family. In some way the Gothic is usually about some "son" both wanting to kill and striving to be the "father" and thus feeling fearful and guilty about what he most desires, all of which applies as well to Gothic *heroines* who seek both to appease and to free themselves from the excesses of male and patriarchal dominance in Sophia Lee's *The Recess* (1783–85), Ann Radcliffe's romances of the 1790s, Charlotte Brontë's *Jane Eyre* (1847), and many "female Gothics" thereafter.[7] Beneath this tangle of contradictions, moreover, is the deeper lingering fear for readers of the Gothic that Fiedler recognizes: the terror or possible horror that the ruination of older powers will haunt us all, not just with our desires for them, but with the fact that what "grounds" them, and now their usurpers, is really a deathly chaos. Beneath his quest to manufacture life, after all, Victor Frankenstein confronts a desire to reunite with his dead mother and somehow engender artificial life from her and his biological decay. Through the Gothic, we remind ourselves, albeit in disguise, that something like a return to the confusion and loss of identity in being half-inside and half-outside the mother, and thus neither entirely dead nor clearly alive, may await us behind any old foundation, paternal or otherwise, on which we try, by breaking it up, to build a brave new world (see Kahane, "Gothic Mirror" and Kristeva, *Powers of Horror*).

This pattern of hyperbolically verbalizing contradictory fears and desires over a possible "base" of chaos and death, and in a blatantly fictional style, remains a consistent element in the Gothic even as the terms and features of this combination change with the transformations of western society in the nineteenth and twentieth centuries. By the time of *Frankenstein,* the many dilemmas for its hero stem from alterations in the anatomical, electrical, and chemical sciences *and* the acceleration of an industrial revolution that may lead to the greater mechanization of life *and* the concomitant rise of a homeless urban working class displaced from the land by the creations of the bourgeois economy *and* the concern that an expanding British Empire may bring Anglos face to face with the very racial others (like the multicolored creature) that are supposed to be kept distant from "us" even while we depend on them economically (see Malchow, *Gothic Images*, pp. 9–40). Even so, the intermixed transitions of this era, where each cultural position seems capable of blurring into its opposite *and* some others besides, become embodied in, even scapegoated on, the half-alive/half-dead, half-organic/half-artificial, and obscurely desirable/obviously repellant specter/creature. He/it locates and focuses our longings and fears as though they are *and are not* ours, allowing them to be visible as part of our present fearfully threatening us and yet making them either a relic of the decaying past or perhaps the avatar of a mechanistic or racially other future. Such a Gothic construction, altered from Walpole's but not leaving his oversized and stalking ghosts behind altogether, conflates the major changes in modes of cultural production by 1818 *and* the contradictory hopes and fears that these arouse in white middle-class readers while permitting that same audience either to face or to avoid these multiple implications, all in a fiction as sewn together from different types of previous writing as the creature is fabricated from different portions and classes of older bodies (see Hogle, "*Frankenstein*").

The Gothic has lasted as it has because its symbolic mechanisms, particularly its haunting and frightening specters, have permitted us to cast many anomalies in our modern conditions, even as these change, over onto antiquated or at least haunted spaces and highly anomalous creatures. This way our contradictions can be confronted by, yet removed from us into, the seemingly unreal, the alien, the ancient, and the grotesque. Some Gothic tales, such as *Frankenstein* or *Dracula,* have a lasting resonance of this kind, so much so that we keep telling them over and over again with different elements but certain constant features. Such recastings help us both deal with newly ascendant cultural and psychological contradictions and still provide us with a recurring method for shaping and obscuring our fears and forbidden desires.

The Gothic, in other words, provides the best-known examples of those strange and ghostly figures that Freud saw as examples of "the Uncanny" (or *Unheimlich*) in his 1919 essay of that name. For him what is quintessentially "uncanny," as he reveals most by analyzing a German Gothic tale, "The Sandman" (1817) by E. T. A. Hoffman, is the deeply and internally familiar (the most infantile of our desires or fears) as it reappears to us in seemingly external, repellant, and *un*familiar forms. What is most familiar to Freud, to be sure, are strictly psychological or visceral drives from our earliest existence, such as sheer repetition-compulsions and the castration anxiety born of desiring the mother and thus risking the wrath of the father (which some Gothic tales do indeed include). But the devices he isolates for rendering the symbolic disguises of such drives in fiction can also be employed, as *Frankenstein* has revealed, for configuring quite familiar and basic social contradictions engulfing middle-class individuals who must nevertheless define themselves in relation to these anomalies, often using creatures or similarly *othered* beings to incarnate such mixed and irresolvable foundations of being.

Since Freud and partly in line with his kind of psychoanalysis, the French theorist and therapist Julia Kristeva has gone on more recently in her book *Powers of Horror* (1980) to see the return of the repressed familiar in "the uncanny" as based on a more fundamental human impulse that also helps us to define the cultural, as well as psychological, impulses most basic to the Gothic. Kristeva argues for ghosts or grotesques, so explicitly created to embody contradictions, as instances of what she calls the "abject" and products of "abjection," which she derives from the literal meanings of *ab-ject*: "throwing off" and "being thrown under." What we "throw off," she suggests, is all that is "in-between . . . ambiguous . . . composite" in our beings, the fundamental inconsistencies that prevent us from declaring a coherent and independent identity to ourselves and others (p. 4). The most primordial version of this "in-between" is the multiplicity we viscerally remember from the moment of birth, at which we were both inside and outside of the mother and thus both alive and not yet in existence (in that sense *dead*). It is this "immemorial violence" that lies at the base of our beings and is one basis of the primal chaos calling us back, yet it is that morass from which we always feel we must "become separated in order to be" a definable person (p. 10).

Whatever threatens us with anything like this betwixt-and-between, even dead-and-alive, condition, Kristeva concludes, is what we throw off or "abject" into defamiliarized manifestations, which we henceforth fear and desire because they both threaten to reengulf us and promise to return us to our primal origins. Those othered figures reveal this deeply familiar foundation while "throwing it under" the cover of an outcast monster more vaguely archaic and filled with contradictions than supposedly normal human beings, as in the cadaverous creature of *Frankenstein,* the aristocratic vampire in *Dracula,* or the shrunken and gnarled other-self-*in*-the-self of Robert Louis Stevenson's *Dr. Jekyll and Mr. Hyde* (1886; see Hogle, "The Struggle"). By these means all that is abjected is thrown under in another fashion: cast off into a figure or figures criminalized or condemned by people in authority and thus subjected to (again, thrown under) their gaze and the patterns of social normalcy they enforce. The process of abjec*tion*, then, is as thoroughly social and cultural as it is personal. It encourages middle-class people in the west, as we see in many of the lead characters in Gothic fictions, to deal with the tangled contradictions fundamental to their existence by throwing them off onto ghostly or monstrous counterparts that then seem "uncanny" in their unfamiliar familiarity while also conveying overtones of the archaic and the alien in their grotesque mixture of elements viewed as incompatible by established standards of normality. The Gothic is the form of western fiction-making, from novels to films to videos (witness Michael Jackson's

Thriller of 1982), where such symbolic "abjection" most frequently occurs precisely because its highly mixed form allows both the pursuit of sanctioned "identities" and a simultaneously fearful and attractive confrontation with the "thrown off" anomalies that are actually basic to the construction of a western middle-class self.

One reason the Gothic as a form symbolizes this process of abjection so well is its cross-generic status from the start and its resulting combination of "high culture" and "low culture" throughout its varied history. When Walpole proposed blending "two kinds of romance," he was referring in part to his own cross between medieval chivalric romances and neoclassic tragedies oriented toward the old aristocracy, on the one hand, and the newly ascendant bourgeois novel (or so it was later called) directed in its comic elements and probabilities of common existence toward the increasingly dominant middle classes, on the other. His choice of the Gothic label for this uneasy marriage, while not widely adopted as rapidly as some have supposed, was therefore a marketing device designed to fix a generic position for an interplay of what was widely thought to be high cultural writing (epic, verse romance, tragedy) with what many still regarded as low by comparison (servant-based comedy, superstitious folklore, middle-class prose fiction). The most immediate result was a tortured mixture in Walpole's text and those of his earliest imitators, such as Clara Reeve in *The Old English Baron* (1777–78), whereby characters – and thus readers – were torn between "traditional signs of identity ... based on social rank and blood lines" and the refashioning of themselves, as well as fiction, to suit "the vagaries of exchange value ... associated with capitalist-class imperatives and the growing strength of the market economy" (Henderson, " 'An Embarrassing Subject,' " p. 226).

By 1797, when Samuel Taylor Coleridge reviewed Matthew Lewis's *The Monk* (1796), for many the archetype of the horror Gothic then and since, "the multitude of the manufacturers" of the "horrible and the preternatural" for the broad "public taste" by this time – clearly an attack on the "lowness" of romances targeted at the widest popular market – has become associated with both an oxymoronic, class-mixing style ("phrases the most trite and colloquial" applied to exalted subjects requiring "sternness and solemnity of diction") and a "level[ing]" of "all events ... into one common mass" where events from different spheres of existence "become almost equally probable" (Coleridge in Clery and Miles, *Gothic Documents*, pp. 185–87). The Gothic has thus become the subject of intense debate, which continues today, over its blurring of metaphysical, natural, religious, class, economic, marketing, generic, stylistic, and moral lines. This debate has had great influence, as Michael Gamer, Jeffrey Cox, Misha Kavka, and Steven Bruhm show in this book, over how counter-Gothic as well as admittedly Gothic writers, dramatists, or filmmakers have incorporated or altered the most established features of the Walpolean and Radcliffean romance over the last 200 years. In the meantime the Gothic has also come to deal, as one of its principal subjects, with how the middle class dissociates from itself, and then fears, the extremes of what surrounds it: the very high or the decadently aristocratic and the very low or the animalistic, working-class, underfinanced, sexually deviant, childish, or carnivalesque, all sides of which have been abjected at once into figures ranging from Lewis's monk Ambrosio and Radcliffe's class-climbing villains to the title character in C. R. Maturin's *Melmoth the Wanderer* (1820), Stevenson's Mr. Hyde, Wilde's Dorian Gray, Stoker's Count Dracula, and the carnival-magician "Opera Ghost" hidden in the depths of a palace of high culture in Gaston Leroux's original *Le Fantôme de l'Opéra* (1910; see Wolf, *Essential Phantom of the Opera*). Still classified for many as betwixt and between "serious" and "popular" literature and drama, the Gothic is thus continuously about confrontations between the low and the high, even as the ideologies and ingredients of these change. It is about its own blurring of different levels of discourse while it is also concerned with the interpenetration of other opposed conditions – including life/death, natural/supernatural, ancient/modern, realistic/artificial, and unconscious/conscious – along with the abjection of these crossings into haunting and supposedly deviant "others" that therefore attract and terrify middle-class characters and readers.

Concurrently, too, as feminist critics of this mode have seen for decades now, the Gothic has long confronted the cultural problem of gender distinctions, including what they mean for western structures of power and how boundaries between the genders might be questioned to undermine or reorient those structures. Even as early as *The Castle of Otranto* – and certainly in Walpole's Gothic play *The Mysterious Mother* (composed in 1768 but never staged before the author died) – women are the figures most fearfully trapped between contradictory pressures and impulses. It is *Otranto*'s Isabella who first finds herself in what has since become the most classic Gothic circumstance: caught in "a labyrinth of darkness" full of "cloisters" underground and anxiously hesitant about what course to take there, fearing the pursuit of a domineering and lascivious patriarch who wants to use her womb as a repository for seed that may help him preserve his property and wealth, on the one hand, yet worried that, fleeing in an opposite direction, she is still "within reach of somebody [male], she knew not whom," on the other

(p. 28). From the start, then, the oppression and "othering" of the female seen from her point of view has been a principal Gothic subject, even to the point of depicting her reduced to an object of exchange or the merest tool of child-bearing between men (see Sedgwick, *Between Men*). Hence it is hardly surprising that the Gothic attained its first great effulgence in the hands of Ann Radcliffe, the most popular English woman novelist of the 1790s. Female readership was increasing by leaps and bounds in the middle classes from the 1760s on, so she and her many imitators had great encouragement to develop the primal Gothic scene of a woman confined and turn it into a journey of women coming into some power and property by their own and other feminine agency, albeit within a still-antiquated and male-dominated world full of terrors for every female.

Even more striking, though, is the frequent goal of that journey in the Gothic, even for Walpole: the recovery of a lost or hidden maternal origin by both women and men. In this motif a patriarchal lineage and house turns out to be explicitly dependent on and rooted in the unpredictable possibilities of a forgotten, but finally uncovered, womanhood (see Walpole, *Castle of Otranto*, pp. 114–15, and Radcliffe, *Mysteries of Udolpho*, pp. 638–49). The confinement of woman by patriarchy in a great deal of Gothic, we ultimately find, is based fundamentally on an attempt to repress, as well as a quest to uncover, a potentially "unruly female principle" (Williams, *Art of Darkness*, p. 86) that antiquated patriarchal enclosures have been designed to contain and even bury, as in Poe's "The Fall of the House of Usher" (1839). The Gothic often shows its readers that the anomalous foundations they seek to abject have become culturally associated with the otherness of femininity, a *maternal* multiplicity basic to us all (see Kahane, "Gothic Mirror"). Social gender divisions have been designed to deny, even as they make us desire, this boundary-blurring source of ourselves that initially stems, the Gothic reveals, from the body of a woman. Here is the reason, a key factor in the history of the Gothic, why Kristeva can link horrifying abjection with our throwing off of the memory that we have archaically been both inside and outside the mother whom we now fear and desire at the same time. The Gothic is quite consistently about the connection of abject monster figures to the primal and engulfing morass of the maternal; Victor Frankenstein not only seeks his mother's dissolving body through the construction of his male monster, but shows his greatest fear and commits his strongest act of repression by feverishly destroying the female creature that his first creation has asked him to make (Shelley, *Frankenstein*, pp. 163–64). It is woman whom he has avoided most in his onanistic creation because it is the ultimate uncontrollability of the life-giving female that most crystallizes all of his many fears and abjections.

Some historians of the Gothic have made sharp distinctions between works of female Gothic (in the sublimated terror vein of Radcliffe) and male Gothic (in the graphic horror tradition of "Monk" Lewis; see Williams, *Art of Darkness*, pp. 99–158), and there is some accuracy in these categories, particularly when we note the vast twentieth-century market for feminine Gothic romances (see Radway, *Reading the Romance*) epitomized by the highly Radcliffean *Rebecca* (1938) by Daphne du Maurier, the source of the Oscar-winning David O. Selznick/Alfred Hitchcock film of 1940. Yet even male-oriented Gothic works, such as *Frankenstein* but also *Dracula* and *The Phantom of the Opera*, are bedeviled by the threat of and longing for the deeply maternal abyss of nonidentity that ultimately beckons to all the characters, especially the heroes. Jonathan Harker in Stoker's novel is most aroused and horrified deep in Dracula's castle by the multiple bevy of female vampires who threaten to seduce, drain, and thereby unman him (*Dracula*, pp. 41–44), while Leroux's original phantom cannot build his subterranean lair of music rooms and carnivalesque halls of mirrors under the Paris Opera without centering it around a *petit bourgeois* bedroom fashioned to duplicate exactly the *boudoir* of his mother, possibly the site of his own conception and now the location for him to which all things in the Opera must descend – and regress (Wolf, *Essential Phantom of the Opera*, pp. 174–75, 316–18). The repressed, archaic, and thus deeply unconscious Feminine is a fundamental level of being to which most Gothic finally refers, often in displacements of it that seem to be old patriarchal structures, and all the blurred oppositions that are abjected onto monsters or specters by Gothic characters face their ultimate dissolution into primal chaos as they approach this feminized nadir that is both the ultimate Other and the basically groundless ground of the self.

The greatest horror in the Gothic, however, is not simply the pull of the masculine back toward an overpowering femininity. The deep Feminine level, as the Gothic mode has developed, is but one major form of a primordial dissolution that can obscure the boundaries between all western oppositions, not just masculine–feminine or the other pairs already noted. The reason that Gothic others or spaces can abject myriad cultural and psychological contradictions, and thereby confront us with those anomalies in disguise, is because those spectral characters, images, and settings harbor the hidden reality that oppositions of all kinds cannot maintain their separations, that each "lesser term" is contained in its counterpart and that difference really arises by standing against *and* relating to interdependency. While *high* versus *low* and *serious* versus *popular* tend to blur in the malleable Gothic genre, so do all of the cultural distinctions it takes on thematically, whether these are based on gender, sexual orientation, race, class, stages of growth, level of existence, or even species. The original Dracula, for instance, can disgorge blood from his breasts as much as he can penetrate flesh with his phallic teeth (Stoker, *Dracula*, p. 247); can be attracted by Jonathan Harker (and vice versa) as much as Mina Murray (p. 31); can be western and eastern simultaneously in his whiter-than-white visage linked to "aquiline" stereotypes of the Jew in the 1890s (pp. 23–24); can be extremely aristocratic and cavort among homeless gypsies (p. 45), threatening the stability of class boundaries; can seem the supremely mature sophisticate (very evolved) and manifest a primeval "child-brain" (quite *devolved*) at the same time (p. 264); can be nearly all things on the continuum between a very earthy being bound by time and the unearthly demon (like Melmoth) surviving across centuries; and can of course become an animal – a wolf or bat – as easily as he can remorph into various human guises from different eras and cultures.

Threats of and longings for gender-crossing, homosexuality or bisexuality, racial mixture, class fluidity, the child in the adult, timeless timeliness, and simultaneous evolution and devolution (especially after the middle of the nineteenth century): all these motifs, as possibly evil *and* desirable, circulate through Gothic works across the whole history of the form, differing mostly in degree of emphasis from example to example. Social and ideological tensions about all these "deviations" at different times thus find expression in the Gothic mode, which offers hyperbolic temptations toward these possibilities disguised in aberrant and regressive forms but also fashions means of othering them all so that standard, adult, middle-class identities can seem to stand out clearly against them. This remains the Gothic gambit, as several of our contributors will show, as much in the recent *Alien* films and Stephen King novels on demonic vampire-children as in *The Mysterious Mother, The Monk*, Radcliffe's *The Italian* (1797), *Frankenstein, Dracula, The Phantom of the Opera*, and (most obviously) *Dr. Jekyll and Mr. Hyde*, whether one refers to the original novels or more recent adaptations of them. The Gothic clearly exists, in part, to raise the possibility that all "abnormalities" we would divorce from ourselves are a part of ourselves, deeply and pervasively (hence frighteningly), even while it provides quasi-antiquated methods to help us place such "deviations" at a definite, though haunting, distance from us.

All that is linked to the Gothic as both high and low fiction, we have to say, raises the perpetual question of whether it is primarily a conservative or a revolutionary genre composed from other genres. Students of this form have long noted its first widely popular use during and after the French Revolution (1789–99) and have echoed the views of the Marquis de Sade, a frequent adapter of Gothic devices, who in 1807 saw this "genre [as] the inevitable product of the revolutionary shocks with which the whole of Europe re-sounded" because it was able "to situate in the land of fantasies" the violent challenges to established orders that by now were "common knowledge" (Sade as quoted in Mulvey-Roberts, *Handbook to Gothic Literature*, p. 204). Certainly there are hints of similar revolutions in aspects of *The Monk*, where a tyrannical prioress is torn apart by a mob of oppressed common people (pp. 355–56), and in *Frankenstein*, where Victor's refusal of responsi-bility for his working-class creature parallels his failure to see the value and equality of women, a problem already addressed by the author's mother, Mary Wollstonecraft, in her occasionally Gothic *The Wrongs of Woman* (1797)[8] and taken up a century later in Gilman's "The Yellow Wallpaper." But there are just as many instances, we have to admit, of a conserva-tive ideology that presents revolutionary horrors as the results of declines in social order or refusals of cultural proprieties and distinctions. Lewis's novel, through its ultimately happy characters, finally condemns the licenses it presents as flawed challenges to valuable social hierarchies;[9] Bram Stoker in *Dracula* unquestionably castigates all the crossings of boundaries that his count inspires and embodies, especially the "liberated" sexuality; and the *Frankenstein* films of the 1930s directed by James Whale constrain the creature's suggestiveness greatly by giving him a criminal's brain and making him finally the enemy of a Depression-era crowd of workers, who scapegoat their problems onto him and his creator, rather than those with corporate power, in an antiquated mill that they finally burn up along with much of the original novel (see Whale, *Frankenstein*).

Most often, though, Gothic works hesitate between the revolutionary and conservative, as when Ann Radcliffe allows her heroines independent prop-erty and ultimate freedom of choice within the fervent worship of their fathers and an avoidance of all direct political action, rebellious or reac-tionary. Partly because it comes from mixing discourses and postures so bla-tantly, often with their incompatibilities fully in view, the Gothic can both raise the sad specters of "othered" and oppressed behaviors, crossings of boundaries, and classes of people and finally arrange for the distancing and destruction of those figures or spaces into which the most troubling anoma-lies have been abjected by most of the middle class. No other form of writing or theatre is as insistent as Gothic on juxtaposing potential revolution and possible reaction – about gender, sexuality, race, class, the colonizers versus the colonized, the physical versus the metaphysical, and abnormal versus normal psychology – and leaving both extremes sharply before us and far less resolved than the conventional endings in most of these works claim them to be. In this respect, as the book's chapters will show in proceeding through historical stages of the Gothic oscillation, writing, theatre, and films of this kind enact and reflect the most intense and important ambivalences in modern western culture, if only in a distortion mirror that ostensibly places these quandaries long ago or far away from us.

These cultural functions are made possible, this book wants to show, by the ways the Gothic exaggerates its own extreme fictionality – and does so through long-lasting and creatively changing techniques. The hyperbolic *unreality*, even *surreality*, of Gothic fiction, as subject to parody and critique as it has been, is in every way essential to its capacity to abject cultural and psychological contradictions for modern readers to face or avoid. This is partly because, as Walpole reveals in his 1765 *Otranto* preface, the recipe for the "Gothic Story" from the start is to give "fancy" the "liberty to expatiate through the boundless realms of invention" while still constraining the "agents" of a fiction within "the rules of probability" in *their* reactions and behaviors. In this statement as well as others, Walpole (as a fellow Whig in the British Parliament) is developing the specific sense of the "sublime" in several forms of art proposed by Edmund Burke in *A Philosophical Enquiry into the Origin of our Ideas of the Sublime and Beautiful* (1757; see Mishra, *Gothic Sublime*). Burke's definition confines the sublime (traditionally the "grand style," literally a "rising from beneath a threshold") to "whatever is fitted in any sort to excite the ideas of pain, and danger," including the threat of "death" and the dissolution of the self, by "operat[ing] in a manner analogous to terror" so as to produce "the strongest emotion of which the mind is capable" (Burke, *Enquiry*, in Clery and Miles, *Gothic Documents*, p. 112). Sublimity is thus aroused for Burke and then Walpole by linguistic or artistic expansions into "Vastness" or "Infinity" or even "notions of ghosts or goblins" (clearly expatiations into the boundless) because they terrifyingly threaten the annihilation of the self (ibid., pp. 112, 114), but such stretchings of immediate credulity are nevertheless valuable for Burke ("according to the rules of probability") because the "mortal agents" who observe those potentials are reacting as they should, as he sees them in a treatise focused primarily on the empirical psychology of emotional affect.

What most enables this seeming paradox, moreover, is Burke's additional claim that life-threatening descriptions prompt an aesthetically worthwhile reaction because each one is so thoroughly artificial that "no idea of [genuine] danger [is really] connected with it" and the "mental powers" are beneficially expanded while "the pain and terror are modified so as not to be actually noxious" (Burke, *Enquiry*, in Clery and Miles, *Gothic Documents*, pp. 120–21). The extremes that sublime or Gothic images point toward, in other words, are distanced and blunted enough by transformative representations to be pleasant in their terror. They not only lead to mixed but safe reactions that can be called sublime, but they do so (as Freud might say) by "sublimating" what would be unacceptable to consciousness so as to trans-figure that deathly otherness into the merest and most harmless figures, as when chemical sublimation turns a hard solid into an airy gas without pass-ing it through the liquid stage.[10] The Gothic mode begins, we have found, by employing the deliberate fictionality of the "terror sublime" to both draw us toward and protect us from virtually *all* that we might associate with the destruction of our presumed identities. The Gothic intermixture of the sublime with what Burke calls the unthreatening "beautiful" *and* with the comically bathetic and other incongruous elements only adds to the delib-erately forced unreality that allows this mode to symbolize the threatening inconsistencies – including irrational desire and the immanence of death – in the personal and the political unconscious.

A related reason for this insistent artificiality, too, is the fact that its repre-sentations and even its Gothicism are so pointedly fake and counterfeit from the beginning. Walpole's *Otranto* in its first edition not only fakes its being a translation of a manuscript by a Renaissance priest – a very ironic decep-tion, given Walpole's open opposition to Catholicism (see the first preface in Walpole, *Castle of Otranto*, pp. 5–8) – but populates the actual tale with specters who are ghosts of what is *already artificial*: the gigantic, fragmented shade of an *effigy* on an underground tomb (p. 20) and the walking figure of a *portrait* which descends from the wall where its picture hangs (p. 26). As much as these sublime "ghosts or goblins" are signifiers of repressed pri-mal crimes, one of which is in fact a "fictitious will" transferring Otranto to a false heir (p. 113), they play such roles as shades of figures; they are not just counterfeits but ghosts of counterfeits (see Hogle, "*Frankenstein*"). The Gothic is founded on a quasi-antiquarian use of symbols that are quite obviously signs only of older signs; by the time of the Gothic revival in archi-tecture of the eighteenth century, there had already been "Gothic" revivals, even in the Middle Ages. The earlier signs had themselves been broken off from many of their past connections and now existed more as mere sig-nifiers than as substantial points of reference or human bodies. Indeed, in using symbols from a highly Catholic past in an ultimately anti-Catholic way, as he did in his Gothicized house at Strawberry Hill (Walpole, *Castle of Otranto*, pp. vii–viii) and Radcliffe, Lewis, and others proceeded to do after him, Walpole made his references to the distant past distinctly *hollowed-out* ones, allusions to what was largely empty as well as distant for him, even though Gothic relics could be effective for establishing a useful myth of Gothic ancestry that often proved to be as effective for class-climbing as it was ultimately counterfeit.[11] Such a use of the emptied past in ghosts of counterfeits has consequently allowed the *neo*-Gothic to be filled with antiquated repositories into which modern quandaries can be projected and abjected simultaneously.

Even the use of the Gothic label, which has become even more common today compared to its very sporadic use to describe romantic fiction in the eighteenth century, turns out to be equally counterfeit, though quite usefully so, partly because *Gothic* as an aesthetic term has been counterfeit all along. It was first used by early Renaissance art historians in Italy to describe pointed-arch and castellated styles of medieval architecture, as well as medieval ways of life in general – but to do so in a pejorative way so as to establish the superiority of more recent neoclassic alternatives, because of which the designs of the immediate past were associated with supposedly barbaric Goths who had little to do with the actual buildings in question.[12]

Consequently, *Gothic* has long been a term used to project modern concerns into a deliberately vague, even fictionalized past. It has thus served over the years to refer, with equal fictionality, to Moors and other orientals (hence as a term of racial othering) and to uneducated members of the rural working classes, but also, by Walpole's time, to a mythic past of Anglo-Saxon freedom from foreign oppression connected with the Magna Carta that Whigs of the 1760s liked to use as a reference point for their anti-Tory arguments.[13] Like the ghosts of counterfeits it employs, then, the Gothic is inherently connected to an exploitation of the emptied-out past to symbolize and disguise present concerns, including prejudices.

It has thus been an ideal vehicle throughout its history in which, as David Punter has put it, "the middle class displaces the hidden violence of present social structures, conjures them up again as past, and promptly falls under their spell" (*Literature of Terror*, II, 218–19). The Gothic and its ghosts of the already counterfeit can serve this cultural purpose *first* because the exploited relics from the past are emptied of much former content but *also* because such figures are unusually betwixt and between, like "Gothic" itself; they look back to a past existence which can never be recovered and so can be reconceived, yet they also look ahead to marketable recastings of old remnants in modern technologies (from Walpole's printing press at Strawberry Hill to the computer systems and software of today) in which what is already counterfeited can be transformed into a simulation among other simulations directed at a newer purpose and market. What better symbolic mechanism can there be, multidirectional as Gothic figures are, for abjecting betwixt and between, anomalous conditions where opposed positions of many kinds keep blurring into each other and threatening us with the dissolution of our normal cultural foundations for the identities we claim to possess? The Gothic has been and remains necessary to modern western culture because it allows us in ghostly disguises of blatantly counterfeit fictionality to confront the roots of our beings in sliding multiplicities (from life becoming death to genders mixing to fear becoming pleasure and more) and to define ourselves against these uncanny abjections, while also feeling attracted to them, all of this in a kind of cultural activity that as time passes can keep inventively changing its ghosts of counterfeits to address changing psychological and cultural longings and fears.

The chapters that follow seek to explain and exemplify the several stages and manifestations through which this cultural project has gone from the later eighteenth through the turn of the twentieth into the twenty-first century. There is not sufficient space for these experts on the Gothic to account for every form it has taken over 250 years, as chronological as our progression endeavors to be. Collectively, however, we hope to help our readers understand how and why the Gothic has developed as it has in different time periods and sometimes in different media. While each of us focuses on the Gothic of a specific era or location, we all attempt to answer the same fundamental questions. What were the historical, cultural, and aesthetic forces that shaped a certain stretch of the Gothic, and how and why did those forces interact as they did? What transformations took place in earlier versions of this form? What characterized these changes? What do these show about both the symbolic techniques and the cultural functions of the Gothic at particular times and in particular places? What longings, fears, and contradictions are most abjected into the Gothic at different times? What conceptions of human psychology do these variations manifest? How is the Gothic's essentially betwixt-and-between nature, including its slippage between conservative and revolutionary impulses or what is thought to be high as opposed to low culture, drawn in one set of directions or another at a given time or place – and why those results, as opposed to others, at that point? How do the gender, racial, generational, and national or colonial politics of particular times in western history get played out in these wildly fictional disguises? What are the relationships between pervasive cultural changes and stylistic transformations in the Gothic across its many forms? What happens to the Gothic's extreme artificiality (its ghosts of the already counterfeit) over time, particularly as a predominantly print culture gives way to film, video, and computer-based cultures? Do the cultural functions of the Gothic remain primarily the same or change radically or become what is finally a combination of both?

My introduction to this succession of studies has attempted an overview of this field that necessarily draws examples from mostly eighteenth- and nineteenth-century Gothic, since that is where the chapters most immediately after mine will focus their attention. This book ends with an essay by Fred Botting designed to look backwards from the digitized present in a widely comparative way, much as I have primarily looked forward from the Gothic's beginnings in Walpolean fiction. Between these framing pieces, we offer accounts of how the Gothic has moved from one toward the other in the revolutionary *and* counterrevolutionary eighteenth century in England from the 1760s to the 1780s (E. J. Clery) to the explosively Gothic 1790s (Robert Miles); on the continent of Europe in France and Germany as the eighteenth century passed into the nineteenth (Terry Hale); in the so-called Romantic period in early nineteenth-century England, where the Gothic was both strongly resisted and often replayed (Michael Gamer); in Scotland and Ireland, the nearby soil of the conquered in the nineteenth century, where the politics of subjection and resistance altered the Gothic significantly for future use in several such places (David Punter); in the English theatre of the Romantic into the Victorian periods, where the theatricality inherent in Gothic fakery came more into its own on actual stages (Jeffrey N. Cox); in the Victorian prose Gothic of Britain visible in a wide range of novels and short stories with surprisingly various political leanings and placements of women (Alison Milbank); in the developing United States, where the Gothic proved amazingly right for symbolizing the contradictions in a supposedly new world still drawn by the old (Eric Savoy); in the English Gothic of the *fin du siècle* and the early twentieth century, as this pliable mode addressed the most wrenching series of cultural changes in its history (Kelly Hurley); in the filmed Gothic, which accelerated rapidly in post-1930 America and later in Europe to offer alternative techniques of representation to deal with numerous post-Depression hopes and fears (Misha Kavka); in a much transformed Gothic with cross-racial ingredients in what used to be distant colonies of European countries, here exemplified most by the Caribbean (Lizabeth Paravanisi-Gebert); and in the wide range of contemporary Gothic horror in the west after the Second World War, from novels to films to television, in which growing audiences came to confront, in new kinds of disguise, the traumas peculiar to postmodern life and our ways of protecting ourselves from them even as we continue to fear them (Steven Bruhm).

In each of these accounts, our readers will find, the purveyors and receivers of Gothic fictions all face different versions of a similar choice in how they construct or respond to this highly exaggerated, and still controversial, range of fictions. Because of the Gothic's conservative leanings and its capacities for disguising its abjections in highly displaced locations and specters, on the one hand, authors and audiences can choose approaches that emphasize surface shock value, luridness of setting, exoticism of character, and a posture of convenient middle distance from these that both admits their attractions and condemns their excesses in the end, claiming "that's entertainment!"

On the other hand, since the Gothic also serves to symbolize our struggles and ambivalences over how dominant categorizations of people, things, and events can be blurred together and so threaten our convenient, but repressive thought patterns, its creators and onlookers have the opportunity to make Gothic show us our cultural and psychological selves and conditions, in their actual multiplicity, in ways that other aesthetic forms cannot manage as forcefully or with such wide public appeal. Such self-exposures can create occasions for us to reassess our standard oppositions and distinctions – and thus our prejudices – at which point Gothic can activate its revolutionary and boundary-changing impulses and lead us to dissolve some of the rigidities and their otherings of people by which we live and from which much of the Gothic takes its shape. We are always poised on the fulcrum of this choice when we read or consider Gothic fictions: do we let them mainly protect and justify us as we are (which most of them can, if we seek that through them) or do we let them arouse us to reconsider and critique the conventional norms of western middle-class culture, which can confront disguised challenges to them in the Gothic (if we let it) more vividly than anywhere else? Will the fear that Gothic works to arouse keep us from facing the longings and anomalies behind those terrors that the Gothic also depicts? These chapters do not finally answer that question, but they do collectively pose it in analyzing key examples of the Gothic's tempestuous history, which, we now see, is intimately bound up with the history of modern western culture over the last three centuries.

NOTES

1 See Joseph Wiesenfarth, *Gothic Manners and the Classic English Novel* (Madison: University of Wisconsin Press, 1988), pp. 41–160; Judith Wilt, *Ghosts of the Gothic: Austen, Eliot, and Lawrence* (Princeton: Princeton University Press, 1980), pp. 173–231; Robert Mighall, *A Geography of Victorian Gothic Fiction* (Oxford: Oxford University Press, 1999); and especially Alison Milbank, both *Daughters of the House* (London: Macmillan, 1992) and her chapter in this volume.

2 On the satirizing of Gothic, see E. J. Clery and Robert Miles, eds., *Gothic Documents: a Sourcebook, 1700–1820* (Manchester: Manchester University Press, 2000), pp. 201–22, and Roxana Stuart, *Stage Blood: Vampires of the Nineteenth-Century Stage* (Bowling Green, OH: Pennsylvania State University Press, 1994), pp. 164–78.

3 Here I gratefully parallel the attempt to distinguish the *Gothic* tale clearly from other kinds of ghost stories in Chris Baldick, ed., *The Oxford Book of Gothic Tales* (Oxford: Oxford University Press, 1992), pp. xi–xxiii.

4 These extremes of the Gothic were first defined theoretically in Ann Radcliffe's posthumously published "On the Supernatural in Poetry" (Clery and Miles, *Gothic Documents*, pp. 163–72), which appeared in 1826 first in the *New Monthly*

Magazine and then as a preface to her posthumous novel, *Gaston de Blondeville.* See also ibid., pp. 168–71. The same distinctions were best reinvoked for recent critical discussion in the 1969 essay by Robert Hume.

5 The highly pre-Freudian nature of Poe's work was established most forcefully by Marie Bonaparte in *The Life and Works of Edgar Allan Poe* (1933), trans. John Rodker, introduced by Sigmund Freud (London: Hogarth, 1949). The presagings of psychoanalysis in nineteenth-century French fiction have been discussed in Joan Kessler, *Demons of the Night: Tales of the Fantastic, Madness and the Supernatural from Nineteenth-Century France* (Chicago: University of Chicago Press, 1995), pp. xi–li.

6 See the chapters by Paul O'Flinn, Chris Baldick, Anne K. Mellor, Margaret Homans, and Gayatri Chakravorty Spivak in *New Casebooks: Frankenstein,* ed. Fred Botting (London: Macmillan, 1995).

7 For the best histories of the female Gothic, see Julianne Fleenor, ed., *The Female Gothic* (Montreal: Eden Press, 1983); Kate Ellis, *The Contested Castle: Gothic Novels and the Subversion of Domestic Ideology* (Urbana: University of Illinois Press, 1989); Eugenia DeLamotte, *Perils of the Night: a Feminist Study of Nineteenth-Century Gothic* (Oxford: Oxford University Press, 1990); Anne Williams, *Art of Darkness: a Poetics of Gothic* (Chicago: University of Chicago Press, 1995); Susan Wolstenholme, *Gothic (Re)visions: Writing Women as Readers* (Albany: SUNY Press, 1993); Diane Hoeveler, *Gothic Feminism: the Professionalization of Gender from Charlotte Smith to the Brontës* (University Park: Pennsylvania State University Press, 1988); and Susanne Becker, *Gothic Forms of Feminine Fictions* (Manchester: Manchester University Press, 1999) (in recommended order of reading).

8 See Wollstonecraft's *Mary* and *The Wrongs of Woman,* ed. Gary Kelly (Oxford: Oxford University Press, 1976), pp. 75–81.

9 See Daniel P. Watkins, "Social Hierarchy in Matthew Lewis' *The Monk*," *Studies in the Novel* 18 (1986): 115–24.

10 This definition of sublimation is indebted to Stuart Sperry, *Keats the Poet* (Princeton: Princeton University Press, 1973), pp. 33–49.

11 See Mark Madoff, "The Useful Myth of Gothic Ancestry," *Studies in Eighteenth-Century Culture* 8 (1979): 337–50. My sense of the counterfeit is also heavily indebted to Jean Baudrillard, *Symbolic Exchange and Death* (1976), trans. Iain Hamilton Grant (London: Sage, 1993), especially pp. 50–61.

12 Here I am beholden to pp. 259–60 of Paul Frankl's, *The Gothic: Literary Sources and Interpretations Through Eight Centuries* (Princeton: Princeton University Press, 1960) a book which provides a definitive genealogy of *Gothic* as an aesthetic term.

13 See Madoff, "Useful Myth"; Samuel Kliger, *The Goths in England: a Study in Seventeenth- and Eighteenth-Century Thought* (Cambridge, MA: Harvard University Press, 1952); Clery in this volume; and Susie I. Tucker, *Protean Shape: a Study in Eighteenth-Century Vocabulary* (London: Athlone Press, 1967), pp. 149–55.

2

E. J. CLERY

The genesis of "Gothic" fiction

The attachment of the term *Gothic* to the literature of terror is quite a recent development – and almost entirely accidental. Horace Walpole's *The Castle of Otranto* is generally regarded as the first Gothic novel, but when it was published on Christmas Day 1764 it was subtitled simply *A Story*. The preface puts forward an elaborate counterfeit origin for the text, presenting it as an Italian work printed in 1529 and speculating that it may have been written between 1095 and 1243, at the time of the Crusades, when the story is set. But "Gothic" is nowhere mentioned. It was only when Walpole published a second edition in April 1765 and confessed that it was in fact a modern concoction that the word *Gothic* was added to the title: *The Castle of Otranto: a Gothic Story*. The addition was a flippant paradox chiefly intended, one infers, to annoy stuffy critics who objected to the experiment. After all, how could a Gothic story have a modern author?

For Walpole's contemporaries the Gothic age was a long period of barbarism, superstition, and anarchy dimly stretching from the fifth century AD, when Visigoth invaders precipitated the fall of the Roman Empire, to the Renaissance and the revival of classical learning. In a British context it was even considered to extend to the Reformation in the sixteenth century and the definitive break with the Catholic past. "Gothic" also signified anything obsolete, old-fashioned, or outlandish. *Otranto* may have been set in Gothic times, but the term does nothing to describe what was ground-breaking and influential about the novel, and Walpole does not use it again in his preface to the second edition, which constitutes a manifesto for a "new species of romance." After *Otranto* the only significant work in which "Gothic" appears in a subtitle was Clara Reeve's *The Old English Baron*.[1]

The "Gothic novel" is thus mostly a twentieth-century coinage.[2] The most obvious justification for its employment as a literary term was by analogy with the Gothic Revival in architecture, which also began in the mid-eighteenth century. In addition, histories of the literature of terror written from the 1920s onwards routinely identified Walpole as the progenitor of a genre, and hence the maverick subtitle *A Gothic Story* began to gain academic weight. Interesting work has been done on the etymology of "Gothic" and most monographs on "Gothic" as a genre have something to say on the matter, but when determining what is distinctive or innovative about eighteenth-century fiction in the terror mode it is essentially a red herring. During the 1790s the mode acquired a number of categorizing names, none of them involving "Gothic."[3] In the period dealt with here (the mid to late 1700s), the earliest experiments were universally referred to as "romances."

The novel in its "realist" form evolved in the first half of the eighteenth century in reaction to the romance tradition that had flourished up to the late seventeenth century. Daniel Defoe, Samuel Richardson, and Henry Fielding all made the claim for the originality and relevance of their fiction by distinguishing it from otherwordly, outdated "romance." In Richardson's novels the worst accusation leveled at the heroines is that they are readers of romances; in other words, fantasists and time-wasters. Fielding devoted the introductory chapter of book 8 of *Tom Jones* (1749) to a satire of the use of the marvelous in fiction. The "novel" means literally "the new," and it marked itself off as a new, more credible and progressive genre of fiction for an enlightened age by denigrating "the old," the romance. The classical keystones of this attitude were Aristotle, who in the *Poetics* insisted on probability in the drama, and Horace, whose dictum *"incredulus odi"* ("what I cannot believe disgusts me") from the *Art of Poetry* is a cliché of neoclassical criticism. Only if a fiction is true to life can it become the vehicle of useful instruction or moral improvement.

The target of attack was a somewhat amorphous entity. A common view of medieval romance can be found in Tobias Smollett's preface to *Roderick Random* (1748): "when the minds of men were debauched by the imposition of priest-craft to the most absurd pitch of credulity, the authors of romance arose, and losing sight of probability, filled their performances with the most monstrous hyperboles." By this light, romance was a Roman Catholic imposition. Another was derived from Cervantes' *Don Quixote* (1605, 1615), which satirizes chivalric romances like *Amadis de Gaul*. Here the object was seen as a perversion of the educative function, unfitting the reader for life in the real world. But hostile judgments were unlikely to be based on first-hand knowledge of pre-1600 literature. When critics and writers condemned romance, they had in mind above all the French heroic romances such as *Cassandre* (10 vols., 1644–50) by La Calprenède and *Le Grand Cyrus* (10 vols., 1659–63) by Madeleine de Scudéry, which were for a time enormously popular. Most of these in fact contained no supernaturalism, but were characterized by artificial diction, numerous coincidences, the promiscuous mixing of history and fiction, absurd idealism, and over-the-top heroics. It might seem surprising that their spell was regarded as potent enough still to require exorcism in Charlotte Lennox's satire *The Female Quixote* (1752). But the novel *needed* romance as the measure of its own achievements; there was a dialectical relation between the two, an interdependency.[4]

It follows that in spite of the rhetoric the dividing line between novel and romance was not absolutely clear-cut. Novelists quibbled over the boundaries of probability and attempted to balance the demands of instruction and entertainment. Moral messages would be useless if not joined to compelling narratives that stirred the emotions of the reader. Some of the most successful works contained episodes that would not be out of place in Gothic fiction. The imprisonment and madness of Richardson's Clarissa looks back to the melodramatic "she-tragedies" of Nicholas Rowe and forward to Sophia Lee's *The Recess* (1783–85). The scene from Smollett's *Ferdinand Count Fathom* (1753) in which the Count finds himself trapped in a bandit's den with a fresh corpse was undoubtedly a source for a similar adventure in *The Monk*, and later enthusiasts for the terror mode praised it as an extraordinarily effective example of "natural horror" (Clery and Miles, *Gothic Documents*, pp. 129, 162). But natural horror was as far as novelists were prepared to go at this stage: there could be no appeal to the imagination that went beyond rational causes.

The Castle of Otranto was presented to the public, especially in the preface to the second edition, as an outright challenge to this orthodoxy. Romances had been called improbable; now Walpole accused modern fiction of being too probable: "the great resources of fancy have been dammed up, by a strict adherence to common life" (p. 9). The chief enemy of fancy in his view was Samuel Richardson (p. xiii), whose narrative practices had been raised to the level of absolute moral prescription by Samuel Johnson in a well-known essay in the journal *The Rambler* (no. 4, 31 March 1750). In order to carry out its true function of instructing the young, fictions should "exhibit life in its true state, diversified only by accidents that daily happen in the world." The novel must be exemplary, and "what we cannot credit we shall never imitate" (Johnson in Clery and Miles, *Gothic Documents*, p. 175). In his fiction Walpole flouts this principle by bringing divine punishment to bear on the heir of a usurper through the intervention of a vengeful ghost and assorted gargantuan pieces of armour. By no stretch of the imagination could the tale offer a useful lesson for real life. The moral, as Walpole observes himself, is scarcely very edifying: "that *the sins of the fathers are visited on their children to the third and fourth generation*" (p. 7). Walpole's business is not instruction, but the pleasures of the imagination.

Walpole was uniquely well qualified to spearhead a revival of romance. He was the son of the late Prime Minister, Robert Walpole, Earl of Orford, and had a patrician's disregard for common opinion. He could also afford to be controversial. His income came largely from government sinecures, not from writing. He was even able to set up his own independent printing press at his home, Strawberry Hill, a modest villa remodeled as a feudal castle in Twickenham near London. His days were spent in dilettante antiquarianism, some light politicking at the House of Commons (he was an MP from 1741 to 1768), arduous socializing, and voluminous letter-writing (the modern edition of his correspondence stretches to 48 volumes). He had the maverick nature required to champion a lost cause and the status to make the public take note of the enterprise. When he came forward as author of *Otranto* in 1765, he carefully presented the "rules" for "a new species of romance" that would otherwise be dismissed as a piece of eccentric whimsy (Walpole, *Castle of Otranto*, p. 14). The story was "an attempt to blend the two kinds of romance, the ancient and the modern" (note the delicate insistence that modern fiction, in spite of its probability, remains romance); it also subsumed the opposition by "leaving the powers of fancy at liberty to expatiate through the boundless realms of invention, [hence] of creating more interesting situations" while making the characters "think, speak and act, as it might be supposed mere men and women would do in extraordinary positions" (pp. 9–10). In other words, Walpole wanted to combine the unnatural occurrences associated with romance and the naturalistic characterization and dialogue of the novel. Just as the novel contained traces of romance, so Walpole's experiment drew on the innovations of realist and sentimental fiction. The formula was offered as a "new route" for "men of brighter talent to follow" (p. 10).

The rules laid out by Walpole accurately describe the method of *Otranto*'s narrative from the opening pages. In the first paragraph a wedding is overshadowed by a troubling ancient prophecy. In the second, the supernatural intervenes in the form of a giant helmet which crushes the bridegroom to death. The next few pages are devoted to the reactions of various characters: the horror and inexplicable anger of the father, Prince Manfred, the grief of the mother, Hippolita, the daughter Matilda's eagerness to comfort others, the sympathy of the bereaved bride Isabella combined with relief, and the nervous panic of the crowd. The fluctuations of rage, hysteria, and crafty manipulation in Manfred's dealings with the mob are detailed at length, with the narrator playing the active part of an astute but slightly baffled observer. Yet the representation of feelings and motives will seem primitive to a reader of today, and the lightly archaic dialogue does not improve matters. What is required is a leap of imagination and a sense of context. According to the critic of the *Monthly Review* (23 February 1765), "the disquisitions into human manners, passions, and pursuits, indicate the keenest penetration, and the most perfect knowledge of mankind" at that time (p. xvii). Consequently, this novel provides the template for all future fictions of supernatural terror, including film. The credible emotions of the characters connect us to incredible phenomena and events and allow terror to circulate via processes of identification and projection.

Although the fusion of the probable and the improbable is the most vital aspect of the narrative, Walpole also brought to his "new species of romance" a curious assemblage of elements which owed more to the fashionable tastes of his day than to any very strict definition of the romance genre as it had previously been understood and criticized. Among the contemporary developments that became intertwined with the revival of romance were revisionist accounts of medieval culture, the aesthetics of original genius and the sublime, and the growing cult of Shakespearean tragedy.

An earlier work by Walpole, *Catalogue of Royal and Noble Authors* (1758), is evidence that he had read some genuine early romances, but *Otranto* bears little relation to them. Early apologists for ancient romance were mainly concerned with identifying the principles of composition for a text like *The Faerie Queene* by Edmund Spenser, which seemed lacking in internal connection and overburdened by detail. They often reached for an analogy with Gothic architecture, especially cathedrals, where the proliferation of forms nevertheless obeyed a certain hierarchy. But this issue is irrelevant to Walpole, who is at pains to note in his first, counterfeiting preface that the story seems to obey the theory of the "three unities" laid down by Aristotle, where representation of action, time, and place is simplified in the interests of coherence: "There is no bombast, no similes, flowers, digressions, or unnecessary descriptions. Every thing tends directly to the catastrophe" (p. 7). Although *Otranto* was first published as a translated romance and fooled at least one critic, it has more to do with new theories about the social origins of medieval literature than with actual imitation of them.

Two important works of literary history appeared in the decade preceding *Otranto*: *Observations on the Faerie Queene of Spenser* (1754; enlarged edition 1762) by Thomas Warton and *Letters on Chivalry and Romance* (1762) by Richard Hurd. Both stressed that medieval romances should be seen as the product of their times and both took a particular interest in the customs of chivalry as a foundation for romance. Warton interpreted the fanciful and supernatural elements in romance as allegories of social realities, a point also taken up by Hurd. Thanks to the appearance of St. Palaye's historical study *Mémoires de l'Ancienne Chévalerie* in 1759, Hurd was able to provide a detailed account of feudal society and manners and argue, more persuasively than any previous commentator, the relativist point that Gothic literature was as valid a form of artistic expression as Grecian art when seen in context.[5]

The historicist approach of Warton and Hurd informs Walpole's treatment of the relation between the medieval setting and manifestations of the supernatural. Hurd had speculated that tales of enchantment "shadowed out" the class conflict of their times; "oppressive feudal Lords" were imaginatively transposed by the peasantry into fictional giants, "and every Lord was to be met with, like the Giant, in his strong hold, or castle."[6] In *Otranto*, too, exaggerated fantasy is the natural outgrowth of the violent appropriation of power.[7] The benevolent Prince Alfonso, we discover, was murdered by his chamberlain Ricardo, the line of succession has been perverted, and two generations later Alfonso has returned as a spectral giant to reclaim the property for his own descendant. The castle is central to the fable and seems to have a life of its own. It traps and conceals; its walls frame almost all the main events with a specificity on which Walpole prided himself ("The scene is undoubtably laid in some real castle" he fibbed in the first preface, p. 8, though some have drawn comparisons with his own house Strawberry Hill). Its alien modes of ingress and egress give rise to the prototypical scene of Isabella's desperate flight from the villain through an underground tunnel and to the display of chivalric pageantry when Prince Frederick arrives at its gates incognito to challenge Manfred, accompanied by a large entourage of harbingers, heralds, pages, foot-guards, liveried footmen, and "an hundred gentlemen bearing an enormous sword, and seeming to faint under the weight of it" (p. 65). In *Lives of the Novelists*, Walter Scott praised Walpole's attention to "the costume of the period."[8]

In the counterfeiting first preface, the inclusion of ghosts and miracles is justified with the claim that the tale is "faithful to the *manners* of the time" (p. 6). If chivalry and feudalism provide one explanatory context, the dominance of the Catholic Church in medieval times provides another. Walpole (posing as translator) initially suggests that the original story was written to reinforce "the empire of superstition" when the growth of learning threatened to dispel it: "such a work as the following would enslave a hundred vulgar minds beyond half the books of controversy that have been written from the days of Luther to the present day" (pp. 5–6). A factor in the dismissal of ancient romance was the association with Catholic superstition. The disenchanted novel was felt to be the appropriate fictional mode for an enlightened Protestant culture. Hence the outrage of one reviewer when the true authorship of *Otranto* was revealed: "It is, indeed, more than strange that an Author, of a refined and polished genius, should be an advocate for re-establishing the barbarous superstitions of Gothic devilism!"[9] Nearly thirty years later, Radcliffe was to introduce the device of the "explained supernatural" in order to reconcile Protestant incredulity and the taste for ghostly terror. Walpole's "authentic" representation of medieval ghost beliefs is ambivalent. On the one hand the church effigy with a nosebleed and the uproarious reaction to every supernatural phenomenon of the benighted servants and peasants have the quality of spoof; it is notable that the "noble" characters, Manfred and the hero Theodore, retain their skepticism almost to the end. On the other hand Father Jerome is represented by and large as a man of integrity, Manfred and Hippolita finish by seeking redemption in holy orders, and the climactic incarnation of the giant ghost shaking the castle to its foundations is undeniably real. Ultimately, therefore, Walpole eschews irony and takes the radical option of reviving discredited beliefs for the entertainment of a modern audience.[10]

The revisionist view of medieval culture did not stop at historical analysis. To grant that medieval Gothic literature had its own unique character was to grant that it had its own virtues; dissection made way for enthusiasm. Warton and Hurd suggested that the Gothic age, precisely because of its relative barbarity, was especially conducive to the free play of imagination and that what the modern era had gained in civility it had lost in poetic inspiration. Historicism in literary studies shaded into primitivism, a questioning of the certainty that civilization meant progress.[11] And once a sense of loss had been acknowledged, it was only another small step to take the view that modernity must learn from the uncivilized past and aspire to imitate it.

The Castle of Otranto was one of various attempts around this time to cut a new path in literature by looking back to the past; the poets William Collins, Edward Young, Walpole's friend Thomas Gray, and the fabricator of "Ossian," James Macpherson, were all important innovators of this kind. In every case there was impatience with the limitations of neoclassical taste and an investment in alternative theories about art and its reception, human nature, and the workings of the mind. These did not always relate directly to romance but they helped to create a climate of opinion favorable to revival. The concept of the sublime originated in a classical text, the treatise *On the Sublime* (*Peri hupsous*) attributed to Longinus. In 1674 this text was translated into French by Boileau, and the resulting account of the "grand style" of writing which provokes powerful emotion became immediately influential. Writers and critics from John Dryden to John Dennis began using this classical concept to counter other classical concepts, most notably *mimesis*, the imitation of nature. The inclusion of supernatural or fantastical beings in a drama was justified as a means of stimulating the sensation of "transport" that Longinus commended. Joseph Addison acknowledged that traditional tales of ghosts and fairies arouse "a pleasing kind of Horrour in the Mind of the Reader" and are an excellent resource for a poet. He cited Shakespeare in evidence, but warned that "it is impossible for a Poet to succeed in it, who has not a particular Cast of Fancy, and an Imagination naturally fruitful and superstitious."[12]

As if in answer to Addison's challenge, the poem "A Night Piece on Death" (1721) by Thomas Parnell launched the so-called "Graveyard school," which had its heyday in the 1740s with Edward Young's *The Complaint, or Night Thoughts on Life, Death, and Immortality* (1742–45), Robert Blair's "The Grave" (1743), and James Hervey's prose *Meditations Among the Tombs* (1746–47). All used superstitious suggestion to raise the mind to a pitch sufficient to embrace the idea of mortality, but without representing a "real" ghost. It was a critical balancing act: the differentiation between the rational beliefs of Protestantism and irrational Catholicism was at stake. William Collins went much further in embracing the aesthetic possibilities of the supernatural with two poems, "Ode to Fear" (1746) and "Ode on the Popular Superstitions of the Highlands of Scotland" (written 1749, published 1788). It struck some observers as entirely in keeping that he lapsed into insanity soon after. Samuel Johnson's judgment on Collins after his early death was strict: "He had employed his mind chiefly upon works of fiction, and subjects of fancy; and, by indulging some peculiar habits of thought, was eminently delighted with those flights of imagination which pass the bounds of nature, and to which the mind is reconciled only by a passive acquiescence in popular traditions."[13]

But towards the end of the 1750s the case for expanding the imagination was strengthened. Edmund Burke's *A Philosophical Enquiry into the Origin of Our Ideas of the Sublime and Beautiful* (1757) was the most ambitious and methodical consideration of the sublime yet published. It presented imaginative transport not only as desirable – one rhetorical option among others – but as a necessity, mentally and even physiologically. Burke begins by outlining the problem of indifference, a state of mental lethargy brought about by a steady diet of the familiar. Positive pleasure, the type of novelty associated with beauty, is one way of relieving the problem, but it is only a mild and temporary cure. Far more effective is a peculiar kind of pain mixed with delight, "the strongest emotion which the mind is capable [of feeling]" (Burke, *Enquiry*, p. 36; also in Clery and Miles, *Gothic Documents*, p. 113). The sublime is an apprehension of danger in nature or art without the immediate risk of destruction; it is a "state of the soul, in which all its motions are suspended, with some degree of horror" and "the mind is so entirely filled with its object, that it cannot entertain any other" (*Enquiry*, p. 53; *Documents*, p. 113). Just as the muscles of the body must be kept in tone, so the imagination must be "shaken and worked to a proper degree" by images and ideas of the terrible sublime (*Enquiry*, p. 123; *Documents*, p. 121).

The relevance of Burke's *Enquiry* to Walpole's experiments with romance is twofold. First, there is the emphasis on terror as the "ruling principle" of the sublime. Walpole picks up the idea in the first preface to *Otranto*: "Terror, the author's principal engine, prevents the story from ever languishing; and it is so often contrasted by pity, that the mind is kept up in a constant vicissitude of interesting passions" (p. 6). After all, like Burke's theory, *Otranto* originates in the problem of boredom and satiety. They are both products of a commercial society in which stability, leisure, and plenty lead to a demand for artificial excitements, and most appositely, in which the rapid growth of the reading habit in the middle class breeds obscure longings for novelty. Burke contributed to a mounting sense of crisis in literary culture, an increasing impatience with borrowed forms and mere social utility. He was forcefully seconded by Edward Young in *Conjectures on Original Composition* (1759): "We read *Imitation* with somewhat of his langour, who listens to a twice-told tale; Our spirits rouze at an *Original*; that is a perfect stranger, and all throng to learn what news from a foreign land" (cited in Clery and Miles, *Gothic Documents*, p. 122).

In spite of this pressure in favor of originality, the path of innovators did not necessarily run smoothly. There was still strong resistance from the literary establishment. A case in point was that of Thomas Gray, a close friend of Walpole, who like Collins was deeply versed in folklore and mythology, admired Spenser and Shakespeare above all poets, and revived the Pindaric ode, the most irregular and thus "sublime" of metrical forms. His *Odes* were the first volume to be published at the Strawberry Hill press in 1757, and one of the poems, "The Bard," contains several of the ingredients later to be found in *Otranto*: a tyrant, a prophecy, and ghosts demanding vengeance. It is based on the tradition that after his conquest of Wales, Edward I condemned to death the bards for reciting seditious stories. Gray's treatment brought together primitivism and the natural sublime and has been credited with launching the "Celtic revival" in literature.[14] In the figure of the Poet, the bard who confronts Edward, curses him, and commits triumphant suicide, Gray also created a potent emblem of the resistance of the spirit of imagination to tyrannical laws, aesthetic and political. But in the short term the *Odes* met with a frosty critical reception and sold badly. By contrast, the next import from the Celtic fringe just five years later, the "Ossian" epics – *Fingal* (1762) and *Temora* (1763) – became one of the publishing phenomena of the century. The prose poems were presented to the public as the work of a Gaelic bard of the fourth century AD, but were actually concocted by James Macpherson. There was debate over their authenticity but most admirers, until well into the next century, preferred to take them as irrefutable evidence of primitive genius. There seems little doubt that Walpole's initial decision to disguise *Otranto* as an ancient manuscript was informed by his comparing the reception of "The Bard" with that of "Ossian."

Unlike Macpherson, Walpole quickly confessed his authorship, but when he did so in the second preface, he chose "to shelter [his] own daring under the cannon of the brightest genius this country, at least, has produced" (Walpole, *Castle of Otranto*, p. 14). With this stratagem we come to the third, and arguably the most significant, added factor in Walpole's romance formula. It would be impossible to overestimate the importance of Shakespeare as touchstone and inspiration for the terror mode, even if we feel the offspring are unworthy of their parent. Scratch the surface of any Gothic fiction and the debt to Shakespeare will be there. To begin with there are the key scenes of supernatural terror that are plundered by Walpole and then by many other fiction writers: the banquet scene, the vision of the dagger, and the visit to the cave of the three witches in *Macbeth*; the phantasmagoria of the tent scene in *Richard III*; and above all, the ghost scenes from *Hamlet*. In Walpole's time these episodes had already acquired autonomous fame in the theatre through the thrilling naturalism of David Garrick's acting style, capable of persuading a skeptical audience that they too witnessed the supernatural (see Clery, *Rise of Supernatural Fiction*, pp. 37–46). When Walpole in the first preface talks of the "inspired writings" of the past that serve as his model, in which "witnesses to the most stupendous phenomena, never lose sight of their human character" (Walpole, *Castle of Otranto*, p. 10), he is thinking primarily of Shakespeare's tragedies and Garrick's interpretations of them.

Shakespeare had a very specific value for the romance revival in Britain. Historically, he was situated on the cusp between Gothic and enlightened times. His plays were believed to combine the benefits of Protestantism and Renaissance learning with ready access to the resources of popular folklore and Popish superstition, so conducive to the imagination. Even his language was regarded as striking a perfect balance between ancient and modern. Hurd suggested that the English language was at its best in the age of Elizabeth, "somewhere between the rude essays and uncorrected fancy, on the one hand, and the refinements of reason and science, on the other."[15] Ideologically, Shakespeare also played an important part in the nationalist myth surrounding the reign of Elizabeth. It was no accident that the cult of the Immortal Bard intensified during the period of the Seven Years' War, 1756–63, when France's living national poet Voltaire chose to launch an attack on the English dramatic tradition. Walpole's second preface, partly addressed to Voltaire, was a notable contribution to the war of words and a ringing defense of one aspect of Shakespeare's practice that remained controversial even in Britain: the inclusion of comic scenes in the tragedies. Walpole adopted this practice in *Otranto*, and it was to remain a feature of Gothic romance through to Ann Radcliffe, "Monk" Lewis and beyond.

For several years, however, no other contenders appeared to capitalize on the possibilities of a modern romance genre. Walpole himself turned his attention to drama. The design of *The Mysterious Mother: a Tragedy* (1768) was as rebellious in its way as *Otranto* had been. The Countess of Narbonne, maddened by learning of the death of her husband, secretly and in disguise committed premeditated incest with her son, bore a child from that union, and in spite of attempts to expiate the sin through good works, has suffered years of inner torment before killing herself when father/son and daughter/sister unwittingly fall in love and the truth is exposed. With this story Walpole aimed to create a character "quite new on the stage."[16] The play in fact never reached the stage: even in print, it was suppressed by its author and withheld from public sale until 1791. The problem was the nature of the crime, which many of those who read it felt was too revolting to be offered as part of an entertainment and unredeemable by any kind of moral counterweight in the drama.

Walpole was happy enough to impose self-censorship for a while, but he stubbornly resisted attempts by a well-meaning friend to get him to water down the plot.[17] It was vital to his purpose to maintain the stark contrast between the manifest goodness and nobility of the heroine and the enduring stain of a moment of passion. *The Mysterious Mother* is set "at the dawn of the Reformation" and is in the historical sense anti-Gothic. A large part of the Countess's heroism lies in her resistance to the superstitious "mumming" of the devious Catholic priests Benedict and Martin, who seek to frighten her into a confession of her secret and then appropriate her estate.

In spite of its notoriety and long suppression, the play had a growing underground reputation. Ann Radcliffe cites it on three occasions in *The Italian*. As an example of natural horror and an investigation of the extremes of human nature, it was unquestionably influential on a developing strand of psychological Gothic, distinct from supernatural fiction, found in the work of William Godwin, Joanna Baillie, Mary Shelley, Lord Byron, and the Americans Charles Brockden Brown and Edgar Allan Poe.

In the meantime *Otranto* was gradually achieving the recognition Walpole sought for it as a hybrid "new species." The eminent man of letters William Warburton praised it for going beyond its setting "in *Gothic Chivalry*" and putting into "effect the full purpose of the *ancient Tragedy*, that is, *to purge the passions by pity and terror*, in colouring as great and harmonious as in any of the best Dramatic Writers."[18] In 1773 brother and sister John and

Anna Laetitia Aikin published *Miscellaneous Pieces in Prose*, which included in its subjects "The Pleasure Derived from Objects of Terror." They draw the connection between Shakespearean tragedy and traditional tales of the marvelous, whether "old Gothic romance" or eastern fable, "with their genii, giants, enchantments and transformations." *Otranto* is identified as "a very spirited modern attempt upon the same plan of mixed terror ["the terrible joined with the marvelous"], adapted to the model of Gothic romance." For an explanation of the pleasure in fictions of the terrible, they reiterate Burke's theory of the sublime: "A strange and unexpected event awakens the mind, and keeps it on the stretch; and where the agency of invisible beings is introduced, of 'forms unseen, and mightier far than we,' our imagination, darting forth, explores with rapture the new world which is laid open to its view, and rejoices in the expansion of its powers" (the Aikins in Clery and Miles, *Gothic Documents*, p. 129).

When the Aikins speak of "passion and fancy co-operating" to "elevate the soul to its highest pitch," they echo Walpole's central doctrine, the combination of the natural and the supernatural. And like Walpole they set aside the issue of moral justification. They argue that there are no moral feelings involved in the response to this type of fiction, in contrast to the sympathetic response to scenes of distress in novels of sensibility. To demonstrate the effect, a short fragment "Sir Bertrand" (also 1773) was included in the Aikin volume. It consists of a series of astonishing and horrific occurrences undergone by a lone knight, unsubordinated to any overarching narrative logic or didactic message.[19] The fragment offers instead pure sensation, and, with its freedom from the conventional moral rubric of the novel, it is as much a founding text of the terror mode as *Otranto*.

The return of romance to eighteenth-century fiction needs to be seen in economic context, as a symptom of the vicissitudes of the publishing industry and a response to the search for novelty. As a consequence of Ian Watt's landmark study, we are accustomed to the idea of the "rise of the novel" and the corollary that it never looked back. Works such as Samuel Richardson's *Pamela* (1740–41) and *Clarissa* (1747–48), Henry Fielding's *Tom Jones* (1749), Laurence Sterne's *Tristram Shandy* (1759–67), and Jean-Jacques Rousseau's *Julie; ou La Nouvelle Héloïse* (1761) were not only huge publishing successes, but "media events" that launched numerous spinoffs such as journalistic responses, spoofs, theatrical adaptations, print engravings, and sermons, as well as a host of imitators. But by the 1770s the lack of new and original contenders was sending the novel into what appeared to be a terminal decline. Between 1776 and 1779 an average of seventeen new novels per year were published, a slump from a high of sixty in 1771 (see

Garside, et al., *English Novel 1770–1829*, I, 26–27). There were no doubt various factors at play, including the contingencies of war in the American colonies and changes in copyright law, but it seems likely that generic exhaustion was much of the problem. For years would-be heirs to Richardson and Sterne had been churning out feeble imitations. The reading public were beginning to tire of these, and publishers and booksellers were becoming discouraged. The arrival of Frances Burney's *Evelina* in 1778 helped to reverse the fortunes of the novel form and created another wave of imitations. But it was also precisely at this point that Clara Reeve decided to take up Walpole's challenge to develop a "new route" in fiction and wrote *The Old English Baron* (first published in 1777 under the title *The Champion of Virtue*). It was her well-timed initiative that turned Walpole's half-serious novelty into a viable commercial mode.[20]

Clara Reeve was a specialist in romance. In 1772 she published a translation of John Barclay's seventeenth-century romance *Argensis* from Latin, and in 1785 she was to produce a substantial work of criticism, *The Progress of Romance*, which I will discuss shortly. Between these two, *The Old English Baron: a Gothic Story* appeared and, as her preface puts it, brought the technique introduced in *Otranto* "within the utmost *verge* of probability" (p. 4). Reeve presented her own slightly revised formula for combining "the ancient Romance and modern Novel": "a sufficient degree of the marvellous to excite the attention; enough of the manners of real life, to give an air of probability to the work; and enough of the pathetic, to engage the heart in its behalf" (ibid.).

In practice, she takes a story very similar to that of *Otranto*, of a young peasant discovered to be the rightful heir to a usurped estate. She reduces the supernatural element, expands the description of everyday actions and events, and develops the emotional bonds among the different characters in relationships of friendship, patronage, and family piety (the villain scarcely registers, though the suffering of his victims does). A notable instance of her revisionism comes early in the narrative, when the hero Edmund, like Walpole's Theodore, undertakes to sleep in a reputedly haunted chamber. The scene is set more thoroughly than in Walpole, with detail of the bed "devoured by the moths, and occupied by the rats" (p. 42). There is a hint of supernatural rustling in the hall, but fear is immediately quashed by the hero's fortifying prayers. A visitation by the ghosts of his parents seems like a pleasant dream. What is gained by this method is an extension of the aim of moral improvement to embrace a degree of the marvelous; what is sacrificed is terror and sublimity.[21] As far as the "Gothic" nature of the story is concerned, Reeve went to some trouble to evoke the age of chivalry, with a battle scene, a joust, and the device of interruptions to the tale caused by a fragmented manuscript. A critic at the time observed that it was set too late (in the fifteenth century) to be strictly "Gothic."[22]

Due to our own anachronistic usage of "Gothic" and unwillingness to take into account the contemporary term "modern romance," the 1780s have been almost universally misrecognized as a fallow period before the boom of the 1790s. In fact this is a decade of escalating debate on the origins and character of romance, which had an immediate bearing on innovative fictions. Through the 1760s and 1770s, rival theories had been taking shape: the eastern theory (with William Warburton at its head), arguing that romances derived from eastern tales imported to Europe at the time of the Crusades – or earlier, during Moorish rule in Spain; the northern theory (championed by Thomas Percy) locating the source of romance in the Norselands, with the Normans as disseminators; and a Celtic theory put forward by the Welsh antiquarian Evan Evans.[23] In line with the universalist assumptions of neo-classical criticism, all schools of thought presumed there must be a single source, though Hurd's more historicist approach opened the way for an alternative view that romance develops out of native social structures, not through migration. In *The History of English Poetry* (1774–81), Thomas Warton argued strongly for an eastern origin for what he called "Romantic fiction." In doing so, he ran counter to the previous northern trend represented by Percy and Gray and the Celtic revivalism of James Macpherson and Hugh Blair, chief apologist for the authenticity and greatness of "Ossian." Warton's theory was matched by orientalist elements in *Otranto* and *The Old English Baron* (both with Crusade contexts) and the Aikins' singling out of *Arabian Nights* for its "many striking examples of the terrible jointed with the marvellous" (cited in Clery and Miles, *Gothic Documents*, p. 129).

The "romance wars" of the 1780s took place both at the level of theory and practice, and there was considerable interchange between the two. James Beattie and Clara Reeve produced major critical works on the genre. Novice fiction writers Sophia Lee (*The Recess*, 1783–85), Charlotte Smith (*Emmeline, the Orphan of the Castle*, 1788), and Ann Radcliffe (*The Castles of Athlyn and Dunbayne*, 1789) all to a greater or lesser extent embraced the Celtic revival, while William Beckford with *Vathek* (1786) produced the first full-fledged orientalist tale of terror. Although the latter work figured in the notable anthology *Three Gothic Novels* (1968) edited by Mario Praz, it has been omitted from most recent surveys of the terror mode. This is a loss; a sense of the diversity of experiments in modern romance at this stage throws into relief the remarkable convergence of motifs that took place in the 1790s.

James Beattie's essay "On Fable and Romance" in *Dissertations Moral and Political* (1783) is a strange hotchpotch of derivative ideas (mainly Hurd's) but also shows the impact that the success of modern romance was having on the thinking of critics. He repeats the common view of *Don Quixote* as a romance-buster: "This work no sooner appeared, than chivalry vanished, as snow melts before the sun. Mankind awoke as from a dream" (Beattie in Clery and Miles, *Gothic Documents*, p. 92). But his account of chivalric romance sounds just like the "Gothic stories" of Walpole and Reeve, with castles in an eternal state of delapidation, complete with winding passages, secret haunted chambers, and creaking hinges, and narratives revolving around tyranny, rapine, and the ravishing of maidens. In other words, literary history had become infected with present-day fantasy. The revival of romance seems to have encouraged Beattie to apply the term freely, as Walpole did, to every kind of modern fiction including the works of Richardson and Fielding. This, however, does not save the genre from a final unexpected condemnation: "Let not the usefulness of Romance-writing be estimated by the length of my discourse upon it. Romances are a dangerous recreation . . . and tend to corrupt the heart, and stimulate the passions."[24]

Clara Reeve's *The Progress of Romance* (1785) was a campaigning work. The very idea that "romance" *could* "progress" was contentious; the two words had not previously been used together. The work is presented as a series of adversarial dialogues between a woman of letters, Euphrasia (Reeve herself), and Hortensius, a rather facetious strawman of conventional opinions, while Sophronia arbitrates from the sidelines. Euphrasia delivers a knock-out blow in the first round by demonstrating that the prized epics of Homer and Virgil were really a species of romance, comparable to the *Arabian Nights*. After that she is easily able to carry her main point, that "Romances are of universal growth, and not confined to any particular period or countries."[25] Reeve's terminology is distinctive. She distinguishes clearly between romance "which treats of fabulous persons and things" and the novel as "a picture of real life and manners."[26] The "modern romance" describes the heroic romances of La Calprenède and Scudéry. She slides the contemporary revival of romance in through the back door by creating a wholly new category, "Novels and Stories Original and Uncommon," to encompass *The Castle of Otranto* alongside whimsical and fantastical fictions like *Tristram Shandy*, *Gulliver's Travels*, and even *Robinson Crusoe*. *Contra* Beattie, she finds no difficulty in declaring them all "of moral tendency."[27]

Originality, not a medieval setting, is the vital component of the evolving literature of terror. What such texts share is a revolt against the representation of common experience and familiar situations. A case in point is Sophia Lee's *The Recess: a Tale of Other Times* (1783–85). Set in the reign of Elizabeth I, it concerns the tumultuous lives of the fictive twin daughters of Mary Queen of Scots, secretly raised in an underground habitation. Some critics were by now primed to respond to the promise of romance with swooning anticipation. Samuel Badcock writes in the *Monthly Review*, "*The Tale of Other Times* is a romantic title. It awakens curiosity; it sets us at once on *fairy* land – while Fancy, equipped for adventure, sallies forth in quest of the castle, the giant, and the dragon." He confesses disappointment that the fiction turns out to be founded on fact.[28] The *Critical Review* was more receptive to the mixture of fiction and history and excited about its novelty: "This little volume is full of surprising and yet not improbable events. The author, Miss Lee, properly observes, that the age of Elizabeth was that of romance, and she has accordingly chosen it for the era of her heroines...It is new; it is instructive; it is highly interesting; and we wish that this mode of writing were more frequent."[29]

Vathek renewed the claims of the Spanish–eastern theory by reminding the public of the unparalleled imaginative freedom of the genuine oriental tale (it was first published under the title *An Arabian Tale*). William Enfield writing on *Vathek* in the *Monthly Review* indicates he had a contrast with Gothic romance in mind when he echoes the language of Reeve's preface to *The Old English Baron*, a work he had reviewed eight years earlier: "it preserves the peculiar character of the Arabian Tale, which is not only to overstep nature and probability, but even to pass beyond the verge of possibility, and suppose things, which cannot be for a moment conceived."[30] Earlier British versions of the oriental tale, such as Samuel Johnson's *Rasselas* (1759) and Frances Sheridan's *The History of Nourjahad* (1767), had been subject to a didactic imperative as strict as that of the realist novel. Although Beckford gestured toward this model, it was not a wholly convincing gesture. The eponymous villain and his equally loathsome mother Carathis burst the bounds of moral instruction with their extravagant desires and grotesque cruelty, and there is no divine tempering of the magic powers of the genii. Like Walpole, Beckford attempts a Shakespearean contrast of comedy and terror, but instead of interweaving the two, the black humor of the major part of the tale is finally overtaken by a scene of extraordinary tragic power. Vathek discovers that the reality of the ultimate empire, for which he has committed so many crimes, is an eternity of aimless wandering among a multitude of lost souls in the vast domains of the devil Eblis.

The eastern tale of terror had no immediate successor, but the example of *Vathek* was not wholly abandoned. It is evident that Matthew Lewis borrowed some of Beckford's ideas for the handling of his villain Ambrosio in *The Monk* and perhaps took encouragement from *Vathek* for scenes of sorcery beyond the now-standard spectral appearances found in romances of a medieval kind. In the short term, however, a new winning formula for modern romance was coalescing. The heroine-centered adventures in atmospheric settings of Lee's *The Recess* and Smith's *Emmeline* provided one staple; the poetic picturesque of Radcliffe's *Castles of Athlin and Dunbayne* offered another. When they combined in the full-fledged "Radcliffe romance" of the early 1790s, the experiment begun by Walpole achieved unimagined levels of critical and commercial success. Beckford, a sore loser, remained a dissenting voice. His satires on Radcliffe in *Modern Novel Writing* (1796) and *Azemia* (1797) may be seen as postscripts to the era dealt with in this essay, when the creation of imaginary terrors was still an eccentric and highly speculative venture.

NOTES

1 A handful of fictions feature "Gothic" in their titles after Reeve, including Richard Warner's *Netley Abbey: a Gothic Story* (1795) and Isabella Kelly's *The Baron's Daughter: a Gothic Romance* (1802). "A Romance" is by far the most common subtitle among writings of the period now described as "Gothic." See Alfred E. Longueil, "The Word 'Gothic' in Eighteenth-Century Criticism," *MLN* 38 (1923): 453–60 for a few rare early instances of the term being applied in a literary critical sense.

2 *Gothic* as a generic term appears in two literary overviews in 1899: Henry A. Beers, *History of English Romanticism in the Eighteenth Century* (New York: Henry Holt) and Wilbur Cross, *The Development of the English Novel* (New York and London: Macmillan). It was established in Britain by Edith Birkhead in 1921, and in 1932 J. M. S. Tompkins followed suit with a chapter on "Gothic Romance." Cf. Montague Summers, *The Gothic Quest: a History of the Gothic Novel* (London: Fortune Press, 1938).

3 See the chapter by Robert Miles in this volume.

4 See Michael McKeon, *The Origins of the English Novel* (Baltimore: Johns Hopkins University Press, 1987). For an often-cited discussion of novel vs. romance as a gendered opposition, see Laurie Langbauer, *Women and Romance: the Consolations of Gender in the English Novel* (Ithaca: Cornell University Press, 1990); but it should be noted that most heroic romances were written by men, and for the eighteenth century the archetypal romance reader was Cervantes' Don Quixote.

5 On Hurd and antiquarian discourse, see Mark Madoff, "The Useful Myth of Gothic Ancestry," *Studies in Eighteenth-Century Culture* 8 (1979), and Harriet Guest, "The Wanton Muse: Politics and Gender in Gothic Theory After 1760" in *Beyond Romanticism*, ed. Stephen Copley and John Whale (London: Routledge, 1993), pp. 118–39.

6 Hurd, *Letters on Chivalry and Romance*, Augustan Reprint Society, no. 101/02, 1st facsimile edn (Los Angeles: University of California Press, 1963), pp. 28–29.

7 For political readings of *Otranto*, see Robert Miles, *Gothic Writing, 1750–1820* (London: Routledge, 1993), pp. 105–12, and E. J. Clery, *The Rise of Supernatural Fiction, 1762–1800* (Cambridge: Cambridge University Press, 1995), pp. 68–79.

8 Peter Sabor, ed., *Horace Walpole: the Critical Heritage* (London and New York: Routledge and Kegan Paul, 1987), p. 92. Note also John Allen Stevenson, "*The Castle of Otranto*: Political Supernaturalism" in *The British Novel: Defoe to Austen* (Boston: G. K. Hall, 1990), pp. 90–109.

9 *Monthly Review* 32 (May 1765): 394.

10 For an interpretation of *The Castle of Otranto* focusing on religion and superstition, see Victor Sage, *Horror Fiction in the Protestant Tradition* (London: Macmillan, 1988).

11 A related challenge to the Enlightenment narrative was simultaneously arising in the field of philosophy, most influentially in Jean-Jacques Rousseau's *Discourse on the Origins of Inequality* (1754).

12 *Spectator* 419 (1712) in E. J. Clery and Robert Miles, eds., *Gothic Documents: a Sourcebook, 1700–1820* (Manchester: Manchester University Press, 2000), p. 105.

13 Samuel Johnson, *The Poetical Calendar* (1763), cited in Roger Lonsdale, ed., *Thomas Gray and William Collins: Poetical Works* (Oxford: Oxford University Press, 1877), p. xxii.

14 Sam Smiles, *The Image of Antiquity: Ancient Britain and the Romantic Imagination* (New Haven and London: Yale University Press, 1994), p. 18.

15 From "Dialogue III: on the Golden Age of Queen Elizabeth" in *Moral and Political Dialogues*, reprinted in Richard Hurd, *Letters on Chivalry and Romance, with the Third Elizabethan Dialogue*, ed. Edith J. Morley (London: Henry Frowde, 1911), p. 71.

16 *The Yale Edition of Horace Walpole's Correspondence*, ed. W. S. Lewis, 48 vols. (New Haven: Yale University Press, 1937–83), XXVII, 9.

17 On the publication history of the play, see E. J. Clery, "Horace Walpole's *The Mysterious Mother* and the Impossibility of Female Desire" in Fred Botting, ed., *The Gothic*, in the English Association Essays and Studies series (Cambridge: D. S. Brewer, 2001), pp. 23–46.

18 *The Works of Alexander Pope* (1770), IV, 165–67, reprinted in Sabor, ed., *Walpole: the Critical Heritage*, p. 75.

19 This was written by John Aikin; see Lucy Aikin, ed., *The Works of Anna Laetitia Barbauld, with a Memoir*, 2 vols. (1825), I, xiii–xiv.

20 For an illuminating investigation of the emergence of Gothic romance from changes in the publishing trade, see Edward Jacobs, both in "Anonymous Signatures: Circulating Libraries, Conventionality, and the Production of Gothic Romances," *ELH* 62 (1995): 603–29, and in *Accidental Migrations: an Archeology of Gothic Discourse* (Lewisburg: Bucknell University Press), pp. 157–235.

21 For recent readings of *The Old English Baron*, see James Watt, *Contesting the Gothic: Fiction, Genre, and Cultural Conflict, 1764–1832* (Cambridge: Cambridge University Press, 1999) and E. J. Clery, *Women's Gothic from Clara Reeve to Mary Shelley* (Tavistock: Northcote House Publishers, 2000).

22 "[T]he title therefore seems a kind of contradiction in terms. The mistake seems to arise from the Gothic style in building, which then prevailed"; *Gentleman's Magazine* 48 (July 1778): 324–25.

23 René Wellek, *The Rise of English Literary History* (Chapel Hill: University of North Carolina Press, 1941), pp. 153–56.

24 Ioan Williams, ed., *Novel and Romance 1700–1800: a Documentary Record* (London: Routledge, 1970), p. 327.

25 Clara Reeve, *The Progress of Romance* in Gary Kelly, ed., *Bluestocking Feminism: Writings of the Bluestocking Circle, 1738–1785*, 6 vols. (London: Pickering and Chatto, 1999), VI, 167.
26 ibid., VI, 210.
27 ibid., VI, 244.
28 *Monthly Review* 68 (May 1783): 455–56.
29 *Critical Review* 55 (March 1783): 233–34.
30 *Monthly Review* 76 (May 1787): 450.

3

ROBERT MILES

The 1790s: the effulgence of Gothic

It is the business of literary criticism to test the myths of literary history. The contemporary reception of what we now call the Gothic has furnished us with two enduring stories about its rise: that the Gothic novel began with Horace Walpole's *The Castle of Otranto* and that the 1790s witnessed an explosion in what was most commonly referred to then as the "terrorist system of novel writing." The chapters prior to mine in this volume address the first proposition. My purpose here is to explore the second, of which there are two main aspects. Was there in fact an effulgence of terror fiction in the1790s?[1] And if so, what did it mean?

Was the novel-writing market flooded by the Gothic in the 1790s, as the reviewers claimed? With only one small qualification, the answer is a resounding "yes." The qualification rests on the meaning of "Gothic." As E. J. Clery in the previous chapter reminds us, the term *Gothic novel* was retrospectively applied to such works, for the most part. Although this ought to caution us against overlooking the heterogeneous nature of 1790s romance, the fact remains that terror fiction of the period is easily identifiable, despite its variety. The recently published *English Novel 1770–1829: a Bibliographical Guide* (Garside et al.) permits a simple yet decisive exercise. It contains the full titles of virtually all of the novels published during the period, which generally include key items of marketing information, thus giving us useful generic pointers. It also includes extracts from the *Monthly* and *Critical Review*, which dominated reviewing at this time, so that we can observe the period's own acts of critical categorization.

The marketing cues can be broken down into several categories: geographical features (the recess, ruins, the rock, Alps, black valley, black tower, haunted cavern); architectural features (priory, castle, abbey, convent, nunnery, ancient house, cloister); generic pointers (historical romance, legends, tales, memoir, traditions); ghost and its cognates (apparition, specter, phantom, the ghost-seer, sorcerer, magician, necromancer, weird sisters); exotic names (Manfredi, Edward de Courcy, Wolfenbach); and generic or historical figures (the monk, the genius, the minstrel, knights, the royal captives, Duke of Clarence, Lady Jane Grey, John of Gaunt). In terms of contemporary classifications, critics used "romance" and "historical" judiciously, but their main device for sorting through their reviewing was reference to the example of other authors. As regards the Gothic, three in particular stand out from the decades before the 1790s: critics refer to the examples of Walpole, the Aikins, and Sophia Lee (see previous chapter for details). In the 1790s themselves, Ann Radcliffe, Friedrich Schiller, and Matthew Lewis are added to the list. Clara Reeve's *The Old English Baron* (1777–78) is also mentioned, although critics tend to see her as consolidating Walpole's experiment rather than adding something substantially new. The first three writers are particularly important for delimiting the Gothic, as each added something distinct: Walpole contributed the haunted, usurped castle, plus the element of pastiche; the Aikins were credited with integrating the Burkean aesthetic of terrific sublimity into the tale of feudal ruins through their theoretical essay "On the Pleasure Derived from Objects of Terror" and in the tale "Sir Bertrand";[2] while Sophia Lee was seen as pioneering the use of history through her exploitation of the politically resonant legend of Mary, Queen of Scots.

Putting together both kinds of information produces figure 1. It depicts the number of such works published in the period 1770–1800, indicated by year. It includes works with a "gothic" marketing cue and novels associated by the reviewers with the examples of Walpole, Lee, the Aikins, Radcliffe, Schiller or Lewis. As this figure shows, the upsurge in Gothic works is indeed dramatic during the 1790s. There is a sharp increase in Gothic "product" starting in 1788, followed by a further upward deflection point in 1793. From 1788 until 1807 the Gothic maintains a market share of around 30 percent of novel production, reaching a high point of 38 percent in 1795, then dipping to around 20 percent in 1808. Thereafter its market share dwindles, with 1820 the last year of double-digit figures (Garside et al., *English Novel*, II, 56). Terror fiction breaks down into two, broad phases: from 1788 to 1793, when the Gothic bursts onto the literary scene after a long period of intermittent gestation; and a plateau of market dominance from 1794 (the year in which *The Mysteries of Udolpho* and *Caleb Williams* were published) to 1807, when the Gothic begins its decline. If there is a peak, it is in 1800, the year in which the largest number of Gothic novels were published.

Having confirmed that there was a Gothic craze during the 1790s, we can now ask, further, why did it happen? Once again literary history provides us with a piece of received wisdom: the Gothic explosion was collateral damage from the French Revolution. The most famous version of this opinion comes from the Marquis de Sade, who argued that the Gothic novels of

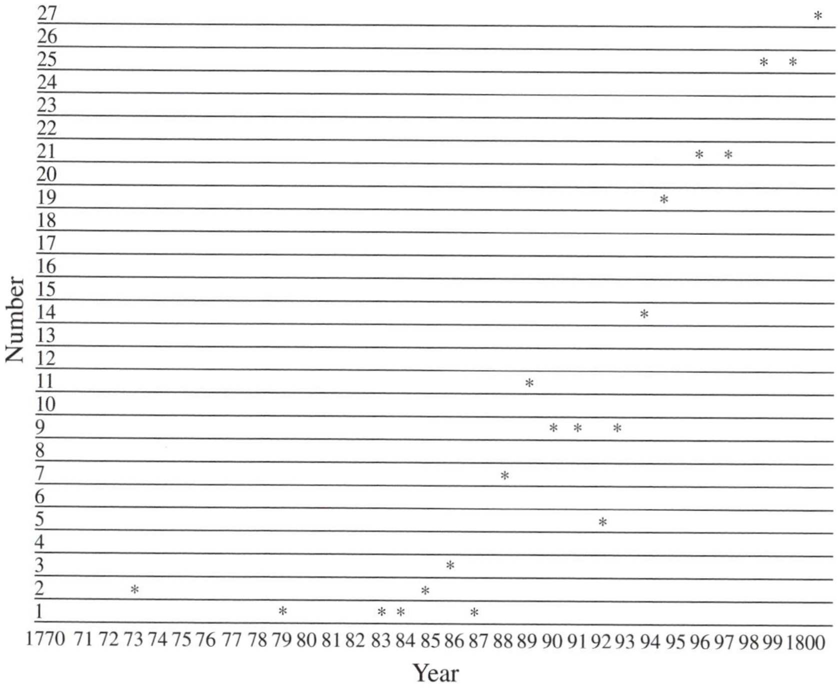

Number

27   *
26
25   *   *
24
23
22
21   *   *
20
19   *
18
17
16
15
14   *
13
12
11   *
10
9   *   *   *
8
7   *
6
5   *
4
3   *
2   *   *
1   *   * *   *

1770 71 72 73 74 75 76 77 78 79 80 81 82 83 84 85 86 87 88 89 90 91 92 93 94 95 96 97 98 99 1800

Year

Fig. 1   Publication of Gothic novels, 1770–1800.

Radcliffe and Lewis were "the necessary fruits of the revolutionary tremors felt by the whole of Europe."[3] According to Sade's view, the bloody horrors of the revolution pushed novelists to new extremes of imaginary violence, as they strove to compete with the shocking reality. William Hazlitt's way of putting matters strikes me as more balanced. Radcliffe's romances "derived part of their interest, no doubt, from the supposed tottering state of all old structures at the time."[4] Equating the Gothic with the French Revolution was a contemporary, rather than a retrospective phenomenon, as we can see from the currency of the smearing pun "the terrorist system of novel writing" employed by reviewers during the latter half of the 1790s (Clery, *Rise of Supernatural Fiction*, pp. 147–48). The reviewers knew full well that Gothic terror derived from the Burkean cult of the sublime, as the Dissenting critic Anna Laetitia Aikin famously explained in her essay, "On the Pleasure Derived from Objects of Terror." The recourse to the sublime adopted by Radcliffe and her school was partly a desire to exploit contemporary aesthetic fashions and partly an attempt to pitch their work toward the high end of the literary market, for sublimity and terror were associated with tragedy and epic, the two most prestigious literary forms – a strategy that would later pay off handsomely for William Wordsworth.[5] By linking Burke's terror with Robespierre's in the limited case of romances by women writers, critics stripped the Gothic of its high literary pretensions, implicitly accusing its authors of being social incendiaries, while figuring them as literary sansculottes: in other words, as a semiliterate mob. One needs to be careful about overstating the case. The adjective "terrorist" smeared, but it also condescended by making "terror" writers the object of a risible pun. The smear worked, not because writers of "hobgoblin romance" were dangerous, but because they palpably were not.

Still, as Hazlitt points out, the connection between Radcliffe's terror and revolutionary fervour was merely "supposed." As an oppositional critic, Hazlitt draws attention to the dubious political rhetoric of the anti-Jacobin forces. His careful formulation suggests that the Gothic derived its interest for readers, not because it was the necessary art of a revolutionary age (de Sade's argument), or because it was itself revolutionary (the view of the anti-Jacobins), but because there was a widespread perception that all old structures were in a tottering condition, such as, for instance, castles, or the constitution, with its feudal, Gothic foundations (William Blackstone's characterization of the constitution as a Gothic structure refurbished for modern living was at once typical and influential [Clery, *Rise of Supernatural fiction*, p. 124]). In other words, the Gothic vogue fed off the revolutionary anxieties of its readership. As there was an explosion in the latter, so was there a burst in the former. Of the three versions of the connection between the French Revolution and the Gothic, Hazlitt's seems to me to be the only one worth testing. But to test it, we first of all need to disaggregate the Gothic.

I started with a cautionary note about nomenclature because I wanted to draw attention to the instability of the very "thing" we are investigating. In constructing figure 1, I concentrated on similarities, on the family resemblances between texts. These similarities conceal significant generic fault lines. For instance, we might ask of a specific work of this period: is it a revived romance, or an historical novel? Like families, genres branch off into distinct lines as they incorporate new genetic material. Thus critics generally concur in arguing that only with Scott does the historical novel come into recognizable being as a distinct subgenre. But Scott manifestly has his precursors, including, if not beginning with, Walpole. To put the matter another way, during this period works with an historical or antiquarian setting and texts featuring castles, the supernatural and sublimity coexist, sometimes overlapping, sometimes not. In order to analyze the proliferation of the Gothic in the 1790s, we need to be more precise about the phenomenon that lies before us.

The 1790s: the effulgence of Gothic

The first point to note is that the fad for Gothic romances predates the French Revolution, or at any rate, the fall of the Bastille in July 1789. Two of the eight Gothics published in 1788 are directly compared by the *Monthly* or *Critical Review* with Walpole's romance (*The Apparition* and *The Castle of St. Mowbray*), while a third, *Oswald's Castle*, is compared with Frances Burney's non-Gothic *Cecilia* (Raven, "Novel Comes of Age," pp. 418, 427, 442). Charlotte Smith's *Emmeline; or the Orphan of the Castle* is tangentially Gothic in that it is set in the present day and does not feature the supernatural. In other respects it merely anticipates the Gothic of William Godwin by a few years, which locates the remains of feudalism, not in a material castle from a bygone age, but in the immaterial manners and class structure of the present day. The final three are *Historical Tales*, *Powis Castle*, and *St. Julian's Abbey*. Collectively these texts are no less varied in their mix of terror and history than those appearing later on in the next decade; so it seems unanswerable that the Gothic lift-off occurs before the literal tottering of the first old, oppressive structure, in France. The counterargument would be that the figures sustain the general proposition (Gothic-related texts begin their effulgence in 1788), but not Hazlitt's view about the origin of this bulge, which would require that the romances follow *Otranto* in featuring a castle teetering under the weight of past sins and auguring renewal through collapse, which is to say revolution. Some of the 1788 Gothics do this, but not all; some appear to be simply exploiting the current antiquarian vogue. But this is only to reiterate the main point, which is that 1790s Gothic is not a unitary object. It is composed, rather, of schools or strands and undergoes phases. We therefore need to break it down.

The best place to begin is with the phases we have already identified. The first phase, from 1788 to 1794, is distinguished by something that happens within the emerging genre and by something that happens outside of it. The internal event is the advent of Ann Radcliffe. Her first novel, *The Castles of Athlin and Dunbayne* (1789), is highly dependent upon Walpole's example. It features a usurped castle, a Manfred-like villain, differing only in being even more evil than Manfred, a ghost, albeit explained, a noble foundling, and plenty of terror and suspense. If Radcliffe had followed the example of the great majority of first-time novelists of the period and not written another book, the literary history of the Gothic might have been very different. But she did not. She went on to become the dominant novelist of the decade, certainly as far as commercial success is concerned – and for many readers critically too (Raven, "Novel Comes of Age," p. 52; Miles, *Ann Radcliffe*, p. 7). John Keats referred to her as "Mother Radcliff," and to a very real extent 1790s Gothic writing happened within her shadow.[6] Her importance lies partly in the fact that she raised landscape description, the verbal art

of the sublime and picturesque, to a new level of perfection,[7] thus investing
Walpole's novel form of romance with poetic kudos, and partly in the fact
that she changed Walpole's formula. Much has been made of her development of the explained supernatural, but her most significant innovation was
to expand a particular element of *Otranto*, the heroine in flight from a patriarchal ogre in a European setting. Walpole's text features a heroine who
retreats ever deeper into the castle's labyrinth. Radcliffe picks this up, but she
also included a period of extended escape and flight, a device that allowed her
to track her heroines' progress through the picturesque and sublime scenery
of southern Europe. Such travelogs called upon Radcliffe's descriptive powers, for which she became justly famous.[8] Her changes also helped throw
history into relief as a distinct theme. *The Castles of Athlin and Dunbayne*
is set in some vague time in pre-Reformation Scotland, whereas *A Sicilian
Romance* (1790) occurs at the advent of the Italian Renaissance. The temporal vagueness of her first romance means we find no thematic contrast
between the past and present within it, but *A Sicilian Romance* is historically explicit. The narrator refers to the historical process where the "dark
clouds of prejudice break away from the sun of science" and where "rude
manners...yield to learning." Her story is set at the beginning of this epoch,
when there appeared "only a few scattered rays."[9] From *A Sicilian Romance*
onwards, Radcliffe's texts will always feature a heroine representing a bright
bourgeois future of enlightened sensibility in conflict with at least one explicit representative of the old, dark, feudal order. As such, Radcliffe's plots
express common liberal attitudes of her time. In the same year that Radcliffe
wrote *A Sicilian Romance*, the radical Whig newspaper, the *Gazetteer and
New Daily Advertiser*, edited by her husband William,[10] enthusiastically
welcomed 1790 as a year in which we might expect "the amelioration,
if not the perfect deliverance, of mankind. Prejudices are encountered in
every kingdom; and establishments, erected by tyranny, are surrendering to
reason."[11]

An important event happening outside the genre, but within the Gothic's
discursive shadow, was the publication of Edmund Burke's *Reflections on
the Revolution in France* in 1790. The *Reflections* imparted to the word
Gothic a new political charge. In one of his most celebrated set pieces, Burke
imagines the recent events in Paris, where the French queen was menaced by
a mob of fish wives:

> I thought ten thousand swords must have leaped from their scabbards to avenge
> even a look that threatened her with insult. But the age of chivalry is gone.
> That of sophisters, economists, and calculators has succeeded; and the glory
> of Europe is extinguished forever. Never, never more shall we behold that

generous loyalty to sex and rank, that proud submission, that dignified obedi-
ence, that subordination of the heart, which kept alive, even in servitude itself,
the spirit of exalted freedom. The unbought grace of life, the cheap defence of
nations, the nurse of manly sentiments and heroic enterprise, is gone! (Burke,
Reflections, in Clery and Miles, *Gothic Documents*, p. 232)

This may seem an expression of nostalgia. It is in fact a deeply meditated
political philosophy, the essence of which may be summed up in Burke's
own paradox: "the old feudal and chivalrous spirit of fealty" is the source
of modern freedom. By being bound, we are free; by submitting ourselves
to the ancient order, we maintain our proud liberty; by exalting the weaker
sex, we gain strength. For Burke, chivalry was no mere outmoded system of
manners. It was Europe's proud cultural patrimony, an inherited instinct for
deference, fealty, and service. As such, it acted as an intangible lubricant for
the civilized interchange between rulers and ruled. By "freeing kings from
fear," chivalric fealty "freed both kings and subjects from the precautions
of tyranny" (Burke, *Reflections,* in Clery and Miles, *Gothic Documents*,
p. 234). All this was personified, and made visible, in the act of devotion
to the female monarch, the national incarnation of the chivalric code. The
undefended body of the French queen and the eclipse of chivalry it signifies must inevitably mean a period of darkness and barbarism. For English
readers the clear lesson was that political innovation was to be resisted, as
demands for greater rights naturally threatened the delicate balance of deference and place that was not just the work of centuries, but the glory and
security of the British nation.[12]

In 1790 Burke was something of a lone voice. The liberal intelligentsia were
overwhelmingly against him. As Mary Wollstonecraft put it, their task was to
"unravel" the "slavish paradoxes" of his rhetoric (Clery and Miles, *Gothic
Documents*, p. 236). A key term in the radical counterattack was "gothic,"
a word Burke's enemies interpreted in the old eighteenth-century sense of
"barbaric" or "Medieval." Where Burke employs "chivalry," his critics
use "gothic" or "feudal." Thomas Christie accuses Burke of "cherishing
in his mind the principles of gothic feudality," prostituting his language to
seduce his readers into a "Temple of Superstition" with a "miserable deformed Gothic idol" in the middle of it (Christie in Clery and Miles, *Gothic
Documents*, p. 245). Mary Wollstonecraft uses "gothic" seven times in
A Vindication of the Rights of Men, each instance bringing out another
negative sense of chivalry. For Joseph Priestley, Burke defends "the superstitious respect for kings, and the spirit of chivalry, which nothing but an age
of extreme barbarism recommended" (Priestley in Clery and Miles, *Gothic
Documents*, p. 246).

Prior to the French Revolution, for any of those subscribing to Whiggism in its many varieties, "Gothic" possessed a positive rather than negative political valence. It was a common belief among Whigs and radicals alike that the English Parliament traced its origins to an ancient, or Gothic, constitution brought to England by the Saxons.[13] As Montesquieu famously put it, citing the authority of Tacitus, the "beautiful system" of English parliamentary government was first "invented in the woods" of Germany (Montesquieu in Clery and Miles, *Gothic Documents*, p. 63). Chivalry, in turn, was considered to be the cultural expression of Saxon manners, just as the Witangemot, or parliament, was its political one. Burke's high-profile ideological capture of chivalry and the widespread radical condemnation of it fundamentally transformed the semantic field of the word *Gothic*.

Such a change naturally impacted on the way romances of the terror school were consumed. For instance, take Mary Wollstonecraft's attack on primogeniture, one of the Gothic customs defended by Burke: "Who can recount all the unnatural crimes which the laudable, interesting desire of perpetuating a name has produced? The younger children have been sacrificed to the eldest son; sent into exile, or confined in convents, that they might not encroach on what was called, with shameful falsehood, the family estate" (Wollstonecraft in Clery and Miles, *Gothic Documents*, p. 237). The Gothic plot of children rebelling against their father's command that they should marry to aggrandize the family, rather than for love, existed long before Burke defended the principle or Wollstonecraft attacked it. In the context of the feverish revolution debates, the plot acquired a new edge, as did the Radcliffean theme of historical change. Tyrannical fathers who insisted their children marry according to the necessity of "alliance" resembled the feudal remnants attacked by Jacobins. On the opposite side, the chivalric devotion the hero habitually displays toward the "lovely" heroine looks very much like a resuscitation of the corpse of chivalry, although this apparently Burkean position is almost always qualified by the fact that the hero is defending the heroine, not from attacks by the mob, but from some powerful and frequently sex-mad aristocrat.

In the first years of its 1790s phase (1788–94), the romance structure dominates the Gothic form principally through Radcliffe's overwhelming influence. In the romance structure dynastic ambitions are pitted against the love interest, a conflict generally resolved in the heroine's favor, but only after the revelation of the familial secrets that have been haunting the action. The pivotal year appears to be 1794: it witnessed an upsurge in Gothic production; it saw the publication of *The Mysteries of Udolpho*, the last great example of the romance structure; and it was marked by Godwin's *Things as They Are, or the Adventures of Caleb Williams*, the first ostensible

Jacobin Gothic. Politically, it was also the year of the treason trials, one of the most significant events of the decade, where even authors, publishers, and booksellers were tried for "seditious libel."

What *Caleb Williams* ushered in, however, was not a spate of radical Gothic novels, but a rush of political ones, some of them explicitly anti-Jacobin.[14] The literary history is again complex. There was, to be sure, a strand of Jacobin-Gothics, featuring Godwin's work above all (Kilgour, *Rise of the Gothic Novel*). His underlying premise is neatly explained by John Thelwall, one of the accused in Pitt's treason trials and a fellow radical. Thelwall attacks Burke's *Thoughts on a Regicide Peace* (1793), from which he quotes:

> Are these the institutions which Mr. B. wishes to support? . . . Are these . . . the regular and orderly fabrics of the ancient legitimate "government of states" whose plans and materials were "drawn from the old Germanic or Gothic customary" and of which those famous architects, "the civilians, the jurists, and the publicists" have given us such flattering draughts, ground plots, and elevations? If they are, away with your idle jargon of venerable antiquity . . . they are Bastilles of intellect, which must be destroyed. They are insulting mausoleums of buried rights.[15]

Burke recurs to the venerable Whig belief in an ancient Gothic constitution as a means of providing intellectual support for the status quo, a position Thelwall attacks. To use another of Thelwall's metaphors, Burke's political rhetoric of Gothic customs "forged" mental "fetters," which imprisoned the citizen, depriving individuals of their rights.[16] What Thelwall is striving toward is a concept of ideology as false consciousness. The uncritical internalization of the mythology of national origin – of ancient constitutions and chivalric codes – constitutes a mental Bastille or feudal remnant, one that imprisons us, concealing our true identity and our rights. This identification of deference to the past as a mausoleum, a "dead hand" that palsies the living, is represented in *Caleb Williams* as the chivalric code that binds Falkland (pp. 10–11). Caleb may be in flight from Falkland, but Falkland is himself entombed within his own mental Bastille. Moreover, the theme and mode of narration implies that Caleb, too, is ideologically immured. The feudal castle that blights the present is thus not an object out there, but a state of mind that immaterially fetters its victims, burying them, and their rights, alive. Caleb's own lack of ideological freedom is symbolized by his obsessive desire to get into Falkland's ancient, iron chest, the physical symbol of Falkland's benighted mental state. Caleb ought to endeavor to free himself from such a structure, not get into it. In Radcliffean terms, it would be as if Emily St. Aubert were trying to sneak into her prison at Udolpho, rather than break out of it. Caleb reads his own fate as "a theatre of calamity" (p. 3) and Falkland's as the result of a "malignant destiny": to the extent that Caleb literalizes his story as tragedy, he locks himself into his own unhappy fate.

Godwin announces in his preface his intention to critique Burke's Gothic ideology, a critique lent urgency by the treason trials. Godwin tells us that it "is now known to philosophers that the spirit and character of government intrudes itself into every rank of society." As far as the "progressive nature of a single story" allows, he intends "a general review of the modes of domestic and unrecorded despotism, by which man becomes the destroyer of man" (*Caleb Williams*, p. 1). Through his attachment to "honour," the chivalric code of the Gothic gentleman, Falkland unconsciously reproduces the "spirit and character" of the government and through it enacts upon others the despotism implicit in its anachronistic codes. *Caleb Williams* evinces a deep understanding of how old codes lock us in and how they are difficult to destroy. To take the world at face value, to read it literally, is to misperceive how abstract structures imprison us. To understand how we unwittingly find ourselves locked within Bastilles of the intellect is to begin to see the world metaphorically, which is to say analytically. In Caleb's case, the genre of tragedy is itself a prison. By regarding himself theatrically, as a bit player caught up in a hero's destined fall, Caleb renounces free will while conceding the class differences, the institutional despotism, that afflicts him. Until Caleb realizes this he will remain fast within a feudal, Gothic "customary." Jacobin Gothics turn on a strong sense of the metaphorics of imprisonment, as in Mary Wollstonecraft's *Maria; or the Wrongs of Woman* (1798), whose given condition (to be "Bastilled in marriage") echoes Thelwall's phrasing.[17]

In 1793 Eliza Parsons published *The Castle of Wolfenbach*, a Radcliffean tale of a heroine marrying against parental wishes. It was also the harbinger of a new vogue, the "German tale," to quote Parson's subtitle.[18] Goethe's *Sorrows of Young Werther* (1774) had introduced an overwrought note into the novel of sensibility, but the really influential German writer, as far as the Gothic novel goes, was Friedrich Schiller. His play *The Robbers* (*Die Räuber*) created an immense fad for stories of Banditti, a subgenre that turned on the ethical question of whether it was right, in corrupt times, to form an outlaw society. From Radcliffe to Goya, Gothic artists found Banditti to be an irresistible source of picturesque terror. After the horrors of the French Revolution, positive representations of Banditti became increasingly uncommon, being associated instead with treachery, mayhem, and bloodshed, as in *The Monk* (1796). *The Necromancer* (1794), the first German Gothic translated into English, follows this pattern.

Schiller's *The Ghost-Seer* (*Der Geisterseher*) proved a more politically ambiguous and finally more influential model for a new kind of Gothic.

Although *The Ghost-Seer* was first published in English in 1795, it was conceived in the late 1780s. The Masonic charlatan, Count Cagliostro, was then headline news across Europe. Cagliostro was in fact of obscure birth from Palermo, Sicily. Styling himself a master of Egyptian mysteries and friend of mankind, Cagliostro cut a swathe through the capital cities of Europe. He foretold the future (using a crystal ball); dispensed nostrums freely to the poor; and held séances for the wealthy. It was also rumored that he was a member of the Illuminati, a revolutionary band of Freemasons allegedly founded in Ingolstadt (the future site of Dr. Frankenstein's experiments) by the shadowy Adam Weishaupt.[19] It was said that the Illuminati secured converts by bamboozling their initiates through a series of visual and aural tricks employing magic lanterns, magnets, electrical devices, and exploding powders. Once the reason of initiates had folded under the stress of inexplicable mysteries, their minds would be putty in the hands of their masters, who plotted the overthrow of monarchies across Europe. Schiller fictionally exploited these rumors in *The Ghost-Seer*. The protagonist, referred to simply as a German Prince, is imposed upon in one of these Masonic séances by a "Sicilian," an evident reference to Cagliostro. A mysterious figure with a preternatural knowledge of the Prince's affairs, known only as "the Armenian," exposes the séance as a sham. The discovery is itself a confidence trick arranged by the Armenian, who is in fact a secret agent of the Inquisition. The Prince is second in line to a significant Protestant throne in Germany. A freethinker, he is also prone to a belief in the marvelous. Realizing this, the Inquisition plots a double game of fiendish ingenuity, whereby the Prince's liberal leanings and freethinking are turned against him through the exposure of the Illuminati as charlatans, an exposure designed to induce the Prince's belief in the Armenian's true supernatural powers. Once under the latter's sway, the Inquisition plan to convert the Prince into a Catholic zealot willing to murder his way to the throne in order to subvert his country's allegiance to Protestantism.

The year 1795 was an appropriate time to translate *The Ghost-Seer*. In Rome, Cagliostro, the "Sicilian" himself, perished at the hands of the Inquisition. In Paris, the spectral technologist Etienne-Gaspard Robertson played the role of the Armenian by staging a show (for which he coined the buzz-phrase *phantasmagoria*) in which the apparitional tricks of the Illuminati were exposed.[20] Members of the public would file into a darkened, smoke-filled room designed to resemble a chamber from a Radcliffe novel, only to be startled and terrorized by a visitation of phantoms (Castle, *Female Thermometer*, pp. 144–49). In London more people were being put on trial for treason to staunch the threat of revolution. The populace was gripped by the idea of living in a society riddled with conspirators,

spies, and informers. It was a time of paranoia, a mood stoked by the publication of the Abbé Barruel's influential *Memoirs, Illuminating the History
of Jacobinism* (1797), which portrayed a Europe riddled with secret cells
of revolutionary Freemasons. In terms of their popular representations,
the Illuminati and the Inquisition were doubles of each other: they were
both underground organizations with their own laws and codes, plotting
dark ends; and they conducted "secret tribunals" in which deviant members
were fatally disciplined. Their interchangeable character was presumably
Schiller's point. According to the *Monthly Review*, Schiller's novel gave rise
to "numberless imitations" in Germany (Raven, "Novel Comes of Age,"
p. 651). None of those translated into English – such as *The Necromancer*
by Carl Friedrich Kahlert (trans. 1794), *The Victim of Magical Delusion* by
Cajetan Tschink (trans. 1795), and *Horrid Mysteries* by Karl Grosse (trans.
1796) – maintained Schiller's balance, preferring instead to feed Barruel's
anti-Jacobin paranoia by concentrating on the tricks of the Illuminati, a tendency Grosse takes to an extreme by exploiting yet another alleged trait of
Weishaupt's followers, their penchant for promiscuous sex. An exception,
curiously enough, is Radcliffe, who in *The Italian* (1797) models her villain, Schedoni, on Schiller's Armenian,[21] while maintaining a focus on the
Inquisition as the truly dangerous "secret tribunal."

It appears that *The Italian* in turn set off its own minifad for Inquisitional tales. *The Inquisition* appeared in 1797, followed by the anonymous
The Libertines in 1798, and a translation of Kotzebue's *The Escape* in 1799.
Mrs. F. C. Patrick's *The Jesuit* (1799) marked a return to Schiller's premise
that the true masters of the dark arts were Catholic agents. Godwin's *St. Leon*
(1799) followed suit. The most influential post-*Ghost-Seer* text was Matthew
Lewis's *The Monk* (1796). Its treatment of the Inquisition was the least of
its notoriety. In many respects *The Monk* belongs with William Beckford's
Modern Novel Writing and Jane Austen's *Northanger Abbey*, two other
works published or conceived in the late 1790s. What all three have in common is an impulse to satirize the common fare of the circulating library.

Of the three, *The Monk* is the most extraordinary owing to its desire to
represent everything that had gone before in transgressive excess. In Lewis's
novel, everything was the same and yet everything was different. We have
the familiar plot of the young couple wishing to marry against their parents'
dynastic wishes, with the young cavalier romantically striving to protect his
mistress. And then every taboo is broken: the couple have premarital sex;
the hero fails to rescue the heroine; the baby dies; and the hero spoofs, rather
than embodies, sensibility. In *The Romance of the Forest*, Radcliffe politely
horrified her readers with the suggestion that the Marquis de Montalt meditated the unwitting seduction, if not rape, of his own daughter, a thought

doubly defused: the attempt is foiled and Adeline is only his niece. In *The Monk*, Ambrosio not only rapes his sister but stabs her as well after earlier strangling his mother. Lewis includes both the explained and unexplained supernatural, but by reversing their proper order, makes a mockery of both: we are given the natural explanation first (Agnes frightening the servants by dressing up as the ghost of the Bloody Nun) and the supernatural cause second (the real Bloody Nun turns up).

German Gothics, such as *Horrid Mysteries*, allegedly introduced a franker depiction of sexuality than was common in romance Gothics. This too Lewis includes, taking it to a new degree of "libidinous minuteness," as Coleridge put it (see Clery and Miles, *Gothic Documents*, p. 188). Lewis's violence is equally explicit, as in the graphic description of Ambrosio's violated and broken body or the Baroque depiction of Agnes emaciated in her crypt cradling her child's decayed, worm-eaten corpse. And whereas earlier Gothics were content with restricting ghosts, where they were not explained away, to *Hamlet*-like specters of the possibly damned (*Otranto* is the obvious model), *The Monk* goes a step further in presenting an actual demon. So it is with nearly every feature of *The Monk*: one can find a precedent for everything, and yet *The Monk* was shockingly new, because it inverted, parodied, or exaggerated the features it cannibalized.

The Monk was not just generically transgressive. Lewis's depiction of the mob's gruesome revenge on the Abbess could be seen to be an apologetic reflection on the violence in France: the mob's actions might have been excessive, but on the other hand the Abbess is presented to us as the incarnation of "class" evil, who deserves what she gets. Lewis's comments in his novel on the obscenity of *The Bible* were the occasion for much critical outrage, including the threat of an action for obscene libel that forced Lewis to expurgate his text. There is reason to believe that the legal threat was the pretext for a greater discontent with Lewis's transgressions, where Lewis's status as an MP notoriously shortened the authorities' patience.[22] Such observations would strengthen the view that *The Monk* was politically motivated in the way that Thelwall's, Wollstonecraft's, or Godwin's novels were, a view supported by T. J. Mathias's reactionary lampoon, *The Pursuits of Literature*, which segues effortlessly from its attack on the revolutionary dangers of a Paine-reading populace to women novelists to the incendiary perils of *The Monk* (see Mathias in Clery and Miles, *Gothic Documents*, p. 190). Lewis inherited wealth, including slave plantations, and while it is true that he held liberal views similar to those of Lord Byron, it would be dangerous to read a narrow political message into Lewis's text. Like many other terror novelists, Lewis is less concerned with developing characters and a consistent point of view and more interested in creating arresting tableaux, or scenes that shock, something he achieves through his inversions of generic expectation. To a degree *The Monk* is a series of these scenic inversions. Spectacle, not narrative, is Lewis's motivating force. Although now chiefly remembered as the author of *The Monk*, Lewis was in fact one of the period's leading dramatists. As a dramatist, he sought to electrify his audience, an ambition he achieved so well in *The Captive* (1803) – a Gothic tableau apparently featuring a key scene from Wollstonecraft's *The Wrongs of Woman* – that the play had to be discontinued owing to audience hysteria (Cox, *Seven Gothic Dramas*, pp. 44–45, 225). Lewis did possess a dissident sensibility, but it was artistically expressed through a diffuse rebelliousness and a general desire to shock. *The Monk*'s sensationalism was its main contribution to 1790s Gothic. Its most celebrated progeny is Charlotte Dacre's *Zofloya; or the Moor* (1805), a work of equal eroticism, violence, and diffuse transgression. But there were others in the 1790s and after which followed Lewis's sensational example, such as William Henry Ireland's *The Abbess* (1799) and *Gondez; the Monk* (1805) and Edward Montague's *The Demon of Sicily* (1807).

With the foregoing in mind, we can begin to generalize about the Gothic's proliferation in the 1790s. During the decade the tale of terror is bound up with its revolutionary times, but the nature of that relationship changes, depending on whether we are talking about pre- or post-1794 Gothic. As we have seen, the pre-1794 phase revolves around Burke's critique of the revolution and his idealization of chivalry as a culturally transcendent force. During the early part of the 1790s Gothic romances do not allegorize the revolution or revolutionary ideas. Instead such works are *ideologically inflected*. Once we have understood the position of "chivalry" within debates about innovation and reform, we begin to see more clearly how Gothic narratives interweave with the contemporary English understanding of the revolution's social meaning. And like contemporary debate, the Gothic lagged behind events in France. Up until 1794 much of the discussion was still conditioned by a late Enlightenment sense of the desirability of society emancipating itself from feudal structures. Hence in Radcliffe true horror is reserved for the fear of finding oneself thrust back into the dark medieval heart of the *ancien régime*, as the modern English traveler believes himself to be at the start of *The Italian*. After 1794 a new sense of modernity emerged as the inrushing of an unrecoverable chaos. Hester Piozzi's contemporary sense of this moment is worth attending to: "science herself suffered from revolutions; and taste, no longer classical, cried out for German plays and novels of a new sort, filled with what the Parisians call…*phantasmagorie*."[23] Her characterization of this moment is suitably dramatic and portentous: "the celebrated fraternity of illuminated free-masons burst their self-created shackles, avowed their secret, and confessed their meditated emancipation of mankind from all subordination and government, exclaiming, 'France is free, the universe will quickly follow her example.'"[24] Meeting in their gaslit caves, with their Rousseau (especially *The Social Contract*) and their revolutionary agendas, the Illuminati were the acme of the modern.

After 1794 the Gothic thus became a way of speaking the unspeakable. The salient historical facts are these: the September massacre of 1792, the execution of the Louis XVI in January 1793, and the fall of Robespierre in 1794. The first event (in which citizens took it upon themselves to butcher the revolution's enemies in the streets of Paris) exemplified the point that a people brutalized and infantilized by the *ancien régime* were bound to act accordingly once their shackles were burst. The execution of the king revealed that violence within the new regime was institutionalized rather than simply mob-related. The episode of Robespierre and the Terror, in turn, raised the possibility that the revolution ate its own and was itself an out-of-control monster (see Paulson, "Gothic Fiction, French Revolution"). French violence, of the mob and of the state, strongly suggested that the French experiment had run past what could be contained by the English model of the Glorious Revolution, which was how Dissenters and English Jacobins had initially viewed events across the channel. The revolution now called up a host of unwelcome associations, of moments of chaos and violence within England's own recent history, beginning with the Gordon Riots of 1780 and extending back to the English Civil War. For the British middle-class mind, English revolutionary violence was indelibly linked to "enthusiasm," or radical Protestantism. Mad George Gordon, who inspired the violence that bore his name, was a Protestant zealot; while the excesses of the English Civil War were laid at the feet of Levellers, antinomians, and now, retrospectively, the Illuminati through their diabolical influence on Cromwell.[25] With all this in mind, we can perceive the real relevance of the scandalous fad for German plays and novels referred to by Piozzi. If German Illuminati were identical with French Jacobins, they were also convertible into English Dissenters. Illuminati, Protestant visionaries, English Dissenters were all essentially one; at least they were to conservative opinion as exemplified by the *Anti-Jacobin*, which from its first issue linked all three together as desperados whose intent it was "to undermine and blow up the constitution."[26] When the *Anti-Jacobin* belatedly reviewed Radcliffe's *The Italian* in 1801, it saw her in this new, dangerous light: "the wildness, the mysterious horror of many situations and events in Mrs. Radcliffe are rather German than English: they partake of Leonora's spirit: they freeze, they 'curdle up the blood.' They are always incredible: they are, apparently, supernatural."[27] Whereas pre-1794 Gothic tended to focus upon Catholic superstition as the enemy of reason and modernity, the German Gothics fixed upon the blind enthusiasm the Illuminati fostered through their "supernatural" tricks. As in Schiller's *Ghost-Seer*, such tricks were used to divorce would-be adepts from their commonsense attachment to the status quo, from their understanding of the established order as a product of nature and providence. According to these paranoid narratives, once liberated into a "higher reason," the adepts of the Illuminati were ready for any manner of mayhem and bloodshed. In being called "rather German than English," Radcliffe is being compounded with the sanguinary enemies of Burkean "reason."

For English readers, German tales of Illuminati were ghostly narratives of English revolution, as they portended the unspeakable English fear: the resurrection of Protestant extremism within England's own political body. These German tales did not feature revolution *per se*; rather, they represented plots and conspiracies and took place in a myriad of hidden places: in forest houses, gaslit caves, or secret gardens. They were hair-raising narratives of domestic revolution, told by proxy, via German translations, including, for instance, James Boaden's *The Secret Tribunal* (1794) and Peter Will's two translated novels, *Horrid Mysteries* and *The Victim of Magico-Delusion* (see above). Despite the scandalous vogue for German tales of Illuminati, English writers avoided the topic themselves other than as translators, as if the subject were governed by a cultural taboo. If so, it is perhaps fitting that the taboo was first broken by the young Percy Bysshe Shelley, with his two juvenile Gothic tales, *Zastrozzi* and *St. Irvyne* (1810), both of which exploit the sensational terrain of revolutionary conspiracy.

During the 1790s Britain seemed closer to chaos, revolution, and violence than at any other time in recent history, save perhaps for 1780. As an example, the smallish provincial town of Sheffield (population 25,000) was the center of much revolutionary unrest. In the early 1790s, on the anniversary of the fall of the Bastille, citizens would dress up as Burke's "swinish multitude" while burning him in effigy. There were mass meetings on the outskirts of the town, with gatherings of 10,000 or so to protest against the war and the lack of political reform. But then Pitt suspended the normal *habeas corpus* regulations for bringing people to trial; the editor of the local newspaper and other radicals were forced into self-exile to escape banishment to Australia; and troops were sent up from the south and established in new barracks to suppress further unrest. The picture was the same in many other parts of the country. But rather than being imagined in literature, English revolutionary violence was the great unmentionable that could be expressed only through displaced representations.

According to Ronald Paulson, in this paranoid context acts of repression and transgression of almost any kind might assume a symbolic force when

represented in fiction. For example, he argues that Ambrosio's monastic upbringing invites itself to be read as a mimic form of *ancien régime* repression;
his sexual mania as a form of uncontrollable revolutionary libertinism; and
the mob's lynching of the Abbess as an allegory of the crowd's berserk moral
economy in which a brutal ruin is brought down upon their despotic masters,
themselves, and everyone around them.

Jane Austen's *Northanger Abbey* best expresses the unspoken threat of
revolutionary violence that pervaded the time and its literature, in a manner
that is both comic and shrewd. For the most part written at the end of
the 1790s, it is a novel exactly of its moment. Eleanor and Catherine find
themselves at cross-purposes. In a solemn tone of voice Catherine says

> "I have heard that something very shocking indeed, will soon come out in
> London."
>
> Miss Tilney, to whom this was chiefly addressed, was startled, and hastily
> replied, "Indeed! – *and* of what nature?"
>
> "That I do not know, nor who is the author. I have only heard that it is to
> be more horrible than any thing we have met with yet."
>
> "Good heaven! Where could you hear such a thing?"
>
> "A particular friend of mine had an account of it in a letter from London
> yesterday. It is to be uncommonly dreadful. I shall expect murder and every
> thing of the kind."
>
> "You speak with astonishing composure! But I hope your friend's accounts
> have been exaggerated – and if such a design is known beforehand, proper
> measures will undoubtedly be taken by government to prevent its coming to
> effect." (p. 100)

Catherine, of course, refers to rumors of the latest product of the terror
system of novel-writing, which Eleanor interprets as a reference to rioting
in London on a scale unknown since 1780. Eleanor accidentally makes the
connection readers would automatically have understood, between narratives of repression, violence, and liberation on the one hand, and the present
revolutionary context on the other. Austen draws the distinction between
early 1790s Gothic, principally associated with Radcliffe, and the later wave
of German Gothics heavily represented in Isabella Thorpe's must-read list of
"horrid" novels (of the seven mentioned, six have a German link). As a reader
of Radcliffe, Catherine is unable to make the connection between fictional
and revolutionary terror, and that is because Radcliffe herself, with the possible exception of *The Italian*, keeps the two separate. The German Gothics
are quite different, as revealed by an odd turn of phrase neither Catherine nor
Eleanor picks up. When Catherine says she does not know who the "author"
is, we might expect Eleanor to grasp her friend's drift that Catherine is talking about books. Eleanor does not, because the late eighteenth century did

not habitually think in sociological terms, of mass unrest being produced by impersonal economic and political causes. Riots, like books, had authors. Unrest must have human agents, or conspirators. That is what the German Gothics provided: the terror of revolutionary conspiracy.

Ironically, Eleanor makes the connection between a description of Gothic horror and revolutionary violence because she is not a reader of the terror system of novels. Her brother Henry is, and being a sophisticated reader he is able to fathom both perspectives and so unravel the confusion. Catherine continues to read the world Gothically, famously interpreting General Tilney as *Udolpho*'s Montoni, meaning a rapacious aristocratic villain, or like the Marquis Mazzini from *A Sicilian Romance*, an apparent wife-killer. She is later cruelly disabused of her Radcliffean fantasies by Henry, who humiliates her through his patient depiction of a modern England policed by neighborhoods of voluntary spies, where roads and newspapers lay everything open. Against Eleanor's paranoiac fears and Catherine's Gothic imagination, Henry sets everyday English common sense where revolutionary unrest and patriarchal despotism do not exist. But then the General acts true to Gothic form and sets Catherine upon the road without a penny, thus subverting Henry's homily. Where contemporary terror novels draw their charge from coded references to the great unspoken, *Northanger Abbey* does something different. It balances the two views together: the paranoiac vision of Freemasons mustering in London and repressive aristocrats fomenting revolution through despotic cruelty on the one side, and complacency as to England's civil superiority on the other. As such, *Northanger Abbey* is not so much an expression of unspeakable revolutionary anxiety as a reflection and comment upon it.

What does this review of the terror writing of the 1790s tell us? Above all else, it reveals that the Gothic follows the first law of genre: to deviate and make it new. During the 1790s the Gothic does not just simply burst forth. It multiplies, branches out, and proliferates. But there is yet another force at work that we have not mentioned, and that is the entry into the market of William Lane, the proprietor of the Minerva Press, the era's most prolific publisher of novels. Much of it produced cheaply by first-time or anonymous novelists, Minerva's output was geared toward the circulating libraries where novels were marketed by type rather than author. If the Gothic is anything to go by, Lane followed, rather than led, the market. No work of note from the 1790s which we now designate as Gothic was first published by the Minerva Press. This tendency to follow had a conservative effect on generic change within the novel market, since, once a successful "formula" was established it was (and this was certainly the opinion of wearied and exasperated reviewers) done to death. Once a particular kind of Gothic begins, it does not go away, a phenomenon that tends to inflate the quantity of Gothic works published during the period. Gothic writing proliferates into the various strands we have identified: Radcliffe's historical romances; Godwin's Jacobin Gothics; Lewis's "blasphemy"; the German tales of revolutionary Illuminati; conservative tales following Clara Reeve's "Loyalist" example (Watt, *Contesting the Gothic*, pp. 42–68); or satires and pastiches. But it is also shadowed by formulaic writing where nothing changes at all. Radcliffe's *The Italian* differs from her pre-1794 work in reflecting the new mood of paranoia and conspiracy; Regina Maria Roche's *Clermont* (1798), published by Minerva, repeats the conventions of early Radcliffe, as the *Critical Review* sourly notes (Raven, "Novel Comes of Age," p. 759). *Clermont* is the only non-German tale among those Isabella Thorpe cites as truly "horrid." Austen gives us an indication of the latest German fashion, plus one example of the staple product. The *Critical Review* might sniff, but horrid writing, whether the latest German fare or not, still sold, hence William Lane's lucrative and terror-ridden list.

Which takes us back to Hazlitt's balanced view: the immense popularity of the Gothic during the 1790s was "doubtless" owing to the perception of the tottering nature of all old structures at the time. Hazlitt's formulation does not attribute particular political allegiances to either the producers or consumers of Gothic texts; rather it is consonant with the view that narratives are consumed partly because they allow writers and readers to rehearse, to imaginatively air and work through, anxieties that perplex the culture. Thus whether one anxiously hoped for the fall of Pitt and the politically exclusive status quo he supported, or dreaded it, one might draw interest from a tale featuring the Gothic order *in extremis*, especially if it was safely displaced on to the continent.

Cultural fashions are both trivial and profound. By definition they refer to the ephemeral, to that which comes and goes. During the last part of the eighteenth century and the first part of the nineteenth the Gothic was just such a passing fad. In 1816 Charles Maturin ruefully observed that the tale of terror (a form to which he was imaginatively addicted) was already "out" in 1807, the year in which he published *The Fatal Revenge*, his own first essay in the genre. But the fact that it was a fad should not blind us to its importance. For a start, during the decade the tale of terror produced its own fair share of major works: *The Mysteries of Udolpho*; *The Italian*; *Caleb Williams*; *The Monk*; *Northanger Abbey*; *Christabel*; *The Rime of the Ancient Mariner*; and some of Joanna Baillie's *Plays on the Passions*. Its ratio of major and minor works is doubtless little different from, say, the sonnet, which during the same period witnessed the achievement of Wordsworth, but also the product of William Lisle Bowles. Fashions are also profound because they key us into movements and changes deep within the culture. One such change was the development of a certain kind of literary snobbery, which for many years blinded critics to the obvious fact that many of the decade's canonical texts were first and foremost tales of terror. Such snobbery was undoubtedly connected to the material fact that for the first time women, at least as readers, were associated with a form that challenged (or was perceived to challenge) traditional literary authority. In other words, much of the tension between "high" and "low" literature which has pulsed through the institutionalization of "literature" over the last 200 years is first generated by the effulgence of the 1790s tale of terror. A further point to consider is its pertinacity: after 1820 the Gothic does not go away, but migrates into other forms and media, or undergoes generic recrudescence. Given this afterlife – given, too, the potency of the paradigm of the unconscious, now so instrumental in modern critical thought – the 1790s might seem a crucial moment for the study of the Gothic, as being the time of its first popular efflorescence. And so it is. But as we have seen, the Gothic is not a unitary object during the decade. We must be aware of differences, as well as similarities. Without doing so, we will not be able to move much beyond Hazlitt's generation of what it was that fueled the Gothic rage. On the other hand, providing an articulated picture of its differences may help us understand more deeply what the tale of terror signified to the diverse constituencies that produced and consumed it at the end of the eighteenth century.

NOTES

1 In this chapter I concentrate solely on the novel, although the reader should be aware that the Gothic phenomenon also included poetry and drama. As Paula Backscheider and Jeffrey Cox have pointed out, "Gothic" drama dominated the theatre during the 1790s. The poetic tale of terror was another significant subgenre – see Robert Miles, *Gothic Writing, 1750–1820* (London: Routledge, 1993) and Michael Gamer *Romanticism and the Gothic: Genre, Reception and Canon Formation* (Cambridge: Cambridge University Press, 2000) – as was the "magazine" story. On the latter, see Robert D. Mayo, *The English Novel in the Magazines, 1740–1815* (Oxford: Oxford University Press, 1962).

2 According to Lucy Aikin, the author's niece, Anna Laetitia Aikin, wrote the essay while her brother John Aikin wrote the fictional fragment (E. J. Clery and Robert Miles, *Gothic Documents: a Sourcebook* [Manchester: Manchester University Press, 2000], p. 127). After her marriage, Anna Laetitia Aikin was known as Mrs. Barbauld.

3 Marquis de Sade, "Ideas on the Novel," in Victor Sage, ed., *The Gothic Novel: a Casebook* (London: Longman, 1990), p. 49.

4 William Hazlitt, *Lectures on the English Comic Writers* (Oxford: Oxford University Press, 1907), p. 73.

5 See E. J. Clery, *Women's Gothic: from Clara Reeve to Mary Shelley* (Northcote House, 2000), pp. 53–57.

6 *Letters of John Keats: a Selection*, ed. Robert Gittings (Oxford: Oxford University Press, 1979), p. 212.

7 As judged by the *Critical Review* (see Robert Miles, *Ann Radcliffe* [Manchester: Manchester University Press, 1995], p. 54).

8 Ellen Moers, *Literary Women* (London: W. H. Allen, 1977).

9 Ann Radcliffe, *A Sicilian Romance*, ed. Alison Milbank (Oxford: Oxford University Press, 1994), p. 117.

10 Rictor Norton, *Mistress of Udolpho: the Life of Ann Radcliffe* (London and New York: Leicester University Press, 1998), pp. 60–61.

11 Cited by Robert Miles in the introduction to his edition of Radcliffe's *The Italian* (Harmondsworth: Penguin, 2000), p. xix.

12 See Claudia Johnson, *Equivocal Beings: Politics, Gender, and Sentimentality in the 1790s* (Chicago: University of Chicago Press, 1995).

13 See Samuel Kliger, *The Goths in England* (Cambridge, MA: Harvard University Press, 1952); also R. J. Smith, *The Gothic Bequest: Medieval Institutions in British Thought, 1688–1863* (Cambridge: Cambridge University Press, 1987).

14 For the strand of conservative or anti-Jacobin Gothic, see James Watt, *Contesting the Gothic: Fiction, Genre, and Cultural Conflict, 1764–1832* (Cambridge: Cambridge University Press, 1999), pp. 42–69. Watt aptly calls this mode "Loyalist Gothic Romance."

15 John Thelwall, *The Rights of Nature Against the Usurpation of Establishments. A Series of Letters to the People of Britain, Occasioned by the Recent Effusions of the Right Honourable Edmund Burke* (London and Norwich: H. D. Symonds and J. March, 1796), p. 15.

16 ibid., p. 2.

17 Mary Wollstonecraft, *Mary* and *The Wrongs of Woman*, ed. Gary Kelly (Oxford: Oxford University Press, 1980), p. 155.

18 The interrelationship between the German tale of terror and what came to be known as the English Gothic novel is a complex one. See Michael Hadley, *The Undiscovered Genre: a Search for the German Gothic Novel* (Berne: Peter Lang, 1977), as well as E. J. Clery, *The Rise of Supernatural Fiction, 1762–1800* (Cambridge: Cambridge University Press, 1995), pp. 156–71. For the relationship between German and Gothic drama, see Gamer, *Romanticism and the Gothic*, pp. 126–62.

19 For recent treatments of the Cagliostro story, see Roberto Gervaso, *Cagliostro: a Biography*, trans. Cormac O'Cuilleanain (London: Victor Gollancz, 1974), and François Ribadeau Dumas, *Cagliostro*, trans. Elisabeth Abbott (London: Allen and Unwin, 1966).

20 Barbara Stafford, *Artful Science: Enlightenment Entertainment and the Eclipse of Visual Education* (Cambridge, MA: MIT Press, 1994), pp. 14–16.

21 According to Norton in *Mistress of Udolpho*, p. 127.

22 For a detailed history of the obscene libel charges with which Lewis was threatened, see Michael Gamer, "Genres for the Prosecution: Pornography and the Gothic," *PMLA* 114 (1999): 1043–54.

23 Hester Lynch Piozzi, *Retrospection: Or a Review of the Most Striking and Important Events, Characters, Situations, and Their Consequences, Which the*

Last 1800 Years Have Presented to the View of Mankind (London, 1801), ii, 511–12.

24 ibid., ii, 50.

25 Ian McCalman, "Mad Lord George and Madame La Motte: Riot and Sexuality in the Genesis of Burke's *Reflections on the Revolution in France*," *Journal of British Studies* 35 (1996): 343–67. For the contemporary association of the Illuminati with Cromwell and Puritan enthusiasm, see Piozzi, *Retrospection*, ii, 487, and the *Life of Joseph Balsamo, Commonly Called Count Cagliostro*, translated from the original proceedings published at Rome by Order of the Apostolic Chamber (Dublin: P. Byrne, 1792), pp. 103–20. The latter work represented Cagliostro's confession to the Roman Inquisition.

26 *Anti-Jacobin Review and Magazine* 1 (1798): 626.

27 *Anti-Jacobin Review and Magazine* 7 (1801): 27–30.

4

French and German Gothic: the beginnings

Literary genres do not emerge overnight, nor do they arise in cultural isolation. This is especially true of the Gothic, which not only underwent an initial period of gestation, development and decline (broadly speaking, from the publication of Walpole's *The Castle of Otranto* in 1764 to some moment after Charles Maturin's *Melmoth the Wanderer* of 1820) but also, from the very outset, borrowed liberally from a vast range of sources, foreign and domestic, literary, aesthetic, and scientific.

In light of the burgeoning academic interest in the Gothic in Britain and the Americas over the last decades of the twentieth century, it is easy to forget that the English Gothic genre was by no means the only example of a popular aesthetic of horror in late eighteenth- and early nineteenth-century Europe. Indeed, in France a tradition of sentimental adventure stories, stories which generally contained more than the occasional macabre *frisson*, had existed since the 1730s (and been equally popular elsewhere, particularly in Britain); while in Germany, at almost exactly the same moment as the vogue for the Gothic reached its apogee in Britain, the reading public devoured a succession of novels and tales featuring knights, robbers, and ghosts (thus giving rise to a tripartite genre generally thought of as the *Ritter-*, *Räuber-*, and *Schauerroman*). At some moment in the late eighteenth century, moreover, under the impact of translated English and German works, the French sentimental adventure story transmuted itself into yet another distinct genre, termed the *roman noir*, which appropriated genre markers from translated foreign literature while generally obeying local norms with regard to narrative structure and ideological content. This new form underwent further modifications as a result of the evolving social and political landscape in the wake of the restoration of the French monarchy during the 1820s and 1830s, at which point a new term was coined to describe it: the *roman frénétique*. Broadly speaking, the *roman noir* may be seen as a late flowering of eighteenth-century sensibility, while the *roman frénétique*, which is much more innovative in terms of thematic interest and narrative technique, is clearly a product of the rise of Romanticism which, it should be remembered, occurred much later in France than in Britain.

Each of these developments will be analyzed in turn here, so that these often neglected branches of the Gothic's growth can be given their full place in its history. A select group of representative texts will be examined in an attempt to establish the underlying motivations and most distinctive features of these generic developments. Beneath this activity, it should also be remembered that other forces were at work. In 1764, when Walpole smuggled his new literary creation into the cultural marketplace in the guise of a translation (a ploy used by many others before him), English was by no means the language of power and prestige that it would become a century and a half later. The European intelligentsia in the late eighteenth century and early nineteenth century communicated with each other in French, and British writers, especially those who had received a formal education, notwithstanding the independent literary tradition which existed in their own country, were as likely to be aware of developments on the Continent as they were of those at home. The outbreak of the French Revolution in 1789, in fact, permitted British and German fiction to develop along new lines, as if suddenly liberated from Francophone interference, and may be held partially responsible for the sudden growth in literary exchanges between these two countries which occurred in the mid-1790s. The Gothic was a widely European phenomenon from its very beginnings and became even more so as its early features were transformed in several continental variations well into the nineteenth century.

The French sentimental adventure story

In his *History of Prose Fiction*, first published in 1814, John Dunlop recounts an apocryphal story concerning the death of the Abbé Prévost (1697–1763). This noted author, it is claimed, was walking through some woods on the way to his home in Chantilly when he was struck down by apoplexy. Some peasants, finding his body stretched out at the foot of a tree, carried it to the nearest village, where it was laid out in the church. As was customary when a dead body was found, it was decided to proceed to an autopsy, and the local surgeon was called. However, as the surgeon made his first hasty incision, Prévost suddenly recovered consciousness. "The surgeon immediately stopped; but too late, the incision was a mortal one. The Abbé Prévost had just the time to see the cruel instrument which menaced him and to realize the horrible manner by which he had been deprived of his life."[1]

In all likelihood, Prévost died peacefully in his bed, reconciled with the Church. But this turning of his death into a story modeled after his own

fictions recalls what a willful and unpredictable servant he had been to or-
thodox Christianity most of his life. Indeed, he spent a considerable proportion of his youth on the run from the authorities, secular and religious.
As a young man he had been initiated into the Benedictine order, but had
soon tired of the austerities of monastic life and spent six years in exile in
England and Holland (where he also got into further trouble over unpaid
debts); later, in 1741, his involvement in the publication of court scandal em-
broiled him in fresh problems. By this stage in his life, however, Prévost had
established himself as one of the most popular authors in Europe, where his
three long novels continued to interest readers well into the nineteenth century: the *Mémoires et aventures d'un homme de qualité* (1728–31; *Memoirs
and Adventures of a Man of Quality*), which recounts the sufferings of the
narrator-hero and then the adventures of the young nobleman whose men-
tor he becomes; *Le Philosophe anglais ou Histoire de monsieur Cleveland*
(1732–39; *The English Philosopher, or the History of Monsieur Cleveland*),
which will be discussed shortly; and *Le Doyen de Killerine* (1735–40; *The
Dean of Killerine*), a novel set in Ireland at the time of the Jacobite struggles.

It was James R. Foster who first noted the link between the French sentimental adventure story in the manner of Prévost and the English Gothic
novel.[2] But it was readily apparent in the late eighteenth century. One of the
most important early Gothic novels, Sophia Lee's *The Recess* (1783–85),
largely follows the plot outline of Prévost's *Cleveland*. The changes she
makes, however, are as striking as the extent of her borrowings. Crucially,
Lee's decision to foreground female subjectivity and reengineer the gender
relationships in the text seems to indicate a sharp understanding of the
new, predominantly female, audience for such works and an almost modern
gender consciousness. Thus, while Prévost's sprawling novel concerns the
attempt of an illegitimate son of Oliver Cromwell to escape persecution at
the hands of his father, Lee's version is set in the reign of Elizabeth I and
centers on the attempts of the two main female protagonists (twin sisters),
who are the offspring of a secret marriage between Mary, Queen of Scots
and the Duke of Norfolk, to avoid the equally tyrannical persecution of their
monarch.

In the case of both novels, all manner of exciting incidents overtake their
respective heroes and heroines, including shipwreck, piracy, abduction, and
robbery. Indeed, it might be said that the two works essentially consist of an
unending pursuit during which the hero and heroine, though they may move
from one exotic location to another, can never escape their destiny. Prévost
is clearly aware of the effect that can be achieved by more deathly (and
thus pre-Gothic) descriptions. At an early stage in *Cleveland*, for example,
the hero stumbles across the crypt of a certain Lady Axminster, another of

Cromwell's victims; later in the novel, progressing from the lugubrious to the macabre, the hero is obliged to have his own daughter embalmed so as to transport the body back to France. The story recounted earlier concerning Prévost's death is entirely within such a tradition, especially in the light of his own biography, itself a catalogue of transgressive actions and behavior.

In any case, Sophia Lee was not the only early Gothic novelist to turn her attention to Prévost. In 1785, Charlotte Smith, a writer who would have her own distinguished career as a Gothic novelist, published a translation of his *Histoire du Chevalier des Grieux et de Manon Lescaut* (1731) as *Manon Lescaut, or, The Fatal Attachment*. Although Smith eschews Lee's preference for adaptation, she nonetheless considerably modifies Prévost's novel: the emotional and psychological portrait of the heroine is greatly augmented, the criminal behavior of the hero is moderated, the language and style throughout becomes more elegant and ornate, and, on occasion, distinctly Gothic-sounding flourishes are introduced which probably derive in part from Burke's theory of the terrific sublime.[3] Other early Gothic novelists would be drawn to the works of Prévost's closest disciple, Baculard d'Arnaud (1718–1805), whose sentimental stories and plays emphasized the more lugubrious aspects of the French tradition. Sophia Lee, for example, penned a sentimentalized version of his *Varbeck* (from *Nouvelles historiques*, 1774–84) as *Warbeck: a Pathetic Tale* (1786), while Clara Reeve's *The Exiles; or, Memoirs of the Count de Cronstadt* (1788) is really an amalgam of several stories from the pen of d'Arnaud.

While none of these works is generally seen, perhaps wrongly, by British or American commentators as central to the Gothic tradition, collectively they bring many of the central elements of the Gothic into focus. This is notably the case with regard to the use of historical settings, the juxtaposition of sentimentality and the macabre, the sense of breathless flight and pursuit, and the occasional exploitation of supernatural possibilities. Significantly, many of the writers engaged in the Gothic experiment began their literary careers as translators (a term which was, in itself, extremely fluid at the time, embracing practices which, as we have seen, might be more accurately described as adaptation). As such, Clara Reeve, Sophia Lee, and Charlotte Smith became the main conduits for considerable French input into the development of the sentimental Gothic novel in England.

The *Ritter-*, *Räuber-*, and *Schauerroman* traditions

The tradition of the author-translator as cultural innovator was continued a decade later by figures such as M. G. Lewis and Robert Huish (together with a host of others), who were part of a similar process of assimilation, this time of German horror-writing into England. But the traditional taxonomy of the German Gothic itself has been to divide the genre into three distinct subgenres: *Die Ritter-, Räuber- und Schauerromane* (novels of Chivalry, Banditry, and Terror). This classification was first proposed as early as 1859 and has tended to be followed, with only slight modification, by later commentators.[4] Since the *Räuberroman* is, superficially, the most straightforward of these three categories, it is as well to start there.

The concept of the romantic outlaw surely derives from the model of Karl Moor in Schiller's play *Die Räuber* (1781; trans. *The Robbers*, 1795). "Twelve years after the appearance of Schiller's drama," writes Agnes Murphy, "a flood of robber-novels appeared in the [German] loan libraries. The heroes were all Karl Moors: that is, they were of noble birth, had been maltreated by society, and were fired with a desire for revenge. Mere wealth had no appeal for them. They were determined to fight for the good of humanity, and the only way they could do this, so they thought, was to destroy all persons possessing money and power." Principal among these works was Heinrich Zschokke's *Aballino, der grosse Bandit* (1793), which was adapted/translated for an English-speaking audience by M. G. Lewis as *The Bravo of Venice* (1804). Though Schiller's play was set in Germany, it was Zschokke who transported the action to Venice and, as Agnes Murphy points out, virtually every German robber novel written subsequently employs a Mediterranean background. However, although Zschokke's novel proved popular in Lewis's version, the relative tardiness of the translation implies that the *Räuberroman* never enjoyed quite the same prestige in Britain as it had in Germany.

The same is probably true of the *Ritterroman* (or novel of chivalry). This second type of German popular novel should be construed as broad enough to include such exercises in medievalism as Goethe's *Götz von Berlichingen* (1773), translated by Sir Walter Scott in 1799, Christiane Naubert's *Hermann von Unna* (1788), and later imitators such as Christian Vulpius's *Der Maltheser* (1804; trans. *The Knight of Malta*, 1997). Medievalism, in this context, must be understood to entail stories of tournaments, jousting competitions, magic mirrors, mortal combat, knightly honor, endangered heroines, treachery and betrayal, and secret tribunals. The activities of these secret tribunals (i.e. illegal courts in which summary justice was supposedly meted out, often after the infliction of torture, by the rich and powerful who appear as masked judges) gave rise to some interest among British writers after Naubert's novel, now entitled *Hermann von Unna: a Series of Adventures of the Fifteenth Century*, was published in English translation in 1794. Purporting to contain a record of the Proceedings of the Secret Tribunal under the Emperors Winceslaus and Sigismond in Westphalia, this work effectively introduced the subject to the British market. Ann Radcliffe's descriptions of the Tribunal of the Inquisition in *The Italian* (1797), for example, are clearly modeled on Naubert's novel. Surprisingly, the *Critical Review* of September 1797 published a notice of *Hermann von Unna*, by no means unflattering, that ran to more than eight pages, quoting extensively from a passage in the novel detailing the workings of the Secret Tribunal, which is clearly portrayed as dispensing terror rather than justice. As Devendra P. Varma has noted, Naubert's novel further contains a range of "typical gothic motifs: the distressed heroine, the separated lovers, the malignant rival; the secret dungeon, the imprisoned heroine in a lone convent; her persecution by the wicked and diabolical monk, and finally the union and nuptial of the courageous hero and exquisite heroine."[5] But it was the sinister descriptions of the proceedings of the early fifteenth-century Secret Tribunal of Westphalia that represented the real interest of this work for British readers.

Both the *Räuber-* and the *Ritterroman* probably had more immediate effect in France than in Britain, though the influence of such works on the later development of the "penny dreadful" was far from negligible. Significantly, reprints of late eighteenth-century German texts, such as the anonymous *Rinaldo Rinaldini, Captain of Banditti* and *Woman's Revenge; or, The Tribunal of Blood* by Veit Weber (i.e., Georg Philipp Ludwig Leonhard Wächter), tended to resurface in the 1840s in publications such as William Hazlitt's *The Romancist and Novelist's Library*, which published popular works in weekly installments at the competitive price of twopence.

In the mid-1790s, though, it was the *Schauerroman* (or terror novel) which excited the greatest interest. In Germany, Schiller's unfinished *Der Geisterseher* (1789; trans. *The Ghost-Seer, or Apparitionist*, 1795) gave rise to an entire subgenre of works intended to expose the machinations of secret societies. But this was by no means the only direction that the genre could take. As early as 1791 the prolific Hans Christian Spiess published a novel which is generally regarded as best typifying the "spirit tale" side of the *Schauerroman*: *Das Petermännchen: Geistergeschichte aus dem dreyzehnten Jahrhundert* (i.e. *Little Peter: a Ghost Story of the Thirteenth Century*). It was translated almost immediately into English (as *The Dwarf of Westerbourg*, 1792) and a short while later into French (*Le Petit Pierre, ou Aventure de Rodolphe de Westerbourg*, 1795). The work is the very antithesis of the explanatory rationalism favored by Schiller. Closely allied to the German *Märchen* (or fairy tale) on the one hand, and Christian apologetics on the other (the author does not fail to drive home the moral of his tale, which concerns man's duty to exercise free will, at every turn), Spiess's novel is an unrepentant exercise in the supernatural, during which two demons fight over a man's soul. It would prove an extremely popular formula in Germany, even if British audiences preferred the more earthly conundrums of the Schiller-type tale.

Developments in France, 1789–1820

The French Revolution and its aftermath had tremendous consequences – some immediate, others delayed in their effect – in all kinds of cultural production throughout the fields of literature, theatre, music, and the fine arts. Censorship, one of the main buttresses of the *ancien régime*, disappeared almost overnight. For the sixty or so years prior to 1789, strict laws had remained in force against all those "who printed or caused to be printed, sold, exposed for sale, distributed or peddled" works prejudicial to religion, the king, the state, good morals, or the honor and reputation of individuals or specific families. Moreover, in order to publish a particular work, official sanction was required (though a quasi-official system of works which were tolerated, if not actively approved, also developed). Between 1745 and 1789 the number of censors directly employed by successive chancellors in this capacity rose from 73 to 178. Censorship laws even applied to tourists, as Tobias Smollett discovered to his cost when he landed at Boulogne in 1763: his private reading matter was confiscated and he was obliged to retrieve it, on payment of the appropriate fee, from the authorities at Amiens.[6]

Control was not only exerted by means of censorship, however. A variety of cultural/political support mechanisms also operated. In the realm of theatre, for example, 1789 marked the end of the quasi-monopoly enjoyed by the *Comédie-Française*, whose support for neoclassical productions not only did much to further French cultural imperialism in Europe, but also served to bolster the principle of absolutist government. Nor were such mechanisms directed only at cultural elites. In the sub-literary domain, an entire tradition dating back to the 1620s of absolutist apologia, which frequently took the form of simple homilies comprehensible by the widest possible readership, likewise came to a very abrupt end.[7]

For the more learned, the revolution was responsible for providing access to all manner of historical, literary, and political documentation, as the great libraries of the *ancien régime* were broken up and dispersed. The banks and bridges of the Seine, the auction rooms, and the covered galleries were submerged beneath a tide of old books and bundles of papers for decades after 1789. Indeed, the first half of the nineteenth century represents the greatest epoch in the history of French bibliophily, as writers and collectors sought to find a pathway through this maze of human knowledge. As the *ancien régime* shriveled up in the face of revolutionary activity, new political

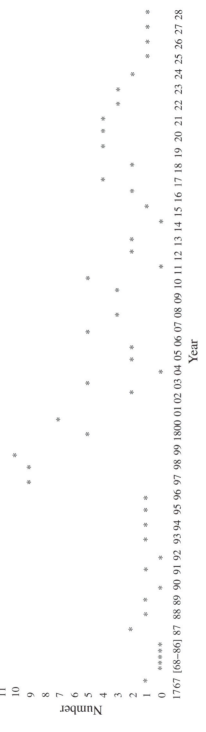

Graph based on Maurice Lévy's 1974 bibliography of English Gothic novels in French translation.

Fig. 2   Publication of English Gothic novels in French translation, 1767–1828.

and social discourses rapidly emerged. How, if at all, was the Gothic novel, or *roman noir* as the genre was called in France, implicated in that process?

Historically, French commentators have been primarily interested in the development of the English Gothic novel. That is partly because, as figure 2 makes abundantly clear, very little translation occurred prior to 1797.[8] Walpole's *The Castle of Otranto* (1764) made its way into French quickly enough (1767), as any such novelty might be expected to do, but this did not start becoming a trend until 1787, when Clara Reeve's *The Old English Baron* (1777–78) was issued in French by two different publishers. Over the course of the next eight years a further six Gothic novels were published in French translation, including Charlotte Smith's *Emmeline, The Orphan of the Castle* (1788; trans. 1788), Sophia Lee's *The Recess* (1783–85; trans. 1793), Radcliffe's *The Romance of the Forest* (1791; trans. 1794), and William Godwin's *Things As They Are; or, The Adventures of Caleb Williams* (1794; trans. 1795 and 1796).

This late acceleration of production can be explained by a number of factors. Censorship may have been temporarily abolished in 1789, but that by no means meant that it was safe to publish or that the economic circumstances were favorable to the publication of fiction. This was especially true after 1792, when a systematic campaign of suppression aimed at the newspapers began and lasted throughout the period of "the Terror," which commenced in September 1793. Not until the fall of Robespierre did revolutionary fervor begin to abate. Nor should it be forgotten that from January 1793 Britain was at war with France. However, though Prime Minister Pitt's policy of forming a European coalition against France was initially successful, it ultimately proved a costly failure, so much so that the British prime minister was forced to sue for peace with France in May 1796.

Thus the rise of the *roman noir*, at least with regard to the translation of British fiction, coincides very clearly with the so-called "*réaction thermidorienne*," commencing with the restoration of freedom of the press by the constitution of 1795 and the paralysis of the British war effort thereafter. Figure 2 shows nine titles published in 1797 and 1798, ten titles published in 1799. Over the course of the next few years these numbers steadily declined as British hostility to French expansion stiffened. Indeed, by 1804–05, with Napoleon planning an invasion and Pitt hastily assembling a new coalition with Russia, Austria, and Sweden, translation almost comes to a standstill: there are no known new titles for 1804 and only two for the year in which the Battle of Trafalgar was fought. After that moment has passed a more or less steady trickle of translations of English Gothic novels occurs between the years 1806–10 and 1817–23. The dip in the number of works published between these two sets of dates is probably explained by the presence of the

Duke of Wellington's British army in Spain, who represented a very considerable threat as far as Napoleonic policy was concerned, and the political uncertainty surrounding the restoration of the French monarchy in 1814.

Useful as these figures are, they say very little about the French attitude toward the Gothic or what happened to the genre in the hands of local writers. In this respect, it is helpful to examine a number of domestically produced texts. As might be expected, the titles of translated English Gothic novels published in France reveal similar geographical, architectural, and generic features as those to be found in the English Gothic novel. An examination of texts in the Gothic tradition by French writers, however, suggests that though some such features may be present, the act of writing a *roman noir* was seen as an opportunity for making points about the political situation in France itself. Significantly, the vast majority of texts are either critical or openly hostile to the political transformations taking place in the country.

As with the translations from the English, these texts tend to date from the period of the *réaction thermidorienne*. Mercier de Compiègne's anonymous *Les Nuits de la conciergerie* (i.e. *Night (Thoughts) at the Conciergerie*), for example, which appeared in 1795, is ostensibly intended to appeal to opponents of, or at least those ambivalent toward, the French Revolution.[9] The *conciergerie* of the title is the famous prison in Paris situated next to the Palais de Justice, where those awaiting execution during the Terror were imprisoned.

The link with the Gothic novel, however, is not restricted to the macabre subject of the work but is also related to the form of six interconnected "visions" which constitute its main organizing feature. As we shall see, Mercier de Compiègne was by no means the only author of the epoch to look to Edward Young's lugubrious blank-verse poem *The Complaint, or Night Thoughts on Life, Death and Immortality* (1742–46; translated by Le Tourneur, 1760) for a model. The visions in this case, which largely represent an exercise in sentimentality, are supposed to be those of a young man shortly to be guillotined. The most curious of these visions is certainly the sixth, in which the author imagines himself reincarnated in the body of a Republican soldier who has been fighting valiantly for his country. Returning home, though upset to find his wife remarried, he is overjoyed at discovering that the utopian vision of the revolution has been realized. It is at that point, as if to underline the intended irony of the preceding passage, that he is disturbed by the jailer who has come to escort him to his execution.

Mercier de Compiègne (1763–1800) was a Parisian bookseller at the time of the revolution, who published a variety of slight or lighthearted works during his short working life, including a number of erotic texts. *Les Nuits de la conciergerie*, which is by no means typical of his literary output, cannot be considered as much more than a minor historical curiosity. But the same is not true of all such texts. J. B. I. P. Regnault-Warin's *Le Cimetière de la Madeleine* (i.e. *The Graveyard of the Madeleine*; 1800) was popular enough to be reprinted several times during the first half of the nineteenth century in French,[10] while Spanish editions were published in 1811, 1817 (described as corrected and expurgated), 1829, 1833 (in which the expurgated passages are said to have been restored), 1878, and 1920 ("*Con censura eclesiástica*" – i.e. with the approval of the ecclesiastical authorities). In Spain at least, this was a text which enjoyed some longevity and, arguably, a much greater readership than that of any English Gothic novel. There is also evidence that the work found readers in Italy and Portugal. Regnault-Warin (1771–1844) also published numerous works in the field of political history, though *Le Cimetière de la Madeleine* would appear to have been by far his most popular novel even in France, where the work even aroused the disapproval of Napoleon, who tried to have it suppressed. Interestingly, one of Regnault-Warin's slightly earlier works was published in English translation by the Miverva Press under the title *The Cavern of Strozzi* (1800).

As with Mercier de Compiègne's excursion into the *roman noir*, *Le Cimetière de la Madeleine* is orientated around a series of visions in the manner of Young's *Night Thoughts*. Like the *conciergerie*, the *église de la Madeleine* has considerable revolutionary significance, for it was in the cemetery of this church, a few hundred meters from the *Place de la Révolution* (renamed the *Place de la Concorde* in 1830), that the body and severed head of Louis XVI were buried the same day as his execution on 21 January 1793. As if to bury the Bourbon monarchy beyond any hope of resurrection, it was ordered that the grave should be dug 10 feet deep.

Louis XVI's execution was an historical event which immediately gave rise to a diversity of narratives. According to Daniel Arasse, two distinct tendencies emerge from this mass of material. At the highest symbolic level, the desanctification in death of Louis XVI also served to sanctify the revolution itself. The republican version of this event, seeking to make political capital from it, emphasized the king's apparent belief that his supporters would still rescue him even as he mounted the scaffold (thus, giving credence to the idea of an aristocratic plot); in royalist accounts, many of which have an inherent mystical tendency, "the king offers himself of his own free will as an expiatory victim."[11]

Regnault-Warin's *Cimetière*, which deals directly with the execution of Louis XVI, cannot be seen as anything but a contribution to the literature of royal apotheosis. In order to achieve this, however, the author employs a mixture of techniques derived from Edward Young and the French tradition of political pamphleteering. The narrative is divided into eleven nocturnal visions, while a mass of historical documentation is incorporated into the narrative, a considerable amount of it relating to the problematic status of Marie-Antoinette. Thus the novel commences with a quite "Gothic" account of the narrator's nocturnal ramblings across Paris from the bridge across the Seine near the Place de la Révolution to what was then the "half-built church of the Madeleine":

> The name of Vernet invoked itself at the sight of these beautiful tricks of the light which his brush has so delicately captured; my lips were already murmuring it when the baneful thought crossed my mind that this building was a monument to death and destruction. This double circle of damaged walls and half-destroyed columns, I reminded myself, was the pit in which the revolution heaped up the victims of its murderous inclinations. Here, wrapped in eternal sleep, slumber the bones of those celebrated for their virtue, their power, their crimes, and their talents! There, lost in dusty embrace, lie the victims of the public executioner. Vergniaud, struck dumb, seems to have forgiven Robespierre; and a tiny worm nourishes itself on the heart of a king of France!
>
> These sombre and lamentable images made a knot in my stomach. I cannot say what secret horror caused me to shiver. Such are the wondrous effects of terror on the imagination! From the gaping holes in the building, I thought I saw a mass of hideous, blood-stained ghosts leap forth. They flitted about the colonnades, chasing and fighting with each other furiously, and only leaving off in a state of high dudgeon. Suddenly they emitted a terrible scream, after which I neither saw nor heard anything more.[12]

These supernatural apparitions are not treated as necessarily having an objective existence. Indeed, the implication is that they are in some sense the product of the narrator's disordered imagination. After he regains consciousness, he encounters the shade of the Abbé Edgeworth de Firmont, Louis XVI's confessor, who, according to some accounts, accompanied the king to the scaffold. Indeed, according to Bigot de Sainte-Croix, the minister for foreign affairs who had wisely escaped to England some months prior to the events he claims to describe, the king's confessor was blessing him at the very moment the blade of the guillotine fell, thus implying a double act of sacrilege.[13] Regnault-Warin does not fail to make use of this lugubrious detail, nor does he fail to add his own innovation to the story in his description of a young man from Marseilles who leaps upon the scaffold just after Louis's head has fallen and covers his naked arms with the royal blood before turning to the people to provide them with a sort of political benediction.[14]

Royalist attitudes toward the queen, however, were subject to greater variation. As a number of recent historians have been at pains to establish, Marie-Antoinette was the victim of an increasingly vicious campaign of pornographic pamphlets and lampoons for more than a decade before the

French Revolution actually broke out. Though the king's trial was restricted to political issues alone, that of the queen, which paid considerable attention to her private life, seems to echo the transgressive sensationalism of these earlier *libelles*. As early as 1779, the author of one well-known pamphlet, after describing the queen masturbating, went on to describe a supposed orgy with her brother-in-law, the comte d'Artois (later Charles X).[15] It now seems more than likely that pamphlets such as *Les amours de Charlot et Toinette* (Charlot remains a common diminutive for Charles to this day; Toinette is, of course, an abbreviation of Marie-Antoinette) not only did much to shape Republican attitudes toward Marie-Antoinette, but also influenced Royalist sentiments as well. Hence Regnault-Warin, writing some six or seven years after the turbulent days of 1793, devotes an entire chapter (or "vision") to such matters. Though he avoids accusing the queen of actually committing adultery, he does convict her of acting in an imprudent manner shortly after her marriage to the Dauphin by participating in a series of flirtatious moonlit promenades with the comte d'Artois (whose identity was not yet divulged to her). These promenades are portrayed as alienating the natural affection she owed to her husband, such that his succession to the French crown in 1774 is marred by his wife's marital transgressions.[16] Later in the same chapter, Marie-Antoinette's attempts to avoid the amorous attentions of the duc d'Orléans, the king's cousin, are also dealt with in some detail. As Marie-Antoinette makes clear in the fictitious historical memoir attributed to her by Regnault-Warin, some responsibility for the outbreak of revolution must be laid at her door due to her scandalous (if unintentional) behavior.

Thus, though undoubtedly a *roman noir*, *Le Cimetière de la Madeleine* is by no means close to what we understand today by the term *Gothic novel*. Indeed, it might be said that the novel merely employs certain style markers inherited from the poetry of Edward Young more or less as a framing device for what might better be described as an historical tale. In other works from the same period, however, such style markers are used to greater effect, and in one novel at least a successful attempt is made to turn Marie-Antoinette into a bona fide Gothic heroine. That work is Reveroni Saint-Cyr's *Pauliska ou la perversité moderne; mémoires récens d'une Polonaise* (i.e. *Pauliska or Modern Perversity; Recent Memoirs of a Young Polishwoman*; 1796).[17]

This peculiar novel concerns the attempted flight and capture of the eponymous heroine, together with that of her principal bodyguard, in the face of a Russian invasion of Poland. Given that the author himself had been involved with the defense of the Tuileries during the French Revolution and been otherwise compromised by his devotion to the royal family, modern critics have been quick to point to the obvious parallel to Marie-Antoinette's abortive flight to Varennes in 1791. Although the novel contains a number of markers which we have come to associate with the Gothic (including a virtuous, distressed heroine, scenes of pursuit and capture, feudal châteaux, mad scientists, and secret societies), the work is quite unlike anything else in the genre.

One reason for this is that the liberalization of the censorship regime meant that authors were capable of describing scenes considerably more erotic than were allowed at other times or elsewhere. (There would even seem to have been a French pornographic pastiche of *The Castle of Otranto* published around 1798, complete with a frontispiece depicting penitents being flagellated by monks.) More generally, though, works such as *Le Cimetière de la Madeleine* and *Pauliska* are engaged with a moment of cultural history which, until recently, has been all but lost to us. Thus, in one sequence, Ernest Pradislas, *Pauliska*'s devoted young captain, is captured by a society of female Freemasons and becomes the unwilling subject of a bizarre experiment intended to prove the purely physical nature of the male sex drive. In short, the women reveal their breasts to him in order to examine the physiognomic effect that this has on him. Similarly, among the various persecutions that Pauliska is forced to undergo is an attempt to inject her with a love serum. In both cases, it seems likely that the author's main purpose – as in the obscene *libelles* directed at Marie-Antoinette – is to create anxieties about women invading the public sphere, organizing themselves into political associations, and ultimately assuming power.

Pauliska was an unusual work in an unusual age. But even more mainstream works in the tradition of the *roman noir* did not ignore the consequences of the French Revolution. Bellin de la Liborlière's *Célestine, ou les Epoux sans l'être* (1800; i.e. *Célestine, or Husband and Wife Without Being Married*) features a melancholic hero, d'Orméville, whose parents have fallen victim to the guillotine.[18] Clearly French authors by now did not have to reach back into the feudal past in search of themes for their work. This novel, moreover, is based largely on French literary models rather than English ones. The sentimental nature of the work looks back to Baculard d'Arnaud and his master, the Abbé Prévost. Indeed, d'Orméville's principal function in the work is to rescue the heroine, Célestine, from a bewildering sequence of abductions and attempted abductions reminiscent of the eighteenth-century French adventure story. The mystery, such as it is, relates to the identity of the persecutor and the "inexplicable" nature of some of the adventures which befall the couple. The former is revealed midway through the work however, while the latter, which shows the author has also learned the lessons of Ann Radcliffe, is explained during the lengthy death-bed scene with which the work concludes.

Likewise, Mme. Herbster's *Le Souterrain, ou les deux soeurs* (1806; trans. *The Two Sisters or, The Cavern*, 1807), a work perhaps intended for the juvenile market, makes use of the device of the underground cavern deriving from Prévost via Sophia Lee.[19] In this case, the hiding place is constructed in the face of mounting revolutionary fervor in 1792 and is intended to shelter the Count de Roseville and his family and servants. On the strength of the many editions of this work published in London (it had reached its eighth edition by 1833, many of these issued by the *émigré* publishing house of Dulau), there is every likelihood that the author herself was a French refugee in Britain.

The above examples might lead one to believe that the *roman noir* was largely, if not exclusively, a literary genre utilized by writers with royalist sympathies. This would seem to be generally true, even of the French translators of English Gothic novels. When Jean Cohen translated Charles Maturin's *Melmoth the Wanderer* (1820; trans. *Melmoth, ou l'homme errant*, 1821),[20] for example, as much as a fifth of the original text disappeared. Detailed analysis of the French edition, which is still in print today, suggests that the anti-Catholicism of the original was considerably toned down during the translation process and that remarks critical of the Society of Jesus were systematically removed. Significantly, Cohen (1781–1848) was a legitimist in politics (i.e. loyal to the Bourbons) and had even served as censor with specific responsibility for foreign-language publications a decade earlier. In light of the prolonged right-wing reaction occurring in France at the time the French translation of *Melmoth* was published, such alterations were probably essential to keep the book from being banned.

Not all authors connected with the supernatural and mysterious were inherently conservative in outlook, however. Collin de Plancy (1794–1881), one of the more prolific authors of the 1820s, would perhaps have considered himself an Enlightenment skeptic. The majority of Collin de Plancy's works were no doubt intended for a newly literate urban audience. Typical of these are collections of curious or mysterious stories, culled from a wide variety of sources (including the Gothic novel), such as the *Anecdotes du dix-neuvième siècle* (1821; i.e., *Nineteenth-Century Anecdotes*). Although Collin de Plancy clearly set out to thrill his readers, his intention was also to instruct: "Unfortunate peasants, as you well know yourselves to be. You are terrified of devils, the thought of ghosts or even a dead body makes you quake; you are the victim of every fear; and you are refused the very illumination [*lumières*] which would render you less miserable."[21] The author's most significant contributions to the *roman noir*, however, were the three substantial compendiums he published in the fields of the supernatural (*Dictionnaire infernal*, 1818; expanded edition 1825–26), feudalism (*Dictionnaire féodal*, 1819), and religious relics (*Dictionnaire critique des reliques et des images miraculeuses*, 1821–22). Contemporary authors such as Victor Hugo would be indebted to Collin de Plancy for a host of superstitious legends and folklore.[22]

Developments in France, 1821–1830

The history of French horror fiction over the period from the restoration of the monarchy until the eve of the revolution of 1848 is one of increasing narrative sophistication. This can be seen particularly clearly in the case of the novelist and short story writer Charles Nodier (1780–1844), who is often considered one of the founding figures of the French Romantic movement. Among Nodier's earlier works is a robber novel, *Jean Sbogar* (1818),[23] in the tradition of Zschokke's *Aballino*. Indeed, the similarities between the two works are considerable, including the Venetian setting, the concealment of the hero's identity, and his ambiguous social status as nobleman or bandit. In light of the fascination – one might almost say obsession – of previous writers with revolutionary history, it is not surprising that Nodier's main contribution to the robber story is the skillful manner in which the tale is politicized. Sbogar is leader of the feared *Frères du bien commun* (Brothers of the Common Weal), whose main tenets seem to owe not a little to the revolutionary leader Babeuf. Nodier also makes telling use of the imagery of the bloodshed of the revolution, not least in the passages in which the heroine catches sight of a disembodied head in a mirror, an image which later comes back to her in a delusion.

Nodier is frequently credited with being one of the first French writers to employ oneiric devices of this kind successfully. Several of his later works, especially tales such as *Smarra ou les démons de la nuit* (1821; trans. *Smarra, or The Demons of the Night*; see Kessler, *Demons of the Night*, pp. 1–29), while also making extensive use of violent imagery, employ dream sequences in a manner intended to deliberately puzzle or perplex the reader while also serving to reveal the unconscious in a pre-Freudian way. As if to mark the coming of age of French horror-writing, Nodier was also responsible in 1821 for coining the term *roman frénétique*, a neologism which has been taken up by recent scholars as a useful way of differentiating the older *roman noir*, with its essentially eighteenth-century resonances, from the new kind of writing ushered in with the late flowering of the Romantic movement in France. According to Nodier, the term *frénétique* might be applied to those writers who, whether in prose or in verse, "flaunt their atheism, rage and despair over tombstones, exhume the dead in order to terrify the living, or who torment the reader's imagination which such horrifying scenes as to suggest the deranged dreams of madmen."[24] As with the development of the

Gothic novel in England in the 1780s, it is significant to note that translated works, at least initially, would seem to have played a major role in this new school of writing. Indeed, Nodier's first use of the term occurred in a review of a new French translation of the same German spirit tale by Christian Spiess, *Das Petermännchen*, which we encountered earlier.

Between 1821 and 1848 more than 200 novels and collections of short stories, excluding translations, were published which might be classified as *frénétique*.[25] As with the Gothic, not all these works recognized themselves as such. Some writers referred to the genre by other names. Théophile Gautier, in his celebrated preface to *Mademoiselle de Maupin* (1835), called it *le roman-charogne* ("the novel of decaying carcasses"); Honoré de Balzac in a preface later omitted from *La Peau de Chagrin* (1831) describes it as a literature *sanguinolent* and *bouffon* ("bloody" and "clown-like"); Hippolyte Castille, writing as late as 1853, calls it variously *la littérature cadavérique, la littérature enragée, paradoxale et lycanthropique*, and *la littérature succube* ("the literature of cadavers," "rabid, paradoxical, and lycanthropic," and "succubus-like").[26] Many of the writers involved were on the fringes of the Romantic movement, and, indeed, some of the early works of authors such as Victor Hugo incontestably belong to the genre (particularly *Hans d'Islande*, 1823; trans. *Han of Iceland*, 1825).

In thematic terms, the *frénétique* genre is extremely wide-ranging. On one hand, as we shall see, it encompasses historical novels, especially those dealing with figures such as Gilles de Rais, the medieval child-murderer and practitioner of black magic (the subject of a novel by the almost entirely forgotten Hippolyte Bonnellier in 1834, who also wrote *frénétique* accounts of the lives of Nostradamus and Urbain Grandier, the priest convicted of sorcery in 1634 following allegations of demonic possession at the convent of Loudon), or revolutionary leaders such as Robespierre (the subject of an advertised but unpublished work by Pétrus Borel). On the other hand, just as *Frankenstein* did, the *frénétique* also embraces a host of contemporary subjects ranging from dissection in the Parisian medical schools to the sale of children for medical experimentation, galvanism, the causes and effects of the cholera epidemics, hermaphroditism and impotence, gender transgression, and so on.

In this vein, one of the most successful novels of the early 1820s was a work entitled *Le Solitaire* (i.e. *The Recluse*) by the vicomte d'Arlincourt.[27] Indeed, it could be said that *Le Solitaire* was the first *frénétique* best-seller on a European scale. German, English, Dutch, and Italian translations were all brought out in 1821, the same year as the French first edition, while by 1824 it had been translated into Danish, Polish, Spanish, Swedish, Russian, and Portuguese. Perhaps one reason for the work's success was that it dealt with Napoleon Bonaparte, who died the same year as the book came out and whose military campaigns and political ambitions had had such tremendous consequences for Europe as a whole. Napoleon, however, is never directly mentioned in the course of d'Arlincourt's novel. Indeed, the work purports to be an historical novel dealing with Charles the Bold, presumed to have died during the Battle of Nancy in 1477, but who the author implies is still alive some 344 years later. The vicomte d'Arlincourt's Charles the Bold is a deeply ambiguous figure, however. On one hand he is capable of tremendous acts of bravery and inspiring great tenderness on the part of the heroine; on the other hand his attempts to usurp the French crown result in appalling loss of human life and, on occasion, gratuitous acts of violence, so much so that parallels with the career of Napoleon hardly need emphasizing. *Le Solitaire* manages to collapse all these different issues of time, identity, and political ideology into a single coherent narrative which, presumably, could have been read in different ways by an extremely diverse audience.[28]

Another *roman frénétique* that manages to collapse political meanings is Henri de Latouche's *Fragoletta, ou Naples et Paris en 1799* (1829; i.e. *Fragoletta: Naples and Paris in 1799*).[29] This dense novel follows the fortunes of Marius d'Hauteville, a dashing lieutenant in command of French troops seeking to export revolutionary democracy to an unwilling Italy, who falls in love with the beautiful Eugénie (the Fragoletta of the title) at the same time as he becomes a close friend of her brother, Philippe Adriani. Marius has a hard time of it. He witnesses at close hand the manner in which the working clergy fan the superstitious population into rebellion by fabricating miracles during the short-lived experiment with republican government in Naples at the end of the eighteenth century; later, after the French are forced out, he witnesses the barbarous manner in which the Catholic Church establishes a secret tribunal to punish local democrats. The real surprise in the novel, and one which requires considerable rereading of the work, comes after Marius has fought a duel with Philippe Adriani, who has accused him of seducing his sister. As Philippe is dying, it is revealed that he is a hermaphrodite and that he and Fragoletta are, in fact, the same person. Thus, it turns out, de Latouche's main objective in the novel was to create a complicated metaphor of crisis in sexual identity to explain political failure. At the most simplistic level, Fragoletta is as incomprehensible to Marius (at an earlier point in the novel we see him gazing with incomprehension at a statue of an Androgyne) as are the demands of democratic processes to the Neapolitan populace.

The vicomte d'Arlincourt and Henri de Latouche represent different political extremes in the France of the 1820s. The former was a legitimist who had served in the Napoleonic regime; the latter was a noted liberal. The work of both authors, however, shows evidence of some influence from abroad. A subplot in *Fragoletta* concerning her birth, for example, is not without parallels in Radcliffe's *The Italian*. As the *roman frénétique* developed as a genre, though, it gradually assumed more local features and cast off most signs of foreign influence. One such style marker of the genre is a black humor and self-mockery that is mostly absent from the English Gothic (save for Walpole and Lewis) and certainly from the German *Schauerroman*. This tendency to self-parody, which is clearly visible in the early novels of Victor Hugo, is particularly marked later in the nineteenth century in one of the most famous examples of the genre: Jules Janin's *L'Ane mort et la femme guillotinée* (1829; trans. *The Dead Donkey [and the Guillotined Woman]*, 1851).[30]

With its claustrophobic atmosphere and wealth of dreadful incident (ranging through a description of a dog savaging a donkey, an attempt to recall a dead body back to life by means of an electrical discharge after it has been immersed in the Seine, sexual persecution, details of the working conditions of a prostitute in a low-class brothel, murder, and the heroine's rape by a hideously deformed jailer prior to her execution), Janin's novel contains more concentrated scenes of horror than previous works in the field. The author himself clearly intended the work to be taken as a parody of the genre (though one of the butts of his humor was also Lawrence Sterne), yet he gradually became more enamored of his subject matter. At the very least, the work may be considered a study in the nature of French Romantic misogyny and thus a revealing account of the extent to which literature in the 1820s and 1830s was still seeking to negotiate the intellectual legacy of the French Revolution. Significantly, in *Barnave* (1831), the author's only other major foray into the genre, Janin presents an interpretation of Marie-Antoinette's abortive flight to Varennes in 1791. Like Reveroni Saint-Cyr, Janin chose to present the late queen as an unsullied icon of virtue, though a terrifying scene of female crucifixion toward the end of the novel may be a reminder of the fact that the radical left debated whether this form of death was a more suitable punishment for Marie-Antoinette than the guillotine.

Conclusion

The Gothic novel, the *Schauerroman*, the *roman noir*, and the *roman frénétique* represent a complex network of borrowings, misappropriations, and innovations. It is unlikely than any of these genres would have developed in the manner they did without the initial impetus provided by the translation process; but as literary practitioners became more assured in their manner of creating the effects they desired, each genre took on an increasingly distinctive local character. The cultural disruption caused by the French Revolution, moreover, allowed the Gothic novel to take root, however briefly, on continental soil. As French hegemony reasserted itself following the restoration of the monarchy, it would be the *roman frénétique* that would have the greater impact on European literature in the nineteenth century. This would be particularly true as the genre gave way to the nascent *roman feuilleton* after 1836. The three major practitioners of the serial novel in daily installments – Frédéric Soulié (1800–47), Alexandre Dumas (1802–70), and Eugène Sue (1804–57) – either began their literary careers as *frénétique* novelists or were on the fringes of the movement. Consequently, their later work is never entirely free of the tendency. Henri de Latouche and Jules Janin were too quirky and experimental to have a wide following beyond their own shores, but the early novels of Soulié and Sue were reprinted continuously throughout the nineteenth century in continental Europe and elsewhere.

With the rise of English as a world language in the twentieth century, the Gothic has reasserted itself as a major literary movement. In Russia, France, Spain, and Italy the canonical Gothic texts are increasingly available in reliable scholarly translations. Though the cultural center of gravity may have passed elsewhere, the French and German contribution to horror Romanticism deserves to be studied in more detail. That effort would also reveal our pressing need throughout the coming years to study writing in the horror genre in other languages beyond English, French, and German.

NOTES

1 John Dunlop, *The History of Prose Fiction*, 4th edn (London: Reeves and Turner, 1876), p. 440 (my translation).
2 James R. Foster, "The Abbé Prévost and the English Novel," *PMLA* 42 (1927): 443–64.
3 See my "Translation in Distress: the Construction of the Gothic" in Avril Horner, ed., *European Gothic: a Spirited Exchange, 1760–1960* (Manchester: Manchester University Press, 2002).
4 See Michael Hadley, *The Undiscovered Genre: a Search for the German Gothic Novel* (Beme: Peter Lang, 1977), plus Agnes C. Murphy, *Banditry, Chivalry, and Terror in German Fiction, 1790–1830* (Chicago: University of Chicago Libraries, 1935), cited in my next paragraph from p. 5.
5 "Introduction" to Marquis of Grosse, *Horrid Mysteries*, trans. Peter Will, Northanger Set of Jane Austen Horror Novels (London: Folio Press, 1968), p. ix.
6 John Lough, *Writer and Public in France from the Middle Ages to the Present Day* (Oxford: Clarendon Press, 1978), pp. 173–79.
7 Carol Blum, "Representing the Body Politic: Fictions of the State" in James A. W. Heffernan, ed., *Representing the French Revolution: Literature, Historiography, and Art* (Hanover, NH: University Press of New England, 1992), pp. 125–26.

8 Figure 2 is based on the bibliography provided by Maurice Lévy, "English Gothic and the French Imagination: a Calendar of Translations, 1767–1828" in G. R. Thompson, ed., *The Gothic Imagination: Essays in Dark Romanticism* (Olympia: Washington State University Press, 1974), pp. 150–76. As Lévy himself admits, it is not exhaustive, including as it does only works for which there is a known location.

9 See anonymous [Mercier de Compiègne, C. F. X.], *Les Nuits de la conciergerie. Rêveries mélancoliques, et poésies d'un proscrit. Fragmens éshappes au vandalisme* (Paris: La veuve Girouard, 1795).

10 See Regnault-Warin, *Le Cimetière de la Madeleine*, 4 vols. (Paris: Lepetit, 1801).

11 Arasse, *The Guillotine and the Terror*, trans. Christopher Miller (Harmondsworth: Penguin, 1989), p. 57.

12 *Le Cimetière*, I, 5–7; my translation. The allusions in this passage are to Joseph Vernet (1714–89), the French painter celebrated mainly for his landscapes, and Pierre Victurnien Vergniaud (1753–93), the politician and orator who died on the scaffold during the Terror.

13 *The Guillotine and the Terror*, pp. 70–71.

14 *Le Cimetière*, III, 85–92.

15 See Robert Darnton, *The Literary Underground of the Old Regime* (Cambridge, MA: Harvard University Press, 1982), pp. 200–01 and Lynn Hunt, "The Many Bodies of Marie-Antoinette: Political Pornography and the Problem of the Feminine in the French Revolution" in *Eroticism and the Body Politic*, ed. Lynn Hunt (Baltimore: Johns Hopkins University Press, 1991), pp. 116–18.

16 *Le Cimetière*, III, 128–35.

17 See Reveroni Saint-Cyr, *Pauliska ou la perversité moderne*, ed. Béatrice Didier (Paris: Deforges, 1976).

18 See Anna Grenwil Bellin de la Liborlière, *Célestine, ou les Epoux sans l'être*, 4 vols. (Paris: Billois, 1800).

19 For a translation, see Mme. F. Herbster, *The Two Sisters; or, The Cavern* (London: T. and R. Hughes, 1807).

20 Jean Cohen, trans., *Melmoth, ou l'homme errant* by C. R. Maturin, 6 vols. (Paris: G. C. Hubert, 1821).

21 J. A. S. Collin de Plancy, *Anecdotes du dix-neuvième siècle, ou collection inédite d'Historiettes et d'Anecdotes récentes*, 2 vols. (Paris: Charles Painparré, 1821), II, 69 (my translation).

22 See Edmond Huguet, "Quelques sources de Notre-Dame de Paris," *Revue d'histoire littéraire de la France* 8 (1901): 46–79, 425–55, 622–49.

23 See Charles Nodier, *Jean Sbogar*, ed. Jean Sgard (Paris: Champion, 1987).

24 Nodier in "Critique Littéraire: *Le Petit Pierre, traduit de l'allemand*, de Speiss (1)," *Annales de la Littérature et des Arts*, 16e livraison (1821): 82.

25 Some examples of the *frénétique* short story are available in Terry Hale, ed., *The Dedalus Book of French Horror: the Nineteenth Century* (Cambridge: Dedalus, 1998).

26 These three statements can be found in Gautier, *Mademoiselle de Maupin*, ed. Geneviève van den Bogaert (Paris: Garnier-Flammarion, 1966), p. 37; Balzac, *La Comédie humaine*, ed. Pierre-Georges Castex et al., 12 vols. (Paris: Gallimard, 1976–81), X, 54; and Castille, *Les Hommes et les moeurs en France sous le règne de Louis-Phillippe* (Paris: Henneton, 1853), pp. 277–305.

27 Charles Victor Prevot, vicomte d'Arlincourt, *Le Solitaire*, 2 vols. (Paris: Le Normant, 1821).

28 See Terry Hale, "A Forgotten Best Seller of 1821: *Le Solitaire* by le Vicomte d'Arlincourt and the Development of European Horror Romanticism," *Gothic Studies* 2 (2000): 185–204.

29 H. J. A. Thabaud, *dit* Henri de Latouche, *Fragoletta, ou Naples et Paris en 1799*, 2 vols. (Paris: Levavasseur, 1829).

30 See *The Dead Donkey and the Guillotined Woman*, ed. Terry Hale (London: Gothic Society, 1993).

5

MICHAEL GAMER

Gothic fictions and Romantic writing in Britain

> That Gothicism is closely related to Romanticism is perfectly clear, but it is easier to state the fact than to prove it tidily and convincingly. There is a persistent suspicion that Gothicism is a poor and probably illegitimate relation of Romanticism, and a consequent tendency to treat it that way. There are those, indeed, who would like to deny the relationship altogether.
>
> (Robert Hume, "Gothic Versus Romantic," p. 282)

This was the way matters stood in 1969 when Robert Hume published "Gothic Versus Romantic: a Revaluation of the Gothic Novel" in the flagship journal of America's Modern Language Association, *PMLA*. To reread Hume's essay today is to be surprised by the modesty of its claims – since it points to conventions, aesthetics, and reading experiences shared by Gothic and Romantic texts and their readers – and by the energy with which these claims were attacked by another scholar, Robert Platzer, in a "Rejoinder" published as a companion piece to it. Their exchange resembles another, better-known dispute between Arthur Lovejoy and René Wellek over the nature of Romanticism.[1] There Lovejoy had attacked Wellek's holistic definition of Romanticism by pointing to its exceptions. Here Platzer took a similar approach: attacking the fundamental vagueness of the categories of "Gothic" and "Romantic"; allowing for common thematic preoccupations but no closer relation; and arguing for the two terms as part of an overarching "continuum" of print culture. Sharing subject matter and themes, he claimed, did not amount to sharing consciousness, and only the most selective account of both movements could point to real common ground or direct and unmediated influence (Platzer, "Gothic Versus Romantic: Rejoinder," pp. 270–71).

Ironically, many of the ideas put forward by both Hume and Platzer have proven fruitful in the succeeding decades for literary historians writing about the Gothic, many of whom are featured in this volume. Beginning with Platzer's suggestion that generic categories are neither fixed nor preeminent, we have moved to perceiving the Gothic as a "mixed" genre, assembled, like Frankenstein's monster, out of other discourses. While taking up Hume's question of what kinds of reading experiences Gothic texts offered to their readers, we have let go of his notion that Gothic is fundamentally a kind of prose fiction and instead have viewed it more accurately as an aesthetic crossing the genres of narrative, dramatic, and lyric writing. Taking up this question of the relation between Gothic and Romantic writing, we have embraced each critic's assessment that the relation is complex while abandoning the notion that it should be described through a precise delineation of direct influence. Rather, we have begun looking to the intricacies of late eighteenth-century print culture in our search for more sophisticated ways of describing Romantic and Gothic writing's dealings with one another. The language of influence between writers, whether of direct borrowing or of willful misreading, cannot adequately represent the mediating forces at work here, let alone capture the richness of the appropriations that do occur.

While "Gothic" may be a notoriously shifting and complex object of study for any literary historian interested in genre, its rapid changes and instabilities at the end of the eighteenth century, rather than frustrating us, should form part of our definition of the term. Certainly late eighteenth-century readers considered it thus. When they first began to group specific writers into the category or group we now call "the Gothic," they were aware that they were responding to a "new" literary fashion. At the same time, they were alarmed by the sudden appearance of so many similar texts across so many genres. Londoners walking the streets around St. Paul's Cathedral or Covent Garden in the spring of 1794, for instance, would have found Ann Radcliffe's *The Mysteries of Udolpho* (1794) to be on every fashionable person's lips, appearing as it did during the same weeks that saw James Boaden's stage triumph with *Fountaineville Forest*, a successful dramatic adaptation of Radcliffe's *Romance of the Forest* (1791).[2] Two springs later, these same residents would have found Gothic entertainment even more plentiful and nearly impossible to avoid. Aside from Radcliffe's fictions and those by writers like Matthew Lewis and Eliza Fenwick, they would have attended new plays like George Colman the Younger's controversial *Iron Chest* (adapted from William Godwin's *Caleb Williams*), Charles Farley's *Raymond and Agnes* (adapted from *The Monk*), Andrew Franklin's *The Wandering Jew*, and Robert Jephson's *The Conspiracy*. Among new books of poetry, they would have found among their fellow readers what amounted to a craze for supernatural ballads. Lewis's ballads had quickly become the most critically celebrated and reprinted parts of *The Monk*, and in subsequent months they were imitated by several poets, including Walter Scott,

Robert Southey, and Mary Robinson. The poetic sensation of 1796, however, was the supernatural ballad *Lenore* by Gottfried Augustus Bürger. Depicting a young woman's midnight ride with the ghost of her lover to his grave, the ballad was first translated into English by William Taylor of Norwich for the *Monthly Magazine* in March of 1796. Over the next nine months, Taylor's translation was reprinted multiple times and inspired no fewer than four other translations in book form, including attempts by Poet Laureate Henry James Pye and Walter Scott.[3]

As Scott's recent biographer John Sutherland has noted, Scott referred to the next five years of his life as his "German-mad" phase, in which he penned "drum and trumpet exhibitions" full of ghosts and conspiring secret societies.[4] The same can be argued for British popular culture in general. Here we see Lewis's surprising power as a trailblazer of literary fashion. In the autumn of 1796, following Lewis's acknowledgment of authorship of *The Monk*, the "German" Gothic quickly became both fashionable and controversial in Britain. While social conservatives like Thomas Mathias, Hannah More, and Richard Polwhele attacked Lewis particularly and "German" writing generally for its pernicious social tendencies, such works dominated British poetry, drama, and fiction between 1796 and 1800. By the first decade of the nineteenth century, readers grouped together texts as disparate as James Boaden's dramas, Matthew Lewis's ballads, and Charlotte Dacre's fiction under a single categorical umbrella. Several names may have existed for this rubric – "the terrorist school," "modern romance," "the trash of the Minerva Press," "the German school" – yet what is clear from these groupings is the recurrence of specific writers, readers, and publishers under a single heading.

To focus on the reception and production histories of Gothic texts, then, is to arrive at a more dynamic and heterogeneous sense of "the Gothic" than can be achieved through constructing a genealogy only of the Gothic novel. While William Wordsworth's early poetic efforts may show debts to contemporary poets of sensibility, his first undeniably "mature" work – the semi-Gothic drama *The Borderers* (1797) – makes specific homages to Renaissance and German tragedy (particularly *The Robbers*, first translated into English in 1792). Samuel Coleridge's tragedy *Osorio* (1797) and Matthew Lewis's *The Monk* and *The Castle Spectre* (1797–98), moreover, provide equally instructive examples of this process of assimilation and appropriation across genres. Both writers echo Schiller and the ghostlier parts of Shakespeare, with Lewis invoking additional German sources and Ann Radcliffe's fiction. A letter from Coleridge to Robert Southey nicely captures the energy with which Schiller and writers like him were read during the 1790s:

'Tis past one o'clock in the morning – I sate down at twelve o'clock to read the "Robbers" of Schiller – I had read chill and trembling until I came to the part where Moor fires a pistol over the Robbers who are asleep – I could read no more – My God! Southey! Who is this Schiller? This Convulser of the Heart? Did he write his Tragedy amid the yelling of Fiends? – I should not like to [be] able to describe such Characters – I tremble like an Aspen Leaf – Upon my Soul, I write to you because I am frightened – I had better go to Bed. Why have we ever called Milton sublime? That Count de Moor – horrible Wielder of heart-withering Virtues – ! Satan is scarcely qualified to attend his Execution as Gallows Chaplain.[5]

Coleridge was hardly alone in holding such sentiments. In these same years a number of periodicals and writers of note made public and private eulogiums, including the *Monthly Review* and *Monthly Magazine*, William Hazlitt, Elizabeth Inchbald, Henry Mackenzie, Mary Robinson, and Helen Maria Williams. A generation later John Keats would affectionately refer to "mother Radcliffe," Percy Bysshe and Mary Shelley would write Gothic fictions based in German *and* French sources in the tradition of Lewis and Charlotte Dacre, and Lord Byron would praise Walpole as "the father of the first romance, and of the last tragedy in our language, and surely worthy of a higher place than any living writer, be he who he may."[6]

Praise, furthermore, produced translation and appropriation, especially by younger writers fired by the theatrical potential of this new literature. Thus, the 1790s saw an explosion both of dramatic translations and of stage adaptations, the most popular being translations of the dramas of August von Kotzebue and adaptations of Radcliffe, Godwin, and Lewis.[7] Among these translators were Coleridge, Lewis, and Scott, all of whom published translations of German dramas before the close of the eighteenth century.[8] Lewis, furthermore, would prove instrumental to getting Scott's *House of Aspen* read by London theatre managers, while his own astounding success with *The Castle Spectre* late in 1797 proved a source of irritation and envy to Wordsworth and Coleridge, both of whom had submitted their own Gothic tragedies to Drury Lane at about the same time. Like Scott, Wordsworth and Coleridge were unsuccessful in their respective bids to write for the stage. They received rejections, expressed mortification, dismissed the theatre as bankrupt of taste, and went back to writing poetry. While in their respective correspondences Scott condemned the quality of London theatre audiences and Coleridge the quality of Lewis's play, Wordsworth pithily dismissed the quality of both in a single sentence to William Hazlitt, reporting that *The Castle Spectre* "fitted the taste of the audience like a glove."[9]

Given the disparaging words made by all three writers about the theatre after they had received rejections, we might wish to end our account here, laconically speculating (with an appropriate shudder) on the horror that would have resulted had great writers like Coleridge, Wordsworth, and Scott experienced popular and sustained success writing Gothic plays. Or we might simply wish to consider these early texts as aberrations, as necessary lapses into a false taste that had to be purged before Romanticism could fully flower in Britain. The Gothic would then figure into our models of literary history and periodization as a juvenile fancy – an immature and sensationalistic aesthetic that any mature writer must reject for the more serious business of writing about nature, imagination, sublimity, dejection, and interior consciousness. Indeed, when pressed, we would even be able to find scattered confirmation of the need for such a rejection in the critical and satirical writings of the Romantics themselves: in Mary Wollstonecraft's and Coleridge's reviews of Gothic fiction; in the preface to the second edition of *Lyrical Ballads* (1800); in Mary Robinson's *Memoirs* (1801); in Coleridge's *Biographia Literaria* (1815); in Scott's correspondence; and in Byron's *English Bards and Scotch Reviewers* (1809) and *Don Juan* (1819–24). Such a reading, however, would demand we exercise selective memory and require we overlook that these same writers in these same years produced recognizably Gothic texts. At the very least, we would need to ignore Wollstonecraft's *The Wrongs of Woman* (1797), Coleridge's *Rime of the Ancient Mariner* (1798) and *Christabel* (1797–1800), Wordsworth's ballads, several of Robinson's *Lyrical Tales* (1800), Scott's *Lay of the Last Minstrel* (1805) and *Marmion* (1808), and the bulk of Byron's poetic production between 1813 and 1818.

In a sense, the question of the relationship between Gothic and Romantic writing becomes one of explaining this contradiction. What was it about the cultural standing of the Gothic in these years that made it at once an object of appropriation and of vilification? Without question the Gothic's popularity after 1794 rendered it an attractive and potentially lucrative aesthetic, particularly for writers ambitious for popular success who sought a wide readership. But associating oneself with Gothic writers was at best a risky business. As the experience of Matthew "Monk" Lewis suggests, an author once identified with the Gothic found it difficult to shake the association. Lewis's first prose romance not only literally named him ("Monk") but also negatively shaped the way that his subsequent work – even his best tragedy *Alfonso, King of Castille* (1805) – was received by reviewers. Coleridge's own experience points to similar difficulties. Desperate for funds after returning home from Germany in 1799, he found London theatres gleefully satisfying popular demand for German and Gothic drama.[10] Eager to exploit the similar demand for translations of German drama, Coleridge sold his translation of Schiller's *Wallenstein* to Longman and Rees in 1800. Reviews, however, were sparse and dismissive, and when the *Monthly Review* labeled Coleridge a "partisan of the German theatre," Coleridge responded tellingly with a flat denial:

> I am numbered among the Partisans of the German Theatre. As I am confident that there is no passage in my Preface or Notes from which such an opinion can be legitimately formed; and as the truth would not have been exceeded, if the direct contrary had been affirmed, I claim it of your justice that in your answers to Correspondents you would remove this misrepresentation.[11]

It is worth pausing here to contemplate this staggering rebuttal, or at least to consider what it means for a translator flatly to deny the merit of his source materials. The explanation of financial need, moreover, only goes so far, especially when we place it next to Coleridge's six years' enthusiasm for German literature and his willingness to travel to Germany during wartime to learn the language and to read the works of its poets, dramatists, and philosophers. Instead, what registers most strongly here is Coleridge's strong disinclination at being associated with a "German" aesthetic.

As Coleridge's later correspondence confirms, this horror at "German" literature extended to its English Gothic counterpart and to writers associated in any way with it. The most stunning of these documents is a letter of 1804 to Mary E. Robinson, in which Coleridge refused her request to include his poem "The Mad Monk" in *The Wild Wreath* (1804), an anthology of poems compiled in honor of her deceased mother Mary Robinson.[12] For Coleridge, the prospect of appearing in a volume of poetry alongside Matthew Lewis – and through a poem whose title recalled that of Lewis's infamous novel – produced nothing less than panic. "[M]y dear Miss Robinson!," he pleads, "I have a wife, I have sons, I have an infant Daughter – what excuse could I offer to my own conscience if by suffering my name to be connected with those of Mr. Lewis... I was the *occasion* of their reading the Monk?... Should I not be an infamous Pander to the Devil in the seduction of my own offspring? – My head turns giddy, my heart sickens, at the very thought of seeing such books in the hands of a child of mine."[13] One sees similar responses to the work of Charles Robert Maturin, whose associations with Lewis were noted by Scott in an ultimately damning review of *The Fatal Revenge* (1807).[14] Usually considered one of the few defenders of Gothic writing in these years, Scott himself condemned Maturin's novel to a circle of literary hell below even that occupied by novels of scandal, those "lowest denizens of Grub Street narrating... all that malevolence can invent and stupidity propagate."

Scott's review directs us away from the political and moral status of the Gothic and toward the questions of literary taste and social class that

Gothic writing consistently raised as the nineteenth century turned. Echoing Wordsworth's and Coleridge's earlier dismissals of the taste of theatre audiences, he constructs a cultural divide between what he understands to be "high" and "low" culture:

> Amid these flat imitations of the *Castle of Udolpho* ... and, in defiance of the very bad taste in which it [*The Fatal Revenge*] is composed, we found ourselves ... impressed with no common degree of respect for the powers of the author. We have at no time more earnestly desired to extend our voice to a bewildered traveller, than towards this young man, whose taste is so inferior to his powers of imagination and expression, that we never saw a more remarkable instance of genius degraded by the labor in which it is employed.

Associating the Gothic with the unthinking mass production ("flat imitations") of hack writers ("the lowest denizens of Grub Street") writing solely for gain, this review opposes the "bad taste" of *The Fatal Revenge* to the "powers of imagination and expression" of its author, who has "degraded" himself by the "labor" with which he has "employed" himself. Scott's logic is as clear as it is dualistic: Gothic, the lowest of genres, should only be written by the "lowest denizens of Grub Street" because the "bad taste" of Gothic's audience shows them to be the lowest of all possible readers.

More fundamentally, however, reviews like Scott's demonstrate how Gothic writing's ascent to popularity in the 1790s forced writers and reviewers to reconsider and redefine what constituted literary value. For half a century periodicals like *The Monthly Review* and *The Critical Review* had extolled literature as a vehicle for social improvement and national education. In their formulation, legitimate authors wrote for fame or for the social good; worthy readers, in turn, read either for wholesome improvement or for innocent pleasure. Using Fredric Jameson's formulation of author–reader relations as a "social contract," we can begin to see how such assumptions about legitimacy shape Scott's criticisms of *The Fatal Revenge*.[15] First placing Gothic writing back into its proper position at the bottom of the literary ladder, Scott presents *The Fatal Revenge* as the product of a violated authorial social contract, where Maturin has committed a gross breach of duty by wasting his genius upon a worthless production. Within this social economy of literary production, Maturin's perverse mixing of "genius" and "bad taste" threatens to undermine the conceptual and class divisions that ensure the stability of existing social hierarchies, as Pierre Bourdieu's writings on the social function of "taste" make clear: "There is an economy of cultural goods, but it has a specific logic ... To the socially recognized hierarchy of the arts, and within each of them, of genres, schools or periods, corresponds a social hierarchy of the consumers. This predisposes tastes to function as markers of 'class.'"[16] Looking back to Gothic writing as it is represented in Scott's review, then, we begin to understand how its associations with female readers, circulating libraries, repetitive narratives, and mechanistic production served to define its class position within late eighteenth-century literary hierarchies. Thus, for writers wishing to exploit popular conventions associated with Gothic writing in their own work, the challenge became one of dissociating oneself from the very readers and forms of publication that made Gothic a recognizably "low" generic entity in the first place.

That Scott penned his review still glowing from the popular and critical success of his own long poem *Marmion* – a poem featuring a host of Gothic effects including a dark and troubled hero, chivalrous intrigue and betrayal, supernatural combat, and a wronged nun sentenced by an inquisitional tribunal to be buried alive – suggests at best a very mixed relationship to the Gothic. While representing himself as "an initiated Ghost-Seer" and "ghost-raiser" in his own private correspondence,[17] Scott always took care to occupy the position of enlightened and rational skeptic in his own literary criticism and in the notes to such works as *Minstrelsy on the Scottish Border* (1802–03) and *Letters on Demonology and Witchcraft* (1830). This same critical stance, furthermore, occurs in the literary criticism of other Romantic writers as well. We find it, for example, in Wordsworth's condemnation of "frantic novels" and "sickly and stupid German tragedies" in the 1800 preface to *Lyrical Ballads*, as well as in Byron's chastisement of Lewis in *English Bards and Scotch Reviewers* (1809):

> Oh! wonder-working LEWIS!, Monk, or Bard,
> Who fain would'st make Parnassus a church-yard! –
> Lo! wreaths of yew, not laurel, bind thy brow,
> Thy Muse a Sprite, Apollo's sexton thou!
> Whether on ancient tombs thou tak'st thy stand,
> By gibb'ring spectres hailed, thy kindred band;
> Or tracest chaste descriptions on thy page,
> To please the females of our modest age,
> All hail, M.P.! from whose infernal brain
> Thin sheeted phantoms glide, a grisly train;
> . . .
> Even Satan's self with thee might dread to dwell,
> And in thy skull discern a deeper hell.[18]

While more gentle in its criticisms than most attacks on Gothic writing in these years, Byron's satire nevertheless recounts a series of familiar, damning traits. His representation of the Gothic as a satanic aesthetic and his placement of it in a Dantesque "deeper hell" anticipates the language of Scott's review of Maturin a year later. The remainder of the passage is far more familiar; allying the Gothic with female readers and with a sexually suspect morbidity, Byron anthologizes more than a decade of critical abuse of *The Monk* and its imitators – a discourse in many ways inaugurated by Coleridge's own review of Lewis's romance in the *Critical Review* twelve years earlier.[19]

Like Scott, Byron himself would achieve popular acclaim through a series of long poems heavily influenced by the very texts from which he distances himself in the above passage. To modern eyes, this almost simultaneous writing of Gothic-influenced poems and anti-Gothic criticism suggests something akin to duplicity. Certainly Romantic writers, given the contentious and polarized context into which they wrote, were forced to publish defensively and with care, and sought to prevent reviewers from associating their productions with objectionable ones. Yet the ease with which Romantic writers moved from criticizing Gothic texts to appropriating Gothic conventions stemmed less from a heightened sense of self-defense and self-marketing than from a strongly hierarchical sense of genre and of print culture – one far stronger than, and perhaps even foreign to, our own sensibilities. Coleridge and Scott may playfully admit to Gothic predilections in their personal correspondence, but such sentiments do not find their way into their literary reviews. Each instead takes on the solidly institutional voices of their respective periodicals, often even adopting their assumptions about literary value.

Looking to the example of Mary Robinson, meanwhile, students of her prose will remember 1796 as the year of her best-known Gothic novel, *Hubert de Sevrac*; these same months, however, saw her publish a book of far more serious and scholarly tone, *Sappho and Phaon*, an ambitious sonnet sequence that included essays on Sappho and on the sonnet as a form. Similarly, Byron may freely glut his taste for Gothicism and orientalism in his early lyrics and later verse romances, but his tone and assumptions change markedly when he shifts to the more traditional and elevated modes of Juvenalian and Horatian satire, as he does with *English Bards and Scotch Reviewers* and *Hints from Horace* (1811). In all of these examples, generic ascent accompanies greater seriousness of subject matter and higher elevation of tone. Perhaps more importantly, these instances suggest that Romantic writing, in spite of its penchant for producing generic hybrids (whether they be historical tragedies, metrical romances, *Elegiac Sonnets*, *Descriptive Sketches*, or *Lyrical Tales*), was nevertheless received and criticized by a literary culture that strongly valued cultural hierarchy, aesthetic unity, and generic purity and definitiveness.

One need not, however, look to the critical prose and verse satire of Romantic poets to find Romantic writing's attraction to, and repulsion from, its Gothic relations. These same ambivalences occur plentifully within the individual texts themselves. Sometimes they manifest themselves structurally, as with the rift in "The Rime of the Ancient Mariner" between Coleridge's pious glosses and his grisly subject matter, or with Joanna Baillie's tendency in *Ethwald I* and *Ethwald II* (1802) to question, through her appended historical and scholarly notes, the very supernaturalism she creates in the text of her work. We see this schism between text and footnote perhaps most markedly in a work like Scott's *Lay of the Last Minstrel*, one of the first poems in these years to tap the Gothic's popular potential and produce spectacular sales while still receiving critical acclaim. The poem itself employs a series of motifs familiar to students of the Gothic: a "withered" monk guarding a magic book both he and William of Deloraine are forbidden to open, the undecaying corpse of a wizard, and halls that echo with "voices unlike the voice of man."[20] These textual moments, interestingly, also see Scott's scholarly commentary at its lengthiest and most historical. Of Michael Scott, the wizard in the poem who raises both evil secrets from the crypts of abbeys and embodies ancestral *virtu*, Scott notes, "he appears to have been addicted to the abstruse studies of judical astrology, alchemy, physiognomy, and chiromancy. Hence he passed among his contemporaries for a skilful magician."[21] Here and elsewhere in Scott's poetry the effect is to bestow upon a text's most Gothic moments an historicized and enlightened distance, and to inscribe a degree of irony into its formal features. Scott's readers, therefore, are free within the text of the poem to indulge in a host of supernatural effects, from shape-shifting to raising spirits from the grave; these readerly fantasies, in turn, are safely framed within a scholarly apparatus of enlightened antiquarianism.

Scott's tendency to insulate supernatural moments with enlightened and historicizing commentary performs ideological functions as well. The Scottish–English conflict dramatized in *The Lay*, for example, depends entirely on the device of Lord Cranstoun's goblin page, who steals the magic book procured by William of Deloraine and uses a spell within it to lure the young heir of Branksome Tower away from his home until an army of English soldiers captures him. With the young boy as hostage, the army then marches to Branksome to demand William of Deloraine in exchange, and the threatened battle is only broken up when Cranstoun uses the same spell to assume the form of Deloraine and win a single combat. The effect of *The Lay*'s most Gothic scenes, then, is to celebrate British martial prowess in the face of invasion while simultaneously attributing the causes of English–Scottish disputes to supernatural agency. In this light, perhaps the most striking passage of the poem is canto 5's dramatization of the two armies passing the time until the single combat at brotherly play:

> Now, noble dame, perchance you ask
> How these two hostile armies met,
> Deeming it were no easy task
> To keep the truce which here was set;
> Where martial spirits, all on fire,
> Breathed only blood and mortal ire.
> By mutual inroads, mutual blows,
> By habit, and by nation, foes.
> They met on Teviot's strand;
> They met and sate them mingled down,
> Without a threat, without a frown,
> As brothers meet in a foreign land:
> . . .
> Visors were raised and faces shown,
> And many a friend, to friend made known,
> Partook of social cheer.
>   (canto 5, lines 88–99, 103–05)

Aligning "habit" with the English and Scottish armies' sense of "nation," Scott opposes these two concepts to the grander and more compelling idea of the British nation, which he argues is the natural nation-state of men who share fraternal ties as obvious as those shared by the Scottish and English. Meeting in the "foreign land" of warfare, the sides know themselves to be "brothers" by each other's faces. The passage, then, suggests that the conflicts arising from outdated petty factions are in and of themselves a blindness, the result of men who, their visors not "lifted," cannot see their own kin in front of them. It also confirms Scott's ideological tendency to locate Scottish–English strife in the machinations of power-hungry individuals rather than in any real or lasting cultural differences. In this light, Scott's linking of Gothic supernaturalism with this state of cultural and national adolescence seeks to portray the causes of such border wars as Gothic and therefore trivial, the products of a protracted national adolescence so long outgrown it has been forgotten. Put another way, without a magic book and a goblin page to create mischief with it, no English–Scottish conflict would occur in this re-presentation of history.

By the first decades of the nineteenth century this combination of generic exploitation and ideological recasting had become almost a standard move among writers seeking to tap the Gothic's popular readership while at the same time distancing themselves from its low cultural status. Such acts of generic appropriation began in earnest, however, before the end of the eighteenth century in texts like *Lyrical Ballads*, a work marketed as an "experiment" whose ballads sought to harness the Gothic's remunerative potential while criticizing its reliance on suspense and sensationalistic plot devices.[22] Unlike traditional ballads, therefore, very little actually happens in poems such as "The Thorn" and "The Idiot Boy." Both present us with characters whose obsessive patterns of thought serve to illustrate the workings of a mind beset by superstitious fancy while simultaneously functioning as parodies of prototypical Gothic scenes. "The Idiot Boy," for example, provides us not only with Betty Foy's wild imaginings but also with the comic burlesque of Johnny's midnight pony ride, itself a pointed deflation of Lenore's gallop to her grave with her skeleton bridegroom. Even "Goody Blake and Harry Gill," the poem in the collection most like a traditional supernatural ballad, subverts the typical experience of reading ballad poetry through its unexplained and open ending. Abjuring its readers to "think, ye farmers all, I pray / Of Goody Blake and Harry Gill" (lines 127–28), the poet leaves the question of *what* we should think unaddressed. Like "Simon Lee," the poem gently chides readers away from the gratifications of plot and suspense and instead exhorts them to the active role of making their own meaning.[23]

While such experiments in poetic narrative are important to our understanding of emerging Romantic notions of value, they also function as defensive gestures – particularly at the turn of the nineteenth century, when Gothic's popularity with readers and unpopularity with reviewers make the costs and benefits of marking one's text as "Gothic" extremely high. When the strategies undertaken by Coleridge and Wordsworth proved unsuccessful and reviewers of *Lyrical Ballads* singled out the volume's ballads for criticism, Wordsworth, not surprisingly, responded by opening both volumes of the 1800 edition with even more explicit manifestos, declaring himself to be free of the several "corruptions" supposedly current among other Gothic writers. While in the first volume the preface to *Lyrical Ballads* rejected "frantic novels [and] sickly and stupid German tragedies," the first lines of part 2 of "Hart-Leap Well" (1800) opening volume II attempted to inoculate the collection against the kinds of criticisms to which the "supernatural" poems of the first edition of *Lyrical Ballads* (1798) had been subject:

> The moving accident is not my trade;
> To freeze the blood I have no ready arts:
> 'Tis my delight, alone in summer shade,
> To pipe a simple song for thinking hearts.[24]

These lines not only reject "freez[ing] the blood" as "trade," but also insist that the poetry of *Lyrical Ballads* is a philosophical vehicle for reconnecting thought to feeling, embodied in the declarative, oxymoronic "thinking hearts."

The structure of "Hart-Leap Well" works along similar lines, performing an exorcism of its own Gothic content. Part 1 opens by providing the originary narrative of Sir Walter killing the Hart and commemorating its leap with three pillars and a well; part 2, after opening with the lines just quoted, follows with the shepherd's superstitious interpretation of the decayed well as haunted only to have Wordsworth revise and naturalize its supernatural content:

> Grey-headed Shepherd, thou hast spoken well;
> Small difference lies between thy creed and mine:
> This Beast not unobserved by Nature fell;
> His death was mourned by sympathy divine.
>
> The Being, that is in the clouds and air,
> That is in the green leaves among the groves,
> Maintains a deep and reverential care
> For the unoffending creatures whom he loves.
>
> (lines 157–64)

Like "Goody Blake and Harry Gill," the poem models appropriate poetic interpretation even as it performs it; it provides a history of the monument's construction and then performs first "low" and next "high" interpretations of these "facts." Of the two interpretations, Wordsworth may place them side by side, but it is clear from his elevated tone – and his position as the one who utters the final word – that we should prefer the lesson of his high interpretation to the shepherd's stories of "murder," "blood," and "dolorous groan[s]" (lines 132–34). His primary goal in the poem, then, is to do more than teach his reader to distinguish between popular supernaturalism and poetic naturalism. The obsessive retelling of Sir Walter's story, with its accompanying progression from apparently straightforward narrative to metaphysical interpretation, suggests that such histories are valuable primarily as raw material to be transformed into fuller meaning. In many ways the poem's practice resembles that of *The Lay of the Last Minstrel* by allowing Wordsworth and his readers first to indulge in the supernatural speculation of low and rustic characters and then to ally themselves with a more philosophical and chastened interpretation of the same events. The poem's structure thus works to distance author and reader from the poem's Gothic materials and from the ballad's supernatural predilections even as it taps both as sources.

If a discernible pattern of Gothic appropriation emerges in Romantic writing, it lies in the ability of authors like Scott and Wordsworth to find

the formal means of neutralizing the Gothic's negative critical reputation –
usually by setting their works in the distant past or in distant lands or
cultures, or by locating Gothic effects in the minds of immature readers –
while at the same time legitimizing its conventions by self-consciously putting
them to acceptably intellectual and ideological uses. With this pattern in
mind, we can see a poem like Byron's *The Giaour: a Fragment of a Turkish
Tale* (1813) calling upon a host of conventions familiar to readers of Gothic
and oriental fiction while at the same deploying an array of legitimating
strategies common among Romantic writers. Published in the wake of the
sensation created by the first two cantos of *Childe Harold's Pilgrimage*
(1812), *The Giaour* went through an astounding seven editions in its first
six months of publication. With each successive edition, furthermore, Byron
added further passages and notes, effectively creating several distinct versions of what he came to call his "snake" of a poem. While outstripping
even the poems of Scott in popularity, aspects of *The Giaour* nonetheless
strongly resemble Scott's own *Marmion* and *The Lady of the Lake*,[25] particularly its dark and unpenitent hero and the way the poem hurled itself
forward through the motif of the Giaour furiously riding on horseback:

> On – on he hastened – and he drew
> My gaze of wonder as he flew:
> Though like a demon of the night
> He passed and vanished from my sight;
> A troubled memory on my breast;
> And long upon my startled ear
> Rung his dark courser's hoofs of fear.[26]

A "demon" propelled by "hoofs of fear," the figure of the Giaour finds ample
precursors in Gothic writing. His evening gallop, breathlessly narrated by
Byron, recalls Bürger's *Lenore*, while his fixed and gloomy expression resembles that of similarly "dark" figures like Osmond in *The Castle Spectre* and
Montoni in *The Mysteries of Udolpho*. Possessing a "haughty mien" (256)
and an "evil eye" (196), the Giaour's complexion is characterized by "ghastly
whiteness" (239) while his countenance is "scath'd by fiery passion's brunt"
(195). Like Radcliffe, then, Byron foregrounds the ways in which extreme
emotions imprint themselves permanently on the body and on the psyche:

> 'Tis twice three years at summer tide
>   Since first among our freres he came;
> And here it soothes him to abide
>   For some dark deed he will not name.
>   . . .
> Dark and unearthly is the scowl

> That glares beneath his dusky cowl –
> The flash of that dilating eye
> Reveals too much of times gone by –
> Though varying – indistinct its hue,
> Oft will his glance the gazer rue –
> For in it lurks that nameless spell
> Which speaks – itself unspeakable –
>
> (lines 798–801; 832–39)

Haunted by his own dark deeds and mixed allegiances, the Giaour becomes, in effect, an embodiment of the Gothic. Like the character Schedoni in Radcliffe's *The Italian* (1797), the Giaour ends the poem cowled yet godless, confessing unpenitently to a priest who understands neither his violent actions nor the motivations that have produced them.

Still, even within this most unrepentantly Gothic of Byron's works, we see him adopting, especially in the poem's earliest editions, legitimizing strategies similar to those we saw undertaken by Scott in *The Lay of the Last Minstrel*. When *The Giaour* was first published in June of 1813, Byron presented the poem as a piece of oriental antiquarianism, a tale recovered from an original source and archaeologically represented, however imperfectly, through "disjointed fragments." "The Story, when entire," he states, "contained the adventures of a female slave . . . [and] a young Venetian, her lover, at the time the Seven Islands were possessed by the Republic of Venice" (advertisement). In addition, Byron included a modest dedication to Thomas Moore and copious notes. Serious in tone, these early notes show a similar antiquarian anxiety about providing documented sources. Addressing various aspects of Islamic culture, they also show Byron at his most learned when commenting on his poem's most sensational and Gothic passages. Thus, Byron's notes systematically debunk as baseless "superstitions" the very materials – the scorpions' suicides (line 434n), "evil eyes" (612n), vampires (755n), and episodes of second sight (1077n) – that he indulges in most strongly in the text of his poem. The notes to later editions, however, change considerably in both tone and content, becoming less anxious about their own authority, determinedly skeptical about religious faith, and increasingly facetious about their own scholarly affect. Glossing the "Djerrid, a blunted Turkish javelin, which is darted from horseback with great force and precision," for example, Byron humorously notes "It is a favourite exercise of the Mussulmans; but I know not if it can be called a *manly* one, since the most expert in the art are the Black Eunuchs of Constantinople" (line 251n). Here and elsewhere, the changing tone of the notes in later editions suggests a change in their function. "The monk's sermon is omitted," Byron wryly comments, because "[i]t seems to have had so little effect upon the patient [the Giaour], that it could have not hopes from the reader" (line 1207n). Apparently, once he considered *The Giaour* as an established critical and popular success, Byron no longer felt the need to cultivate antiquarian and ideological respectability through the formal manipulation of his poem's editorial apparatus.

As these examples suggest, such formal gestures can be as simple as dividing supernatural incident from historical footnote, as strategic as displaying Gothic materials and then subjecting them to critique, or as complex as aligning primitive factionalism with superstition and modern nationalism with enlightenment. Romantic appropriations of the Gothic, however, in no way are limited to this legitimating enterprise. Mary Robinson's "The Haunted Beach," for instance, attempts to bring poetic form, metaphor, and Gothic subject matter to bear upon the problem of how to describe a murderer's conscience as a kind of haunted landscape:

> And since that hour the fisherman
>   Has toil'd and toil'd in vain;
> For all the night the moony light
>   Gleams on the specter'd main!
> And when the skies are veil'd in gloom,
>   The murderer's liquid way
> Bounds o'er the deeply yawning tomb,
>   And flashing fires the sands illume,
> Where the green billows play.[27]

In a poem where each stanza ends with the same refrain, the repeated image of crashing waves combines with Robinson's portrait of a barren, storm-lit coast to create both a formal and metaphorical representation of the workings of guilt on the human mind.

Mary Shelley and Byron, meanwhile, increasingly find in the Gothic a language for philosophical and psychological inquiry, taking their cues from writers like Radcliffe and Maturin while redirecting the focus of their texts away from romance narratives and toward the representation of extreme states of consciousness. *Frankenstein* (1818, revised 1831) is perhaps most famous for its creation scene and for the various confrontations that occur between Victor Frankenstein and his creation throughout the novel, scenes which combine Miltonic language and sublime imagery with descriptions of violence, horror, and decay. But the emphasis is on mental state.

> Unable to endure the aspect of the being I had created, I rushed out of the room, and continued a long time traversing my bed-chamber, unable to compose my mind to sleep. At length lassitude succeeded to the tumult I had before endured; and I threw myself on the bed in my clothes, endeavouring to seek a few moments of forgetfulness. But it was in vain: I slept indeed, but I was

disturbed by the wildest dreams. I thought I saw Elizabeth, in the bloom of health, walking in the streets of Ingolstadt. Delighted and surprised, I embraced her; but as I imprinted the first kiss on her lips, they became livid with the hue of death; her features appeared to change, and I thought that I held the corpse of my dead mother in my arms; a shroud enveloped her form, and I saw the grave-worms crawling in the folds of the flannel. I started from my sleep with horror; a cold dew covered my forehead, my teeth chattered, and every limb became convulsed; when, by the dim and yellow light of the moon, as it forced its way through the window-shutters, I beheld the wretch – the miserable monster whom I had created.   (p. 53)

This nightmare – in which Victor's creation is replaced by Elizabeth, who then mutates into the rotting corpse of Victor's mother Caroline, who, as Victor wakes, again becomes the creature – shows Shelley providing a stunning account of Victor's extreme psychological state, one which anticipates the insights of Freud into dreaming, death, and the family. The scene, consequently, has provided psychoanalytic critics with rich material for interpretation. While Fred Botting has found the creation functioning within Victor's dream as "the inverted image of Frankenstein's narcissistic project, its animation overturning the creative ideals in a process of complete and monstrous reversal,"[28] Paul Cantor has argued that the creation becomes an agent through which Victor freely can associate love and death: "He himself sees that the monster serves his own destructive urges . . . [and] seems to know intuitively what the monster has done . . . Frankenstein knows the monster's intentions because deep down they are his own."[29] Much of the same emphasis, it can be argued, can be found in Dr. John Polidori's novella *The Vampyre*, begun near Geneva in the summer of 1816 alongside *Frankenstein* and published in 1819 under Byron's name, a text that gestures repeatedly toward a similar idea of the "unconscious" (see pp. 33–49).

In many ways, then, the structures of Shelley's and Byron's (and Polidori's) works present us with compelling, albeit different, representations of consciousness, as well as foregrounding the extent to which the Gothic presented Romantic writers with a conventional language through which they could explore fundamental problems of representation, knowledge, interpretation, and consciousness. The fragmented structure of *The Giaour*, for example, becomes a metaphor for its title character's state of mind, while the rapid cuts and multiple perspectives of its protocinematic technique put forward a phenomenological model of experience – one requiring interpretation to construct coherence from its pieces while simultaneously representing such interpretive acts as self-serving and doomed to failure. *Frankenstein*, in turn, deploys a narrative structure that buries its story under multiple layers of hearsay testimony. Resembling Chinese boxes, the novel begins with

Margaret Saville receiving letters from her brother Robert Walton. Within Walton's discourse is the story of Victor Frankenstein, and within Victor's accounts are the narratives of his creature, the De Lacy family, and, finally, Felix De Lacy's betrothed, Safie. The effect is similar to the linguistic one of "live burial" described by Eve Kosofsky Sedgwick in *The Coherence of Gothic Conventions* (1980), since as readers we find ourselves often two and three times removed from the events of the novel, making the question of interpretation hopelessly vexed (Sedgwick, *Coherence of Gothic Conventions*, pp. 57–58). Aside from shrouding Victor's incredible story within a series of second-hand accounts told by implacable enemies, Shelley creates a situation in which it becomes impossible to know the reliability of a given narrator, let alone determine the credibility of the other testimonies contained within a given narrator's discourse. This reading experience, in turn, leads us to examine our own processes of interpretation, since as readers we are confronted by psychological challenges similar to those faced by Shelley's characters.

Examining these and other works, then, we begin to gain a sense of how far Romantic writers went to transform potentially dangerous generic materials into something at once legitimate and, by certain class and aesthetic standards, respectable. As such, the examples within this chapter not only suggest a rich and varied relation between Romantic and Gothic texts; they also function as case studies for how Romantic assumptions about literariness and literary value – most influentially dubbed "Romantic ideology" by Jerome McGann in his book carrying the same name[30] – are constituted and articulated in terms of genre. Looking again to "Hart-Leap Well," we can read the poem as doing more than merely exemplifying the centrality of genre in Wordsworth's poetry. It also illustrates the extent to which a preference for "high" literary forms and aesthetics depend upon, and emerge out of, other "lower" aesthetic forms and points of view. Thus, when we consider the ways in which this poem situates itself in relation to Gothic superstition – as both *a result of* Gothic's negative critical reception and as *a response to* Gothic's low cultural status within existing hierarchies of genre – we begin to discern links between Gothicism and Romanticism other than those of simple influence. The social dynamics of their relation, mediated by Gothic's reception and by a political and economic context that dominated all forms of discourse in these years, shows us that the formative texts of Romanticism emerged self-consciously and with an astute sense of the prevailing critical landscape and literary market. Romantic writers' appropriation of the conventions and practices of their Gothic contemporaries, therefore, exemplifies something more fundamental about Romantic aesthetic practice itself. It shows us that Romanticism's privileging of specific literary forms and aesthetics depends upon an ostentatious rejection of others, and that in these rejections – and through the hierarchies of genre that are their byprod-ucts – we can trace the processes by which Romantic ideology is constituted.

NOTES

1 See A. O. Lovejoy, "On the Discrimination of Romanticisms," *PMLA* 39 (1924): 229–53, and René Wellek, "The Concept of Romanticism in Literary Scholar-ship," *Comparative Literature* 1 (1949): 1–23, 147–72.

2 For information about individual plays at the Drury Lane and Covent Garden theatres, see Charles Beecher Hogan, *The London Stage 1660–1800, Part V: 1776–1800* (Carbondale, IL: Southern Illinois University Press, 1968). On Boaden's play, see Jeffrey Cox in this volume.

3 Five translations were published: Henry James Pye, *Lenore, a Tale* (London: the author, 1796); J. T. Stanley, *Leonora. A Tale* (London: William Miller, 1796); W. R. Spencer, *Leonora: a Poem* (London: Hookham, 1796); Walter Scott, *The Chase, and William and Helen* (London: T. Cadell, 1796); and William Taylor, "Lenore," *Monthly Magazine* 1 (March 1796): 135–37.

4 John Sutherland, *The Life of Walter Scott* (Oxford: Blackwell, 1995), p. 43.

5 See Coleridge to Robert Southey, 3 November 1794, in *The Collected Letters of Samuel Taylor Coleridge*, ed. Earl Leslie Griggs, 6 vols. (Oxford: Oxford University Press, 1956), I, 122. Coleridge's sonnet "To the Author of 'The Robbers'" is printed in the *Collected Poems*, ed. E. H. Coleridge, 2 vols. (Oxford: Clarendon Press, 1912), I, 72.

6 Lord Byron, preface to *Marino Faliero: Doge of Venice* (London: John Murray, 1821).

7 For a fairly exhaustive list of translations published in Britain between 1760 and 1830, see Violet A. A. Stockley, *German Literature as Known in England 1750–1830* (London: G. Routledge, 1929).

8 See Matthew Lewis, trans., *The Minister: a Tragedy* (London: J. Bell, 1797); Samuel Coleridge, trans., *Wallenstein* (London: Longman, 1800); and Walter Scott, trans., *Goetz of Berlichingen, with the Iron Hand* (London: J. Bell, 1799).

9 See Walter Scott, *The Letters of Sir Walter Scott*, ed. H. J. C. Grierson, 12 vols. (London: Constable and Co., 1932), I, 124; Samuel Coleridge, *Collected Letters*, ed. Earl Leslie Griggs, 6 vols. (Oxford: Clarendon Press, 1956–71), I, 378; and William Hazlitt, "On My First Acquaintance with Poets," *Complete Works*, ed. P. P. Howe, 21 vols. (London: Dent, 1930–34), XVII, 118.

10 Between 11 October 1798 (the opening of Elizabeth Inchbald's translation of *Lovers' Vows*) and 7 February 1800 (the final showing of Richard Cumberland's translation of *Joanna*), audiences at Drury Lane and Covent Garden had been pre-sented with a staggering 240 separate performances (40 percent of all mainpieces) of dramas adapted from Kotzebue over the 300 nights in which the theatres were open to perform dramas. These figures have been compiled from Charles Hogan's *The London Stage* (noted above).

11 *Monthly Review* 33 (1800): 336.

12 Coleridge did not deter her. His "Mad Monk" appears in M. E. Robinson, *The Wild Wreath* (London: Richard Phillips, 1804), pp. 142–44.

13 Coleridge in his *Collected Letters*, II, 905.

14 See Walter Scott, review of *The Family Revenge* by Dennis Jasper Murphy [Charles Robert Maturin], *Quarterly Review* 3 (1810): 339–48, reprinted in *Miscellaneous Prose Works of Sir Walter Scott, Bart.*, 28 vols. (Edinburgh: Cadell, 1834–36), XVIII, 157–72. All further quotations of this review will be from this latter volume and appear there on pp. 161–62.

15 See Fredric Jameson, *The Political Unconscious: Narrative as a Socially Symbolic Act* (Ithaca: Cornell University Press, 1981), p. 160.

16 Pierre Bourdieu, *Distinction: a Social Critique of the Judgement of Taste*, trans. Richard Nice (Cambridge, MA: Harvard University Press, 1984), pp. 1–2.

17 See Scott in *Letters*, I, 121.

18 *English Bards and Scotch Reviewers*, in volume I of *The Complete Poetical Works*, ed. Jerome J. McGann, 7 vols. (Oxford: Oxford University Press, 1980), lines 265–74, 281–82.

19 Coleridge's review of *The Monk* was published in the *Critical Review* 19 (1797): 194–200.

20 See *The Lay of the Last Minstrel* (London: Longman, 1805), canto 2, lines 58, 192, 259. All further references to this poem are cited parenthetically in the main text by canto and line numbers.

21 Walter Scott, *Complete Poetical Works* (Boston and New York: Houghton Mifflin, 1900), p. 517.

22 For an excellent treatment of the origins of *Lyrical Ballads*, see James Butler and Karen Green, "Introduction" to William Wordsworth, *Lyrical Ballads and Other Poems, 1797–1800*, ed. James Butler and Karen Green (Ithaca: Cornell University Press, 1992).

23 See Don Bialostosky, *Making Tales: the Poetics of Wordsworth's Narrative Experiments* (Chicago: University of Chicago Press, 1984).

24 *Lyrical Ballads and Other Poems, 1797–1800*, ed. Butler and Green, lines 97–100. Further references to this poem or to other poems in *Lyrical Ballads* will be made from this edition and cited by line number.

25 See *The Lay of the Last Minstrel* I, canto 17, lines 1–3, and *The Lady of the Lake* I, canto 3, lines 1–5.

26 Byron, *The Giaour*, in *The Complete Poetical Works*, III, canto 46, lines 200–06. All further references to this poem will be from this edition and quoted by line number.

27 Mary Robinson, "The Haunted Beach," in *Lyrical Tales* (London: Longman and Rees, 1800), lines 64–72.

28 Fred Botting, "Frankenstein, Werther and the Monster of Love," in *News from Nowhere: Theory and Politics of Romanticism*, ed. Tony Pinkney, Keith Hanley, and Fred Botting (Keele: Keele University Press, 1995), p. 162.

29 Paul Cantor, *Creature and Creator: Myth-Making and English Romanticism* (Cambridge: Cambridge University Press, 1984), p. 118.

30 See Jerome McGann, *The Romantic Ideology: a Critical Investigation* (Chicago: University of Chicago Press, 1983).

6

DAVID PUNTER

Scottish and Irish Gothic

I want to focus in this chapter on qualities particular to Scottish and Irish Gothic fiction, wider histories of which are already available.[1] More specifically, I propose to inquire into some of the general relations between history and the Gothic for Scotland and Ireland and to exemplify these issues through an extended consideration of two texts, one Irish and one Scottish, that might both, in very different ways, make some claim to have an "originary" status in the history of Gothic fiction. One of these is, perhaps, inescapable in any contemplation either of the Gothic in general or of the "Irish Gothic": Charles Robert Maturin's *Melmoth the Wanderer* (1820). My epitome of Scottish Gothic is less obvious, but carries, as I hope to show, a freight of themes that touch at many points on the Gothic: Walter Scott's *The Antiquary* (1816).

I have in mind also the curious way in which current critical discourse seems to be forming itself round a certain terminology that owes much to the Gothic tradition. I have looked elsewhere at the contemporary preoccupation, in literary as well as in psychoanalytic theory, with crypts, phantoms, and processes of spectralization.[2] Here I want to use different terms, principally the monument and the ruin. Both of these notions, I believe, point us toward the "uncanny," in that they speak always of history, but of a history that is constantly under the threat of erasure. They speak of history not as a living presence nor yet as an irrecoverable absence, but as inevitably involved in specific modes of ghostly persistence which may occur when, particularly in Scotland and Ireland, national aspirations are thwarted by conquest or by settlement, as they have been so often. I want to show how the Gothic is especially powerful in rendering the complex hauntings in such conflicted histories.

As I write, there are plans for the replacement of two statues in that heartland of the celebration of the British Empire, Trafalgar Square in London. The statues are of General Sir Charles Napier and Major General Sir Henry Havelock. Napier is known to history principally as the conqueror and later governor of Sindh in 1843–47, but also as a suppressor of Chartist domestic uprising; Havelock fought in the Anglo-Burmese war of 1824–26 and the first Afghan war of 1839–42 before presiding over the siege of Lucknow. Questioned by a journalist as to the significance of these figures, a passing Londoner recently replied dryly that, although she had no idea who they were, they were "in keeping with the rest of the area. Everywhere you look round here there's a statue of some bloke on a horse."

These monuments, then, appear to gain their significance, not in the context of any specific knowledge about heroism or imperialist opportunism, but from their participation in the general chain of monumentalization that constitutes the memory of the nation-state. Their very erasure as aids to individual memory permits a return of a different sort and offers them as part of a general process of state legitimation – from statue to state, one might say, in a single bound. Alternatively, they place a seal on the traumas that accompany the attempt to establish a cohesive genealogy. In any case, the location and realization of such genealogies is always responsive to the current dispositions of power. These particular monuments are themselves clearly not ruins, despite being prone to pigeon droppings; nonetheless they testify to a problematically ruined memory and hold out the prospect of being replaced by other monuments, newer and more seemingly appropriate testaments to a history that strives to be read as continuous, explicable, a constant reassurance of the validity of national destiny.

The histories of Scotland and Ireland, subsumed by Britain off and on, are also, of course, replete with monuments themselves: records of battles lost and won, celebrations of famous victories and defeats, relics from savored or lamented moments from the past. But for Ireland as for Scotland, the gesture that continually retrieves these moments is a different one; it is one that includes within itself the question "What if?," the implicit possibility of a history that could have been "done differently," the possibility of a writing that would now be speaking from a position of political power rather than from one of subjugation to the invader, the settler, the conqueror. It is one thing, it seems, to reinscribe the names of London streets and squares with names like Nelson Mandela or Steve Biko; to do something similar in Edinburgh or Northern Ireland is right now quite distant on the political or cultural horizon.

There seems little doubt, however, that in both Scotland and Ireland Gothic at a certain point became a way of articulating these suppressed histories, as indeed it continues to do. But this "task" for the Gothic permits of two very different approaches. We might think of the "domestic Gothic," in which the traumas and defeats of the past are enacted on a home terrain, and the "foreign Gothic," in which they are displaced on to a fictionalized "third location." In English terms, for example, we might think of Clara Reeve's *The Old English Baron* (1777) as "originating" a version of the domestic Gothic; but far more frequently, as in Horace Walpole's *The Castle of Otranto* (1764) or Ann Radcliffe's *The Mysteries of Udolpho* (1794), the conflicts are displaced so that civil and religious disputes can be reenacted under a different banner, reterritorialized into a phantom or simulacrum and thus recoded within the supposed logic of a foreign body.[3]

There is a continuous history in Scottish writing of both these types from the heyday of the "original Gothic" to the present day. Among earlier writers, one thinks not only of Scott but also preeminently of James Hogg and the extraordinary depiction of the psychology of Calvinist religion and its relation to Scottish culture in *The Private Memoirs and Confessions of a Justified Sinner* (1824). One would want also to note the effect of specifically Scottish religious disputes on the work of George MacDonald, minister and author of *Phantastes* (1858) and *Lilith* (1895). Also, in the later part of the nineteenth century, Robert Louis Stevenson wrote not only the supernaturally influenced "domestic" fiction of the highly Scottish *Master of Ballantrae* (1889) – not to mention *Dr. Jekyll and Mr Hyde* – but also far-flung and displaced tales like "The Isle of Voices" (1893). One can even find certain traditions of the Gothic, from the haunted castle to the notion of the double, reappearing in different forms in very modern Scottish writers as diverse as Elspeth Barker, Iain Banks, and Janice Galloway.

In Ireland, one can similarly point to a Gothic tradition that deals with Irish issues in a variety of guises. J. S. Le Fanu's work, for example, includes Protestant religious and political polemics, novels about eighteenth-century Ireland, and such well-known Gothic works as *Uncle Silas* (1864) and the collection *In a Glass Darkly* (1872; site of the vampiric "Carmilla"), but common themes about the unreliability of history and the perverseness of power run through all his writings. It may be surprising to some to learn that not only was Bram Stoker, the author of *Dracula* (1897), born in Dublin, but also that his first book was *Duties of the Clerks of the Petty Sessions of Ireland* (1879), although the relation between this and his later work is indeed more tenuous. A more recent history of Irish Gothic would take us from Lord Dunsany, a favorite of Yeats, who wrote a long series of "Celtic" fantasies during the first fifty years of the twentieth century, to the haunting "great house" stories of Elizabeth Bowen, and then on to such recent writers as the eloquent and intricate John Banville.

My chief example from Scotland, *The Antiquary*, is a work of domestic Gothic. The story unfolds in the northeast of Scotland during a period of some four weeks in July and August 1794; it is replete with local knowledge and thus includes a whimsical understanding – and in some cases a misunderstanding – of local dialect. It also speaks, like so many of Scott's other novels, of Scottish folklore and legend and of powers of resistance and endurance. Its central figure, Jonathan Oldbuck, is the "antiquary" of the title, and as such he embodies a particular attitude toward history, the attitude of the collector. Indeed, Oldbuck is so much of a collector that he frequently risks being overwhelmed by history: "the abundance of his collection often prevented him from finding the article he sought for" (Scott, *Antiquary*, pp. 84–85), since the private museum in which he seeks to articulate the bones of the past remains uncatalogued.

At one point, for example, he is searching through his collection for a letter relating to his unending dispute with the villainous MacCribb, but he fails to find it, thus remaining unable to substantiate the accusation of forgery so apparent in his rival's name. What he finds is something else instead, a different text. "There, Mr Lovel," he remarks,

> there is the work I mentioned to you last night – the rare quarto of the Augsburg Confession, the foundation at once and the bulwark of the Reformation, drawn up by the learned and venerable Melancthon, defended by the Elector of Saxony, and the other valiant hearts who stood up for their faith even against the front of a powerful and victorious emperor, and imprinted by the scarcely less venerable and praiseworthy Aldobrand Oldenbuck, my happy progenitor, during the yet more tyrannical attempts of Philip II, to suppress at once civil and religious liberty. (Scott, *Antiquary*, p. 85)

This quasi-miraculous "finding" of the founding document of the Lutheran Church in 1530 performs a variety of functions. It establishes Oldbuck, through the Gothic device of the lost manuscript, as the accidental custodian of a "true history," as the possessor of a document crucial to Scottish religious life and thus to Scottish nationhood. But it simultaneously aggravates the comparatively trivial dispute about the "authenticity" of Ossian, the supposedly ancient "bard" created by James Macpherson in the 1760s, which is also being negotiated in *The Antiquary* by the assertion of a further, unquestionable authenticity in a document contained within "a case made of oak, fenced at the corner with silver roses and studs" (p. 85). This discovery removes the site of authenticity from Scotland and places it, for safekeeping, within a different, continental chain of monuments. In addition, it asserts the crucial contribution of writing and print culture to the preservation of national identity – in a chain to which Scott, of course, sees himself as belonging – by inserting Oldbuck himself into the continuity of history. The question of the "venerable" is here of some importance: does it refer simply to antiquity, to the age of the person described, or does it rather seek within itself to establish a *necessary* connection between antiquity and respect so that the depth of the root becomes a guarantee of the stability and authority of the result? At all events, what is being crucially explored here is the history of Scottish Protestantism and thus inevitably the actual and potential attempts of the authorities to suppress it. Scott's novel thus participates directly in the history of Scottish national self-conception.

Yet Scottish history is perhaps more resistant to clarification than Oldbuck would like to believe. Lovel is exhorted to look upon the equally "venerable effigies" of the "older" Oldenbuck and to "respect the honourable occupation in which it presents him, as labouring personally at the press for the diffusion of Christian and political knowledge" (Scott, *Antiquary*, p. 85). Oldbuck in particular presents Lovel with his ancestor's motto, "*Kunst macht Gunst,*" which he translates as "Skill, or prudence, in availing ourselves of our natural talents and advantages, will compel favour and patronage, even where it is withheld, from prejudice, or ignorance." This interpretation produces in Lovel "a moment's thoughtful silence," after which he asks: "that then is the meaning of these German words?" He is right to be skeptical. A German dictionary refers indeed to art, skill, and dexterity as meanings of *Kunst,* and to favor, goodwill and kindness under the heading *Gunst*; but *Kunst* can also refer to trick, knack, artifice, sleight-of-hand, while *Gunst* as "favour" can also figure in phrases like "courting a favour" or "doing a person a favour." "*Kunst macht Gunst*": it is possible, we might alternatively translate, to make a favorable impression on anybody by underhanded means. We need to keep in mind that Gothic history is itself always liable to employ such means, because it presents its own distortions and exaggerations while simultaneously playing a part in claiming to expose the distortions of history imposed by a generally accepted ideology or a falsely unproblematic narrative of the past.

History, then, slips and slides in *The Antiquary*. The search for a stable base is in constant danger of being undermined both by the overabundance of primary materials and by the indeterminacy of language. Instead of verifying a single history, what Oldbuck ends up doing – in a move which effortlessly encompasses the Gothic and its "antiquarian" forebears – is placing in question the very act of historical interpretation. The notion of a firm origin, a monument of unquestioned authority, slides into its opposite, the ever-present possibility of a fantastical distortion by means of which history will become irrecoverable, occluded by a wealth of tales and always receding into the geographical and chronological distance.

Even so, in *The Antiquary* some ancient enmities, particularly that between the Scots and the English, are inveterate and never appeased; they are held particularly within the dialect-laden statements of characters such as Elspeth Cheyne, who has imbibed her hatreds from her feudal masters, the lords of

Glenallan. There is her hatred, for example, of the anagrammatically named Eveline Neville:

> I hated Miss Eveline Neville for her ain sake – I brought her frae England, and, during our whole journey, she gecked and scorned at my northern speech and habit, as her southland leddies and kimmers had done at the boarding-school as they ca'd it (and, strange as it may seem, she spoke of an affront offered by a heedless school-girl without intention, with a degree of inveteracy, which, at such a distance of time, a mortal offence would neither have authorised or excited in any well-constituted mind) – Yes, she scorned and jested at me – but let them that scorn the tartan fear the dirk! (Scott, *Antiquary*, p. 261)

History, it would seem, is founded on and articulated around three kinds of offense. The offense committed by Eveline's fellow schoolgirl back in England is, it would seem, condonable; it was offered "heedlessly," "without intention." The offense, however, that Eveline offers to Elspeth now is inexcusable. Although Eveline may be a schoolgirl herself, an offense offered in the context of unequal national difference is in a totally different sphere. This means that the third kind of offense, that which Elspeth offers to Eveline in return, is not merely legitimate; it is required. It takes on the contours of a participation in Scottish national destiny. The "well-constituted mind," it would appear, is not to be assessed free from the constraints of history or nationality; it is indeed a matter of "constitution," but that term here takes on a political as well as a personal or psychological cast.

Eveline's real offense, that which lies further back down the chain, is her betrothal to the son of the Countess Glenallan, an offense that the Countess herself wishes to deal with straightforwardly in "the old way": by throwing Eveline into the "Massymore of Glenallan" and chaining her son in the "Keep of Strathbonnall." Alas, however, these rollicking old times are no more, "and the authority which the nobles of the land should exercise, is delegated to quibbling lawyers and their baser dependents" (Scott, *Antiquary*, p. 261). Scott here touches on one of the most basic of all themes in early Gothic: the supplanting of an older, more violent authority by the middling (and meddling) rule of law. Throughout Gothic, whether in the mountains of the Abruzzi or in the towers and keeps of medieval Britain, one can sense the fascination with the past that flows from a mingled yearning and terror for a set of simpler verities, an unquestioned legitimation.[4] This nostalgia goes through a further twist of intensification in Scottish Gothic, for that supplanting, real or imagined, is forcibly juxtaposed by the native Scots with the destruction of a "national way of life." Scottish culture is seen as a territorialized, appropriated land, a place where a foreign body has been violently installed in the very heart of the country. There the writing of the past has been distorted, perverted by a "law" that professes equality and justice but merely serves to prevent the "proper settling of accounts" of which the Countess speaks, one that would vindicate an aristocracy that is seen as having been starved out of power.

Accordingly, the character Lord Geraldin undergoes a fate that reads like a textbook of Gothic infirmities. A Catholic, and thus the subject of a different but massive political exclusion, he "had been a young man of accomplishment and hopes," but "such fair dawns are often strangely overcast." He "led a life of the strictest retirement. His ordinary society was composed of the clergymen of his communion, who occasionally visited his mansion; and very rarely, upon stated occasions of high festival, one or two families who still professed the Catholic religion were formally entertained at Glenallanhouse" (Scott, *Antiquary,* p. 220). Those guests thus privileged to gain an insight into this site of ruined hopes return from such entertainments "without knowing whether most to wonder at the stern and stately demeanour of the Countess, or the deep and gloomy dejection which never ceased for a moment to cloud the features of her son." Reports gather after his mother's death

> that the earl's constitution was undermined by religious austerities, and that, in all probability, he would soon follow his mother to the grave. This event was the more probable as his brother had died of a lingering complaint, which, in the latter years of his life, had affected at once his frame and his spirits: so that heralds and genealogists were already looking back into their records to discover the heir of this ill-fated family, and lawyers were talking with gleesome anticipation of a "great Glenallan cause." (pp. 220–21)

Precisely what "constitution," one might ask, is being undermined by "religious austerities," a frequent motif of early Gothic fiction that now has added resonances in the context of Scotland's religious struggles. Whatever the case, we are here in the presence of a "sickness unto death," of an ailing that has come down the family, of a "house of Usher" all too ready to collapse[5] – unless it is propped up by the despised and mercenary acolytes of the law. The coherence of the family is no longer a guarantee of longevity, as it had been in imagined aristocratic times. On the contrary, it is an indicator of death, a carrier of disease, even an early signal of the inevitable corruption of the grave.

But here we have a specifically Scottish resonance, for during the eighteenth century the Scottish nobility had indeed lost a great deal of its power. Many of them were impoverished and unable to resist the spread of a different, invading power from the south. To this was added the general humiliation of Scotland, and of sections of its aristocracy in particular, by the bitter failure of the 1745 rebellion. All in all, the rule of the lawyer and the political manager had already replaced what lingering strength the nobility had once possessed. The "great Glenallan cause" is a parody of the kind of "cause" – national or religious – that could occasion genuine political adherence. It is now a "cause" reduced to a legal "case," an emptied shell of the passions that apparently once throve in such families as the Glenallans. These drives are in ruins, abandoned to melancholy and decay, inverted monuments to the passing of history and the impossibility of "restoration."

Yet times past are not times past; in *The Antiquary*, as in many other Gothic texts, the separations of history blur and waver. There comes a moment, for example, when Lovel is led by a "beggar" to "a cave, as narrow in its entrance as a fox-earth" which "was indicated by a small fissure in the rock, that the screen of an aged oak...concealed effectually from all observation":

> It might indeed have escaped the attention even of one who had stood at its very opening, so uninviting was the portal at which the beggar entered. But within, the cavern was higher and more roomy, cut into two separate branches, which, intersecting each other at right angles, formed an emblem of the cross, and indicated the abode of an anchoret of former times. There are many caves of the same kind in different parts of Scotland. I need only instance those of Gorton, near Roslin, in a scene well known to the admirers of romantic nature.
>
> (Scott, *Antiquary*, p. 165)

If we were to speak of this passage in terms of territorialization, we would encounter more fissures, more cross-cuttings, than those that appear to describe this cave. For example, we here confront the complex nature of the secret. This fissuring of the earth's surface represents, at one level, a secret from the outside, the invisible persistence of a "native" Scottish religious tradition in the face of persecution by a foreign body; at the same time, it is displayed to us quite vigorously by the narrator, to such an extent that he adds his own personal endorsement, buttressed with a mechanism of verification that reminds us of the present-day context of these things of the past. We should also note a curious cross-cutting of nature and culture, as of genre and the real: like Sophia Lee's "recess" in her novel of the 1780s, this cave is, presumably, not "natural," or at least not wholly so, but it is nonetheless redolent of scenes attractive to the "admirers of romantic nature." Perhaps that which is constructed or "improved" by the labors of a subjugated people becomes assimilated to the "natural"; but it also points to the subaltern as taking on the ambiguous mantle offered to it by the conquering power, resigning itself to the fate of the primitive, allowing itself to be seen, if at all, as merging with the forced habitat of forest and glen, abandoning its prospects of modernity and culture.[6]

Indeed, such a point would seem to be emphasized by Scott's own comments in his "Advertisement" to the novel (Scott, *Antiquary*, p. 3), in which he describes it as the third and last of a series of "fictitious narratives," of which *Waverley* (1814) and *Guy Mannering* (1815) are the others, wherein he has sought his "principal personages in the class of society who are the last to feel the influence of that general polish which assimilates to each other the manners of different nations." Scott adds that he has placed some of the scenes within the confines of this class "to illustrate the operation of the higher and more violent passions" and goes on to agree with Wordsworth that "they seldom fail to express [their feelings] in the strongest and most powerful language," especially, he says, in the case of the Scottish peasantry, since "the antique force and simplicity of their language" is "often tinctured with the oriental eloquence of Scripture."

What is going on here, I believe, is a complex series of deterritorializations and reterritorializations. The Scottish middle and upper classes in the late eighteenth century, Scott claims, were set on an inevitable trajectory that would eliminate national difference; what they were also leaving behind was the force of powerful feeling, subsumed beneath the veneer of a "general polish." What is left as this tide recedes – the remaining monument to Scotland conceived as an "antique" nation or, perhaps, the ruin of national strength of feeling – is a peasantry possessed of a curious blend of simple force (sanctioned, ironically, by an English poet) and a Baroque rewriting of biblical prose, a version of prophecy (as emphasized in the person of the archetypal wanderer Ochiltree) that comes – but only temporarily – to occupy the vacuum produced by the decay of Scottish society's upper echelons. The adjective used by the distinguished Scottish historian J. D. Mackie in connection with the major features of the national condition at the time is still a very precise word for it: *supine*.[7]

It is perhaps in this sense more than any other that the entire text falls under the spell of the "antiquary." Scott himself goes on to admit to Oldbuck's own failing when he says that he has been unable in the novel to reconcile the minute description of manners with "an artificial and combined narration" (Scott, *Antiquary*, p. 3). Minute attention to the past does not facilitate narrative; on the contrary, it causes narrative to fall apart under the pressure of the detail. The antiquary's collection resists cataloguing; the freight of oddities and curiosities borne to us on the waves of the past overwhelms the telling of any simple story; and narrative fragments striving to contain the "time" of the past, attempts at enduring monumentalization, become ever more complicated and uncertain.

That this sense of temporal complication and uncertainty is endemic also to *Melmoth the Wanderer* should need no emphasizing, given all the studies of this rich – as well as quite Irish – Gothic novel. But it might help our sense of its Irishness if we specified the connections between this looping of time, this mistiness of the past, and the Irish context in which the text was written. It is often said, for example, that Maturin's great strength in *Melmoth* lies in his depiction of extreme emotional and passionate states; but this is accompanied throughout by an anguished historical sense of the impossibility of transition. The condition of the heroine Elinor, for example, caught between the secular and the religious, as between the Protestant and the Catholic, is emblematic. The impossibility of her position, her suspension between incompatible theological and social narratives, is underlined by the narrator.

> Thus it fares with those who wish to make an instant transition from one world to another, – it is impossible, – the cold wave interposes – for ever interposes, between the wilderness and the land of promise – and we may as soon expect to tread the threshold which parts life and death without pain, as to cross the interval which separates two modes of existence so distinct as those of passion and religion, without struggles of the soul inexpressible – without groanings which cannot be uttered. (Maturin, *Melmoth*, pp. 478–79)

There is no linear, coherent history; it is not possible neatly to arrange a set of monuments that will attest to the clean lines of conflicts won and lost. There is the "interposition" of the "cold wave" as the breath of death appears in the fissure between beliefs and persuasions. We might image Maturin's notion of change as a matter of stepping-stones over an abyss; one false move and we are lost forever. Indeed, he says as much at the moment when Melmoth is observing the young Isidora and "might have marked all that profound and perilous absorption of the soul, when it is determined to penetrate the mysteries of love or of religion, and chuse 'whom it will serve' – that *pause* on the brink of an abyss" (p. 365). For Maturin, a Protestant Irish clergyman who was wrestling with his own theological and civil demons, any of these moves may well be fraught with danger. There is an absence of a sense of *scale* according to which such differences can be measured.

This absence – or at best relativity – of scale is omnipresent in the Gothic, where the tiniest of infractions of unperceived rules can place one directly in the hands of the "living God." But what is at stake here can also be seen as the sense of a national history, of individuals groaning as they are made to fit in to the straitjacket of ideological conformity. The point comes out with redoubled force – and with all the strength of displacement on to a "third terrain," of refraction on to the contours of a "foreign body" as the bearer of an otherwise unmanageable difference – when *Melmoth* treats the fate of the Jewish "Don Fernan." In the world of this text all is surveillance, which can hardly fail to remind us of the condition of Ireland under English domination. We could quote, for example, a source as early as the historian G. M. Trevelyan on the trajectory of Irish history during the seventeenth and eighteenth centuries.

> Throughout the war with the French Republic, England had been hampered by her "broken arm." Few countries of the *ancien régime* had been more actively misgoverned than Ireland. In the seventeenth century the national leaders of the Catholic Celts had been destroyed as a class, and their lands given to a garrison of alien landlords ... In the latter half of the eighteenth century ... the gates of political power were still closed on the Catholic, and the peasant tilled the soil to pay tithes to an alien Church, and rent to an alien squirearchy.[8]

In vain, then, does the religiously disadvantaged Jew in Maturin's novel protest to the functionaries of the Inquisition that "when the eye of God is on me, most reverend fathers, I am never in darkness":

> "The eye of God *is* on you," said the officer, sternly seating himself; "and so is another eye, to which he has deputed the sleepless vigilance and resistless penetration of his own, – the eye of the holy office ... You are an old man, Don Fernan, but not an *old Christian*; and, under these circumstances, it behoves the holy office to have a watchful scrutiny over your conduct." (p. 260)

What, after all, is being watched here? Among other things, it is certainly Maturin himself, the Protestant clergyman speaking out from the pulpit against what he considers to be Catholic excesses, the Maturin who can say in *Melmoth* that the Catholic religion is one which is lost in idolatry, false monumentalization, and has abnegated its moral responsibilities at the altar of pomp and ceremony: "In Catholic countries, Sir, religion is the national drama; the priests are the principal performers, the populace the audience; and whether the piece concludes with a 'Don Giovanni' plunging in flames, or the beatification of a saint, the applause and the enjoyment is the same" (p. 165). This is a very important passage, because it clearly shows the way in which Maturin wants to *reuse* Gothic motifs and structures, which are already aging, in the service of a specific religious – and hence political – argument. The excesses, the violent transitions, the impossibility of moving from one position to another, the absence of coherent history: all are elements in the construction of arguments about the legitimacy of the Irish state and about the nature of the Protestant Ascendancy, that process whereby a conquering English supremacy was installed in the heart of Ireland. It is here, I think, that one comes up against the crucial ambivalences and contradictions in this text. *Melmoth* is a novel about persecution, but there are times when the nature of that persecution seems radically to exceed its particular conditions.

In other words, the stance of the narrative may seem to place the Protestant minority at the mercy of a greater power; but it was, as we have seen above, the Catholic majority who were alienated from power in Ireland, and hence some of the contortions and extravagances of Maturin's text really stem from the difficulty of accommodating or making sense of this impossible double perception.

These exact elements are reconstructed in *Melmoth* precisely in the form of monuments. The principal monument, as we might expect both from Gothic conventions and from Maturin's apparently anti-Catholic argument, is the Inquisition, and yet here we find an interplay between the narrator's sense of a present and continuing threat, on the one hand, and an equally strong wish to send this travesty of solid history into the consuming flames of the ruined past, on the other: "Far, far, above us, the flames burst out in volumes, in solid masses of fire, spiring up to the burning heavens. The towers of the Inquisition shrunk into cinders – that tremendous monument of the power, and crime, and gloom of the human mind, was wasting like a scroll in the fire" (p. 241). In this assimilation of the three terms "power," "crime," and "gloom," we can perhaps also see something of the essence of *Melmoth the Wanderer*. What lies behind all this is a terror of the ambiguities of human aspiration: a fear that the very attempt to seek necessarily involves transgression and thereby plunges one into melancholy. True, we have in *Melmoth* the voice of Maturin himself, aware in a melancholy fashion of the potential historical doom of his own religious convictions; but what we also have is a problematic admiration of striving and ambition, even when surrounded by the chattels of Catholicism – or of Hinduism, or of any of the other religions ostensibly attacked in the text.

I would not be the first reader of *Melmoth* to note the way in which, despite the determined partisanship which forms one aspect of the text, the fact remains that all the voices run into each other:[9] it is very difficult to separate imprecations against Catholic excesses from more general railings against fate or, indeed, condemnations of the religious impulse in general. In fact, one could say that, despite the vehemence of his own religious beliefs, what truly appalls and worries Maturin – and hence what continually troubles the textual surface of *Melmoth* – is the problem of the divided mind. It is impossible to decide whether this figures as more of a problem for the Catholic mind (succored, according to Maturin, by false monuments) or for the Protestant mind, a victim to its own inner demons and phantasms, as in Hogg's *Justified Sinner*. At all events, we may usefully note as evidence for this difficulty Victor Sage's comment on Maturin's style: "Narrative in Maturin has a 'broken mirror' effect: from the outset he is interested in allegory, structural repetition, variation, refraction and romance plots of disguise and revelation rather than the assimilation of a point of view to a grand sweep of historical narrative."[10] Catholicism, in this reading, might stand for the impossibility of separating the mind from the external manifestation of its guilt, Protestantism for the impossibility of escape from a disastrous inner troubling, and here we have the Irish situation in the early nineteenth century in a nutshell. A well-known passage from *Melmoth* begins with the "tempter" calling up the ruined image of an "eminent puritanical preacher":

> Half the day he imagines himself in a pulpit, denouncing damnation against Papists, Arminians, and even Sublapsarians (he being a Supralapsarian himself). He foams, he writhes, he gnashes his teeth; you would imagine him in the hell he was painting, and that the fire and brimstone he is so lavish of, were actually exhaling from his jaws. At night his *creed retaliates on him*; he believes himself one of the reprobates he has been all day denouncing, and curses God for the very decree he has all day been glorifying Him for.   (p. 57)

The discourse of the reprobate, as of the tempter and the wailing and gnashing of teeth, again reminds one irresistibly in this context of the doubling in Hogg's *Justified Sinner*, where the question of the origin of the diabolic is placed within the possibility that the self and what bedevils it are born together. The birth of the moral sense, it seems, is already interdicted by the circumstances of the (familial and historical) past and so conjures with it the birth of precisely that force which will ruin any attempt at psychic coherence. The major mode of preaching in Scottish churches at this time, it might be useful to remember, was the violent denunciation of sin.

In the Irish *Melmoth* there is an immense wealth of codes of displacement; it is for this reason that I see it as a text under the sign of the foreign body, as opposed to the domesticity (problematic though it is) of Scott's *Antiquary*. We might consider, for example, the attempt to exile extremities of conduct and punishment to a world characterized by "intoxication," a world that tries to locate itself everywhere except in the British Isles. In these *other* locations, the figures of the other-in-the-self truly violate nature – whether they be in the north, among the Turks or Dervishes, or among the monks who are symbolic of the darkness of Catholicism – and nature always responds by retaliation:

> [She] exacts a most usurious interest for this illicit indulgence. She makes them pay for moments of rapture with hours of despair. Their precipitation from extasy [*sic*] to horror is almost instantaneous. In the course of a few moments, they pass from being the favourites of Heaven to becoming its outcasts...All saints, from Mahomet down to Francis Xavier, were only a compound of

insanity, pride, and self-imposition; – the latter would have been of less consequence, but that men always revenge their impositions on themselves, by
imposing to the utmost on others. (pp. 114–15)

This is one of many passages where Maturin sets up a monumental history,
in this case the history of the saints, precisely in order to rip it down and
cast it to the utmost perdition. Again we have the extremes of transition, but
what we also have is a continual probing of the relation between inner and
outer, what one might fairly call an attention to the mechanisms of projection. It is these mechanisms that fatally trouble the possibility of a unified
national history and which reveal it as an expressionist illusion, giant shadows thrown against the screen which bear little relation to what is occurring
on the ground. The monastery or convent, of course, was throughout the
history of the early Gothic a site of hypocrisy and violent incarceration; in
Melmoth what is revealed more clearly is that there can be no single valu-
ation of this curious phenomenon or set of practices. All response depends
on a habit of perception that is like a process of reading, albeit one bound to
end in ambivalence. Maturin speaks of "the petty squabbles and intrigues of
the convent" and of all that "makes monastic life like the wrong side of the
tapestry, where we see only uncouth threads, and the harsh outlines, without
the glow of the colours, the richness of the tissue, or the splendour of the
embroidery, that renders the external surface so rich and dazzling" (p. 76).
Seen from one side, then, the life of the monastery, however solemnly it may
be denounced in the voice of the Reformation, nevertheless appears perversely to retain the semblance of glow, color, life; seen from the perspective
of the other, of course, it betrays only the contours of a tedious, fractious
intimacy. Nevertheless, in this doubleness of voices, Maturin is in continual danger of betraying himself. Something in his own discourse retaliates
(in glowing terms) against the plainness, the reliance on all that goes on
outside the illusions of "richness of tissue," that should be beloved by the
Protestant sensibility.

Seen from one side, then, the life of the monastery – the enclosed life
which is so frequent a Gothic theme – is a monument: it rises above petty
individuality, it transcends the "squabbling" that we may see as emblematic
of an Ireland divided between historic Catholicism and an imposed Protestant domination. Seen from another angle, though, the monument reveals
itself as a ruin, as a thing of shreds and patches, as a location where, even
if coherence can be felt, it will always be on the other side of a great divide,
never immediately available to a life lived in the present.

But in *Melmoth*, as in early nineteenth-century Ireland, ruins are everywhere. To take an example quite similar to the notions of antiquarianism in

Scott, ruins loom over the strange room, the private museum, which is the location in which we first encounter the Jew Adonijah.

> It was a large apartment, hung with dark-coloured baize within four feet of the floor; and this intermediate part was thickly matted, probably to intercept the subterranean damps . . . There were, amid maps and globes, several instruments, of which my ignorance did not permit me to know the use . . . around the room were placed *four* skeletons, not in cases, but in a kind of upright coffin, that gave their bony emptiness a kind of ghastly and imperative prominence . . . Then I saw figures smaller, but not less horrible, – human and brute abortions, in all their states of anomalous and deformed construction. (pp. 262–63)

The catalogue goes on, a listing of bits and pieces, of body parts and bones, of an inexplicable antediluvian past, which here, as it does also for Scott, represents an attempt to explain and understand the ruins ("of which my ignorance did not permit me to know the use"). Here the possible past of human and animal history shades off into myth ("some gigantic bones, which I took for those of Sampson, but which turned out to be fragments of those of the Mammoth"), and this hybrid antiquity raises itself as an object and progenitor of terror through its conjuring of an unintelligible and menacing past. But this is only one among many sites of ruin; there is also, for example, the island in "the Indian sea, not many leagues from the mouth of the Hoagly" (p. 272) on which Immalee, later to be Isidora, is found by Melmoth. Here we find ourselves in the presence – or rather, the remains of the presence – of a temple that has been overthrown by an earthquake. On this occasion, we learn, "the inhabitants, their dwellings, and their plantations, [were] swept away as with the besom of destruction, and not a trace of humanity, cultivation, or life, remained in the desolate isle" (p. 272). Yet the "besom of destruction" proves singularly inadequate here, as perhaps Maturin hopes it might be when occupied in a different work of overthrowing a certain ascendancy guaranteed by plantations and the like. Immediately after this total evacuation of the island, this forced removal of all traces of the organic and the human, we find the "devotees" still mysteriously consulting their imagination "for the cause of these calamities," since, as Maturin perhaps hopes, there may still be some hope for the Protestant cause in Ireland after the inevitable uprising (which was, of course, not to have a successful outcome for another century).

It is the ruins themselves, however, that cast a spell over the text. The "ruin of the pagoda" had been

> a massive square building, erected amid rocks, that, by a caprice of nature not uncommon in the Indian isles, occupied its centre, and appeared the consequence of some volcanic explosion. The earthquake that had overthrown it,

had mingled the rocks and ruins together in a shapeless and deformed mass, which seemed to bear alike the traces of the impotence of art and nature, when prostrated by the power that has formed and can annihilate both.

(pp. 276–77)

As with Scott, there is a problem, or at least an issue, about the relation between the primitively human and the merely organic. What happens in the process of ruination is that the very differentiation of the human is effaced. Under these circumstances, it is perhaps inevitable that what gets erased is at least partly the process of writing or inscription itself: "There were pillars, wrought with singular characters, heaped amid stones that bore no impress but that of some fearful and violent action of nature, that seemed to say, Mortals, write your lines with the chisel, I write my hieroglyphics in fire" (p. 277). The most relevant comparison here is with P. B. Shelley's "Ozymandias, King of Kings" in his sonnet published in 1818, but there are significant differences. Ozymandias, the pharaoh Ramses II under his Greek name, may be toppled and broken, since his huge stone head (the focus of Shelley's poem) now lies in the desert in Egypt, but the message he wrote continues to shine forth, albeit disfigured by the irony of time and history. By contrast, the "pillars" in *Melmoth* have been subject to much more defacement in the process of their monumental ruin. If the language in which they were inscribed has ever been known, it has certainly faded from memory now, to such an extent that the operation of the human hand in forming these vanished signs can no longer be discerned from the parallel operations of nature.

If "Ozymandias" is a quasi-Gothic myth that has to do with the fallen grandeur of past civilizations while continuing to assert their relevance as a warning to the continuity of national progress, then the myth in *Melmoth* goes one step further, as one might expect in the Irish context, and undermines the entire sense of memory and interpretation on which history is based. Whereas in England even a removed and subverted notion of tradition can remain relevant, here in the Irish context – as with Scott's peasants – there is no bedrock on which to stand. The Gothic removal of history does not suggest analogies to past civilizations or cultures, but rather exposes a terrifying abyss in an occupied land, the looming presence of a nonverbal "history" that might not be human or coherent at all, just as the issue of Catholic emancipation in Ireland hinged on the denial of human rights to the majority of the population.

What, after all, is the distinguishing mark of the human? Melmoth shows Immalee a vision of the monuments of the human race – the "black pagoda of Juggernaut," a Turkish mosque, the "temple of Mahadeva" (p. 276) – but

Immalee is not content with this vision. "The houses are nothing to me," says this child of nature, "shew me the living things that go there." Bring history to life, she suggests, and Melmoth does:

> Immalee looked and saw a vast sandy plain, with the dark pagoda of Juggernaut in the perspective. On this plain lay the bones of a thousand skeletons, bleaching in the burning and unmoistened air. A thousand human bodies, hardly more than alive, and scarce less emaciated, were trailing their scarred and blackened bodies over the sands, to perish under the shadow of the temple, hopeless of ever reaching that of its walls. (p. 292)

There is, then, no life in this history, only slaughter and famine, only another version of the omnipresent "ruins of empire"; when one inspects the monuments of the past closely, it turns out that they preside over an empire of death, that all creeds have really been the same in their unthinking call to sacrifice while providing no reward for those who survive the religious holocaust. Again, whatever "time" Maturin thinks he is writing about, we should heed the historian: "The typical Irish landlord had never been an 'improver.' He did nothing for his estate. He neither built nor repaired the cabins, sheds or fences of his tenantry. He was simply a consumer of rack-rent... The result was periodic famine."[11] Religion, in fact – and one can surmise that this is a lesson Maturin is telling us from his Irish experience – does not preserve and save the spirit. Instead it dehumanizes. It continually threatens to reduce the human to a copy, to a mask, to the very automaton – vividly described in E. T. A. Hoffmann's "The Sandman" (1815–16) and transcribed from there as one type of the "uncanny" (see Freud, "The Uncanny") – which causes us anxiety by seeming to be human while having no soul. Such an automaton can, for example, manipulate famine to its own ends, as the English were to do in Ireland, according to many accounts, during the great potato blight of 1846. This is how the unbelieving novice might feel when his spiritual health is being investigated: "They stated to him my abstraction, my mechanical movements, my automaton figure, my meaningless words, my stupified devotion, my total alienation from the spirit of the monastic life, while my scrupulous, *wooden, jointless* exactness in its forms was only a mockery" (Maturin, *Melmoth*, p. 100). We may take this, then, as a statement, from a specific national and historical viewpoint, about the relation between the human, considered as founded upon a notion of self-motivation and free will, and the larger dehumanizing forces of history, religion, and ideology which menace human authenticity with a different story, a narrative of conquest and subjugation within which individuals are mere puppets. Here we are upon the essential terrain of Gothic but also immersed in visions of national history, both of which teach that the national "subject" is in practice still "subjected" to domination by an external force.

Gothic in general, I am suggesting, incarnates a set of stories within which human individuals are at the mercy of larger powers. The question of where these larger powers "originate" – if they can be said to originate at all – is shrouded in darkness. Sometimes they may be figured as banditti springing from the mountainsides, sometimes as controlling inner voices, sometimes as phantoms, ghouls, zombies, or automata. But once they have appeared they are difficult to lay to rest, and the resonances of the stories they tell, like the aftereffects of the Ancient Mariner's tale in Coleridge's *Rime* of 1798, are always likely to throw a skeptical light upon our own narratives of egotistical importance.

What I have been trying to suggest through looking at *The Antiquary* and *Melmoth*, however briefly, is that in Scottish and Irish contexts this process of narrative reforming history goes through a further twist. Here the dehumanizing force in Gothic generally is brought into alignment, direct or indirect, with that power which reduces or dismembers the national narrative of a people operating under a sign of subjugation. As Fiona Robertson puts it in the context of Scott, the problem is one of what counts as a "legitimate history": "The term 'legitimate'...most immediately conjures up the political context of Scott's work, asking what counts as a legitimate history for Britain within the rapidly changing European framework of Scott's time, and for Scotland after its first (Ossianic) creation of a romantic identity and cultural history."[12] One could seek, and indeed find, similar forces at work in, for example, Le Fanu and Stevenson, to name one further Irish and one further Scottish example: in the peculiar situation, for example, of Uncle Silas and his mysterious house of Bartram-Haugh, or in the mystery-within-mystery of the double-doored house in *Dr. Jekyll and Mr. Hyde* (1886), both of which can be seen as reflecting, among many other things, the impossibility of arriving at a fully verified cultural narrative.

I do not mean to suggest, however, that these motifs are peculiar or exclusive to Scottish or Irish Gothic; Gothic in general is strewn with ruins, endlessly attentive to the "other" stories that can be told about national and cultural monuments. The important thing to realize is that the ways in which these alternative narratives are shaped will always be responsive to the specific conditions of power. The recapitulation of the past is never neutral. History has always to be told from a point of view.

Gothic began as a mode of dealing with the past and thus it has continued to the present day. In the contexts of Scotland and Ireland, different in many ways though they are, that past looks all too often as though it has already been appropriated by another, as though the story of one's own nation has already ceased to be one's own to tell. Scott responds to this problem with a series of cultural moves that appear to reinstate Scottish history while simultaneously consigning it to the margins. The Irish Maturin, less poised about his own cultural marginalization, casts a bitter eye over the whole process of history and historical narration as he *and* Ireland have seen it. By putting them both together, however, we can see how Gothic itself, as a discourse of the marginal and the barbaric, comes together with the discourses of specific cultures themselves regarded – sometimes by their own champions – as other and barbarian. Ultimately it is far from accidental that these cultures of exile and implantation came to play a crucial role in the Gothic, as indeed they have continued to do over the last two centuries.

NOTES

1 See, for example, Ian Duncan, *Modern Romance and Transformations of the Novel: the Gothic, Scott, Dickens* (Cambridge: Cambridge University Press, 1992), and W. J. McCormack, *Sheridan Le Fanu and Victorian Ireland* (Oxford: Oxford University Press, 1980).

2 See David Punter, "Teaching Gothic: Thoughts on Psychoanalysis and Culture," in Diane Lang Hoeveler and Tamar Heller, eds., *Approaches to Teaching Gothic Fiction: the British and American Traditions* (New York: MLA, 2002).

3 See Nicholas Royle, *After Derrida* (Manchester: Manchester University Press, 1995), pp. 143–58.

4 See David Punter, *Gothic Pathologies: the Text, the Body and the Law* (London: Macmillan, 1998), especially pp. 1–18, 200–21.

5 The references are to Søren Kierkegaard, *The Sickness unto Death* (1848), and Edgar Allan Poe, "The Fall of the House of Usher" (1839).

6 See Peter Womack, *Improvement and Romance: Constructing the Myth of the Highlands* (London: Macmillan, 1988).

7 J. D. Mackie, *A History of Scotland*, 2nd edn, ed. Bruce Lenman and Geoffrey Parker (Harmondsworth: Penguin, 1978), p. 286.

8 G. M. Trevelyan, *British History in the Nineteenth Century (1782–1901)* (London: Longman, 1922), p. 99.

9 cf. Richard Haslam, "Maturin and the 'Calvinist Sublime,' " in Allan Lloyd Smith and Victor Sage, eds., *Gothick Origins and Innovations* (Amsterdam: Rodopi, 1994), pp. 44–56.

10 Victor Sage, "Irish Gothic: C. R. Maturin and J. S. Le Fanu," in David Punter, ed., *A Companion to the Gothic* (Oxford: Blackwell, 2000), pp. 81–93.

11 Trevelyan, *British History*, p. 219.

12 Fiona Robertson, *Legitimate Histories: Scott, Gothic, and the Authorities of Fiction* (Oxford: Clarendon Press, 1994), p. 10.

7

JEFFREY N. COX

English Gothic theatre

According to Northrop Frye, "There has never . . . been any period of Gothic English literature, but the list of Gothic revivalists stretches completely across its entire history, from the *Beowulf* poet to writers of our own day."[1] There was, however, a specific period of Gothic English drama. While scholars have identified Gothic elements throughout the dramatic tradition from Euripides and Seneca to Tennessee Williams and *The Rocky Horror Picture Show*, it is important to locate the Gothic drama proper in the late eighteenth and early nineteenth century (that is, during the period we call "Romantic"), when it rose and fell as a major force on the London stage. During an era when English audiences anxiously lived through a series of political, economic, social, cultural, and literary innovations the Gothic drama provided a major new form of entertainment and of reflection upon a world in major upheaval.

Still, Frye's point that the Gothic has always seemed belated, always a revival rather than an origin, does apply to the Gothic on stage. Gothic drama arose in England roughly between 1789 and 1832 under a multiple debt of imitation. As *Gothic* drama, it appeared after and often as an imitation of Gothic novels.[2] As Gothic *drama*, it struck many as an attempt to revive the conventions and motifs of great Elizabethan and Jacobean plays, or alternatively as a dangerous effort to import the suspect German drama of the *Sturm und Drang*, a deliberate theatrical style of anticlassical "Storm and Stress" that began with a German play of that name by F. M. Klinger in the 1770s (Mulvey-Roberts, *Handbook to Gothic Literature*, p. 286). While wildly popular then (as is now its descendent, the horror movie), the Gothic drama has always been found by critics to be second-hand literature: second-rate as literature and secondary to an understanding of the Gothic firmly grounded in the novel. What we need is an account of Gothic drama on its own terms.

While it is possible to trace the Gothic drama back through such eighteenth-century plays as Home's *Douglas* (1756) to the works of Otway, Southerne, and Lee, and then to Elizabethan and Jacobean plays such as Webster's

Duchess of Malfi, the best candidate for the first Gothic drama is *The Mysterious Mother* (1768) by Horace Walpole, the author of the first "Gothic story," *The Castle of Otranto* (1764). Yet, since it dealt with incest, Walpole circulated his play only privately until the early 1790s; it was never performed. As a result, his play never had the impact his romance did. While we can identify some Gothic plays in the 1770s and 1780s – Robert Jephson, for example, adapted *The Castle of Otranto* itself as the *Count of Narbonne* (Covent Garden, 1781), and we could point to Hannah Cowley's *Albina, Countess of Raimond* (Haymarket, 1779), Richard Cumberland's *The Mysterious Husband* (Covent Garden, 1782) or Miles Peter Andrew's *The Enchanted Castle* (Covent Garden, 1786) – the Gothic would become a truly powerful force on the London stage only after 1789, the year of the publication of Ann Radcliffe's first novel, *The Castles of Athlin and Dunbayne*, and of the fall of the Bastille.

Throughout the 1790s Radcliffe's novels would help generate a fascination with the Gothic as a style that could be deployed in fiction, poetry, and the drama. Radcliffe's own novels provided the basis for at least ten plays, with James Boaden being her most important adapter.[3] Other key Gothic novels reached the stage. For example, Boaden also staged Matthew Lewis's *The Monk* as *Aurelio and Miranda* (Drury Lane, 1798), George Colman the Younger dramatized William Godwin's *Caleb Williams* in *The Iron Chest* (Drury Lane, 1796), Benjamin West provided a stage version of Charles Robert Maturin's *Melmoth the Wanderer* (Royal Coburg, 1823), and Richard Brinsley Peake adapted Mary Shelley's *Frankenstein* as *Presumption; or, The Fate of Frankenstein* (English Opera House, 1823). The novelists themselves often turned to the drama, as we can see in the cases of Walpole, Lewis, whose *Castle Spectre* of 1798 was a smash hit, and Maturin, who was better known by his contemporaries for the successful *Bertram; or, The Castle of St. Aldobrand* (Drury Lane, 1816) than for *Melmoth*.

The popularity of the Gothic as drama is attested by the number of "original" plays using a Gothic formula that reached the stage, particularly in the 1790s; a recently compiled list of acted Gothic plays[4] indicates that during this decade there were from two to six Gothic dramas performed each year, the Gothic occupying a significant place in a repertoire that admitted few new plays during a season. There is a recognizable body of Gothic drama produced during the first decades of the nineteenth century, with some playwrights – Lewis, for example, or William Dimond – making their careers through staging the Gothic. One can also begin to identify a canon of "classic" Gothic drama that would include Boaden's *Fountainville Forest* and *The Italian Monk*, Lewis's *Castle Spectre* and *The Wood Daemon* (Drury Lane, 1807), Colman's *Iron Chest* and *Blue-Beard* (Drury Lane, 1798),

Joanna Baillie's *De Montfort* (Drury Lane, 1800), William Sotheby's *Julian and Agnes* (Drury Lane, 1801), John Tobin's *The Curfew* (Drury Lane, 1807), Maturin's *Bertram*, and Peake's *Presumption*, to which we might want to add Coleridge's *Remorse* (Drury Lane, 1813), Byron's *Manfred* (1817), and Shelley's *The Cenci* (1819). Beyond Baillie, we find a number of women writers engaged with the Gothic drama, as John Franceschina has noted, with plays ranging from early dramas by More and Cowley through Sophia Lee's *Almeyda, Queen of Granada* (Drury Lane, 1796) or Harriet Lee's *The Mysterious Marriage* (1798) to Jane Scott's *The Old Oak Chest* (Sans Pareil, 1816). The Gothic remained the dominant form of serious popular drama until the rise of the domestic melodrama in the 1820s.[5]

The Gothic drama's power on stage was not, of course, wholly dependent upon the popularity of the Gothic novel in the closet. The Gothic drama worked because it was able to harness a variety of powerful theatrical forces. In a period when there were few successful new tragedies and when those that gained some critical and popular success (such as More's *Percy*, Baillie's *De Montfort*, and Coleridge's *Remorse*) were arguably Gothic, the Gothic drama provided audiences with a vital new form of serious drama. It may be hard for us to see today that these plays – beyond constant allusions to Shakespeare, as in Boaden's echoes in *Fountainville Forest* from *Hamlet* and *Romeo and Juliet* – seem to reach back beyond the neoclassical drama to the great plays of the Elizabethan and Jacobean period. The Gothic drama, as we will see, was also identified with the "German" drama, that is with the importation of the new drama being forged by Goethe and Schiller but most fully identified at the time with August von Kotzebue. The Gothic drama, then, not only had roots in the "old English drama" but also in the newest dramatic innovations. It was also able to absorb new theatrical techniques that were arising within the increasingly sizeable London theatres. As the two major theatres in London, Covent Garden and Drury Lane, sought to fill their cavernous halls and to cope with increasing competition from the so-called "minor" theatres – appealing as they did to a changing, broader audience – playwrights and theatre managers turned to spectacle, music, and special effects. The Gothic theatre of shock and wonder was arguably the first form to capitalize fully on evolving lighting techniques, new stage effects, and the increasing presence of continuous music behind the action. The extremely powerful and popular apparitions in Boaden's *Fountainville Forest* and Lewis's *Castle Spectre*, the secret chamber with its moving skeleton in Colman's *Blue-Beard*, and the appearance of Sangrida in a chariot pulled by dragons in Lewis's *Wood Daemon* all indicate how the Gothic drama matched perfectly with the theatrical tastes and techniques of the 1790s and beyond.

While there is greater variety to these plays than is sometimes allowed, they can be examined as a body of drama, since they often do rely upon standard settings and situations. Time and again, we find ourselves in a forbidding castle (James Cobb's *The Haunted Tower* [Drury Lane, 1789], Thomas Sedwick Whalley's *The Castle of Montval* [Drury Lane, 1799]); a decaying convent (William Pearce's *Netley Abbey* [Covent Garden, 1794], J. C. Cross's *Julia of Louvain; or, Monkish Cruelty* [Royal Circus, 1797], Lewis's *Venoni; or, The Novice of St. Mark's* [Drury Lane, 1808]); or a dark forest or cave (the anonymous *Mystic Cavern* [Norwich, 1803], Dimond's *Foundling of the Forest* [Haymarket, 1809]). These sites are peopled by gloomy aristocrats, harried young lovers, and comic servants who often hold the key (literally and figuratively) to the lovers' escape and happiness. Play after play traces a movement from an enclosed, prison-like structure dominated by an evil aristocrat to an open space where the lovers can be united and the crimes of their oppressors revealed. Some plays – Lewis's *The Castle Spectre*, for example – focus on the struggle of the tyrannical yet charismatic aristocrat to maintain his power and position and thereby move toward the tragedy of a titanic figure later known as the Byronic hero. Others – Boaden's *Fountainville Forest*, for instance – are more concerned with the oppressed lovers and thus follow an ultimately comic movement toward marriage. However, most of these plays include both tragedy and comedy and thus offer a mixed form of the drama that offended those who liked their dramatic genres "pure." Since these plays also merged music and spectacle with the spoken word, they were seen by theatrical commentators such as John Genest as a "jumble of Tragedy, Comedy and Opera."[6] The Gothic drama, trailing its debts to the novel, to other literary forms, and to developing tactics of stage sensationalism, was seen as an impure generic hybrid, a kind of monstrous form oddly appropriate to the chamber of horrors it displayed on stage.

It was also a form that seemed to engage – sometimes directly, more often indirectly – the turmoil of the days of the French Revolution and Napoleon. It is perhaps difficult for us today to understand how thoroughly the revolution penetrated society and culture. Of course, the revolution itself attempted to remake the world entirely, not only in overturning the old political order by eliminating aristocrat privilege, executing the king, and disestablishing the Church, but also by remaking daily life through such devices as a new calendar, new civic celebrations, and new fashions. England obviously experienced these events at a remove, but not at a great one. Aristocratic French exiles filled British parlors. Supporters and opponents of the revolution argued their positions strenuously, most famously in the war of words around Edmund Burke's *Reflections on the Revolution in France* that brought many responses including key ones by Thomas Paine and Mary Wollstonecraft.

Images of the French Revolution flooded English material culture; one could raise a toast in pro- and anti-revolutionary mugs, sport medallions displaying political allegiance, or enjoy the powerful political prints of the day. More importantly, of course, England would enter into a more than two-decade-long war with revolutionary France which left no family, no life untouched.

The stage could not remain apart from these compelling, contested events. It may seem paradoxical, but the Gothic drama, so clearly a form of fantasy, was a major popular form for representing on stage the ideological struggles of the day. This is not a simple case of literature reflecting reality. The Gothic predates the grand and terrible days of the revolutionary era, and in a sense it provided in advance images and narratives that could be used to understand revolutionary events while the revolution itself provided a new ideological charge to Gothic devices. If Gothic drama re-presents the events and is-sues of the French Revolution, the popular construction of the revolution itself seemed at times to move to Gothic rhythms. When one reads accounts of the liberation of the Bastille, for example, one enters a Gothic world of dungeons, torture, and miraculous liberation, particularly in the tales of such fictitious long-suffering prisoners as the Comte de Lorges, celebrated by 1803 as though he were real in Madame Tussaud's London waxworks. Revolutionary plays staged in Paris such as Sylvain Maréchal's *Le Jugement dernier des rois* (1793) or Jacques-Marie Boutet Monvel's *Les Victimes Cloitrées* (upon which Lewis drew) used Gothic motifs. As Mona Ozouf has shown, revolutionary civic fêtes staged a movement from the narrow, oppressive city spaces of a feudal past into large open spaces redefined by the revolution, a pattern that resonates strongly with the Gothic drama's depiction of the young lovers' escape from a Gothic castle.[7] The Gothic villain/hero, the charismatic yet terrifying figure at the heart of these plays, seems both to presage and to reflect the titanic figures of the revolutionary era, both the aristocrats of the *ancien régime* and such powerfully contro-versial revolutionary figures as Danton, Robespierre, and Napoleon. Images of sacked chateaus and liberated convents, of imprisoned aristocrats and the guillotine, and of old oppression, Terror and counter-terror both fed and were fed by the Gothic imagination.

The British Gothic could also be seen to engage home-grown political life: the necessarily furtive world of persecuted English "Jacobins" and their government pursuers, demonstrations in favor of reform and revolution, counteractions by proroyalist crowds, trials of London radicals, and the re-pression of Irish revolutionaries. Radical thought was not, of course, limited strictly to questions of the political order, and heated arguments over reli-gion, signaled for example in Paine's *Age of Reason* (1794–95), or about gender roles, set forth most famously in Wollstonecraft's *Vindication of the*

Rights of Woman (1792), would also have a place in the Gothic drama. Paula Backscheider has made an important argument that the Gothic drama responded to a specifically British crisis in political, cultural, and gendered social identities, and David Worrall has indicated how the Gothic drama is connected with the political concerns of an increasingly self-aware English plebeian culture.[8]

There is no simple ideological import that can be attached to the Gothic drama, however. Different authors could, of course, use the same devices to different ends. Some authors offer subtler reflections on the ideological struggles of the day. Some texts seem simply confused. The presence of a Licenser of Plays, always ready to strike out political allusions, made it difficult for these plays to offer direct commentary on events in France or at home. Although there were a number of plays that staged the fall of the Bastille in 1789, the censor moved rapidly to forbid such plays, and thus the Gothic drama's commentary on the revolutionary era was largely carried out through resonance and resemblance. Still, the Gothic drama's portrayal of a conflict between a tyrannical aristocrat and young lovers, often offered as being from the lower orders even if later discovered to be nobles in disguise, could not help but be seen as reflecting upon the revolutionary struggle. In an age of religious controversy, the Gothic's exploration of the supernatural could seem suspect. When women's rights were being urged with a new self-consciousness, the Gothic drama's exploration of gender battles and the darker side of the erotic could be seen as provocation. It was this subversive potential that would lead Coleridge to call the Gothic drama "the modern jacobinical drama" with its "confusion and subversion of the natural order of things" (*Biographia literaria*, II, 221). What was finally so compelling and threatening about the Gothic drama was that – despite the fact that most plays offer versions of revolutionary ideas that are tamed down by the author's own convictions, the threat of the censor, or simple aesthetic confusion – its grand theatrical gestures, its sensational theatre, and its very extremism put on stage the possibility that the world might be utterly transformed. Even when the vision offered at the end of the play is conventional, the Gothic drama still allowed a space within which political, religious, and gender hierarchies could be put into question. The Gothic drama was "jacobinical" or revolutionary in that it allowed into the closed world of traditional tragedy and the comedy of manners the possibility of a radically different order of things.

James Boaden provides a strong case for examining the way in which the Gothic drama was derived from a variety of sources to become an enormously powerful force on the stage of the 1790s and beyond, offering a key artistic response to a set of changing literary, theatrical, cultural, social, and ideological conditions. We find him adapting two Radcliffe novels and Lewis's *The Monk*. He draws upon Shakespeare and the "German" drama. His plays offer a wide variety of Gothic settings, plots, and characters. By looking at his plays, and particularly *Fountainville Forest*, we can get a good sense of what the Gothic became within the theatre, as it raised questions about politics, gender relations, and religion.

Boaden's *Fountainville Forest* simplifies Radcliffe's story in *The Romance of the Forest*. It stages the story of Lamotte, a nobleman driven into exile and crime by his gambling debts, who rescues a beautiful young woman, Adeline, and takes her to his hiding place in a ruined abbey. When the local marquis identifies Lamotte as the perpetrator of an attempted robbery, the lustful lord convinces Lamotte to help him to win Adeline in exchange for freedom and promised support. However, we learn that Adeline is, in fact, the daughter of the Marquis's assassinated brother. At the moment when the Marquis is about to imprison Lamotte and kill Adeline, Lamotte's son Louis, who is also in love with Adeline, arrives from Paris – in a kind of judicial *deus ex machina* – with a witness to the Marquis's designs and a lawyer, Nemours. The Marquis stabs himself, Lamotte is freed, and Adeline and Louis live happily ever after. This fairly conventional Gothic plot of virtue in distress, of robbers and evil nobleman, is played out in appropriate settings, a dark forest and an abbey, "the whole much dilapidated," which includes "A Gothic Hall" (I, i).

The most striking and controversial change Boaden made to Radcliffe's novel was to make her ghost, which she eventually explained away as she always does, into a real presence on stage. In his *Life of John Phillip Kemble* (hereafter *Kemble*), Boaden explains why he chose to incarnate his ghost. He grants that in Radcliffe's romances "the sportive resolution of all that had excited terror into very common natural appearances" pleases, but he argues that the case is different in the drama: "While *description* only fixes the inclusive dreams of the fancy, she may partake the dubious character of her inspirer; but the pen of the dramatic poet must turn everything into shape, and bestow on these 'airy nothings a local habitation and a name.' "[9] The Gothic novel from Radcliffe to Henry James and beyond invites us to explore and to enjoy the terrors of the mind, repeated turns of the psychological screw, as the supernatural is seen as most likely a projection of an unbalanced psyche. In the theatre, however, Boaden argues that the audience demands clarity: the playwright must either follow Shakespeare's *Hamlet* in making the ghost real or, as Boaden does in his adaptation of Lewis's *The Monk*, eschew the supernatural. While the Gothic drama thus loses the psychological subtlety of the novel, the debate over whether or not to put a specter on stage indicates that the supernatural in the theatre carried an important ideological charge.

Boaden, over the protests of the theatre's managers and the later objections of some reviewers, insisted that *Fountainville Forest* needed a ghost. The ghost appears in a scene taken from the novel where Adeline uncovers a hidden manuscript in a secret room in the abbey (the very scene that Jane Austen would parody in *Northanger Abbey*). Where Radcliffe uses this scene to demonstrate how the psychology of her character leads her to people her world with terrors, Boaden puts a terrifying specter on stage: we are frightened along with Adeline. Drawing upon Fuseli's painting of the ghost from *Hamlet*, Boaden had a pantomime actor portray the ghost behind a "blueish-grey gauze, so as to remove the too corporeal effect of a 'live actor,' and convert the moving substance into a gliding essence" (*Kemble*, II, 117). Boaden had correctly gauged the effect.

> The whisper of the house, as he [the specter] was about to enter, – the breathless silence, while he floated along like a shadow, – proved to me, that I had achieved the great desideratum; and the often-renewed plaudits, when the curtain fell, told me that the audience had enjoyed "That sacred terror, that severe delight," for which alone it is excusable to overpass the ordinary limits of nature.
>
> (*Kemble*, II, 119, misquoting Jones Thomson's *Seasons*)

This was a key moment in the development of the Gothic drama, for it demonstrated, against repeated complaints inside and outside the theatre, that audiences would respond to the presentation of the supernatural on stage.[10] It indicated that, in the theatre, shock – the Burkean "severe delight" of "terror" – granted great power to the Gothic.

Yet ghostly apparitions as such were rare enough to be famous, as in the case of the ghost in Lewis's *Castle Spectre* or the elaborate horror chamber in Colman's orientalist Gothic play, *Blue-Beard*. More typical was Siddons's *Sicilian Romance; or, The Apparition of the Cliffs*, where we discover that the "phantom" is in fact an imprisoned woman, or the production of Maturin's *Bertram* where, at the insistence of Sir Walter Scott, Maturin agreed to delete the figure of the Dark Knight of the Forest, a sinister figure, perhaps the devil himself. There was a general sense, enforced by the government's Licenser of Plays, who attempted to banish all religious references, that there was something bordering on the sacrilegious in putting "spirits" on stage.

Supernatural presences posed a particular problem, for if they were explained away, one could ask whether similar explanations might be found for the supernatural aspects of religion itself. If the ghostly, the demonic, and the uncanny were left to stand unchallenged, however, it might seem as if there were supernatural forces uncontained by the providential vision of traditional religion, particularly when Lewis, for example, offers a syncretic vision that joins together the supernatural forces of Christianity, classical paganism, and folklore. Staged during a period which saw the French Revolution's disestablishment of the national church and the publication of Paine's *Age of Reason*, when images such as Fuseli's *Nightmare* troubled the imagination and texts ranging from Blake's prophecies to Sir William Jones's translations of Sanskrit offered quite exotic versions of the numinous, these plays had the ability to unsettle, perhaps even to challenge, accepted conventional religious notions. The government's censor and censorious critics were therefore quick to criticize any play that dared dramatize the supernatural. We can see the increasing impact of such restraints when Boaden, who would again use a ghost in his *Cambro-Britons* (Haymarket, 1798), came to stage Lewis's *The Monk*: he eliminated all of Lewis's macabre and demonic machinery and thus considerably weakened his play. Ironically, he still did not evade religious controversy. As the composer Michael Kelly noted of the play's impressive ecclesiastical sets, "many thought it indecorous to represent a church on the stage." Boaden himself, who praises Kemble's portrayal of "Aurelio" (the renamed Ambrosio) as a masterful representation of a religious man torn by passion, tells us that the Duke of Leeds "avowed that his *religious feelings* hardly allowed him to tolerate the powerful effects, which he saw produced upon the stage."[11] Simply seeing a man of religion or the trappings of religious institutions on stage was enough to disturb the audience. It is as if there were a concern that the staginess of the theatre would wear off on the performances of religious practice and thus compromise their power.

The radical potential of Gothic conventions went beyond the staging of religion and the supernatural. The ideological charge of Boaden's *Fountainville Forest* – and by extension the Gothic drama as a whole – is signaled by its prologue,[12] which acknowledges that in 1794 one cannot avoid political allusion when the play, though "Caught from the Gothic treasure of Romance," "lays the scene in France":

> The word, I see, Alarms – it vibrates here,
> And Feeling marks its impulse with a tear.
> It brings to thought, a people once refin'd,
> Who led supreme the manners of mankind;
> Deprav'd by cruelty, by pride inflam'd,
> By traitors madden'd, and by sophists sham'd.
> Crushing that freedom, which, with gentle sway,
> Courted their revolution's infant day.

While in France "The regal source of order, once destroy'd, / Anarchy made the fair creation void," England is held up as a model of "temperate freedom" and "manly sentiment"; thus the stage should remain "Firm to your King, your Altars, and your Laws."[13]

Why would Boaden place such a clearly political prologue before his Gothic play, which is ostensibly a piece of pure entertainment? In part, he may have feared the censor's pen, since the Licenser of Plays tended to ban any play that referred to events in France, whether the play seemed to support or to oppose revolutionary principles. In part, he may have wanted to appeal to the patriotic sentiment of his audience in the early days of England's war with France, when the Terror had come to define the French Revolution which earlier, in its "infant day," had been celebrated by many in England, including Wordsworth, who famously found that "Bliss was it in that dawn to be alive, / But to be young was very Heaven!" (*Prelude* XI, 108–09).[14]

Beyond such matters, however, I think that Boaden recognized and wanted to contain the radical potential of his play and of the Gothic drama in general. If we look more closely at a number of features the play shares with other Gothic dramas we can begin to see how these plays could take on a radical charge. Boaden himself noted the connections between the revolution and the stage: "The present was the age of revolutions. The most surprising events had occurred on the stage of real life, and the mime world followed";[15] or, "The French Revolution had now opened upon the world in all its horrors; and the stage, 'which echoes but the public voice,' was now destined to rave about that cage of tyranny, the bastile [*sic*]" (*Kemble*, II, 11). Boaden knew that in the early days following the fall of the Bastille, the London theatres rushed to portray the exciting events in revolutionary Paris in plays such as John Dent's *Bastille* (Royal Circus, 1789), John St. John's *Island of St. Marguerite*, which tells the story of the Man in the Iron Mask (Drury Lane, 1789), and Charles Bonnor's *Picture of Paris in the Year 1790* (Covent Garden, 1790); these plays combined a spectacular representation of contemporary events with various Gothic situations and settings. As England turned against the revolution, though, it became increasingly difficult to get anything directly political on stage – as one author said of the theatre, "In that paradise ... politics [is] the forbidden fruit."[16] It was impossible to silence the resonances between Gothic structures and revolutionary events, however.

At its core *Fountainville Forest* contains a criticism of the *ancien régime* that fell with the French Revolution and that would be challenged in England as "Old Corruption." The villain of the piece is the local lord, the Marquis of Montault, who is willing to prey upon the impoverished Lamotte and the friendless and apparently lower-class Adeline. While Lamotte lives in a ruined Gothic abbey and speaks in the hyperbolic language of Gothic villain-heroes, his story of a fall from privilege to attempted villainy is grounded in economic fact, as he finds himself "sorely pinch'd / By poverty already" (I, I) and his home and goods seized by "legal harpies" (II, iv). Even the target of his robbery attempt, the Marquis, admits that "He look'd not like a common ruffian" and recognizes that he steals from economic necessity (I, ii). Adeline is also presented to us as a victim of a tyrannical regime. Before we learn of her own aristocratic heritage, we hear from her that she has been subjected to patriarchal oppression and placed within a convent. She has been designated for "the virgin veil, / And banish'd... for ever from the world" (II, i). She speaks especially of the miseries of this confinement.

> A convent is the scene of hopeless tears,
> Of heart-struck melancholy, dumb despair,
> Of visionary guilt and vain repentance,
> Incessant horrors, poor dissimulation.
>
> (II, i)

As in Boaden's other Radcliffe adaptation, *The Italian Monk*, as well as in any number of other Gothic plays such as Lewis's *Venoni; or the Novice of St. Mark's* and J. C. Cross's *Julia of Louvain; or, Monkish Cruelty*, convents are scenes of torture, imprisonment, and thinly veiled libertinism. With the young girl subjected to confinement in a convent, with Lamotte forced into a life of crime by poverty, with the villain an evil aristocrat, *Fountainville Forest* seems to offer a summary picture of the corruption of the old institutions of church, state, and class. The *ancien régime* is also summed up in the image of the ruined abbey (which, of course, should not be in ruins in the beginning of the fifteenth century, when the play is supposedly set), which seems poised to fall completely apart as a turret falls in the midst of a thunderstorm (IV, i). The aristocratic status of villainy is underlined by who opposes it: justice is achieved at the climax of the play not through divine intervention, the assertion of kingly authority, or even the exercise of knightly arms, but through the intervention of a lawyer, Nemours, who is Lamotte's advocate.

The play offers a particularly telling attack upon gender discrimination. Not only is there the criticism of the enforced celibacy of the convent (again, echoed more strongly in Boaden's *Italian Monk* and his adaptation of *The Monk* as *Aurelio and Miranda*); the Marquis' libertinism is also exposed as all too typically aristocratic. He claims to want to court Adeline in an honorable fashion, but when she declines his advances, he makes it clear that he has other designs, that he wants her to join him in "scenes of gay, voluptuous love" (III, ii). He argues that she should trade her sexual favors for his financial ones, and, moreover, he contends that marriage embodies just such an arrangement: "Survey the world, / Its daily tribes of wedded sacrifices! / Most to supposed necessity give up / The boon withheld from humble, faithful love" (IV, iv). When her surrogate father, Lamotte, seems willing to betray her to the Marquis in order to win his own freedom, the Marquis' arguments seem to be born out. Finally, however, unable to woo her with his libertine doctrines, he threatens her with rape: "I would persuade by honourable means, / But once defied, may fall on lower forms" (IV, iv). As she pleads for mercy, he finds "How lovely is this terror!" (IV, iv) as he clearly gains a sadistic pleasure in her struggles.

The Marquis – like Don Giovanni pursuing the erotic within a decaying world or Sade's monstrous noblemen seeking their pleasures amidst Gothic horrors – comes to embody a power and a freedom available to the aristocrat at the very moment that the world of the aristocracy is about to come to an end. It is as if, with his world crumbling around him like the abbey that has long belonged to his family, he is able to unleash an energy – both charismatic and terrible – no longer constrained by any social controls. He has, as he tells Lamotte, "A mind superior to all common forms" (IV, v), and – like Oswald in Wordsworth's *Borderers* or Don Ordonio in Coleridge's *Remorse* (Drury Lane, 1813) or, more precisely, the Count in Shelley's *The Cenci* – this mental superiority and freedom gives him, he believes, the right to rape and to murder in order to get what he wants. Of course the Marquis is finally defeated, at which point he stabs himself; this decision to commit suicide rather than submit to public condemnation is, after all, another mark of the "superior mind" in Gothic plays. It is important that this aristocrat is defeated by the powerless and downtrodden. While there have been attempts from Burke to the right-wing opponents of US President Clinton to link the left's pursuit of liberty with libertinism, Boaden's play offers the libertine as a simultaneously fascinating and horrifying last gasp of the old world brought to an end through the efforts of an abandoned woman, an outcast family, their servant, and a trusty lawyer.

In his second adaptation of Radcliffe, *The Italian Monk*, Boaden offers a fuller portrait of the Gothic villain/hero and changes the novel's plot so as to emphasize a motif that would be central to the melodrama and would be named in the title of Coleridge's Gothic tragedy, *Remorse*. Schedoni is offered as a powerful figure in the play, sternly pious on the exterior and a torrent of passion within.

> Though I seem wedded to austerity,
> The iron scourge my exercise, my day
> Frozen by abstinence and hourly prayer,
> Yet, underneath this icy outside, glows
> As fierce a flame of masterless ambition,
> As e'er informed the conquerors of earth,
> And wither'd nations in its splendid course.
> (I, I)[17]

Having the potential to rule nations and "scorning vulgar modes of action" (II, I), he still finds himself acting upon a smaller stage, working to destroy Ellena and Vivaldi. These two young lovers are opposed by the latter's mother, the Marchioness, who through Schedoni has Ellena abducted and placed in a typically oppressive convent. When Vivaldi penetrates the convent, Ellena is removed to an assassin's hut. But the killer finds himself unable to harm the innocent girl, and when Schedoni enters her room to do the deed himself, he discovers that Ellena is in fact his daughter (in the novel, she is his niece). He is redeemed by familial feeling, and becomes the protector of Ellena and Vivaldi. However, they are all seized by the Inquisition, the lovers for their actions in the present, Schedoni for some ominous crime in the past. Vivaldi is informed by a mysterious monk that Schedoni has murdered his own wife. Not realizing that Schedoni is his beloved's father and his potential savior, Vivaldi is used by the monk to expose Schedoni. Schedoni – contending that "Your iron whips, your fires, your breaking wheels / Are Eden to the hell that burns within me" (III, v) – repents and confesses that he killed his wife in jealousy. The monk who has hounded Schedoni now admits that he was her lover, that she was innocent, and that she in fact still lives, having hidden in a convent all these years. Schedoni, transformed by remorse, is reunited with his wife and child, and the young lovers are allowed to marry.

We see again in this play how standard Gothic moments could touch upon radical issues. In Ellena's interview with the Abbess, the imprisoned young woman argues that there is "No passion better than the love of truth" and that "No one is born too low for justice, Madam. / The humble feel as do the proudly born." To this, the Abbess replies with horror, "What! Would you burst subordination's bounds, / And level all in foul equality?" (I, iii). Here, Ellena's revolt against familial oppression is linked to the larger issues of the age of Burke and Paine. Her demand that she be allowed to marry the man she loves, free from the constraints of class interest, is linked to the attempts to create a more equal society. However, such radical questioning of social and even providential order is limited here by the way in which the plot moves toward a melodramatic embrace of an ultimately conventional order. In the recreation of the family unit at the close of the play, as the villain is redeemed by remorse and reconciliation – rather than dying, like the Marquis in *Fountainville Forest*, through a prideful suicide – the play suggests that both the energy of the Gothic villain/hero and the calls for reform by his young opponents can be contained within traditional pieties and family values. It is neither titanic energy nor revolutionary reform that is needed here, but rather stronger family bonds that restrain energy and provide a cultural containment that, because the family is seen as part of the "natural" order, can resist even radical reform.

Yet Boaden's engagement with potentially subversive motifs does not stop here. While the *Italian Monk* stages the Inquisition, he takes up its German parallel – the *Vehmgericht* – in his *Secret Tribunal* (Covent Garden, 1795), and Worrall has shown how this secretive judicial body can be seen to comment on Pitt's efforts to suppress English political dissent in the years following the French Revolution.[18] Moreover, in turning to a German model (Christiane B. E. Naubert's *Hermann von Unna* of 1778), Boaden also engages the then controversial drama of "foreigners." The Gothic drama of the 1790s becomes conflated with the imported German drama of the *Sturm und Drang* in order to decry it as, in Gamer's words, "culturally invasive, morally corrupting, and politically jacobin" (*Romanticism and the Gothic*, p. 145); as we have seen, Coleridge would go so far in the *Biographia Literaria* as to relabel the German theatre as the "modern jacobinical drama."

The antipathy that the Gothic/German drama raised in conservative critics is most strikingly revealed in the great satire on the "jacobinical" drama published in the *Anti-Jacobin* in June 1798, *The Rovers; or, The Double Arrangement* (this parody would be staged at the Haymarket in 1811 by George Colman as *The Quadrupeds of Quedlinburgh; or, The Rovers of Weimar*, when it would also attack the use of horses on stage in Lewis's Gothic *Timour the Tartar* [Covent Garden, 1811]). The preface to the play, offered by a fictitious Jacobin playwright, sees the German/Gothic drama embracing a new "SYSTEM comprehending not Politics only, and Religion, but Morals and Manners, and generally whatever goes to the composition or holding together of Human Society; in all of which a total change and Revolution is absolutely necessary" (p. 236). The prologue, noting that the play has "borrow'd from the GERMAN Schools," ironically celebrates the Gothic/German as espousing libertinism with liberty. The plot of the satiric play resembles *The Italian Monk* with the genders reversed, for it tells the story of "Rogero," who has been imprisoned in an abbey by his father for loving a woman beneath his station. The description of his dungeon is a satire on Gothic effects.

> SCENE changes to a Subterranean Vault in the Abbey of QUEDLINBURGH; with Coffins, Scutcheons, Death's Heads and Cross-bones. – Toads, and other loathsome Reptiles are seen traversing the obscurer parts of the Stage. – ROGERO appears, in chains, in a suit of rusty Armour, with his beard grown, and a Cap of grotesque form upon his head. – Beside him a Crock, or Pitcher, supposed to contain his daily allowance of sustenance. – A long silence, during which the wind is heard through the Caverns. (p. 238)

The play suggests that the Gothic would be silly if it were not for the Jacobin sentiments that lie behind it. William Cobbett in the *Baviad* summed up the attack upon playwrights who have "their gothic hands on social quiet laid, / And, as they rave, unmindful of the storm, / Call lust refinement, anarchy reform."[19] Conservative critics were adamant about the fact that the Gothic/German drama was not entertainment but subversive propaganda.

In some ways *Fountainville Forest*, with its ghost and its portrayal of a corrupt aristocratic order, had more radical potential than Boaden's later Gothic plays, written for a nation and particularly a government increasingly hostile to what was transpiring in France. We can, in particular, see Boaden moving away from his strong critique of gender relations as his audience is shaped by the backlash against the work of Wollstonecraft and other women writers and particularly against the publication by Godwin of *Memoirs of the Author of a Vindication of the Rights of Women* in 1798, the same year as Boaden's much tamer *Aurelio and Miranda*. With Godwin revealing the fact that the most famous advocate of women's rights had taken several lovers and contemplated suicide, with a backlash growing against women writers in such works as Richard Polwhele's *The Unsex'd Females* (1798) and Thomas James Mathias's *The Shade of Alexander Pope on the Banks of the Thames* (1799), which attacks female writers who "*forget the character* and delicacy of their sex" to take up the "trumpet of democracy, and let loose the spirit of gross licentiousness" (pp. 51–52), and with many women writers – including Radcliffe herself – falling silent or disguising their positions, the Gothic drama, already a suspect form, came under increasing attack. For example, Lewis had to defend his *Castle Spectre*, which opened in December 1797 and ran well into 1798, from charges that the "language was originally extremely licentious" and "that the sentiments were violently democratic."[20]

Of course, the protests against the *Castle Spectre* were nothing compared to the firestorm of criticism that raged over the publication of Lewis's *The Monk* in 1796, which struck conservative reviewers as proof that the Gothic was blasphemous, licentious, and ideologically suspect. In the "Advertisement" to *Aurelio and Miranda*, Boaden indicates that he has undertaken his adaptation of *The Monk* without wishing to enter "into the discussion which that work has produced" and that he hopes to dramatize the tale "without recourse to supernatural agency." This turn from the controversy that surrounded Lewis's novel and from the supernatural that Boaden had introduced into *Fountainville Forest* reflects the changed and charged atmosphere surrounding the Gothic drama in the last years of the 1790s. The result is very much a tamed down version of Lewis's novel, with specters and demons removed, with the extreme sexuality of the romance almost completely eradicated, and with the villain/hero Ambrosio transformed into the sentimental hero Aurelio. In the end, rather than incest and murder, a storming of the convent, and Ambrosio's death at the hands of the devil, we have multiple sets of lovers united, as those who have liberated Agnes from the convent's dungeons rush off to rescue the convent itself from rioters. The political charge of the Gothic is evaded here, and there seems to be a desire also to deny its erotic charge as well, which *The Monk*, or Charlotte Dacre's *Zafloya*, or the quasi-Gothic works of the Marquis de Sade seem to celebrate to subversive ends.

The Gothic drama could, of course, remain a vehicle for a variety of protests. Joanna Baillie's Gothic-inflected plays such as *De Montfort* and *Orra* can be seen to provide a critique of the standard roles of women, and John Franceschina has argued that Elizabeth Polack's *St. Clair of the Isles* does something similar as late as 1838, when it substitutes a controlling villainess for the conventional villain. Byron's *Manfred* continued the Gothic's controversial exploration of man's relation to the divine, while Shelley's *The Cenci* turned to the Gothic and its Jacobean precursors to offer a comprehensive assault upon patriarchal power within the family, state, and religion. In Maturin's *Bertram* we still face a Napoleon-like figure who appears to escape moral codes in the pursuit of his own sense of himself. There is a moment in post-Waterloo London, following the success of Coleridge's Gothicized *Remorse* and Maturin's play, when the Gothic seems to offer a vehicle for Romanticism to offer a new brand of tragedy, an effort to which Robert Lalor Sheil (*The Apostate* [Covent Garden, 1817] or *Evadne* [Covent Garden, 1819]) and Henry Hart Milman (*Fazio* [Covent Garden, 1818]) as well as Byron, Shelley, and Keats (*Otho the Great*) contributed.

Still, the development of the Gothic has less to do with this turn to tragedy than it does with the success of a theatre of sensation and the rise of the melodrama, as we can see in the careers of two key Gothic dramatists of the early nineteenth century, Matthew Lewis and William Dimond. While Matthew Lewis also attempted to convert the Gothic into tragedy in his *Alfonso, King of Castile* and *Adelgitha*, his most successful plays are notable largely for their stage effects: the ghost in the *Castle Spectre*, the dream sequence in *Adelmorn the Outlaw*, the masque in *Rugantino*, and the "Necromantic Cavern" in *The Wood Daemon* complete with an altar sporting two snakes that spew blue fire and ultimately twist around the villain as the whole scene sinks before our sight. Matthew Lewis is the key example of a playwright with serious intentions who is willing to make full use of a new theatre of sound and sight, where one needed a genius for special effects more than for poetic ones. In many ways he dominated the theatre of the first decade of the nineteenth century – with roughly a play a year – and he did so by combining tried Gothic devices with new stage tricks.

However, Lewis's style of the Gothic – filled with supernatural forces, charismatic aristocrats, sublime scenes, and grand gestures – began to fade before another linked dramatic form, the domestic melodrama. We see in the plays of William Dimond how the Gothic drama was slowly displaced by this tamer form, with which it shared certain stage techniques and plot devices. In Dimond's plays, Gothic mysteries resolve into misunderstood familial relations. Dimond repeatedly returns to the question of paternity announced in the title of his 1810 play at the Haymarket, *The Doubtful Son; or, Secrets of a Palace*. In this drama, Malvogli, marked by Gothic "mystery and disguise" (I, i), tricks the wife of a marquis into revealing that she had been secretly married before and had a child. Just as Malvogli's plots to alienate husband and wife, disinherit the son, and win money and a bride for himself are about to succeed, a terrifying stranger – he "looks like nothing human – his sallow bloodless cheeks, his large eyes that scowl and glare beneath his pent house brows, and then his voice like thunder; ah! Such a monster!" (IV, i) – reveals that Malvogli has been involved in past crimes, and he is arrested as a common criminal. The audience is treated to Gothic language and devices, but the action centers around marital deceit and jealousy. The play is resolved as the family comes together and the play's central values are celebrated: "a family united with itself – whole happiness is founded upon mutual confidence, and cemented by reciprocal esteem" (V, i).

Dimond returned again and again to issues of paternity and a resolution embracing family values. His Gothicized *Adrian and Orilla; or, A Mother's Vengeance* (Covent Garden, 1806) hinges upon the fact that Matilda, who has lost her illegitimate child by the Prince of Altenburg, has stolen and raised his legitimate son, Adrian; when Matilda reveals herself and her secret, the Prince forgives her and agrees to marry her – "next a husband's heart, be folded, and absolved for ever" (V, i). Dimond's most successful play, *The Foundling of the Forest* (Haymarket, 1809) – set in a dark forest reminiscent of Boaden's *Fountainville Forest*, illuminated by lightning and the haunt of bravos – again centers around confused parentage and ends with a celebration of the "haven of domestic peace" (III, iv). Even the later *Bride of Abydos* (Drury Lane, 1818), adapted from Byron, concerns a son seized and raised by his father's enemy. While this recurrent theme of the lost son might suggest an obsessive interest on Dimond's part, it also points to the fact that the Gothic drama repeatedly turned to issues of family relations, paternity, and possible incest. When this central plot was finally stripped of the powerful gestures that marked the Gothic – its invocation and question-ing of supernatural presences, its engagement with extreme human acts, its resonance with revolutionary history – what remained would become the domestic melodrama.

As the domestic melodrama came to displace the Gothic drama in the theatre, the stage version of the Gothic would develop in a different direction: the monster story. There are vampire references in a number of Gothic plays, but the first play devoted to this enduring figure is Planché's *Vampyre* at the English Opera House in 1820. *Frankenstein* was staged at the same theatre in 1823 as *Presumption; or, The Fate of Frankenstein* by Richard Brinsley Peake. As the many stage and film versions featuring these figures that followed suggest, the Gothic drama thus survived most clearly as the horror story, filled with monsters that combine features from different levels of existence. In such stories, the titanic struggles of the Gothic hero/villain are redefined as monstrous, concerns with providential order are replaced with worries over science and technology, and the possibility of a radical reordering of the world raised in earlier plays is displaced by a fortuitous turn from the monstrous to the domestic. It is in stage versions of *Dracula* or *The Phantom of the Opera*[21] that the Gothic drama continues to exert an influence in the theatre. While the Gothic drama has thus continued to draw upon the novel and to explore sensational effects – think of the moment when the chandelier swings forward in Andrew Lloyd Webber's *Phantom*, for example, or that play's underground boat scene – whatever cultural power it now possesses is drawn from the issues and struggles of quite different times from those when the Gothic drama dominated the English and European stage.

NOTES

1 Northrop Frye, *Anatomy of Criticism* (Princeton: Princeton University Press, 1957), p. 186.

2 As early as Elizabeth Inchbald's 1808 preface to Colman's adaptation of Godwin's *Caleb Williams* we find critics labeling the Gothic drama as "vain imitation"; see Philip Cox, *Reading Adaptations: Novels and Verse Narratives on the Stage, 1790–1840* (Manchester: Manchester University Press, 2000), pp. 25–27. As Michael Gamer notes, attacks on the Gothic drama "derive their metaphors and logic from the production processes that governed the gothic drama, whose productions of the 1790s were dominated not by original scripts but rather by adaptations from novels" (*Romanticism and the Gothic* [Cambridge: Cambridge University Press, 2000], p. 129).

3 *The Castles of Athlin and Dunbayne*: J. C. Cross, *Halloween; or, The Castles of Athline and Dunbayne* (Royal Circus, 1799); George Manners, *Edgar; or, Caledonian Feuds* (Covent Garden, 1806). *Sicilian Romance*: Henry Siddons, *Sicilian Romance; or, The Apparition of the Cliffs* (Covent Garden, 1794). *The Romance of the Forest*: James Boaden, *Fountainville Forest* (Covent Garden, 1794); *Fountainville Abbey; or, The Phantom of the Forest* (Surrey, 1824). *The Mysteries of Udolpho*: Miles Peter Andrews, *The Mysteries of the Castle* (Covent

Garden, 1795); John Baylis, *The Mysteries of Udolpho; or, The Phantom of the Castle* (1804); *The Castle of Udolpho* (1808). *The Italian:* Boaden, *The Italian Monk* (Haymarket, 1797). Mary Russell Mitford even dramatized Radcliffe's posthumous novel, *Gaston De Blondville*. See Bertrand Evans, *Gothic Drama from Walpole to Shelley* (Berkeley: University of California Press, 1947), p. 91.

4 See Paul Ranger, *"Terror and Pity Reign in Every Breast": Gothic Drama in the London Patent Theatres, 1750–1820* (London: Society for Theatre Research, 1991), pp. 175–79.

5 See Jeffrey Cox, ed., "Introduction" in *Seven Gothic Dramas, 1789–1825* (Columbus: Ohio State University Press, 1992) and "The Ideological Tack of Nautical Melodrama" in *Melodrama: the Cultural Emergence of a Genre*, ed. Michael Hays and Anastasia Nikolopoulou (New York: St. Martin's Press, 1996), pp. 167–89.

6 John Genest on *Kentish Barons* in *Some Account of the English Stage from the Restoration in 1660 to 1830* (1832; rpt. New York: Burt Franklin, 1965), VII, 38.

7 Mona Ozouf, *Festivals and the French Revolution*, trans. Alan Sheridan (Cambridge, MA: Harvard University Press, 1988).

8 See Paula Backscheider, "Gothic Drama and National Crisis" in *Spectacular Politics: Theatrical Power and Mass Culture in Early Modern England* (Baltimore: Johns Hopkins University Press, 1993), pp. 149–233, and David Worrall, "The Political Culture of Gothic Drama" in David Punter, ed., *A Companion to the Gothic* (Oxford: Blackwell, 2000), pp. 94–106.

9 James Boaden, *Memoirs of the Life of John Philip Kemble* (1824; rpt. New York: Benjamin Blom, 1969), II, 97, hereafter cited as *Kemble*. The "airy" allusion here is to Shakespeare's *A Midsummer Night's Dream* (v.i.17–18).

10 For an excellent discussion of the supernatural on stage, see Gamer, *Romanticism and the Gothic*, pp. 127–62.

11 Michael Kelly, *Reminiscences*, ed. Roger Fiske (Oxford: Oxford University Press, 1975), p. 252. The Duke of Leeds is quoted in *Kemble*, II, 230. Both comments are quoted by Steven Cohen, "Introduction" in *The Plays of James Boaden* (New York: Garland, 1980), p. xxxix.

12 It is important to remember that, in the theatre of the day, the play text did not stand alone. It was preceded by a prologue, followed by an epilogue, and was accompanied by music. Most importantly, each play formed part of an evening's entertainment with at least one other play. See Jeffrey Cox, "Spots of Time: the Structure of the Dramatic Evening in the Theater of Romanticism," *Texas Studies in Literature and Language* 41 (1999): 403–25.

13 Boaden, "Prologue," *Fountainville Forest* (London: Hookham and Carpenter, 1794), n. p.

14 I cite *The Prelude* from William Wordsworth, *Poetical Works,* ed. Thomas Hutchinson, revised Ernest de Selincourt (Oxford: Oxford University Press, 1936).

15 Boaden, *Memoirs of Mrs. Sarah Siddons* (1827; rpt. Philadelphia: Lippincott, 1893), p. 435.

16 "Postscript" to the anonymous *Helvetic Liberty: an Opera in Three Acts by a Kentish Bowman* (London: Wayland, 1792), p. vi.

17 Boaden, *The Italian Monk* (London: G. G. and J. Robinson, 1797).

18 See Worrall, "Political Culture," in Punter, *Companion*, pp. 96–97.

19 William Cobbett, *Baviad and Maeviad* (New York, 1789), p. x, quoted in Barry Sutcliffe, introduction to *Plays by George Coleman the Younger and Thomas Morton* (Cambridge: Cambridge University Press, 1983), p. 5.

20 Lewis's own words in his afterword to *The Castle Spectre* in Cox, *Seven Gothic Dramas*, pp. 221–22.

21 See the work of Jerrold E. Hogle in *The Undergrounds of **The Phantom of the Opera*** (New York: St. Martin's Press/Palgrave, 2002), especially chapter 7.

8

ALISON MILBANK

The Victorian Gothic in English novels and stories, 1830–1880

In the gray early morning of 20 June 1837 the young Princess Victoria left her bedroom in a tumbledown St. James's Palace, and with it the enclosure of her isolated youth under the authority of Sir John Conroy, to be greeted on bended knee by the Lord Chancellor and the Archbishop of Canterbury with the news of her accession to the throne. The Victorian age began like the ending of an Ann Radcliffe novel: the bad uncles and despotic guardian give way to the true heir, who is now able to preserve and defend her national inheritance. This moment seemed to fulfill the description of the British constitution by the jurist William Blackstone as "an old Gothic castle, erected in the days of chivalry, but fitted up for a modern inhabitant."[1]

In time the key elements of the Radcliffean Whig Gothic suggested in the above tableau – the politics of liberty and progressivism, freedom from the past, and the entrapped heroine – would indeed be revived in Gothic writing. But in the early years of Victoria's reign, that was not possible. To some extent this was because of the ambivalence of many social groups toward the institution of the monarchy and the gender of the new monarch, all during the 1840s. The influence of this view of the Queen upon the modes of political and literary sensibility during this time may seem surprising, but it can be amply demonstrated. While loyalists heralded the birth of another Elizabethan age of glory and national achievement, utilitarians questioned the relevance of such an irrational institution, and Chartists and moderates such as writers in *Punch* deprecated the cost of the royal family, as well as its isolation from social reality.[2] Victoria's gender and marriage to an unpopular foreign prince in 1840 compromised her legitimacy in the eyes of some, and this problem combined with working-class unrest and political agitation for representation. The upshot for the Gothic in the Victorian era was a bifurcation of the Radcliffe tradition: the trope of the liberated heroine became separated from the trope of release from the prison of the past, in a fashion that I shall now describe. This bifurcation took many different Victorian Gothic shapes, some of which strove to heal the breach, depending on the political and ideological stances of each author or group who took up the Gothic as a mode of writing.

In early Victorian Gothic the heroine who acts as a focus for social critique is lost in the world of her tale, and the liberation from the hold of the past is replaced in such works by a repositioning of the woman to fix her in an architectural and political space. From its beginning, the already Gothic historical novel had provided a means of national self-understanding – and indeed self-creation. In particular, Sir Walter Scott's repeated rehearsals of the shift from a Gothic Highland- or Border-primitive society to commercial capitalism legitimated the Hanoverian dynasty by Gothicizing that transition as the emergence of the modern. His emphasis on usurpation and the disputed succession in the period of the Jacobite Rebellions and earlier periods in *Waverley* (1814), *Rob Roy* (1817), and less politically in *Guy Mannering* (1815) influenced the later romantic fiction of William IV's historiographer, G. P. R. James. The subject of debated succession to the throne dominates his tales of France and England during the sixteenth and seventeenth centuries. In *Darnley* (1830) and *Arabella Stuart* (1844),[3] James writes in a Gothic vein of the incarceration and tragic lives of two female claimants to the British throne. The tragic romance mode serves to legitimize the line that leads to Victoria and turns political opposition into a plot calling for sympathy and pity. However, the trope of liberation from the past is separated from the heroine, who is left imprisoned by her fate (like Victoria?), as Radcliffe heroines are not.

William Harrison Ainsworth, an immensely popular writer during the 1830s and 1840s, was drawn to the same period as James, but with directly Gothic interests both in ancient structures and instruments of oppression. His treatment of the title characters in *The Lancashire Witches* (1848) is sympathetic, but the story is only Gothic insofar as it delineates an oppressive social system haunting the characters. More consciously Gothic in treatment are his three Tudor novels, *The Tower of London* (1840), *Guy Fawkes* (1841), and *Windsor Castle* (1843). *Guy Fawkes* contains supernatural visions; the Tower is constructed of a dizzying succession of trapdoors to yet more secret dungeons, with a variety of demonic jailers; and the ancient oaks of Windsor Great Park contain the headquarters of a monarch to rival Henry VIII in the supernatural figure of Herne the Hunter. This pagan anomaly holds court in a series of underground caves and spites Henry at every turn: "You are lord of the castle, but I am lord of the forest" (*Windsor Castle*, book 2, chapter 8).[4] Despite paeans of praise to Victoria's golden rule in *Windsor Castle*, all Ainsworth's novels imply that human power is contingent and unstable, in a manner appropriate to the "hungry forties" and the rise of Chartism. He plays upon the dual role of the Tower and of Windsor as royal palaces and as prisons: Lady Jane Grey enters the Tower in state at the beginning of volume I of *The Tower of London,* but she ultimately reenters it in volume II as a traitor. Similarly, Ann Boleyn enters Windsor in a cloth of gold as Henry's paramour but leaves it to be executed.

It is the buildings that endure in Ainsworth's fiction, and his lavishly illustrated *Tower of London* often shows a scene of Lady Jane Grey's cell, or the torture chamber, with a contrasting engraving of the same chamber in 1840, now furnished elegantly with sofas and a cheerful fire. Ultimately, one could use Ainsworth's novels as actual guidebooks to the relics of Britain's violent and contested past. That he also intended the reader to draw conclusions about the state of the nation from his contrasts is made plain in his conclusion to the historical survey of *Windsor Castle*: "the Horse-Shoe Cloisters consistently repaired, Windsor Castle would indeed be complete. And fervently do we hope that this desirable event may be identified with the reign of VICTORIA" (book 3, chapter 5). The use of capitals for the Queen's name serves to render it monumental and to include her within the fabric of the restored edifice, as victor over time and Gothic ruination. Only thus, by an organic assimilation to her country, will Victoria evade the supersessions of power. Here, the function of Ainsworth's topographical Gothic is revealed. In order for Victoria to gain legitimacy as both monarch and woman she must become one with Britain, culturally and naturally. However, with her being thus assimilated as a principle of continuity, there ends up being no space for the heroine apart from the structure, and no possibility for critique.

The Gothicizing of Victoria inaugurates the nineteenth century after 1837 as a "Gothic cusp." Robert Miles uses this phrase in his study of Ann Radcliffe to describe the Renaissance setting of much earlier Gothic writing, as poised between the feudalism of the Middle Ages and the Enlightenment (Miles, *Ann Radcliffe,* p. 5). In replaying the trauma of the Reformation from the perspective of a later parallel cultural revolution, the Gothic writers of the 1790s could narrate and thereby recuperate the crisis of their own time. The royal Gothic of the early Victorian era brings the setting of this genre to British shores, but in stressing legitimacy and continuity it loses the ability to narrate change. By contrast to this projection of the present upon the past, one novel feature of *later* Victorian Gothic is its contemporary and localized setting in the Britain of its own century. This shift does not mean that the reference to the past, and the "already having happened" character of the Gothic cusp, has simply disappeared. To the contrary, the Gothic mode remains itself by continuing to evoke the past, and so to clothe the contemporary in Gothic garb is to perpetrate an anachronism, deliberately or not. The point of this device for the novelist G. W. M. Reynolds – as for Charles Dickens – is to speak of the present as if it were already the vanquished past and hence of current tyrants as if they were as archaic as the old defeated ones. This lends a sense of inevitability to calls for social transformation. In such a way Reynolds moves from James and Ainsworth's Gothic of liberation to a new Gothic of subversion. However, the new subversive twist to the theme of liberation still leaves no place for Radcliffe's liberating heroine.

Reynolds was by far the most popular writer in the Gothic genre during the early Victorian period, apart from Dickens. A Chartist supporter, he was the scourge of the aristocracy, whose extreme wealth and irresponsibility he regarded as the direct cause of social misery and crime. His most influential production was *The Mysteries of London*, published in weekly installments from 1844 to 1856 at the cost of a penny each. Like eighteenth-century chap-books (many of which described the trial confessions of famous criminals), Reynolds's *Mysteries* reached working-class readers, whereupon the literate among them could read his salacious, violent, and cunningly plotted narratives to a wider illiterate audience. Reynolds was a shameless but creative plagiarist, who based his form on Eugène Sue's *Mysteries of Paris* (1844), but with significant differences. Sue's long tale does indeed wend its way through a labyrinth of threatening side streets, and his working-class heroine is revealed to be the long-lost daughter of an incognito prince, but generally Sue's treatment of Paris is neutrally realist, with the main emphasis on the protagonists. In contrast, Reynolds centers his vision Gothically, around buildings and institutions which are viewed as producing fear and embedding chains of secret connections. Like Ainsworth's, Reynolds's is a double London that hides underground passageways and secret hideaways behind bland façades.

One spectacular façade penetrated for future burglary is that of Buckingham Palace. Hidden under a sofa, the potboy Holford takes illicit peeps at the diamonds on Victoria's bosom and overhears her conversation. Visiting the empty throne room, he removes the velvet cloth that protects "the imperial seat," and "the splendours of the throne were revealed to him" (chapter 59).[5] The implication of a royal striptease is, perhaps, deliberate. Having penetrated the privacy of the queen in a manner analogous to Ambrosio's invasion of Antonia's apartments in M. G. Lewis's *The Monk*, the narrative proceeds to add to the delineation of Victoria as a Gothic heroine. First, her ignorance and seclusion are indicated, so that, immured in the luxury of her palace and surrounded by courtiers, she is unaware of the reality outside and the plight of the poor. Secondly, two ladies-in-waiting discuss her tainted inheritance of madness and scrofula from George III. On a second visit, Henry learns that she may not even be a legitimate claimant to the throne, since George III contracted a marriage with a commoner before a bigamous union with the Princess of Mecklenburgh. Reynolds employs Gothic here to render Victoria as either an imprisoned heroine or a usurper. His uncertainty mirrors the oscillation of opinion among radicals at the time, such as Thomas Cooper who in his *Purgatory of Suicides* of 1845 both "breathed devotion" at the sight of Victoria as a bride but also warned her of the fate of her executed predecessor, Charles I, if she remained "the dupe / Of tinseled traitors who would thee ensnare / To ease and grandeur" and ignored the poor.[6] The presence of Victoria as ruler thus explains, in part, the eclipse of the entrapped heroine: Victoria can *become* a heroine only if she undoes the entrapment of others.

Cooper, like Reynolds, emphasizes the enclosure, albeit luxurious, of the monarch, and the claustrophobic interior is also the central site of the urban historical fiction of the 1840s. Reynolds adds to the pleasurable prurience of his narrative by suggesting that its perusal is something of an ordeal in the manner of an actual mystery cult, such as that of Eleusis, at which neophytes were taken underground in a mock death before rising to see the unveiled goddess. In this cultic reading of London the city becomes emblematic of the national body of the goddess of truth (of which the queen is the representative) yet also a permeable, albeit enclosed, Gothic structure of imprisonment. In Reynolds's London even the sky, polluted by smog, offers no release but "an everlasting cloud." The trope of the Gothic prison has been extended to cover an entire social system, indeed a nation. C. R. Maturin had anticipated this move somewhat in *Melmoth the Wanderer* (1820), in which the centrality and reach of the Inquisition rendered Spanish society one unified system of oppression. However, although pointedly concerned with the Catholic and Calvinist forces in his own Irish situation, Maturin uses Ireland as a point of judgment as well as the origin for his damned protagonist, not as the scene of his demoniacal operations. A true moving of the Gothic into contemporary settings arrives only with Ainsworth and Reynolds. It is primarily Reynolds who provides the conditions for an indigenous Gothic site in nineteenth-century Britain, although Ainsworth had set the stage historically, not just by Gothicizing English history but by laying his stories almost totally within physical structures of containment. Through Ainsworth and Reynolds the Gothic becomes explicitly a *national* romance, and in the case of *The Mysteries of London* a democratic form that has central roles for the lower classes. It is up to the reader to decide the future: whether to turn to Victoria as Gothic heroine and the people's friend, or decry her as a new Gothic tyrant and call for republican liberation from monarchical tyranny. Here Gothic provides a form of revolutionary education, which can lead to readers either supporting or rejecting revolution itself.

Intriguingly enough, while the Radcliffean element of liberation from the past finds a voice in radical politics, the equally Radcliffean trope of the entrapped heroine migrates to the Tories. This is at a time when Conservatives like Disraeli in his novels *Coningsby* (1844) and *Sybil* (1845) were also trying to find a new social consensus and a way forward. However, since an understanding of national developments as organic, *à la* Edmund Burke, precludes organized change, a conservative Gothic eschews an extensive symbolization of Britain as the prison that one finds in more radical writers. Instead the short stories in the Conservative periodical *Blackwood's Magazine* display a new preoccupation with individual psychology. A significant proportion of these tales are Gothic in offering exotic locales in southern Europe in which dastardly and volatile feudal princes incarcerate their enemies, but others offer a recent British setting and provide the Gothic in their focus on crimes or duelling. In imitation of Maturin's novel of Irish nationalism, *The Milesian Chief*, "Castle Elmere: a Tale of Political Gratitude," published in 1834,[7] sets a typical Radcliffean heroine in contemporary Ireland, in which her traditional responses to the "sublime influences" of the darkening landscape are interrupted by Irish rebels. With the castle here safely associated with the political union of Ireland and Britain, the heroine as threatened heiress is foregrounded without the equally Radcliffean trope of the castle as her prison in the control of a usurper. Thus, the heroine and a local wise-woman are allied as representative of Irish tradition and natural order, which is opposed by Roman Catholicism and modern political insurgency, both conceived as foreign imports. Before the inherent contradictions of this Tory Gothic become too pressing, the tale ends, like Maturin's, with the self-sacrifice of the poor Irish hero to protect the castle and its British inhabitants.

It is such undercurrents that drive the short tale of individual incarceration that is popular in *Blackwood's* and confines its Gothic to a case of individual injustice rather than a broader Whig narrative of liberation and progress. Although the first person is rarely used, there is often an attempt to enter the consciousness of the protagonist and render his sufferings with psychological verisimilitude. In "The Iron Shroud" (1830),[8] Vivenzio knows from the outset that his jailer, Prince Tolfi of Sicily, intends his death. The narrative tension is engendered by the uncertainty, first over the method and then the manner of its execution. Every day Vivenzio notices one window fewer in his prison, until he realizes, "Yes, yes, *that* is to be my fate! Yon roof will descend! These walls will hem me round – and slowly, slowly, crush me in their iron arms." The bodily analogy is appropriate to the mechanism, since the outcome will be an exchange in which the iron walls of the room will substitute for Vivenzio's bed, his bier, his coffin, shroud, and even his skeleton itself, as that will be crushed to dust. Moreover, by anticipation, his mind itself collapses and enacts the death proleptically, becoming its own instrument of oppression. Indeed, in Edgar Allan Poe's version of this story,

"The Pit and the Pendulum" (which was probably influenced by it, since Poe was famously a *Blackwood's* reader), the dreaded horrors of either falling into the pit or being sliced by the descending pendulum are never realized, so that the terrors of anticipation constitute the whole narrative. This turn to the psychological is often hailed as an advance, whereby the unwieldy Gothic machinery of the previous century gives way to a more modern and sophisticated conception of a purely internal drama. However, it must be realized that the turn inwards here serves the project of a Tory rereading of a Whig literary form. It is an inherently conservative turn that avoids the radical implications of the full-length Gothic novel at the time and returns the setting to a safely distant continental arena.

One group of avid readers of *Blackwood's* who, nevertheless, created something radical with the Tory form were the young Brontës in their Yorkshire parsonage. The journal was their resource for history, exploration, and politics, as well as for fictional models, and the imaginary worlds of Gondal and Angria that occupied their youth are structured in its image. At a climactic point of Charlotte Brontë's *Jane Eyre* (1847), when the dominant and persuasive St. John Rivers seeks to impose his will on Jane, she reaches for the language of the *Blackwood's* tale to expresss the intensity of her feelings: "My iron shroud contracted round me; persuasion advanced with slow, sure step" (chapter 34). In this instance the Gothic machinery has, indeed, been internalized, and the threat is not just physical but one that threatens identity itself. However, *Jane Eyre* shows a range of Gothic influences apart from the *Blackwood's* tale which enable a more complete Gothic structure. As a conversation about Radcliffe's peregrinating heroines in chapter 30 of *Shirley* (1849) indicates,[9] Brontë associated female travel itself, as well as female flight, with Radcliffe, while her mad wife in the attic of Thornfield Hall owes something both to the blending of house and asylum in Maturin's *Melmoth the Wanderer* and to a short story by Sheridan Le Fanu, "A Chapter in the History of a Tyrone Family" (1839; see Le Fanu, *Best Ghost Stories*), from which she draws the imprisoned foreign first wife, as well as the veil and the mirror. The Radcliffean and Irish strains impose a more universalizing Gothic vision, which Brontë develops by means of a first-person female perspective. The deployment of full-blown Gothic form, I now want to argue, almost imperceptibly tilts the inherited Tory Gothic writing in a more radical direction.

Critics since Robert Heilman's 1958 article, "Charlotte Brontë's New Gothic," have read her employment of traditional Gothic tropes as metaphorical, particularly as an undercutting of the marvelous in the service of intensification of feeling. A similar interpretation of Gothic as an internal mode of expression for the marginal is given a feminist twist in Sandra Gilbert and Susan Gubar's influential study of nineteenth-century women writers, *The Madwoman in the Attic* (1979). As their title implies, they read the destructive rage of Bertha Rochester as emblematic of the female creative imagination, as well as female anger at patriarchal oppression. In an act of conscious myth-making, Gilbert and Gubar cast the woman writer and her protagonists in a double role as both the Romantic Promethean overreacher, such as Mary Shelley's Frankenstein, and equally his resentful and enraged victim, the creature. In such a model there is a presumed inner conflict between the creative conscious ego and the repressed unconscious.

These interpretations, however, do not do justice to the fact that the Brontës inherited an *already* psychologized Tory Gothic. What they added to this, in terms of genre, was, as we have seen, a *reinstatement* of the more concrete and social facets of the Gothic plot: the terrorizing system and the woman threatened by this system. Certainly there is also, in substantive terms, a deepening of the *Blackwood's* psychological interest. However, in Charlotte Brontë's fiction there is not just an interest in registering the mental effects of social repression, but an effort to escape the "iron shroud" of mental solipsism itself. Thus, for example, Jane Eyre's fearful and violent inner drama is put at the service of an epistemology, a means by which the world beyond the self might be known. An instance of this way of knowing can be found in the very first chapter of *Jane Eyre*, which opens with the child Jane secreted in a window seat reading Bewick's *History of British Birds*, with crimson curtains closed against discovery by her overbearing cousin, John. In imagination, she transforms the realism of the book's Arctic scenes of migrating birds into a Gothic mode, by concentrating her gaze upon a churchyard and reading two ships becalmed as "marine phantoms." Clearly the reddened, curved enclosure stands analogically for her brain and the Arctic scenes, the images that it projects in the manner of magic lantern slides. It also symbolizes Jane's isolation and orphaned status within Gateshead Hall, as well as her tendency toward reserve and privacy. However, in actively seeking enclosure and in her perverse misreading of the Bewick engravings, Jane precipitates Gothic fears quite deliberately, and externalizes and dramatizes her imaginative state, thereby forcing her (itself externally enforced) solipsistic confinement out into the open. Moreover, her chosen seclusion provokes John Reed's anger at her self-possession so that he attacks her, seizes the book, and incites his mother to lock her in a truly Gothic and haunted Red Room, untouched since the death of her uncle. Although Jane will suffer terribly from fear of the dead as a result of her action, it has served to confirm the reality of her mental self-image as an incarcerated victim and to reveal John Reed's character as that of a Gothic villain. So all goes round in a circle: Gothic incarceration engenders solipsistic isolation; but Gothic imagination, by enacting such incarceration differently, breaks out of the solipsistic circle, thereby rendering the imprisoned one a protagonist – even though this process precipitates a worse degree of oppression.

Therefore, in Charlotte Brontë's drive to find external verification for the implicitly feminist self-understanding of her protagonists, she returns to the Radcliffean synthesis of liberation, freedom from the past, and the critical role of the entrapped heroine. All Brontë heroines share an inner life of extraordinary drama, color, and intensity; but each seeks in her own way to connect inner and outer worlds by confirming the reality of her Gothic psychodrama, not merely, as Heilman argued, the intensity of her unmaidenly passions. In so doing, they reconnect the two Radcliffean Gothic modes: the individual suffering of the *Blackwood's* tale and the wider implicit social progressivism of the Whig Gothic. Within the Gothic circle just described, the social outsider and damned genius imposes her will by creative power on the world in a Byronic fashion, yet in so doing she provokes further repression and so retains the status of Gothic heroine. This circle accounts for Brontë's duality more accurately than Gilbert and Gubar's model does; the Byronic thrust produces a dramatization of repression, not totemic gesture, while the provocation of victimage is deliberate, and by no means unconscious. Gilbert and Gubar are indeed right to see that duality is shared by writer and heroine alike. But in the case of Charlotte Brontë as author, this duality concerns the "Gothic circle" and not a play between a would-be male active consciousness and a repressed female sense of victimization. For Brontë as author seeks to dramatize with Gothic metaphors a given social reality and through this artistic performance to expose social hypocrisy, even to provoke society into declaring its true nature. Thus, as Brontë indicated in her preface to the second edition of *Jane Eyre*, society "may hate him who dares to scrutinize and expose, to raise the gilding and show base metal under it, to penetrate the sepulchre and reveal charnel relics; but hate as it will, it is indebted to him." In *Udolpho*, Radcliffe's heroine discovered a corpse that proved to be only a wax image. For Brontë, the reality in the end is an actual corpse (the smashed Bertha Rochester). Reversing Heilman, one can say that Radcliffe had *already* undercut the marvelous in the interests of psychology; Brontë, by contrast, deploys a psychological theatre to disclose the marvel of horror *in* the real. This is not, however, anything like a deliberate strategy springing from a conscious radicalism. Instead, the very act of imagining a Gothic counterpart to real terror reveals the structural extent of that terror and inspires the will to escape it.

The need to activate the Gothic as a means of connecting the mind and the world becomes crucial to survival in Brontë's other Gothic masterpiece, *Villette* (1853). Self-deprecating, secretive Lucy Snowe makes her living in a Catholic boarding school in continental Labassecour. In Maturin fashion, Catholicism is here demystified as a system of surveillance, enacted here by the practical Madame Beck, who searches Lucy's belongings and maintains discipline in her school by an infantilizing indulgence. Sally Shuttleworth reads this surveillance both psychologically, as emblematic of new conceptions of the self constructed through the ordering of physiological pulsations and energies, and socially as "the ideal of [Jeremy] Bentham's panopticon, [a prison fully open to surveillance from nearly every angle above or outside it,] where inmates are trapped, isolated in their cells, subject always to the gaze of authority, without themselves being able to see."[10] This, she argues, "might describe the underlying nightmare of *Villette* from which Lucy is forever trying to escape." However, Lucy Snowe is oddly complacent about these intrusions into her personal effects. Partly this stems from her ironic awareness that Madame Beck has nothing to find, since Lucy's lack of beauty or wealth leaves her without any social value. But it may also point to Lucy's desire to connect her violent and agonistic inner life with some external validation of her existence, albeit a violent one. Lacking any social value that could make her worth confining, Lucy like Jane Eyre must first install herself inside a Gothic narrative in order, paradoxically, to be liberated from its controlling structures. Consequently, during the course of the novel she places herself deliberately in Gothic locales: a forbidden alley said to be haunted by a dead nun, the school attic, and even a Roman Catholic confessional box.

Arguments about *Villette*'s demystification of Gothic machinery depend upon the scene in which Lucy learns that the nun she had glimpsed in the attic and elsewhere was not supernatural, at which point she tears the religious habit to pieces. However, this is not to reject the Radcliffean Gothic but to mirror its explained supernatural, in order that the real, physical threat of the Gothic tyrant or religious system may be uncovered. The supernatural itself does not constitute the Gothic, but rather an awareness of the social order as coercive, spectral, and deathly. The nun's uncovering is the climax to an evening of Gothic initiation and social demystification in which the real threat to her union with M. Paul – the junta of Madame Beck, Madame Walravens, and Father Silas – is revealed. What is new about Charlotte Brontë's Gothic is not demystification but its seductive suggestion that *any* young woman of any class may activate the Gothic, and that it can provide a means of linking the ideal realm of thought with the social "real" through the full extension of the Gothic circle. In reassembling the Radcliffean synthesis, Brontë is led to reveal the fictive nature of the real itself in a way that finally does exceed Radcliffe's vision. Thus, there is no social reality beyond the Gothic in *Villette* that could render the Gothic machinery metaphorical in relation to it. Rather, the protagonist's haunted mind mimics the societal phantasmagoria; Brontë was not unusual in resorting to apocalypse as a response to the riots and unrest of the 1840s. However, the apocalyptic gesture of revelation provides the critical distance that allows the return of the demystifying perspective of the Radcliffean heroine. Thus, while Brontë restores the synthesis, she does so with a dialectical benefit achieved through the intensification of the psychological element. Brontë remained a conservative writer, but she was also constrained to some radicalism by the force of her Gothic imagination. At a conscious level, she seeks no more than to question social hypocrisy (in Byronic mode), not to propose social alternatives. A more radical restoration of the Radcliffean synthesis was attempted by Charles Dickens.

In *The Madwoman in the Attic* Gilbert and Gubar seek to extend the trope of the imprisoned Bertha Rochester to apply to women in general: "almost all nineteenth-century women were in some sense imprisoned in men's houses" (p. 83). Gothic and sensation fiction of the mid-century sought in various ways to register the psychic disturbance of the Victorian middle-class wife, who was confined to the domestic realm at the very time in which that locale ceased to be productive or economically active. It became instead a space to exhibit one's freedom from market forces. Thus, the very circumstances that encouraged female psychological introspection were also those that opened up a critical perspective on social and gender roles in the construction of the trapped woman as one focus of a new generation of fictions. Attempts to explore the flight of the dissatisfied woman in realist novels, such as Flaubert's *Madame Bovary* (imitated by sensation writer Mary Elizabeth Braddon's *The Doctor's Wife*) or Tolstoy's *Anna Karenina*, involved adultery as the marker for transformation and lead almost invariably to failure and death. Paradoxically, it was that promoter of domesticity, Charles Dickens, who was able to conceive a more substantial engagement with contemporary female incarceration and to do so in a Gothic mode. Dickens linked a Whig radicalism about removing social abuses, alongside a progressivist impatience with the entrenched privilege that holds back national development, with a more Conservative anxiety about collectivist solutions and, indeed, group activity of any kind. Thus, he was in a unique position to recombine the Tory Gothic heroine of continuity with the Whig heroine who escapes diachronic and synchronic imprisonment.

From the beginning Dickens's writing is replete with an amazing range of demonic and exciting Gothic villains – so much so that he was accused after the flamboyant Fagin in *Oliver Twist* (1837–38) of glamorizing crime.[11] In that novel the Gothic victim, Oliver, is set in all his pristine innocence as a contrast and a judge of the people and institutions that attempt to corrupt or enclose him: the workhouse and its greedy administrators, the undertaker's shop, the thieves' kitchen, and so on. Yet he only reveals what is already the moral character of those he meets: he effects no change. In *The Old Curiosity Shop* (1840–41), Dickens follows the same procedure of contrasting the child with a range of grotesque companions, but by placing a young *girl* in a setting of an *embalmed past* he imports expectations that equate escape with movement forward in time and the possibility of social change accompanying her rescue and maturation. In a novel that combines fairy-tale, comedy, melodrama, religious allegory and social comment, the Gothic is the motor that truly drives the action. The novel opens with the narrator discomforted and uneasy at the child's musty environment:

> I had ever before me the old dark murky rooms – the gaunt suits of mail with their ghastly silent air – the faces all awry, grinning from wood and stone – the dust and rust, and worm that lives in wood – and alone in the midst of this lumber and decay, and ugly age, the beautiful child in her gentle slumber, smiling through her light and sunny dreams. (*Old Curiosity Shop*, chapter 1)

In the curiosity shop the past is carefully preserved in all its authentic decay. Objects from different periods enjoy a threatening simultaneity, which this passage expresses by repeated connectives and phrases enclosed by hyphens. Although the child sleeps peacefully among objects that would terrorize most children, this is itself disquieting, since it allows no possibility of escape. Indeed, one of the most disturbing aspects of *The Old Curiosity Shop* is its utter inability to imagine any way in which its angelic heroine may be released from the tentacles of a deathly embalmed past, although she evades the sexual threat of the dwarfish villain, Quilp, easily enough. The scene of Nell asleep in chapter 1 is mimicked by her deathbed appearance at the end of the novel. In the illustration of that famous moment, the headboard of her bed takes the form of a medieval stone-carving, as she lies in her portion of a ruined former abbey, next to the graveyard. The Gothic arched window is open to express the departure of her soul.

Despite her journey through the breadth of England, both industrial and rural, there has been no real possibility of a home or settled work and no suggestion of a future. Rather, her death is implicit from the beginning and suggests the impossibility of society to offer her real progress. Instead, it is her death that is effectual for social regeneration and makes "a hundred virtues rise, in shapes of mercy, charity and love, to walk the world and bless it" (*Old Curiosity Shop*, chapter 72). Nell is the shortened form of Eleanor, and her journey across the Midlands is analogous to the route taken by the body of Edward I's Queen, Eleanor of Aquitaine, from Northampton to London, each resting-place marked by the erection of a stone cross. A devoted wife, Eleanor is credited with sucking poison from her husband's wound, in an act parallel to Nell's self-sacrifice for her grandfather. Nell is a queen in the manner of Ruskin's 1865 "Of Queens' Gardens." Just as Nell had turned the graveyard into a garden by planting flowers on the graves, so Ruskin will call women to cultivate the national garden, "to assist in the ordering, in the comforting, and in the beautiful adorning of the state."[12] Thus, in this first attempt at using a Gothic heroine as a moral and social catalyst, Dickens is clearly wedded to the immanence of Ainsworth's royal Gothic. To connect Nell to the land, so that her body will fructify the soil in the manner of a fertility goddess, is to make her a queen rather than a commodity of social transferability, but at the cost of her life.

By the time of his two great social novels, *Bleak House* (1852–53) and *Little Dorrit* (1855–57), Dickens's fiction shows a more optimistic attitude toward social change, which is illustrated, paradoxically, by a reengagement with the Gothic form as a means to delineate and expose the ideological and oppressive nature of contemporary institutions. In both novels the heroine is imprisoned by these structures, and the means to their regeneration lies in her escape. Indeed, Esther Summerson, the illegitimate narrator of much of *Bleak House*, is named after the Jewish queen who saved her people from death. After a guilt-ridden childhood, Esther is eventually able to accept her spiritual equality: "I was as innocent of my birth as a queen of hers; and that before my Heavenly Father I should not be punished for birth, nor a queen rewarded for it" (chapter 36). An outsider, Esther will come to rule over the world of the novel.

Bleak House presents a whole society embalmed like Little Nell in a murky past, and the fog of London that Reynolds used to suggest the ubiquity of evil is here expressive of the mystifications of the antiquated and dilatory Court of Chancery, where cases can outlive their plaintiffs. The Gothic focus is both an actual building, in the heart of the fog, but also an institution that "has its decaying houses and its blighted lands in every shire" (chapter 3). Unlike other Gothic places in Dickens, the court is not directly described, but only invoked as a center, as if to emphasize its incomprehensibility and covert reach. All the many plot-ends of this panoramic novel can be traced back to the operation of Chancery, including the Bleak House of the title, which was named from the suicide of a former owner. Like Madame Beck in *Villette,* engagement with Chancery infantilizes the clients or "wards" of the court. *Bleak House* is a world without energy, erotic drives, or the possibility of future children.

At first merely a housekeeper and literal key-holder in Bleak House, Esther Summerson gradually descends into the Gothic as she comes to hold the keys of life and death. Unlike Nell's Queen Eleanor journey to death during the heart of the winter, Esther's is a royal "progress" (the title of *Bleak House's* chapter 3) toward a summer of restored social relations and her own sexual fulfillment. This she performs, first of all, by her loyalty to Bleak House and the attempts of its owner, John Jarndyce, to act effectively to relieve suffering. By acts of effectual kindness, Esther establishes a network of open and fruitful social exchanges to challenge the covert and guilty connections of the Reynolds-style London of the novel. Secondly, her developing unease with her role, and the proposal of marriage by the elderly Jarndyce, leads her to leave Bleak House to marry with the physician whom she loves – and to a new Bleak House that may form a center for acts of social redemption. In being thus rescued from Bleak House, without any action on her part, Esther Summerson is enabled to make a characteristically Radcliffean double gesture. She remains faithful to tradition and her inheritance while inaugurating a new social grouping and possibility beyond the confines of the Bleak House economy. Only by taking the angelic woman in the house and extending her role outwards is Dickens able to conceive of action in the public realm at all, by women or by men.

In *Little Dorrit*, Amy Dorrit, who returns to the debtors prison in which she had been raised to be with Arthur Clennam, makes a parallel gesture, very much in terms of an intensified Gothic circle. She blesses the prison in which she had been an innocent inhabitant, and also reveals the way to be free of its power, just as Esther Summerson, by virtue of her status as an outsider, is able to redeem Bleak House. In contrast to the perceived patriarchal family in which men work and the women stay at home, *Bleak House* and *Little Dorrit* describe worlds of masculine incapacity – sexual, legal, financial – in which *all* are incarcerated. In the earlier novel, Esther's very transferability as a woman makes possible a movement toward work and productive engagement with the real. However, by the time of *Little Dorrit*, Dickens's Gothic view of reality had extended to embrace the metaphysical. Life itself has become confinement, and the sun's rays form the "bars of the prison of this lower world" (Dickens, *Little Dorrit,* chapter 30). Reality is spatialized in the manner of Ainsworth, but without the mastery of a topographical perspective, so that the reader experiences the panopticon, like the characters, from within. With men as trapped as women in a domestic economic sphere and an irrational world, the threat of a Brontësque collapse back into the solipsism of a haunted mind returns, as witnessed by Arthur Clennam's mental collapse in the Marshalsea. Little Dorrit's apocalyptic gesture here is akin to that of Lucy Snowe: to reveal the fact of inner as well as outer imprisonment and the liberatory potential of an acceptance of a Gothic universe. But whereas Jane Eyre and Lucy Snowe tended to imagine or enter microcosms of the Gothic macrocosm, Amy Dorrit deliberately reenters the Gothic macrocosm itself. All her microcosmic imaginative power is focused upon shining a new light within an imprisoning space, which cannot in this life be entirely escaped even if it can be redeemed.

All that is left, after *Little Dorrit*'s extension of the Gothic into the metaphysical, is a Gothic of demystification. Indeed, in Dickens's later fiction, the weight shifts away from social regeneration achieved through the release of the woman from confinement, to the thralldom of individual men to Gothic fictions. Mrs. Clennam's tyranny over Arthur in the iron fixity of her tortured religion in *Little Dorrit* has a parallel in Miss Havisham's entrapment of Pip in *Great Expectations* (1860–61). Mouldering Satis House, with its time-locked mistress and youthful Estella, offers a false Gothic promise that Pip is the hero come to bring change and new life by rescuing the heroine. In fact, Satis House is a showcase – in the manner of a sensation novel – for a marketable product: a nubile young woman. Here the Gothic has truly become a mental construct, but in a world that is *constituted* by such economic motors. The toy-Gothic cottage, with its diminutive drawbridge and tiny gun to which the law clerk, Wemmick, retires each evening, is both a marker of Wemmick's alienation from his daily employment and an attempt to render his mental division actual. By its cheerful pretence, Wemmick's Castle draws attention to its fictive and self-reflexive character, in contrast to Miss Havisham's festering bridal cake, by which she represents and enacts her dereliction and attributes its cause to events outside the self. This is precisely a *negative* variant of the Gothic circle. By projecting outwards her own delusion, Miss Havisham creates her own solipsism along with an extreme Gothic edifice, instead of escaping from solipsism by means of such a construction as Wemmick does. Indeed, solipsistic imprisonment within the haunted space of the mind, without connection to anything beyond its own constructs, becomes the characteristic Dickens nightmare. It culminates in the opium dreams of John Jasper, the church organist of this novelist's unfinished *Mystery of Edwin Drood* (1870). In his drugged state, a cathedral tower and the rusty spikes of his bed in the opium den combine, and his inability to maintain the separation of the worlds of inner desires and outer reality causes him (most readers assume) to murder his nephew. Here the now metaphysical Gothic circle, unlit by Amy Dorrit's light of Platonic grace, has finally imploded.

At the point when Dickens abandoned the political possibilities of the Gothic novel, however, two other writers engaged directly with female domestic powerlessness in the Gothic mode: Wilkie Collins in *The Woman in White* (1860–61) and Sheridan Le Fanu in *Uncle Silas* (1864). Collins employs a multiple-narrator technique to embed his threatened protagonists in layer upon layer of textual enclosure, as well as providing them with opportunities of self-expression through their control of their own narratives.

Laura Glyde is confined first of all to the neglected portions of a country house, and then to a lunatic asylum by her husband under the name of another woman, who is murdered and buried as Lady Glyde. Marriage results in a complete lack of autonomy and a headlong descent into nonbeing that is implicitly radical in linking the institution itself with female erasure. Despite its classic Radcliffean intensity and aristocratic setting, *Uncle Silas* goes even further to equate the enclosure of woman in the house with live burial. The melancholy heroine, Maud Ruthyn, is only relieved of her deathly fears that make her a virtual bride of death when she faces the social reality of those Gothic terrors. The false window opens to reveal the entry of her murderer, and she is able to flee the house and recognize it as a tomb.

Ultimately, too, *The Woman in White* and *Uncle Silas* are able to sustain a return to the Radcliffean synthesis beyond the one in Dickens by means of an increased reliance on the supernatural. The woman in white herself, who flits in and out of Collins's narrative and Silas's death-in-life ambiguity, renders the ordinary world oddly spectral, even though there is a natural explanation for both versions of this character. Collins employs Radcliffe's explained supernatural for his woman in white, but her repeated disappearances and uncanny duplication of Laura Glyde mean that Gothic liberation is enacted by means of her absence from the text. As in *The Old Curiosity Shop*, social critique is won at the cost of making the feminine disappear or become ghostly. Only in the conclusion to *Uncle Silas* is the Gothic gloom and ubiquitous spectrality finally lifted from the narrative. Nevertheless (as with *Little Dorrit*), this is at the exact point when the heroine acknowledges the earthly as pointing away from itself to the supernatural that is more real: "This world is a parable – the habitation of symbols – the phantom of spiritual things immortal shown in material shape." Here, the supernatural is the guarantor of the natural and that which makes it real. The fusing of social with metaphysical liberation in *Little Dorrit* and *Uncle Silas* should not, therefore, be understood in terms of a mystification of the material, but rather in terms of a Swedenborgian transposition of the qualities of the material and the spiritual. This is most directly exemplified by Le Fanu, but is exhibited also by the protagonist of the ghost story in the 1860s and for some time after.

Influenced by Emmanuel Swedenborg's visions of a mathematically exact parallel afterlife, the Victorian heaven had been utterly naturalized and spatialized into a primary reality and a city of which the earthly world was a suburb. Making the transcendent material thus rendered the actual world spectral, in the manner already revealed in the Brontë novels and as in Marx's sense that increase in bureaucracy and rampant capitalism in the mid-century had rendered reality phantasmal. This transformation has implications for the ghost story, well exemplified in the Christmas production by Dickens, Elizabeth Gaskell, and others of *The Haunted House*, published in *All the Year Round* in 1859, which offered a story for every separate room. However, in every case the revenant is some aspect of the occupier's past self, and Dickens concludes: "we were never for a moment haunted by anything more disagreeable than our own imaginations and remembrances" (Dickens and others, *Haunted House*, p. 158). Still, if the haunted house is the normal world, remembrance does render it uncanny and oddly insubstantial. As Adelaide Proctor concludes in her offering, a poem entitled "The Nun's Portrait," "The hopes that, lost, in some far distance seem / May be the truer life, and this the dream." It is surely no accident that it is the strongly realist novelists who produce so many of the period's most successful ghost stories: Elizabeth Gaskell, Mrs. Riddell, Margaret Oliphant. Even George Eliot wrote one such tale, "The Lifted Veil" (1859). Gothic novelists such as Dickens, Le Fanu, and Collins all wrote wonderfully in this vein also, but using always realist techniques and the impedimenta of Victorian domesticity, such as Le Fanu's "Green Tea" and Collins's "A Terribly Strange Bed." All this realist craft is expended on making the supernatural concrete and eliding it with the natural, which thereby acquires materiality. Thus, while many authors have stressed a "naturalized supernatural" in this period, it is crucial to realize that it had an exact counterpart in a "supernaturalized natural," which means that we are talking here about *anything but* secularization.

One reason for the realism with which the afterlife was described is that it needed to be believable to the bereaved, since the reunion in heaven was central to nineteenth-century religious aspiration. In the figure of the dead (especially female) child, the Victorian imagination was able to envisage the fusion of the domestic and social realms that were fractured in diurnal reality. Margaret Oliphant had lost three children when she wrote "The Beleaguered City" in 1878.[13] This novella points to a removal of centrality from the real to the supernatural in a French town, Semur, whose inhabitants are mysteriously forced out of their homes and outside the gates of the city by the ringing of the cathedral bells. The dead have returned to inhabit their old homes as a judgment on the present citizens, who have neglected remembrance and the justice and charity which this remembering should prompt. Now it is the living who are spectral: "I stood in the city like a ghost." The dead rearrange the furniture in their own homes, and a lost daughter leaves a physical token of their peaceful intentions in the form of "a branch of olive, with silvery leaves." Only by solidarity with the dead will the living become substantial again.

In tales such as "The Beleaguered City" the naturalized supernatural and the supernaturalized natural take the critical stance of the Gothic heroine, together with the Whig liberation plot, to a transcendental extreme. By contrast, a parallel Tory extension of the *Blackwood's* entrapment theme leads similarly to a privileging of the supernatural as the real, but with a negative turn. This is already achieved in the "realist" supernatural within a Gothic plot in Emily Brontë's *Wuthering Heights* of 1847. Here the Gothic house and the supernatural it unleashes act vampirishly to drain the real of any vitality and make resistance impossible. Like her sister, Emily Brontë makes her protagonists provoke the Gothic, whether by Heathcliff's vindictive acts that confirm him as a tyrant or Catherine's willful starvation in order to escape "this shattered prison" of the body and spite him. However, in the naturalized supernatural economy of the novel, to court liberation is only to seek death without the clear assurance of some transcendence that it might provide.

Hence the most vivid materiality is accorded to the ghosts of the novel, such as phantom Catherine's attempt to get in through the window to her old room, now occupied by Lockwood. He recalls that "terror made me cruel; and finding it useless to attempt shaking the creature off, I pulled its wrist on to the broken pane, and rubbed it to and fro till the blood ran down and soaked the bed-clothes" (chapter 3). This bloody dream is vividly physical but its supernatural status is unquestionable, since Lockwood gives his phantom visitor the least likely surname. She is encountered as a cold and physical reality who bleeds as the heartbreaker Lockwood does not. Significantly, Catherine seeks reentry to the house – through the very window of the soul's exit at death – because the supernatural "real" seeks combination with the Gothic narrative. This is achieved finally in Heathcliff's deliberate decision to die by the same lattice in Catherine's room. For it is the Gothic house, and not the Romantic expanse of the moor, that is necessary to embody the intensity of feeling of both of the main protagonists. Its simultaneous articulation of a range of binary oppositions – inside and outside, prison and liberation, body and soul, life and death – makes it a springboard for the supernatural "real." As a site of contestation, identity, and control of the future, Wuthering Heights is the vampiric focus for all the social and psychic energies of the narrative, subsuming them all in an existential metaphysic in which existence itself again becomes the iron shroud of *Blackwood's*' tales. A Burkean conservative stress on the nation as belonging to the dead and those to come, rather than to the living, once more centered on the house and combined with a plot of Gothic usurpation, produces a negative supernaturalism, with only a hint of hope in the survival of the younger Catherine in the context of an ending otherwise replete with exhaustion.

A pessimistic naturalized supernatural can be traced from the 1840s right through to the *fin de siècle* through another Gothic protagonist, the vampire.

Byron's various poetic versions and Polidori's 1819 *The Vampyre* (see chapter 5 above) may be responsible for references to Heathcliff as a ghoul or vampire, but in the same year as *Wuthering Heights* Thomas Preskett published *Varney the Vampire* to enormous popular success. The materiality of the undead who drains the lifeblood of the living is an ultimate figure of a negative natural supernatural that this era sees as a genuine threat.[14] In all his Victorian manifestations he is a feudal relic, battening financially and politically on the social body. *Varney* suggests a certain radicalism in describing Charles II seducing a poor virgin as a sort of sexual vampirism, but the prevailing tone is one of sympathy for a man doomed to everlasting hunger by his accidental killing of his son. Mobs who seek his destruction are described disdainfully, and Varney ends by throwing himself self-sacrificially into the crater of Vesuvius.

In his celebrated tale "Carmilla" of 1872, Le Fanu's female vampire imitates Preskett's Clara Crofton, who preys on other girls, but it also offers a covertly Darwinian critique of vampirism as a negative transcendence. This female vampire uses developmental language to argue that the natural maturation for a girl is to death: "girls are caterpillars while they live in the world" (Le Fanu, *Best Ghost Stories*, p. 297). In her quasiscientific study of ghost appearances, *The Night-Side of Nature* (1853), Catherine Crowe had argued that evolutionary theory had opened a new world of the marvelous, so that the fantastic had become real.[15] Thus in "Carmilla" the vampire ceases to represent the predatory and deenergizing past and instead stands for a natural but sinister progress toward lifelessness. "Carmilla" is a self-reflexive work in which Le Fanu questions, through the vampire's fascination for the living girl, the dangerous tendencies of his own Swedenborgian privileging of the supernatural real. Ultimately, he suggests, a supposedly supernatural real leads to a disparagement of the earthly and an inability to sustain the Gothic heroine's role in a metaphysical Gothic universe, making impossible what Le Fanu prefers: the Radcliffean synthesis of his earlier novel, *Uncle Silas*.

The apogee of the naturalized supernatural in the Victorian age, though, is Edward Bulwer-Lytton's "The Haunted and the Haunters: or, the House and the Brain" (1859).[16] An ordinary London house is the conduit for spectral footprints, moving furniture, and larvae of chaotic forms, as well as the feeling of a malevolent will at work. Eventually the cause of the hauntings is discovered to be a former servant, who had set up a compass with a written curse, saying "so moves the needle, so work my will." What haunts the house is a brain, whose original act of volition sets matter into movement. The house has become the mind's casing in the manner of the skull-shaped house of Usher in Poe's tale. It is an extreme example of an attempt to find a medium to embody one's mental fantasies. Bulwer-Lytton's story seems to fit the thesis of Terry Castle's work on "spectral technology," in which she suggests that this technology's development from the eighteenth into the nineteenth century relocates the supernatural in the imagination, yet, because of that, the mind itself becomes "a kind of supernatural space, filled with intrusive spectral presences" (Castle, *Female Thermometer*, p. 167). While rejecting the view that the supernatural is completely psychologized, my argument is in accord with her spatial reading of Victorian psychology. An awareness of the Victorian account of the mind as a haunted house, which is a wholly spectral space, can question the easy Freudian reading of a binary interiority of realist upper and Gothic lower levels, in which a masterful consciousness represses the "real" unconscious. Instead, the haunted mind at this time traverses constantly, and with semi-consciousness, the Gothic circle between an imaginary realm full of specters and an equally spectral reality.

However, as I have shown, the Victorian Gothic has not reduced the arena of meaning to the haunted mind (as Castle's analysis implies). Bulwer-Lytton's brain inhabits an *actual* house. The mind taken alone had become another barrier to be breached in the period's heroic attempt to return to the critique offered by Radcliffe's Whig synthesis. This motif is reworked through an even more thoroughgoing existential focus on the human spirit trapped in a spectral but material universe. This process begins with Charlotte Brontë and finds its most positive turn in her apocalyptic pro-gressions, Le Fanu's supernaturalism, and again in Dickens's own outsider versions of royal Gothic, in which "queens" such as Esther Summerson and Amy Dorrit guarantee the relation of spiritual and physical worlds, as well as continuity and progress. Without the Gothic heroine's entrapment and liberation, the Victorian Gothic suggests overall, the "real" is drained of meaning, and a negative natural supernaturalism finally offers no way to connect the haunted mind with an equally haunted society.

NOTES

1 William Blackstone, *Commentary on the Laws of England*, 4 vols., 15th edn (London, 1809), III, 268.
2 See, for example, Richard Williams, *The Contested Crown: Public Discourse of the British Monarchy in the Reign of Queen Victoria* (Aldershot: Ashgate, 1997), p. 11, and Elizabeth Langland, "Nation and Nationality: Queen Victoria in the Developing Narrative of Englishness" in *Remaking Queen Victoria*, ed. Margaret Homans and Adrienne Munich (Cambridge: Cambridge University Press, 1997), pp. 13–32.
3 See G. P. R. James, *Darnley; or The Field of the Cloth of Gold* (Paris: Baudry's European Library, 1836), and *Arabella Stuart; a Romance from English History* (New York: Harper and Bros., 1844).

4 I cite the fiction of Ainsworth from *The Tower of London: a Historical Romance* (London: G. Routledge and Co., 1853) and *Windsor Castle: a Historical Romance* (London: G. Routledge and Co., 1855).

5 G. W. M. Reynolds is cited from *The Mysteries of London*, ed. Thomas Trefor (Edinburgh: Edinburgh University Press, 1996).

6 Thomas Cooper, *The Purgatory of Suicides: a Prison Rhyme* (London: J. Watson, 1847), book 7.

7 See "Castle Elmere," *Blackwood's Edinburgh Magazine* 35: 219 (March 1834).

8 *Blackwood's Edinburgh Magazine* 28: 169 (August 1830): 364–71.

9 See Charlotte Brontë, *Shirley*, ed. Andrew and Judith Hook (Harmondsworth: Penguin, 1974).

10 Sally Shuttleworth, *Charlotte Brontë and Victorian Psychology* (Cambridge: Cambridge University Press, 1996), p. 222.

11 I refer here to these editions of Dickens's novels: *Bleak House*, ed. Stephen Gill (Oxford: Oxford University Press, 1996); *Great Expectations*, ed. Margaret Cardwell (Oxford: Clarendon, 1993); *The Mystery of Edwin Drood*, ed. Cardwell (Oxford: Clarendon, 1972); *The Old Curiosity Shop*, ed. Elizabeth Brennan (Oxford: Clarendon, 1966); and *Oliver Twist*, ed. Kathleen Mary Tillotson (Oxford: Clarendon, 1966). The edition I cite for *Little Dorrit*, the most fully Gothic of Dickens's major novels, is the 1978 Clarendon edition, ed. Harvey Peter Sucksmith.

12 John Ruskin, *Sesames and Lilies* (London: Cassell, 1907), p. 87.

13 See Margaret Oliphant's *The Beleaguered City and Other Stories* (Oxford: Oxford University Press, 1988).

14 See Thomas Preskett, *Varney the Vampire*, ed. Devendra P. Varma, 3 vols. (New York: Arno Press, 1970).

15 See Catherine Crowe in *The Night-Side of Nature: Or, the Ghosts and the Ghost-Seers* (London: Routledge, 1853).

16 Edward Bulwer-Lytton's story appears in his *A Strange Story and The Haunted and the Haunters* (London: Routledge and Warne, 1864).

9

ERIC SAVOY

The rise of American Gothic

From the turn of the eighteenth into the nineteenth century and the beginnings of a distinctive American literature, the Gothic has stubbornly flourished in the United States. Its cultural role, though, has been entirely paradoxical: an optimistic country founded upon the Enlightenment principles of liberty and "the pursuit of happiness," a country that supposedly repudiated the burden of history and its irrational claims, has produced a strain of literature that is haunted by an insistent, undead past and fascinated by the strange beauty of sorrow. How can the strikingly ironic, even perverse, career of the Gothic in America be accounted for? Why has it been so at home on such inhospitable ground?

The most common responses to these questions have recourse to conventional metaphors: the Gothic, it is frequently reasoned, embodies and gives voice to the dark nightmare that is the underside of "the American dream." This formulation is true up to a point, for it reveals the limitations of American faith in social and material progress. Yet a simple opposition between the convenient figures of dream and nightmare is overly reductive. These clichés, and the impulses in American life that they represent, are not in mere opposition; they actually interfuse and interact with each other. This realization will take us far in understanding the odd centrality of Gothic cultural production in the United States, where the past constantly inhabits the present, where progress generates an almost unbearable anxiety about its costs, and where an insatiable appetite for spectacles of grotesque violence is part of the texture of everyday reality.

I want to locate the rise of American Gothic and its powerful appeal in certain verbal devices or *figures*. As I broadly define them, these include fictional specters and authorial personae, rhetorical strategies for meditating on America's perplexing history, and strange uses of tropes, such as metaphor and personification, that *turn* language (to "trope" means to "turn") toward suggestions of distinctive and dark American obsessions. Inevitably, the writers of the new republic were deeply influenced by the narrative situations, conflicts, settings, and motifs that made British Gothic so popular on both sides of the Atlantic. The perverse pleasures that acquired conventional status in the Gothic by the early nineteenth century – claustrophobia, atmospheric gloom, the imminence of violence – were generated in early American literature too, and by such standard architectural locales as the haunted house, the prison, the tomb, and by such familiar plot elements as the paternal curse and the vengeful ghost. However, the specificity of American Gothic, what makes it distinctively *American*, does not come just from formulaic plots and situations of an aristocratic genre being adapted to the democratic situation of the new world. More important, as I shall demonstrate, is the *formal* adaptability and innovative energy of American Gothic. Nowhere is all this more evident than in the strange tropes, figures, and rhetorical techniques, so strikingly central in American Gothic narratives, that express a profound anxiety about historical crimes and perverse human desires that cast their shadow over what many would like to be the sunny American republic. Especially important in this tradition of verbal devices is *prosopopoeia*, or personification, by which abstract ideas (such as the burden of historical causes) are given a "body" in the spectral figure of the ghost. It is also the strategy that enables the dead to rise, the ghostly voice to materialize out of nowhere, and objects to assume a menacing pseudo-life. It thus achieves the ultimate effects of the haunted, the uncanny, and the return of the repressed while placing these thoroughly in the depths of American life and the American psyche.

The rise of the Gothic in America, then, was enabled by imitating earlier achievements, yet the figures it generated are emphatically *neither* conventional nor convenient. They are insistently troubling. And what they "trouble" is not only the comprehensibility of America as a subject – including the locus of cultural and political authority after the revolution and the perfectibility of human beings in a democracy – but also the forms and functions of literary expression. For American Gothic is, first and foremost, an innovative and experimental literature. Its power comes from its dazzling originality and diversity in a series of departures that situate the perverse – as forms, techniques, and themes – *inside* the national mainstream and thereby unsettle the implications of Walt Whitman's brave assertion that "The United States themselves are essentially the greatest poem."[1]

Leslie Fiedler has rightly observed in an American context that the whole tradition of the Gothic might best be grasped as "a pathological symptom rather than a proper literary movement" (Fiedler, "Invention of the American Gothic," p. 135). Such an approach helps us to locate the territory of the Gothic not in history exactly, but rather in a particular historical sensibility and even more certainly in *historiography* (literally the study of the *writing* of history), the often convoluted and blatantly constructed discourse of narratives that circle around themes and events that are rarely susceptible to direct exposition. Generally, the sense of the past that pervades Gothic literature does not encourage the writer to explain origins in clear relation to end-points in a seamless linear narrative. Nor does the writer seize on history as a coherent field that is subject to authorial control. Instead, history controls and determines the writer. Gothic texts return obsessively to the personal, the familial, and the national pasts to complicate rather than to clarify them, but mainly to implicate the individual in a deep morass of American desires and deeds that allow no final escape from or transcendence of them.

The historical dimension of American Gothic is entirely congruent with the notion of the Real – of the myriad things and amorphous physicality beyond representation that haunt our subjectivity and demand our attention, that compel us to explanatory language but resist the strategies of that language – according to the definition of "Real" proposed by the French psychoanalyst Jacques Lacan. As Malcolm Bowie explains in analyzing Lacan, "the Real is that which lies outside the Symbolic process, and it is to be found in the mental as well as in the material world: a trauma, for example, is [like sudden physical dissolution] intractable and unsymbolizable."[2] To engage with the Real is to bring the powerful resources of literary form and language to bear on a traumatic "otherness," including much of America's past, that has crucially shaped identity and everyday reality in the present – yet finally to face the limited power of those resources at the same time. In the Gothic approach to the past, the mind of both writer and reader make contact with the limits of their power, with that which – as Bowie asserts – our structures "cannot structure."[3] Yet it is that very struggle to give the Real a language that singularly shapes the American Gothic as broadly symptomatic of cultural restlessness, the fear of facing America's darkly pathological levels. It is also, I suggest, what gives rise to Gothic verbal figures, their urgent straining toward meaning, and their consequent strains upon the limits of language. This tension between an impossible – or at best, ineffable – reference to the Real, on the one hand, and a strange textual surface, on the other, constitute the experimental game played by American Gothic writing. Gothic images in America thereby suggest the attraction and repulsion of a monstrous history, the desire to "know" the traumatic Real of American being and yet the flight from that unbearable and remote knowledge.

In his *Studies in Classic American Literature* (1923), D. H. Lawrence helps us to understand this coalescence of American energy in dark images. For him, these figures cast a spell upon the reader's imagination and stimulate our interpretive curiosity, but in gesturing everywhere – which is to say, nowhere in particular – they only dimly consolidate a definite meaning and thus further excite desire. Writing during the moment of high modernism, Lawrence asserted that European modernists "had not yet reached the pitch of extreme consciousness" that animated the American nineteenth century; whereas the modernists were "*trying* to be extreme," many nineteenth-century Americans "just were it." Lawrence accounts for this essential American modernity – the status of the "extreme" in the literary mainstream – by contrasting nineteenth-century European realism, which was "explicit" and "hate[d] eloquence and symbols, seeing in them only subterfuge," to the Americans who "refuse everything explicit and always put up a sort of double meaning, [who] revel in subterfuge."[4] Given Lawrence's symbolic orientation, it is not surprising that he had little use for Benjamin Franklin, the writer who serves conveniently as a metonym for the American Enlightenment and its ideals of progress and self-advancement and whose popular autobiography (begun in 1771, prior to the revolution, and published in 1818) came to represent the standard American view of the rational individual rising by his own efforts in the marketplace. "The Perfectability of Man! Ah heaven, what a dreary theme!" Lawrence sneers, as he expels Franklin from his American canon. "The ideal self! Oh, but I have a strange and fugitive self shut out and howling like a wolf or a coyote under the ideal windows. See his red eyes in the dark? This is the self who is coming into his own."[5]

Lawrence's vivid sense of this "strange and fugitive self" that has been repudiated by the enlightened and forward-looking American psyche reveals much about the cultural origins and ideological matrix that gave rise to the American Gothic project. In psychoanalytic terms, this "fugitive" – banished, haunting the border of life, determined to return – has the lowly status of the "abject," as defined by Julia Kristeva (see chapter 1 above). The abject is less a specifiable "thing" than a location for throwing off the psyche's *and* a culture's most basic drives, the ones most in need of repression. Radically excluded and driven away by the superego of something like Franklin's national ideology, the abject, as Kristeva asserts, "does not cease challenging its master . . . [It is] a massive and sudden emergence of uncanniness, which, familiar as it might have been in an opaque and forgotten life, now harries me as radically separate, loathsome. Not me. Not that. But not nothing, either. A 'something' that I do not recognize as a thing" (Kristeva, *Powers of Horror*, p. 2). The abject signifies a domain of impossibility and uninhabitability, associated with betwixt-and-between conditions where death keeps invading life, into which the normative American subject must cast the irrational, the desire unacceptable to consciousness, and locate it "over there" in some frightening incarnation of the always inaccessible Real. Moreover, it is precisely this consignment or repudiation that enables the subject to emerge *as* a coherent national subject, a proper citizen of the republic, by contrast to that other. At the same time, as Sigmund Freud has observed, the very point of the repressed is its eventual *return*. Gothic literature is committed to representing that fearful "uncanny" as it reappears in arresting figures[6] that partake generally of the "monstrous" (the Latin origin of which means a showing forth, or something capable of being shown or de*monstrated*). Indeed, Freud theorized the uncanny on the basis of actual Gothic literature (albeit German), which he saw as among the most potent cultural archives of the return of the repressed. The uncanny, he suggests, "is that class of the terrifying which leads back to something long known to us, once very familiar"; it designates the peculiar quality of something "that ought to have remained hidden and secret, and yet comes to light" (Freud, "The Uncanny," pp. 369–70, 376).

Lawrence's "fugitive," then, returns to the house of the American ideal persistently; it has a deeply familiar but thrown-off story, a history, that insists upon being told, however indirectly. Indeed, Lawrence's striking simile comparing the abjected self to a wolf or a coyote (a more American animal) suggests a primordial violence in a figure that strains toward narrative expression. Yet Lawrence's figure of the "fugitive" is itself distinctly fugitive: the monster that returns does not demonstrate; it can at best only "shadow forth," to use one of Nathaniel Hawthorne's preferred expressions, in a symbolic moment that represents a complex unknown. The figure of the wolf (or coyote) could mean *this*, or it could mean *that* – or both and more. The text does not, and probably cannot, commit itself to single explicit significance. The American Gothic, like Lawrence's simile, can be said to strain powerfully but ineffectively in an always fragmentary narrative: it manifests itself often in the strangest of tropes, *catachresis* (as in "howling like a wolf...under the ideal windows"), a figure for which there exists no precise literal referent, merely a "something" that can appear verbally in no other way. All we are left with, ultimately, is the image of the monster's "red eyes in the dark" that follows us as we turn away in baffled unease. This assessment by Lawrence is a sharp critical lesson in the strange narrative unfolding of the repressed's urgent return and its dependence upon figures that cannot be said to "work" in any conventional way. With that insightfulness, as I now hope to show, Lawrence teaches us quite accurately how to read the American Gothic of the late eighteenth and the nineteenth century.

In 1781 an intensely religious farmer in upstate New York ritually murdered his wife and four children after hearing the command of religious "voices." This bizarre and unaccountable story eventually caught the attention of

Charles Brockden Brown, a lawyer from Philadelphia who is often regarded as the first professional author in the United States. Brown used this fragment of American history as the premise of *Wieland; or the Transformation* (1798), the first major novel to adapt the conventions of British Gothic to American circumstances. By any measure, *Wieland* is an awkward novel, a catachresis writ large, marked by a disproportionate relationship between sensational scenic effects and inadequate causal explanation or resolution. Yet it has attracted intelligent commentary from generations of literary scholars, and not simply because of its historical status. Written from the first-person perspective of Clara Wieland, who serves as a register for the dreadful course of events she unfolds – and whose reluctant, traumatized *writing* is the novel's most engaging aspect – the narrative gestures frequently toward pervasive anxieties about the individual's capacity for common sense and self-control within the unstable social order of the new American republic. *Wieland*'s account of the "transformation" into a murderous monster of the benevolent, self-governing, and responsible man – the ideological bedrock of the Enlightenment promise of the free individual's role in the common good – marks the return of the irrational "other" to dismantle the fundamental propositions of the national experiment. More specifically, *Wieland* repudiates the autonomy of the individual and points to a much darker account of why history unfolds in the destructive way that it does. The sins of the fathers – their excesses, their violence and abuses, their predispositions toward the irrational – are visited upon their children, who, despite their illusions of liberty, find themselves in the ironic situation of an intergenerational compulsion to repeat the past. Brown thus inaugurates a historiographical paradigm that will have a long career in American Gothic and will shape the historical imperatives of Nathaniel Hawthorne and William Faulkner, among others.

At the outset of Clara Wieland's retrospective narrative, she and her brother Theodore, along with their friends Henry Pleyel and his sister Catherine, pursue an ideal and harmonious existence of study, conversation, and cultural pursuit at a country estate in the environs of Philadelphia. Buoyed up by wealth and a confidence in their innate goodness, they reveal no cracks in their ideological armature that might render them susceptible to calamity. But after the arrival of a mysterious traveler, Francis Carwin, who turns out to be a ventriloquist – appropriating their voices for what turn out to be dangerous aims indeed – their Enlightenment complacency unravels. Theodore Wieland hears voices and becomes morose and incommunicative; Clara too hears voices emanating from her bedroom closet threatening to rape and kill her. After much rumination on the source, mode, and meaning of "the voice," Theodore acts upon a seemingly spectral command to murder his wife (Catherine) and their children as proof of religious devotion; he then breaks out of jail and attempts to kill Clara too. But this ultimate violence is arrested when Carwin confesses his ventriloquist pranks, which leads Wieland to doubt that it was God's voice he heard. He commits suicide, Clara and Pleyel escape to Europe, and the novel ends. Out of this tortuous, incredible plot, one mystery stubbornly persists: Carwin emphatically denies ventriloquizing the murderous directive to Wieland and thus his own culpability in it. What, then, might explain Wieland's grotesque transformation? Might he be a *personification* of wider and deeper causes, rather than the cause in himself? A possible solution lies in what might be called the historical deep psyche of the American subject.

Nina Baym suggests that the Wieland family is "*shadowed* by a calamitous past in which the threat to their happiness is both contained and predicted."7 The patriarch of the Wielands emigrated to America from Germany in search of freedom of religious expression. A fanatic who acknowledged no authority apart from his own inner light, he built a fantastic temple where he practiced his strange rituals of worship. Increasingly morbid, he became convinced that God would punish him for failing to carry out a divine command, and he eventually died – of spontaneous combustion, no less – in his own temple, which thereby acquired a stark symbolic ghostliness for the next generation. As good Americans, his children turned their backs on the excesses of the father and converted the temple to a pleasure-house dedicated to the pursuit of intellectual beauty. The Gothic turn of narrative in *Wieland* is predicated upon the repression of that past historical gloom. This Real returns with the full ironies of the uncanny – as a darkly familiar imperative – when the son, Theodore, fulfills the destiny required by "divine command" that the father had left unfinished. As Baym argues, "the threat to the family lies in its own depths, in the strain of madness and melancholia" that had been unsuccessfully "exorcised." Given that the threat lies in both the historical and the psychopathological "depths" and is bound up with familial obligations, it is useful to link Baym's "*shadow*" of the past upon the present to the "strains" of melancholia. Freudian theory posits that melancholia arises when the subject has sustained an ambivalent and unresolved relation to a lost object: the mourner turns the residual anger felt for the lost object – a parent, say – inward onto the ego, in a narcissistic identification with the lost object. This identification incorporates the lost object in order to recover and preserve it. Figuratively, the ego altered by such identification becomes a kind of unquiet grave that harbors the living dead. In a sense, the ego seeks to overcome its own fragmentation by bringing the dead back to life. According to Freud, "*the shadow of the object fell upon the ego*, and . . . in this way an object loss was *transformed* into an ego-loss."8

The congruence of Freud's discourse with *Wieland; or the Transformation* shows how the son's conscious disavowal of the father still contains an unconscious identification with the patriarchal mission and the American past that is connected with it. Moreover, the role of the Gothic, we now see, is figuratively to embody an intergenerational tendency when the son finds himself, to his horror, transformed into the very father whose fanaticism he had vehemently rejected. The spectral, disembodied, or ventriloquized voice – instrumental in the Gothic's alignment of present and past – might be understood as an example of what Nicolas Abraham has called "the phantom" in his late twentieth-century "complement" to Freud's theory of melancholy. The departed who are most likely to haunt us, he suggests, are those who were "shamed during their lifetime or those who took unspeakable secrets to the grave" and thus have been thrown away (abjected) by their culture and their descendents. The phantom in any subject's later recollections of it arises from an epistemological predicament, for it "is meant to objectify, even if under the guise of individual or collective hallucinations, the gap that the concealment of some part of a loved one's life produced in us ... Consequently, what haunts are not the dead, but *the gaps left within us by the secrets of others.*"[9] Such gaps and secrets are what surface in Wieland's transformation. One might well inquire "who *is* the protagonist of *Wieland?*": the patriarch, the son who uncannily resurrects his destiny, or Clara, who registers the family's disintegration? Or might the underlying agent of *Wieland* be the shadow of history itself, whether that shadow is understood as an inherited state of mind or the emergence of a ghostly phantom from the depths of the historical psyche?

To respond to these questions is to confront the basic cultural project underlying the Gothic's rise in America. Charles Brockden Brown began to write quite soon after the publication of the great Gothic prototypes – the British romances of Ann Radcliffe and Matthew Lewis – but, unlike his English antecedents, he had neither a rich national history to draw upon nor a valid reason for setting an American tale in Catholic Italy. In a new republic without any visible textures of the past, the Gothic mode proved difficult to adapt to American realities. As Fielder observes, "the generation of Jefferson was pledged to be done with ghosts and *shadows*, committed to a life of yea-saying in a sunlit, neoclassical world. From the bourgeois ladies to the Deist intellectuals, the country was united in a disavowal of the 'morbid' and the 'nasty'" ("Invention of the American Gothic," p. 144). Brown's achievement – which would have tremendous influence upon his Gothic followers – was to resituate "history" in a pathologized return of the repressed whereby the present witnesses the unfolding and fulfillment of terrible destinies incipient in the American past. Even as this redirection of the Gothic focus enabled Brown to anticipate Freud, it also permitted him to reestablish the origins of the American self in the Puritan theology of the colonial seventeenth century – itself quite basic to the American Gothic after Brown – specifically in its acute interests in the marks of sin and transgression and its view of history as a dark necessity, the working-out of a retributive divine plan. If early American Gothic was therefore bent perversely on dismantling the complacencies of ideological investments in human perfectibility through tales of the perverse, it turns out that its mission was a kind of political engagement rather than just escapist storytelling.

To amplify this point I should emphasize the essentially conservative nature of Brown's American Gothic. By raising doubts about the ability of individuals to govern themselves in a full-fledged democracy, Brown participates in Alexander Hamilton's state-oriented Federalist skepticism about the realizability of Thomas Jefferson's confidence in supposedly "free" individualism. *Wieland*, then, is a twice-told tale, narrated once as a Gothic horror story about a son's "transformation" and again as political warning. As Jane Tompkins puts it, the novel "presents a shocking and uncharacteristically negative view of what it meant to survive the War of Independence." Amid the instability of political and social life during the years immediately after the revolution, the Wieland family inhabits "social spaces [that are] empty."[10] They have no authorities of any kind available to tell them what to do, what to believe, how to act. In its twice-telling Brown's novel links the patricide of revolution, by which the newly independent nation threw off its colonizing father, to the son's revolt against the familial and thus all-too-familiar father. As would be the case to a lesser extent in later Brown novels such as *Edgar Huntley* (1799) and *Arthur Mervyn* (1800), *Wieland* demonstrates through the circuits of melancholy and its specifically Gothic features that neither the personal nor the cultural past is dead and that both can uncannily return.

Later generations of American writers would transform Brown's historical sense into a rich recasting of how to rewrite history. In these returns the shadow acquires a more explicit mission and a ghostly embodiment, as an actual moving figure (a revenant) returns from an unquiet grave. Through prosopopoeia – the figure of haunting through personification – the shadow begins to speak. And this shadow *knows* the underbelly of American history, the Real that has yet to be completely represented.

"In the four quarters of the globe, who reads an American book?" taunted the acerbic British critic, Sydney Smith in 1820. Two years earlier, in the *Edinburgh Review*, he opined that "Literature the Americans have none," and speculated that the British would supply that need forever: "why should the Americans write books, when a six weeks' passage brings them, in their own tongue, our sense, science and genius, in bales and hogsheads? Prairies, steam-boats, grist-mills, are their natural objects for centuries to come."[11] Smith could not have predicted that British literary imperialism would be hotly contested in American thought until the end of the civil war in 1865; nor would his prejudices have allowed him to understand that the Gothic productions of Charles Brockden Brown, among others, helped instigate one of the world's first postcolonial literatures. In the half-century following Smith's insult, American writers adapted the major tenets of English Romanticism to their own cultural circumstances with astonishing success. According to Robert Weisbuch's useful survey of the postcolonial impulse in the United States, American responses accelerated in two directions. The transcendentalists – Emerson, Thoreau, Whitman – extended "the visions of the English Romantics to everyday historical living with an unprecedented literalness," while the Gothic tradition realized its greatest artistic brilliance in Poe and Hawthorne, who exposed to "withering skepticism" the Romantic faith in "the individual ego or selfhood."[12] Nathaniel Hawthorne, in particular, redirected the Gothic project and refined its strategies to address the shadows now cast by the past upon the present. He purged American Gothic of its European trappings by avoiding the sensationalism of Brown, yet he consolidated Brown's investment in the ongoing haunting of history's evils and injustices. Most importantly, Hawthorne worked earnestly in the medium of the Gothic to define the identity and historical possibilities of the Anglo-American writer.

Whereas Brown was obliged to strain the limits of credibility in tracing the relation of historical fragments to America's search for authority, Hawthorne located a distinct national subject explicitly in the colonial past, often in the Puritan origins of the American self. This historical archive proved so rich that, with Hawthorne, the Gothic arrived at what it had lacked for several generations: a national way of reconstructing history that arose from a homegrown verbal tradition and a strong engagement with the idea of "America." If Hawthorne's point was to cultivate an underdeveloped historical sensibility in his home country – or, as he puts it in the preface to *The House of Seven Gables*, to "connect a by-gone time with the very Present that is flitting away from us" (Hawthorne, *Novels*, p. 351) – then his style rightly includes not only a lush "atmospheric medium" and a carefully crafted narrative form, but also some recurring figurative techniques by which the past is made to "live" again in striking ghostly images. Generally, Hawthorne's approach to historiographical narrative achieves what might be called a symbolism of *implication*. His novels work at the intersection of history and autobiography to demonstrate both a present indicative of the past and a meshing of the author's subjectivity with ancestral evil. His preferred mode is a Puritan-based allegory, which implies indirectly rather than gesturing explicitly, and his revival of the past is intimately bound up with the success or failure of haunting figures. Perversely, Hawthorne's greatest successes were often predicated upon a certain referential obscurity – and hence a multiplicity – in his symbols.

Nowhere is this paradox more evident than in *The Scarlet Letter* of 1850. Set in the early days of the Puritan colonial experiment in Massachusetts, a society in which sin was indistinguishable from crime, it traces the career of Hester Prynne and the letter *A* which she is forced to wear as punishment for adultery and as a cautionary warning to regulate the behavior of other women. The capacity of the letter to refer proves to be highly unstable as it evolves over time to signify more sympathetic views of Hester: while it slips toward suggesting "Angel" and "Able" – reflecting Hester's generosity toward the community that scorns her – it never entirely sheds its original import. Cumulatively, the narrative turns toward an allegory about reading such symbols to suggest that a conclusive interpretation of texts, particularly historical texts, is a remote possibility. Hawthorne's play with ambiguity has important political implications arising from the early feminist movement of his own time. *The Scarlet Letter* explores the energy of feminine agency in oppressive regimes and interrogates the boundary between private and public life. Yet Hawthorne's response to Hester's protofeminism is ambivalent at best. Indeed, this much discussed novel is centrally engaged with gender politics, particularly with clarifying the stances of male writers who bear witness to the history of wrongs against women in the republic. This quest is exposed in the long preface to Hester's story, "The Custom-House," where Hawthorne offers a distinctly Gothic version of autobiography. Most immediately, "The Custom-House" details Hawthorne's frustration with his job as a civil servant, his fortunate discovery of a few fragments of Puritan historiography pertaining to Hester Prynne, and history's power to stimulate the imagination seeking a "neutral territory, somewhere between the real world and fairy-land, where the Actual and the Imaginary may meet, and each imbue itself with the nature of the other" (a highly Gothic vision already as Hawthorne writes it, reminiscent of Walpole's second preface to *The Castle of Otranto*). In this metaphorical world of romance-writing, we are assured, "Ghosts might enter here, without affrighting us" (Hawthorne, *Novels*, p. 149). "The Custom-House" turns out to be swarming with ghosts – it is surely one of the most deeply emblematic haunted houses in American literature – and they bear messages about the male writer's obligation to affiliate himself with their patriarchal mission, even as he wonders about past wrongs done to women. If such ghostly directives inform a theory of literature, which is a central project of Hawthorne's preface, they also arise gradually from strange accretions of symbols that extend the Gothic's traditional focus on mysterious hauntings in new ways.

The Gothic work of "The Custom-House" is carried out by figures of *exhumation*, a process that links the author's cruel Puritan ancestors to a more literary "father," one Jonathan Pue, who inscribed Hester Prynne's story prior to the revolution. The conjoined authority of *two* writers culminates in the present moment and thus puts pressure on the responsibility of Hawthorne as "author." He begins by speculating whether the "persecuting spirit" of his ancestors, who came to Massachusetts with their Bibles and their swords, might be memorialized by the bloodstains of their victims upon their corpses, "so deep a stain, indeed, that [their] dry old bones, in the Charter Street burial ground, must still retain it" (Hawthorne, *Novels*, p. 126). This forensic and highly Gothic curiosity about the signs of history's evil deeds is bound up with an imaginary exhumation of the family graves; having dug them up, Hawthorne proceeds to personify them: "'What is he?' murmurs one gray *shadow* of my forefathers to the other. 'A writer of story-books!'" Hawthorne's prosopopoeia – the means by which the ghostly "shadow" is endowed with speech – locates his historical project in a melancholic search for affiliation. To recall Freud's image of melancholy's incorporation of the "shadow" of the lost object into the subject, where it functions as a sharp critic of the ego, then, is to confront important clues about the psychological dimensions of Gothic historiography in Hawthorne. For one thing, it suggests a grim determinism, for this writer's repugnance at his ancestors' crimes does not mitigate his recognition that "strong traits of their nature have intertwined themselves with mine" (*Scarlet Letter*, ibid., p. 127). Moreover, the resonant implications of the "shadow" require Hawthorne to pursue his career as a writer in ways that will appease the ghostly fathers, perhaps by continuing their mission of surveying and regulating women's agency and sphere of action. "The past," Hawthorne ominously asserts, "was not dead" (ibid., p. 142). How, then, might the writer approach "the corpse of dead activity" – the fragmentary residues of history that survive into the present – and "raise up from these dry bones an image" (p. 144)?

In "The Custom-House" Hawthorne negotiates his transition from the "office" of civil servant to the "office" of the writer of historical romance. The terms of that negotiation persist as tropes of exhumation, metaphors of unearthing useful residues from the grave of history that are supplemented by exhortations emanating from history's patriarchal ghosts. "The Custom House" is a very important instance of the innovative treatment that the Gothic receives in America, primarily because Hawthorne borrows conventional Gothic elements that he refuses to treat literally. There are no "real" exhumations here, no encounters with actual ghosts: such things enter the text through the syntax of "it was *as if . . . ,*" the grammar of simile, metaphor, and analogy.[13] Hawthorne approaches the legacy of Gothic literature – a set of conventions with which his audience was familiar – as a set of representational practices that can now be used figuratively, in the spirit of irony or parody, within a narrative that is not, strictly speaking, a Gothic story. Rather, he adapts such cliches as graves and ghosts to ground his senses of the suitability of early American history for postcolonial literature, his relation with a gendered past, and the attractions of romance-writing. This playful conversion of the elements of Gothic plot or scene into whimsical rhetoric and elaborately sustained figures is a sophisticated experiment, one that is aware of its own belatedness in the Gothic's evolution. As a result the reader is left wondering about the precise orientation of Hawthorne's ominous hints and forensic autopsies. While his figures give expression to the deep psyche of American history – speaking as they seem to from a melancholic tomb incorporated in the subject as a sort of phantom emanating from the historical unconscious – the reader is never quite certain of their meaning or function as Gothic hauntings.

If Hawthorne might thus be said to produce not only the figures of ghosts but also the "ghosts" of "figure" in "The Custom House," such a blight or palsy soon spreads beyond this extended preface to *The Scarlet Letter* itself, contaminating its central symbol. Hester's *A*, Hawthorne demonstrates, has no singular meaning capable of transcending its historical context or the time in which it was manufactured, since it was read and interpreted by people long dead who never arrived at a consensus. Evidently, Hawthorne refused the Romantic ideology of literary symbol which, according to Coleridge in England, promised stable, transparent, and coherent "meaning" beyond the vicissitudes of history.[14] Instead, Hester's scarlet letter is subjected to scene after scene of reading and interpretation, none of which is corroborated by the text or its author. Given this narrative organization, *The Scarlet Letter* functions as an allegory of reading that focuses on a failed symbol, one that betrays its promise to elucidate and clarify an enduring human truth and so provides no certain knowledge of America's historical origins. The obsession of such other nineteenth-century American writers as Melville, Poe, and James with allegories of reading – narratives that turn upon empty or unreadable signs or texts – might be broadly characterized as a "ghosting" of the text and its interpretive certainty, a literary development coincident with the rise of American Gothic and especially important to Hawthorne.

In the end, though, Hawthorne worried about whether the characters in *The Scarlet Letter* "retained all the rigidity of dead corpses" (*Novels*, p. 148). They do, partly because of the weight of allegorical abstraction they are designed to carry, but more fundamentally because they continually betray their spectral origins in a complex American Real. Arising from the hallucinatory uncanny and incorporating the imperatives of their author's acute melancholia, the characters of this romance stumble through a dark dream. Hawthorne's intervention in American history stems from a profound filial duty that he feels toward the dead, arising from his obsessions with his tyrannical forebears and their unquiet graves, which are the ultimate site of his writing as a reader of their vestiges. His interest in the uncanny therefore emerges in one of his earliest short tales, "Roger Malvin's Burial" (written in 1828, published in 1846), in which a man who abandons his wounded father-in-law to die in the forest is compelled to return to the same site, years later, where he unknowingly murders his own son. This story might be more appropriately entitled "Roger Malvin's Exhumation," for the repressed father returns to demand an ironic compensation. Hawthorne's personified figures of haunting will finally return with greater urgency in *The House of Seven Gables* (1851), in which the latest scion of the Pyncheon family walks the earth as a Puritan revenant and perpetuates ancestral crimes in the name of authority and legitimacy before meeting a retributive end. Throughout his career Hawthorne experimented with many figurative shades of America's historical corpse to augment the political relevance of the Gothic ghost story. However, for a fully realized aesthetics of the corpse and the darkest attractions of death, Hawthorne's work required the supplement of Edgar Allan Poe.

Poe's career was winding down in the 1840s, just as Hawthorne's was starting to accelerate, and so they represent quite different points on the American Gothic continuum. Whereas Hawthorne domesticated the Gothic for the purposes of politicized historiography, cautiously curbing its notorious sensationalism, Poe reveled in Gothic excess with a morbid abandon barely restrained by his tight formal control. While Hawthorne, the friend of presidents and secluded genius of the New England literary scene, was an exemplary bourgeois citizen of the world, Poe was in several senses a denizen of the urban underworld. A dissolute alcoholic, chronically short of money, vituperative in his professional relations, continually scrambling from one journalistic hack job to another, he turned a very dark melancholic despair toward the death drive that appears in his masterful short stories and lyric poems of the 1830s and 1840s. Poe's anatomy of melancholy took the symbolism of exhumation to depths that would have caused Hawthorne to blanch; his horrific scenes transgressed every literary taste, yet at the same time few American writers have been so utterly preoccupied with beauty or have sought such precise aesthetic effects. Of all nineteenth-century

American writers, Poe seems most thoroughly our contemporary in his attempt to give language and a narrative structure to what Freud came to describe as the unconscious. He was empathically *not* a man of his time: as Kenneth Silverman, a recent Poe biographer, observes, "at a time when James Fenimore Cooper, Ralph Waldo Emerson [and others] were creating a feeling of space and self-reliant freedom, he was creating in his many accounts of persons bricked up in walls, hidden under floorboards, or jammed in chimneys a mythology of enclosure, constriction, and victimization."[15]

All Gothic writing seeks to induce in the reader a particular affect from within the spectrum of horror: Brown's aim is abrupt surprise; Hawthorne's might be called the gloomy foreclosure of hope; Poe's characteristic emotional matrix is an acute claustrophobia. Spatial configuration is crucial in achieving this painful sense of imprisonment – while Hawthorne's haunted houses admit escape, Poe's coffins and sealed tombs resonate with finality – but architectural motifs in Poe's writing also function as a symbolic equivalent for characters afflicted with impossible desires that insist upon a grotesque realization. Obsessive melancholics all, Poe's people surrender their defenses in the conventional symbolic order and slide inexorably toward the chaotic and abjected Real. Their power over the reader's affective response is extraordinary; Slavoj Žižek's argument about contemporary Gothic is applicable to Poe: "the spectator is supposed to view [the scene] from close up so that he loses his 'objective distance' toward it and is immediately 'drawn' into it. [The text] neither imitates reality nor represents it via symbolic codes[;] it 'renders' the Real by 'seizing' the spectator."[16] This "Poe effect" arises less from the themes of his stories than from his interest in detailing the processes by which the subject is compelled to pursue a truth that is culturally proscribed; we read on, oriented toward a knowledge that is both a fascination and a fear.

Indeed, a striking quality of Poe's fiction is the progressive narrowing of the safe ground between fascination and fear. This zone is greatly reduced in the course of the story, squeezing the reader between conflicting responses that ultimately collapse into each other in a moment of horrific recognition. Poe's interest in narrative imprisonment was generated, it seems, by his own suspension between cultures and their political values. Unlike most American writers of his time, he set few of his tales in the United States; as Jared Gardner suggests, Poe's contempt for democracy led him to construct "a no-place and a nowhere that might be anywhere but here."[17] However, the "American" Poe – a Southerner who wandered between North and South, finding acceptance and a congenial home nowhere – retained deep, if rather oblique and ambivalent connections to the most urgent and vexed question of his day, the abolition of slavery. Given his preference for the narrative setting of "elsewhere," it seems odd that Toni Morrison would claim that "no early American writer is more important to the concept of African Americanism than Poe."[18] Certainly Poe does not write directly about the repugnant facts, appalling ethics, or national shame of slavery. Yet several of his most celebrated texts are rightly understood now as profound meditations upon the cultural significance of "blackness" in the white American mind. A surprising amount of Poe's work may be said to Gothicize the deep oppression and violence inherent in his culture's whiteness and thus to transform America's normative race into the most monstrous of them all.

Blackness consequently appears, albeit with different resonances, throughout Poe's writings. His poem "The Raven" (1845) exploits the Gothic potential inherent in Victorian America's elaborate rituals of mourning in a manner that turns cultural excess into poetic excess. The poem explores the bereavement of a speaker who may expect no "surcease of sorrow" (Poe, *Poetry and Tales*, p. 81) by incarnating his melancholia in the symbol of a raven who descends upon him, never to depart. The literal blackness of the bird is given figurative resonance by its poetic origin "on the Night's Plutonian shore" (ibid., p. 83); this figure, then, culminates in the Freudian trope of the melancholic shadow falling permanently upon the narrating ego at the poem's close:

> And the Raven, never flitting, still is sitting, *still* is sitting,
> . . .
> And the lamp-light o'er him streaming throws his shadow on the floor;
> And my soul from out that shadow that lies floating on the floor
>   Shall be lifted – nevermore!   (p. 86)

Poe here associates melancholia with a densely symbolic blackness, just as surely as he affiliates the black body with an ontological melancholia, the embodiment of a loss that speaks only of loss. "The Black Cat" (1843) is a more complex beast fable in which the symbolic import of "blackness" conflates the evil perpetrated by the white upon the body of the black, the long and painful memory of the black, and the return of the black as revenant to exact revenge. In this story blackness allegorizes not merely a personal (or even cultural) melancholia, as it does in "The Raven," but the abject underside of a national "normality."

To describe Poe's Gothic fictions as "philosophical" is to suggest that he pursues the question of explanatory origins for the problems of evil and suffering in both the individual and the national psyche. A corollary, as Gardner suggests, is the central issue "of whether there is some ultimate interior thing that can survive the calamities that befall exteriors: . . . does there remain something primal – something buried – that can survive these

calamities?"[19] "The Black Cat" interrogates the impulses of such a calamitous drive toward meaningless, unprovoked violence, and even though Poe
cannot explain how it comes about, he provides a rich Gothic figure to illustrate its temporal consequences. In a parody of the contemporary genre of
the Temperance Tract – a form of witnessing that details the devastation of
alcohol abuse – "The Black Cat's" narrator recounts his escalating violence
against his beloved pet cat, culminating in his murder of the poor animal.
Filled with remorse, he acquires another, almost identical cat, but his abusive
habits continue: attempting to kill the cat and so be rid of it, he turns his
fury upon his wife, whom he also murders. He conceals the corpse behind a
wall, but his crime is apprehended by "a voice from within the tomb," when
the cat – which had somehow become incarcerated within the tomb – emits
"a wailing shriek, half of horror and half of triumph, such as might have
arisen only out of hell, conjointly from the throats of the damned in their
agony" (*Poetry and Tales*, p. 606).

Because his "American" investments are so oblique, Poe's tales require
a historical contextualization. As an abolitionist allegory, "The Black Cat"
aligns the psychoanalytic Real, including the Gothic figure of the undead
come back to settle scores, with the historical real of the sheer perverseness
of American slavery. Lesley Ginsberg has demonstrated the efficacy of such
an allegorical reading by situating Poe's cat in relation to the animal images
of abolitionist literature. If proslavery supporters dehumanized blacks, abolitionists pointed out, by their alternative discourse, the full horror of slavery's
dissolution of the boundary between human and animal. Slave narratives like
that of Frederick Douglass, Ginsberg reminds us, celebrated the "rhetorical
transformation – from the 'beast-like stupor' of slavery to the full humanity
of freedom." Indeed, Ginsberg suggests an important cross-fertilization between the tropes of the Gothic and the slave narrative: Douglass, she notes,
narrates his first act of physical resistance in terms that are both Christian
and the familiar one of the Gothic revenant: "it was a glorious resurrection,
from the tomb of slavery!" The combination of the abolitionist trope of the
slave as domestic animal or chattel and Douglass's assertion of his humanity
as a figurative return from the grave ultimately leads Ginsberg to argue that
"Douglass allows us to reread the irrepressible voice of the dead in 'The
Black Cat' as an explicit metaphor for the silences and repressions upon
which the peculiar institution [of black slavery] was built."[20]

Poe's allegorical experiments with the symbolic potential of blackness are
also congruent with his representations of women, the *other* patriarchal chattel of the American nineteenth century. Female characters enter his fiction,
as black ones do, always already oriented toward the tomb; the point of
the fiction is to dramatize their return from a state of death to fulfill their

erotic mission, one which finds its counterpart in the death drive of his male protagonists. Because Poe so thoroughly identified woman as the object of necrophilial desire, his fictions of the female revenant turn upon a repellant but arresting beauty, a different form of the "perverse" from the violence that drives "The Black Cat," one that now seeks pleasure without shame and remains somehow impervious to the claustrophobia that usually besets Poe's male characters and readers.

Poe's most powerful achievements in the textual macabre gather the writer and the reader together into the spiral of the drive toward death – the inevitable consequence of an unrestrained melancholic absorption. Whereas Freud understood the death drive as a biological urge in *Beyond the Pleasure Principle* (1920), a force on the threshold between the organism and the psyche, Lacan has since reconceptualized it as the return of a sense of the chaotic and othered Real (which always threatens to absorb life into death) that had been precariously excluded by the subject's imaginary sense of its identity. The death drive designates the pressure of the unbound energies of the *id* to drive irrationally toward the Real against the limits enforced by the bound structure of the *ego*. Richard Boothby suggests that the death drive – and its pressure to "unbind" or "dissolve" the ego – is activated by a traumatic event "registered in an indelible image"; the ego obsessively returns to the traumatic image "in an effort to contain it in a repaired *Gestalt*. But at the same time, the memory of the trauma, itself an image of fragmentation and disintegration, provides the forces opposing the ego with their blazon of retaliation against the ego and its strictures."[21] Poe's narratives frequently stage this kind of encounter between the protagonist and a corpse, the emblem of the Real, but the unrequited melancholia that prompts this encounter does not inevitably require that the two be identical. Rather, Poe's Gothic effect is empowered by the confounding figure of *chiasmus* – the symbolism of crossing over, whereby the qualities of one object uncannily imbue the other (as life is invaded by death) – to situate the literally dead in relation to the traumatic shattering of the protagonist's ego, all within a death drive that is now clearly bound up with the process of narration. Between 1835 and 1838 especially, Poe composed several stories that enact this traumatic process.

"Berenice," the most disturbing of these stories, is an account of obsessive-compulsive disorder, or what the nineteenth century pathologized as "monomania," as it proceeds to an appalling fulfillment. Egaeus, Poe's narrator, becomes strangely attracted when, "in a smile of peculiar meaning, *the teeth of the changed Berenice disclosed themselves slowly to* [his] *view*" (*Poetry and Tales*, p. 230). Berenice's teeth constitute for Egaeus a fetish object, for he "felt that their possession could alone ever restore [him] to peace"

(p. 231); just as a fetish acquires meaning by a synecdochic logic, by which the part stands for the whole, the teeth here come to suggest the larger cultural specter of the devouring mother, the myth of woman as *vagina dentata* (a vulva lined with teeth). By this unconscious logic, to possess the teeth is to control the power of feminine sexuality and thus stabilize the contours of the ego. But the drive to possess the desired object as a means of self-possession goes terribly wrong in this story because Poe will allow no refuge in conventional symbolic terms. The abjected Real erupts into the literal when, after Berenice's death, Egaeus violates the corpse to retrieve the white objects of his longing. Poe renders the horrors of the Real by preventing any symbolic containment of it. Egaeus cannot even put the horror into words, only dimly recalling the desecration as "a fearful page in the record of my existence, written all over with dim, and hideous, and unintelligible recollections. I strived to decypher them, but in vain" (p. 232). If Egaeus's narrating ego is unbound by the trauma of his vile act, the narrative process itself is afflicted by its contagion, for it cannot unfold the deeply physical Real in any direct representation; it can but look awry at the corpse's violation. The full horror of Poe's revelation, then, comes in part from its falling back into relentless verbal production at the conclusion of the tale. Egaeus may be able to read what has hitherto haunted him as "a fearful page," but Poe's narrative does not linger to register the extent of his trauma or the extreme consequences of the death drive: "With a shriek I bounded to the table, and grasped the box that lay upon it. But I could not force it open; and in my tremor it slipped from my hands, and fell heavily; and burst into pieces; and from it, with a rattling sound, there rolled out some instruments of dental surgery, intermingled with thirty-two small, white and ivory-looking substances that were scattered to and fro on the floor" (p. 233). According to Kenneth Silverman, Poe extends the moment of horrified recognition in this "copulative ending."[22] By employing the rhetorical trope of *polysyndeton,* a succession of conjunctions, this sentence's series of "ands" helps greatly, in its sheer repetition, to suggest the repetitive death drive and its traumatic unbinding of normal logic, as the final words call attention, with a grisly equality, to the trembling hands, the fall, the shattering box, and the residue of the Real all at once.

The great lessons of Edgar Allan Poe are those of a certain compositional economy: for him chiasmus and prosopopoeia, the tropes of Gothic haunting and the return of the dead, turn perversely toward the literal – the decimated body – in order to assert the residue of history (including racial and gender history in America) as an often horrifying and incomprehensible Real continually calling the subject toward what is dying or has died. In Poe's hands,

Hawthorne's delicately sustained personifications acquire a forceful brevity and a chilling, literal animation; Brown's monstrosities lose their speculative abstraction to achieve a starker, more concise, and more visible animation. Despite his careful tracing of traumatic effects from pathological desires, Poe understood that absence is more unsettling than presence, particularly when the absent manifests itself indirectly as uncanny, the psychological, cultural, or physical otherness just below the threshold of what is conscious and conventional.

These Gothic lessons were not lost upon subsequent writers of the American nineteenth century. Emily Dickinson articulates the process of death in the voices of lyric speakers who address us from beyond the grave in a kind of reverse apostrophe: "I heard a fly buzz – when I died – " (Poem 591).[23] She versifies the inadequacy of poetic figures to capture the ineffable Real at the center of natural phenomena; her famous "Slant of Light" poem details the coming and passing of an oppressive illumination – "When it comes, the Landscape listens – / Shadows – hold their breath – / When it goes, 'tis like the Distance / On the look of Death – " (Poem 320) – but the light itself is the absent object of her intricate personifications and similes. Dickinson's melancholy vision of absences also occurs in Herman Melville's writing: the appalling whiteness of the whale in *Moby-Dick* (1851), by its very "indefiniteness, shadows forth the heartless voids and immensities of the universe,"[24] while the title character's constant refrain of "I would prefer not to" in "Bartleby, the Scrivener" (1853) functions as a catachresis, that rhetorical figure for which there is no literal referent, so as to bring the symbolic order of everyday language into traumatic collision with the blank inaccessibility of the Real. Such occasional Gothic features would consolidate themselves most fully for Melville in his Brockden-Brownish *Pierre or, The Ambiguities* (1852). But if Melville invests the most realistic, documentary narratives with the shadows of Gothic terror, nineteenth-century American Gothic reaches its most complex expression in the late writing of the expatriate Henry James, who not only gives us *The Turn of the Screw* by 1898 but returns to the United States to encounter, both in *The American Scene* (1907) and his last tale of New York, "The Jolly Corner" (1908),[25] the ghosts of the hypothetical selves he might have become had he remained in America. All of these writers refuse the complacent, progressive ideology of their native country. The terms of their refusal – the figures of the melancholic shadow, the "corpse" of an evil history working toward fulfillment, the "shadows" of human action manifested in the unquiet revenant – constitute a brilliantly innovative, experimental literature that perpetuated the life of the Gothic mode and consolidated the underside of writing in the American grain. The Gothic tradition in the

United States reflects not the critic Harold Bloom's model of literary advancement as overcoming the "anxiety of influence" – for these writers were keenly celebratory of their dark antecedents – but rather a haunting *influence of anxiety*, the enduring appeal of the Gothic to our most continuous fears, especially in an America haunted by the dark recesses of its own history.

NOTES

1 Walt Whitman, "Preface to *Leaves of Grass*" (1855) in *Complete Poetry and Collected Prose*, ed. Justin Kaplan (New York: Library of America, 1982), p. 5.
2 Malcolm Bowie, *Lacan* (London: Harper Collins, 1991), p. 94.
3 ibid., p. 105.
4 D. H. Lawrence, *Studies in Classic American Literature* (1923; reprinted Harmondsworth: Penguin, 1977), p. ii.
5 ibid., p. 15.
6 The relation between the abject's will-to-return and figurative innovation in Gothic literature is suggested by Julia Kristeva, who notes that "the subject of abjection is eminently productive of culture. Its symptom is the rejection and reconstruction of languages" (*Powers of Horror: an Essay on Abjection* [New York: Columbia University Press, 1982], p. 45).
7 Nina Baym, "A Minority Reading of *Wieland*" in Bernard Rosenthal, ed., *Critical Essays on Charles Brockden Brown* (Boston: G. K. Hall, 1981), p. 90, my emphasis.
8 Sigmund Freud, "Mourning and Melancholia" in *On Metapsychology*, volume XI of *The Penguin Freud Library*, trans. James Strachey et al., ed. Angela Richards (Harmondsworth: Penguin, 1984), p. 258, my emphasis.
9 Nicolas Abraham, "Notes on the Phantom: a Complement to Freud's Metapsychology," in *The Trial(s) of Psychoanalysis*, ed. Françoise Meltzer (Chicago: University of Chicago Press, 1988), pp. 75–77, my emphasis. Abraham distinguishes between *melancholia* – the loss of a loved one, the unsuccessful mourning, and the consequent incorporation of the lost object as a "tomb within" – and *the phantom*, by which descendents of the dead "objectify those buried tombs through diverse species of ghosts. What comes back to haunt are the tombs of others." The phantom represents, then, "the burial of an unspeakable fact within" the departed ("Notes," p. 76). Abraham's account of its emergence is strikingly resonant with the plot of *Wieland*: "it works like a ventriloquist, like a stranger within the subject's own mental topography" (ibid., p. 78).
10 Jane Tompkins, *Sensational Designs: the Cultural Work of American Fiction, 1790–1860* (Oxford: Oxford University Press, 1985), pp. 44, 52.
11 Sydney Smith, "Travels in America," *Edinburgh Review* 21 (December 1818): 144.
12 Robert Weisbuch, *Atlantic Double-Cross: American Literature and British Influence in the Age of Emerson* (Chicago: University of Chicago Press, 1986), p. xviii.
13 For a fuller analysis of Hawthorne's tropes of exhumation, see my articles " 'Filial Duty': Reading the Patriarchal Body in 'The Custom House,'" *Studies in the*

Novel 25 (1993), and "Necro-*filia*: Hawthorne's Melancholia," *English Studies in Canada* 27 (2001).

14 According to Coleridge the symbol conveys universal truth; it is characterized "above all by the translucence of the eternal through and in the temporal. It always partakes of the reality which it renders intelligible; and while it enunciates the whole, abides itself as a living part in that unity of which it is the representative." Samuel Taylor Coleridge, from *The Statesman's Manual* (1816), in *Critical Theory Since Plato*, ed. Hazard Adams (New York: Harcourt, 1971), p. 468.

15 Kenneth Silverman, *Edgar A. Poe: Mournful and Never-ending Remembrance* (New York: Harper Collins, 1991), p. 228.

16 Slavoj Žižek in *Looking Awry: an Introduction to Jacques Lacan Through Popular Culture* (Cambridge, MA: MIT Press, 1991), p. 174.

17 Jared Gardner, *Master Plots: Race and the Founding of an American Literature* (Baltimore: Johns Hopkins University Press, 1998), p. 127.

18 See Toni Morrison in *Playing in the Dark: Whiteness and the Literary Imagination* (Cambridge, MA: Harvard University Press, 1992), p. 32.

19 Gardner, *Master Plots*, p. 128.

20 Lesley Ginsberg, "Slavery and the Gothic Horror of Poe's 'The Black Cat'" in Robert Martin and Eric Savoy, eds., *American Gothic: New Interventions in a National Narrative* (Iowa City: University of Iowa Press, 1998), p. 104. See also Joan Dayan, "Amorous Bondage: Poe, Ladies and Slaves," *American Literature* 66 (1994): 239–73.

21 Richard Boothby, *Death and Desire: Psychoanalytic Theory in Lacan's Return to Freud* (London: Routledge, 1991), pp. 92–93.

22 Silverman, *Edgar A. Poe*, p. 113.

23 Dickinson's poems are cited from *The Poems of Emily Dickinson*, ed. Thomas H. Johnson (Cambridge, MA: Harvard University Press, 1983). Note also Daneen Wardrop, *Emily Dickinson's Gothic: Goblin with a Gauge* (Iowa City: University of Iowa Press, 1996).

24 Herman Melville, *Redburn, White-Jacket, Moby-Dick*, ed. G. Thomas Tanselle (New York: Library of America, 1983), p. 1001.

25 See Eric Savoy, "Spectres of Abjection: the Queer Subject of James's 'The Jolly Corner'," in Glennis Byron and David Punter, eds., *Spectral Readings: Towards a Gothic Geography* (London: Macmillan, 1999), pp. 161–74.

10

KELLY HURLEY

British Gothic fiction, 1885–1930

The skin, and the flesh, and the muscles, and the bones, and the firm structure
of the human body that I had thought to be unchangeable, and permanent as
adamant, began to melt and dissolve.

> Arthur Machen, *The Great God Pan* (1890; Machen,
> *House of Souls*, p. 236)

I will begin with four Gothic scenarios from the British *fin de siècle*.
Marooned on an obscure island, the protagonist of H. G. Wells's *The Island
of Dr. Moreau* (1896) must contend with "creatures" who are "human in
shape, and yet human beings with the strangest air about them of some
familiar animal" (p. 40). Prendick, unable to classify these anomalous entities,
feels a "queer spasm of disgust," a "shuddering recoil," in their presence
(pp. 25, 31). In *The Great God Pan*, the body of the dying Helen Vaughan
loses its human specificity in a series of rapid transformations as it "descend[s]
to the beasts whence it ascended," dissolves into "a substance as jelly," and
then takes on "a horrible and unspeakable shape, neither man nor beast."
The doctor who attends Helen is convulsed with "horror and revolting
nausea" at the sight of her terrible metamorphoses (Machen, *House of
Souls,* pp. 236–37). The narrator of William Hope Hodgson's *The Boats
of the "Glen Carrig"* (1907) leans over the water and looks into the eyes
of a "thing" with a "white, demoniac face, human save that the mouth
and nose had greatly the appearance of a beak." He recoils with disgust
and a "wild cry of fear" from the "foul and abominable" sight and smell
of this creature, whose two "flickering," tentacled hands clutch at the side
of the lifeboat (Hodgson, *"House on the Borderland,"* p. 30). In Rudyard
Kipling's "The Mark of the Beast" (1890), when a drunken Englishman de-
faces the image of Hanuman, the Indian Monkey-god, Hanuman's priest
changes Fleete into a wolfish creature that howls and bolts raw meat and
makes "beast-noises in the back of his throat." Strickland and the narrator, witnesses to Fleete's transformation, become "actually and physically

sick" at the sight of the "loathsome" spectacle (Kipling, "Mark of the Beast," pp. 202–03).

All of these texts describe human bodies that have lost their claim to a discrete and integral identity, a fully human existence. They are in contrast liminal bodies: bodies that occupy the threshold between the two terms of an opposition, like human/beast, male/female, or civilized/primitive, by which cultures are able meaningfully to organize experience. By breaking down such oppositions the liminal entity confounds one's ability to make sense of the world. Two of the above texts, moreover, describe human bodies in the very act of metamorphosis. As the Machen passage in my epigraph emphasizes, the human form is not reassuringly solid. It can "melt and dissolve" and take on phantasmic, unprecedented shapes. Such a Gothic body – admixed, fluctuating, abominable – can best be called an *abhuman* body (see Hurley, *Gothic Body*, pp. 3–20), borrowing the word *abhuman* from the fiction of Hodgson. The abhuman being retains vestiges of its human identity, but has already become, or is in the process of becoming, some half-human other – wolfish, or simian, or tentacled, or fungoid, perhaps simply "unspeakable" in its gross, changeful corporeality. Or the abhuman being may be some unimaginable "thing" incorporating, mimicking, or taking on a human form, thereby constituting another kind of threat to the integrity of human identity.

Abhumanness is a repulsively fascinating spectacle to which the late nineteenth- and early twentieth-century Gothic returns again and again, in works by such authors as Frank Aubrey, E. F. Benson, Algernon Blackwood, Arthur Conan Doyle, H. Rider Haggard, Hodgson, M. R. James, Kipling, Vernon Lee, Machen, Richard Marsh, M. P. Shiel, Robert Louis Stevenson, Bram Stoker, and Wells. Why do representations of abhuman identity recur so frequently and with such intensity in British Gothic fiction during the modernist era? What are the sociocultural sources of, and need for, such representations, and how does the genre revise its sources and answer that need? This chapter will provide some answers to these questions, and will describe some of the typical images and narratives found in British Gothic fiction from 1885 to 1930. But first I will work to place the modernist Gothic within the history of its genre more generally.

· This part is not to be printed.

Kipling, "The Mark of the Beast," p. 205

Critics of the Gothic agree on little else besides the literary historical fact that a genre that would be known as "the Gothic" came to prominence in Great Britain between 1760 and 1820, a genre distinguished by its supernaturalist content, its fascination with social transgression, and its departure, in formal terms, from the emerging norm of realism. As the preceding chapters show, the Gothic during these years has been quite variously defined in terms of plot (which features stock characters, like the virtuous, imperiled young heroine, and stock events, like her imprisonment by and flight from the demonic yet compelling villain), setting (the gloomy castle; labyrinthine underground spaces; the torture chambers of the Inquisition), theme (the genre's preoccupation with such taboo topics as incest, sexual perversion, insanity, and violence; its depictions of extreme emotional states, like rage, terror, and vengefulness), style (its hyperbolic language; its elaborate attempts to create a brooding, suspenseful atmosphere), narrative strategies (confusion of the story by means of narrative frames and narrative disjunction; the use of densely packed and sensationalist, rather than realistic, plotting), and its affective relations to its readership (whom it attempts to render anxious, fearful, or paranoid).

There is even less consensus on what constitutes literary Gothicism in later periods and on whether the post-Romantic Gothic can usefully be distinguished from adjacent genres such as science fiction, romance, fantasy, and horror. For instance, one might ask whether such *fin-de-siècle* narratives as I have described above shouldn't properly be classed as science fiction rather than Gothic. Of the four texts discussed in my first paragraph, only Kipling's depicts a truly supernatural event, "beyond any human and rational experience" ("Mark of the Beast," p. 202). The Silver Man practices a form of eastern magic, inexplicable to western science, which can only be countermanded by brute force, as when Strickland and the narrator torture the priest to make him undo his transformation of Fleete. *Moreau*'s uncanny Beast People are not supernatural entities, but the products of vivisection, blood transfusion, tissue grafting, and behavioral modification through hypnosis; Wells's novel is a speculative reworking of scientific practices legitimate in his own time. In structural terms, scientific premises are central to – even dictate the logic of – the entire narrative, and these premises are outlined in great detail, especially in the fourteenth chapter, where "Dr. Moreau Explains." Hodgson's fiction in general speculates on what bizarre creatures might evolve through natural selection, particularly in a closed ecosystem like the weed-choked Sargasso Sea, the setting of most of "*Glen Carrig*." Thus, when this novel describes fabulous monsters like the slug-men, their existence is in keeping with turn-of-the-century scientific premises, though these are not spelled out explicitly by Hodgson. *Pan*'s Helen Vaughan is the daughter of a human woman, a nonhuman force, and experimental neurosurgery: Dr. Raymond operates on "a certain group of nerve-cells" in her mother's brain, cells whose function is as yet unknown to other physiologists, in order to bridge the gap between the material and immaterial worlds (Machen, *House of Souls*, p. 173). Dr. Raymond's scientific explanations are far more perfunctory than Dr. Moreau's, and his field of inquiry is not legitimate medicine but "transcendental medicine" (ibid., p. 169), a phrase borrowed from Robert Louis Stevenson's more famous *Strange Case of Dr. Jekyll and Mr. Hyde* (1886). Yet it is notable that in both *Pan* and *Jekyll* seemingly supernatural phenomena are produced *through* scientific practice – by means of physiological manipulation, or chemical experimentation, rather than magical spells.

In "The Inmost Light" (1894), Machen calls such practice "occult science" (Machen, *Tales*, p. 181). And this characterization of science as a liminal art – an empiricist discipline that produces, or describes, phenomena that could best be described as "Gothic" – is prevalent in popular literature of the modernist era. Careless or irresponsible science, in the tradition of *Frankenstein*, results in "monsters manufactured" (Wells, *Moreau*, p. 71) like the beast-people, Mr. Hyde, and Helen Vaughan. But science also describes the unpredictable strangeness of the natural world and the bizarre, shifting nature of the human subject itself. Bram Stoker's *Dracula* (1897), whose characters include two doctor/psychologists, describes its vampire in terms explicitly borrowed from criminal anthropology, degeneration theory, and alienism, late-Victorian sociomedical disciplines that worked to classify and comprehend the abnormal human subject. Though these sciences of the criminal, the unfit, and the insane fail to account for the vampire's longevity or shape-shifting abilities, Dr. Van Helsing has faith that science will explain even these things some day, when it has fully comprehended "all the forces of nature that are occult and deep and strong" – for it is Nature that has shaped Dracula, not some supernatural force. Transylvania, Van Helsing explains in his fractured English, "is full of strangeness of the geologic and chemical world... Doubtless, there is something magnetic or electric in some of these combinations of occult forces which work for physical life in strange way" (Stoker, *Dracula*, p. 278).

Moreover, the thoroughly loathsome nature of the abhuman bodies described in these texts, as well as other characters' thoroughly disgusted responses to them, would indicate that we are in the register of Gothic rather than science fiction, or at least working within some peculiarly modern hybrid genre. But this raises a new problem. For one might argue that these texts' insistence on the gross corporeality of the body – both the admixed, transformative abhuman body and the nauseated body of the human character who confronts it – should lead one to classify the modernist Gothic as horror. Horror is generally understood to be a less restrained, more tasteless genre than Gothic, indulging in more graphic imagery and extreme scenarios as it depicts decomposing, deliquescing, and otherwise disgust-ingly metamorphic bodies, and soliciting a more visceral response from its readership. Noël Carroll's *The Philosophy of Horror*, with its "entity-based" theory of the horrific, argues that the genre is constituted by the presence of a certain kind of monster – a liminal monster, one that is "categorically in-terstitial, categorically contradictory, incomplete, or formless" – that evokes the very particular response of fear "compounded with revulsion, nausea, disgust" (pp. 41, 32, 22). While earlier instances of horror exist, says Carroll, the genre did not really take off until the end of the nineteenth century, when representations of the horrific and the repulsive multiplied and intensi-fied. In her *Skin Shows*, Judith Halberstam associates horror with gruesome spectacles of "embodied deviance" as this has been variously understood since *Frankenstein*, while Gothic is "loosely defined as the rhetorical style and narrative structure designed to produce fear and desire within the reader" (pp. 5, 2). "Gothic" is identified with form and "horror" with content, though Halberstam's distinction is not so simple as that, for narrative and rhetorical strategies must shift in order to accommodate shifts in content. The subtitle of her book (*Gothic Horror and the Technology of Monsters*) thus acknowledges the difficulty, perhaps the futility, of understanding the post-Romantic Gothic as anything *but* a hybridized genre.

As David Punter puts it, we can define the Gothic "as a historically delim-ited genre or as a more wide-ranging and persistent tendency within fiction as a whole" (*Literature of Terror*, I, 12), and some critics have wondered whether the genre Gothic should be said to exist at all after 1825 or so. Nicholas Daly, for one, rejects the formulation of Gothic as a literary "mode" that lingers on, in the Victorian period and afterwards, like "the ghost of eighteenth-century Gothic fiction." Such a formulation, he argues, may be both overly capacious and overly constricting. If we understand Gothic as a genre that reemerges at different historical moments and is designed to ex-plore and manage "the taboo areas of a particular culture," then nearly any text that treats social transgression may be understood as Gothic, rendering the category meaningless. At the same time, it will become difficult to read a text claimed as an instance of the genre as doing anything *except* managing cultural anxieties.[1]

Most critics, nonetheless, have found it useful to retain an understand-ing of Gothic as a transhistorical genre. Its plot elements and setting may change, but its plots still remain exorbitant, piling incident upon incident for its own sake, and its settings are still overcharged with a fearsome and brooding atmosphere. The nature of social transgression may differ from one era to another, and clinical understandings of mental disorder shift as well, but the Gothic still shows a fascination with extreme behaviors and derangements of human subjectivity. The genre is about excess, Fred Botting argues in *Gothic*: excessive imagery, excessive rhetoric, excessive narrative, and excessive affect. Thus we may easily describe a novel like *Moreau* – structured on good scientific principles but marked by its frequent and graphic depictions of grotesquely liminal bodies, the overheated language of its narrator, and hysterical moments of narrative disjunction and refusal – as Gothic rather than (or as well as) science fiction.

Moreover, since the modernist era is the extended moment during which, perhaps, the genre known as Gothic metamorphoses into horror, it is tempting to follow Halberstam's lead and speak of the hybrid genre Gothic horror. But for the moment, at least, I prefer to retain the term Gothic in order to mark a continuity – an ongoing tradition of extravagant representation – between the turns of the eighteenth and of the nineteenth centuries. I understand "Gothic" as a genre comprised of texts that have been deemed "popular"; that deploy sensationalist and suspenseful plotting; that practice narrative innovation despite the frequent use of certain repetitive plot elements; that depict supernatural or seemingly supernatural phenomena or otherwise demonstrate a more or less antagonistic relation to realist literary practice; that actively seek to arouse a strong affective response (nervousness, fear, revulsion, shock) in their readers; that are concerned with insanity, hysteria, delusion, and alternate mental states in general; and that offer highly charged and often graphically extreme representations of human identities, sexual, bodily, and psychic.

> I was conscious of a most horrible smell of mould and of a cold kind of face pressed against my own and moving slowly over it; and of several – I don't know how many – legs or arms or tentacles or something clinging to my body.
> M. R. James, "The Treasure of Abbot Thomas" (1904)[2]

It is also useful to think of genre in terms of what Annette Kuhn calls its "cultural instrumentality":[3] how a genre functions within the culture that produces and consumes it, how it expresses something significant, or negotiates some salient problem, for its readership. The Gothic is rightly, if partially, understood as a cyclical genre that reemerges in times of cultural stress in order to negotiate anxieties for its readership by working through them in displaced (sometimes supernaturalized) form. For instance, critics have linked the resurgence of the Gothic in the late-Victorian period to anxieties about modern urban culture,[4] or about Britain's status as the dominant modern imperial power. In novels such as *Dr. Jekyll and Mr. Hyde*, *Dracula*, Machen's *The Three Imposters* (1895), and Richard Marsh's *The Beetle* (1897), London – both the labyrinthine city itself and its anonymous-seeming suburbs – is envisioned as a dark, threatening mystery, "as unknown . . . as the darkest reaches of Africa."[5] Populated by dangerous hooligans, criminals, perverts, and foreigners, who can conceal and remake their identities at will, the modern city is a space wherein casual, random encounters provoke terrible consequences, and within which any atrocity might be committed and concealed. The "imperial Gothic," as Patrick Brantlinger calls it,[6] describes dangerous encounters between Englishman and colonized subject, like Fleete's with the Silver Man, in the contact zones of the empire. In the colonies the "civilized" man may revert to barbarism with frightening rapidity, like Fleete, and come to wear "the mark of the beast." Or England itself, if weakened by internal stresses and social decay, may itself be the object of imperialist predations by its own colonists, as when London is threatened by supernatural invaders in *The Beetle* and Guy Boothby's *Pharos the Egyptian* (1899).

Along similar lines, the proliferation of Gothic representations of abhumanness at the *fin de siècle* may be partly attributed to the destabilizing effects of nineteenth-century Darwinian science. This science understood species to be impermanent, metamorphic, and liable to extinction. It assumed an uncomfortably intimate relation between "animal" and "human," since the latter was, as Charles Darwin put it famously in *The Descent of Man* (1871), "descended from a hairy, tailed quadruped," which was itself "probably derived from an ancient marsupial animal, and this through a long series of diversified forms, from some amphibian-like creature, and this again from some fish-like animal."[7] The theory of evolution described the human body not as an integral wholeness, but as a kind of Frankenstein monster, patched together from the different animal forms the human species had inhabited during the various phases of its evolutionary history.[8] It posited that natural history (and by extension human history) progressed randomly, moving toward no particular climax, so that bodies, species, and cultures were as likely to move "backwards" as "forwards," degenerating into less complex forms. It destroyed a comfortably anthropocentric worldview: human beings were just a species like any other, developed by chance rather than providential design, and given the mutability of species, humans might well devolve or otherwise metamorphose into some repulsive abhuman form.

"There upon the floor was a dark and putrid mass, seething with corruption and hideous rottenness, neither liquid nor solid, but melting and changing before our eyes . . . I saw a writhing and stirring as of limbs."[9] In the modernist Gothic the human body is fluctuating, admixed, and abominable. Animal species do not remain properly distinct from the human species, but show disturbing traces of an evolving human identity: Hodgson's slug-men; the ape-men in E. D. Fawcett's *Swallowed by an Earthquake* (1894) and

Arthur Conan Doyle's *The Lost World* (1912); the prehistoric survivals of John Buchan's "No-Man's-Land" (1898) and Machen's "The Shining Pyramid" (1895). Humans are transformed into beasts right before one's eyes: into wolfish or simian creatures or unspecifiable human-animal things, as in "The Mark of the Beast" and *Pan*, Algernon Blackwood's "The Wendigo" (1910), Hodgson's "The Adventure of the Headland" (1912), and M. P. Shiel's "The Pale Ape" (1911). Fatally liable to devolution, the human body may even dissolve absolutely, into the primordial slime from whence all life was said to originate, as occurs in the passage above from *Three Imposters*, or in Hodgson's "The Derelict" (1912). Jekyll thinks of Hyde as "something not only hellish but inorganic. This was the shocking thing; that the slime of the pit seemed to utter cries and voices; that the amorphous dust gesticulated and sinned" (*Jekyll and Hyde*, p. 122). Within the terms laid out by materialist science, the human subject is entrapped within the realm of matter – incapable of transcendence, doomed endlessly to demonstrate its gross and changeable physicality. In the modernist ghost story even otherworldly spirits are often disgustingly embodied, materializing into slime-entities in such haunted-house tales as A. M. Burrage's "The Bungalow at Shammerton" (1927) and H. R. Wakefield's "The Red Lodge" (1928), or into the spider-like or octopoid part-human anomalies of M. R. James's "Canon Alberic's Scrap-book" (1895) and "Count Magnus" (1904).

Uncanny human metamorphoses were also the concern of the late-Victorian human sciences that incorporated and revised evolutionism. Criminal anthropology, for instance, argued that deviant individuals, known as "born criminals," were atavists: throwbacks to the species who shared certain savage behaviors and physiognomical traits (jutting jaw, receding forehead, apelike disproportion of the limbs) with other animal species. Degeneration theory posited that certain physical and nervous disorders, spawned by modern industrial and urban life, could be both spread and inherited by social contact, and might even be passed down to offspring in aggravated form. Industrial toxins, drug and alcohol abuse, and unsanitary urban conditions initiated this downward spiral, as did newfangled technologies like railway travel and telegraphy, which increased the pace of modern life and rendered its subjects fatigued and hysterical. The sexologist Richard von Krafft-Ebing and the social theorist Max Nordau believed that moral turpitude (sexual perversion, decadent art, and literature) was an especially repulsive and dangerous cause of degeneration, instigating and exacerbating nervous disorders, all highly "contagious" within modern city life. Not only family lines but also whole societies were thought to be subject to degeneration, whose wildfire progression through a nation could be gauged

by its widespread immorality, political and social unrest, cultural decadence, and the nervous disorders and increasingly deformed bodies of its
subjects.[10]

This entropic plotline, whereby bodies regress and complexity yields to
either increasing indifferentiation or chaotic disorder, also structures Gothic
narratives of degeneration, whether of individual corruption, like Oscar
Wilde's *The Picture of Dorian Gray* (1891), or social decay, like Wells's
The Time Machine (1895) and Hodgson's *The Night Land* (1912). Though
their goal is to accomplish a kind of purification of human identity – the
deviant subject must be identified, diagnosed, and controlled in order to
assure national health – criminal anthropology and degeneration theory
posit human identity as dangerously fluid. The metamorphoses instantiated
by atavism or degeneration are unpredictable and can produce a bewildering variety of admixed bodies: the criminal anthropologist Cesare Lombroso
describes human regressives who display the physical characteristics of mon-
keys, lemurs, dogs, rodents, oxen, reptiles, birds of prey, and domestic fowl,
to name a few. In *The Time Machine* the luxurious indolence of the future
(the "slow movement of degeneration") has caused the human race to split
into two species, one etiolated, shrunken, and intellectually vapid, the other
apelike and cannibalistic, "sickening" in its abhumanness. In *The Night
Land*, a combination of factors – the heat-death of the sun, human "lawless-
ness and degeneracy," scientific experiments that released occult forces into
the world, sexual depravity and miscegenation ("consortings with strange
outward beings") – have combined to produce a "Pandemonium" of abhuman monstrosities that threatens to overwhelm the once-human world.[11]

> "I scratched you yesterday. I bit you. I sucked your blood. Now I will suck it
> dry, for you are mine" ... She came nearer to me and nearer, uttering all the
> time that blood-curdling sound which was so like the frenzied cry of some
> maddened animal. Marsh, "The Mask" (1900)[12]

Thus the Gothic can serve as a sort of historical or sociological index: if
the genre serves to manage a culture's disturbances and traumatic changes,
its thematic preoccupations will allow us to track social anxieties at one
remove, in the register of supernaturalism. Psychoanalytical interpretations
of the Gothic are also concerned with the ways in which social anxieties
are supernaturalized and rendered in displaced form. More specifically, a
psychoanalytic reading of the Gothic might identify the genre's monster
as the "return of the repressed": the embodiment of unbearable or unacceptable fears, wishes, and desires that are driven from consciousness and
then transmuted into representations of monstrosity, just as the unconscious

reshapes repressed material into dream images or hysterical symptoms. The reader remains safely distanced from the threatening contents of the unconscious because they have been defamiliarized by being rendered phantasmic, so that the Gothic can provide a pleasurable catharsis that a realistic genre would not be able to accomplish. This is how Sigmund Freud, writing and practicing during the modernist era, explains an affect he calls "the uncanny": the sensation of "dread and creeping horror" aroused when a well-known thing or person becomes strange, or when something unfamiliar is invested with a haunting familiarity. The uncanny "is in reality nothing new or foreign, but something familiar and old-established in the mind that has been estranged only by the process of repression" (Freud, "Uncanny," pp. 368, 394). Early in *Moreau*, Prendick finds the beast-man M'Ling to be repulsively strange and yet hauntingly familiar, for he cannot comprehend that a human being may be so thoroughly animalized; the symptom of uncanniness identifies him as one who represses the possibility of his own animalism, his own abhumanness.

For Freud, literary instances of uncanniness revive repressed infantile complexes like the Oedipus complex, or "forms of thought that have been surmounted," like belief in animism or the evil eye (Freud, "Uncanny," p. 406). In his influential article on the American Horror film, Robin Wood also reads the uncanny or Gothic representation as a gauge of anxiety, but he is more concerned with culturally specific monsters as they are spawned by culturally specific fears. Wood argues that in all societies "people are conditioned from earliest infancy to take on predetermined roles, as subjects with a certain sexual or class-based identity, perhaps, and to persecute those who fail or refuse to do so" (p. 8). For instance, if reproductive heterosexuality is the social norm, properly normalized subjects will repress their own homoerotic and other inappropriate desires and vilify (as sinners, perverts, barbarians, and so on) those subjects who do not. Gothic monsters, then, are displaced and distorted versions not only of tendencies repressed across a culture, but also of the "bad" subject (the Other) with whom those tendencies have already been identified, and who has already been labeled monstrous. The Gothic may kill off the monster in such a way as to effect catharsis for the viewer or reader, who sees his or her unacceptable desires enacted vicariously and then safely "repressed" again, or it may encourage sympathy for the monster and thus serve to critique the cultural norms which the monster violates.

Along these lines, Elaine Showalter reads Stevenson's Mr. Hyde as the embodiment of late-Victorian anxieties about male homosexuality, whose repudiation within the culture can be charted through both its scientific discourse (Victorian sexology identified the homosexual as a perverse aberration and a degenerate) and its laws (the 1885 Labouchère Amendment made sexual acts between men illegal and punishable by imprisonment). *Dr. Jekyll and Mr. Hyde* depicts an entirely homosocial world – all significant relations, whether based on friendship or rivalry, affection or mistrust, are between men, the bachelors in whose circle Jekyll moves. In this bourgeois professional world from which women (except as servants) are excluded, one would expect to find homoerotic passion as well. But instead one finds joyless repression – characters "mortify" themselves, like Utterson, or simultaneously indulge and conceal their "pleasures … with an almost morbid sense of shame," like Jekyll – and one finds the monster, Hyde. Hyde is a figure of energy, violence, and libidinal excess, a *Doppelgänger* for Jekyll, whose unspecified desires he acts out with impunity, and the object of fascination and fantasy for the self-abnegating Utterson, whose imagination is "enslaved" by Hyde and who is "haunted" by dreams of Hyde appearing suddenly at Jekyll's bedside. "In the most famous code word of Victorian sexuality," Showalter argues, the other male characters "find something *unspeakable* about Hyde":[13] in Wood's terms, Hyde enacts desires that must be banished from both late-Victorian society and the late-Victorian male's consciousness. The cultural figuration of homosexuality as "monstrous" is literalized by Hyde's hideousness and deformity ("there was something abnormal and misbegotten in the very essence of the creature"), while Utterson's "disgust, loathing, and fear" in Hyde's presence is symptomatic of both his attraction toward and repudiation of this dangerous figure of desire (*Jekyll and Hyde*, pp. 37, 103, 48, 99, 52).

During the nineteenth century deviance from sexual norms was identified as both a symptom and a cause of social degeneration, so that by posing a challenge to traditional gender roles, liminal subjects like the homosexual (since the "sexual invert" was said to have a female soul entrapped within a man's body) were seen as causes of social unrest and potential threats to national health. Another such threateningly liminal subject was the "New Woman," or *fin-de-siècle* feminist, an outspoken, independent, and thoroughly modern woman, whose "masculine" behaviors made her something of a monster. The New Woman had abandoned the role prescribed by Victorian gender ideology, that of the "angel in the house," guardian of the private sphere. The domestic angel was defined in relation to her menfolk (as daughter, wife, sister, or mother) and characterized by her childlike innocence, loving tenderness, and selflessness, a moral purity that was often figured as asexuality, her appealing vulnerability and dependence, and a mind that was sympathetic and intuitive rather than rational and intellectual. Maude Redcar, the long-suffering wife whose husband is seduced by a vampire in Dick Donovan's "The Woman with the 'Oily Eyes' " (1899), is "as sweet a woman as ever drew God's breath of life . . . a flawless woman . . . with all the virtues that turn women into angels."[14] *Dracula*'s Mina Harker is another such angelic, asexual wife: she spends her honeymoon in a convent with the convalescing Jonathan and works tirelessly to bring her husband back to health, all the while comforting the broken-hearted suitors of Lucy Westenra. "She is one of God's women," says Van Helsing. "So true, so sweet, so noble, so little an egoist" (pp. 168–69). Victorian men, by contrast, were the breadwinners for and protectors of their gratefully submissive women; courageous, masterful, resourceful, and strong. "How can women help loving men when they are so earnest, and so true, and so brave!," Mina asks rhetorically (p. 308). Adam Salton in Stoker's *The Lair of the White Worm* (1911) is a chivalric defender of his future wife's safety and honor and a cool hand in battle, "ready for any emergency."[15]

While the understanding of male and female sexual identities as complementary, natural, and fixed was contested on many fronts by the turn of the nineteenth century, Victorian gender roles had never been stable to begin with. For instance, social constructions of female identity contradicted one another, so that women might be described as ethereal, essentially disembodied angels within domestic ideology, but also as dangerously embodied creatures – wracked by the upheavals of puberty, menstruation, childbirth, and menopause; incapable of sustained rational thought; prone to emotional outbursts and hysteria – within medical science. Janet Oppenheim shows how definitions of masculinity also shifted drastically during the Victorian period, so that "emotional tenderness" and sentiment, seen as compatible with masculine activity and resolution in the earlier nineteenth century, were considered somewhat effeminate qualities by the century's end, when "physical grace, courage, pluck, and toughness [were] among the highest qualities of manhood."[16] The ideology of separate spheres – only men were to enter the working world, while women accepted domesticity and dependency in exchange for masculine support – was belied by the reality of female experience, as mid-century feminists pointed out. Women who had no male protectors and no means of employment might be left in poverty; a dependent wife might be abused rather than cherished by her husband.

However, if proscriptive ideologies of gender were subject to challenge throughout the century, by the *fin de siècle* it seemed to many that traditional gender roles were becoming undone, especially with the emergence of figures like the New Woman. Many of her goals were not so new; like earlier feminists, she supported education and meaningful employment for women, along with the reform of marriage and divorce laws. But New Women also argued that they had a right to move freely within the public sphere, to engage in frank dialogue about sexuality, contraception, and venereal disease, and to enjoy physical intimacy both within and outside of marriage. As a result, the New Woman was vilified for her unwomanly sexual appetites and her insistence on behaving "like a man."

Using Wood's model, one can argue that the *fin-de-siècle* Gothic contends with this threat in displaced fashion through its numerous representations of monster women and she-devils. For instance, the three vampire women in Dracula's castle are sexual aggressors who attack Jonathan Harker with rapacity and "deliberate voluptuousness." They behave "coquettishly," like more conventional Victorian women might do, but their coquetry is "ribald," and their laughter is "mirthless, hard, soulless . . . like the pleasure of fiends" (Stoker, *Dracula*, pp. 42–43). Even naive and girlish Lucy shows something of a New Womanly sexual appetite when she asks, "Why can't they let a girl marry three men, or as many as want her, and save all this trouble?," so that one is not surprised when vampire-Lucy lures one of her former suitors with "voluptuous wantonness" (pp. 60, 187). It is easy to multiply instances of such supernaturalized sexual predators: *Pan*'s Helen Vaughan ("that woman, if I can call her woman, corrupted my soul," says her dying husband [Machen, *The House*, p. 192]); the snaky villainess of *Lair of the White Worm*; the vampire women in "The Woman with the 'Oily Eyes' "; E. F. Benson's "The Room in the Tower" (1912) and "Mrs. Amworth" (1922); Arthur Conan Doyle's "John Barrington Cowles" (1886); the phantom seductresses of Vernon Lee's "Amour Dure" (1890); Robert Hichens's "How Love Came to Professor Guildea" (1900); Oliver Onions's "The Beckoning Fair One" (1911); and the half-animal, half-magical shape-shifters of *The Beetle* and Shiel's "Huguenin's Wife" (1895).

Fin-de-siècle monster women not only menace sexually, but also display an unwomanly lust for power, like Stoker's Queen Tera in *The Jewel of the Seven Stars* (1903), or the eponymous heroine of H. Rider Haggard's *She* (1886–87), who wishes to "assume absolute rule over the British dominions, and probably over the whole earth."[17] In Frank Aubrey's *King of the Dead* (1903) the priestess Alloyah, driven by her "fiery passions," ambitiousness, and "inflexible will," is described during the course of the novel as a "sorceress," a "beautiful she-devil," an "Amazon Queen," and a "modern Circe." Alloyah is also described as "a devil and an angel mingled in one,"[18] a phrase that could be used to characterize not only the seductive villainesses of the modernist Gothic, but also its winsomely appealing heroines. "It is monstrous that a parent – a father ! – should be subjected to such treatment by his child," says *The Beetle*'s Mr. Linden when Marjorie compares him to a "Russian autocrat" and coolly refuses to obey his orders (pp. 555–56). Mr. Linden is a pompous fool, to be sure, and this scene is played to comic effect, but it is nonetheless true that the modernist Gothic heroine is often described as independent, proud, self-willed, and contemptuous of social mores, rather like the New Woman.

Even Mina Harker, who meekly bows to male authority ("though it was a bitter pill for me to swallow, I could say nothing, save to accept their chivalrous care of me" [Stoker, *Dracula*, p. 214]), and who does not scruple to express her contempt for the New Woman (pp. 86–87), is distinguished by her resourcefulness, technological proficiency, and clear-headed rationality, all culturally coded as masculine. "She has man's brain," says Van Helsing approvingly, "– a brain that a man should have were he much gifted – and woman's heart" (p. 207). Though Mina continues to resist sexual corruption after being seduced by the vampire, she is still imperfectly feminine: not a "ghoulish example of her sex" like the Woman of Songs (Marsh, *Beetle*, p. 462) who changes from female to male and back again, nor Helen Vaughan, whose "form waver[s] from sex to sex" (Machen, *Pan*, in *House of Souls*, p. 237), but a liminal sexual subject nonetheless. What is notable in these texts is not the difference between supernaturalized and normal women, but their similarities and the rapidity with which the latter can change into the former. Within a few hundred pages, Lucy's "sweetness [is] turned to adamantine, heartless cruelty," her angelic "purity" to snarling animalism as she crouches with blood-stained lips over a dying child (Stoker, *Dracula*, p. 187). In Marsh's "The Mask," beautiful Mrs. Jaynes pulls off her costume and becomes the maniac Mary Brooker, blood-thirsty and savage. Remove the mask of feminine innocence and you find beneath it a raging animal, a monster, a "creature with...the face of a devil."[19]

While such representations of monstrous female bodies may be linked to anxieties about the ways in which New Women seemed to be threatening the social order, one must note that the male body, too, is subject to strange transformations in the pages of the modernist Gothic. Victorian science figured the woman as imperfectly human: more entrapped within the body than the man, and thus less intellectual, more animal, more unstable, so that her disgusting metamorphoses are in some senses not unexpected. The man should, by contrast, appear as a fully human subject, powerful and self-sufficient, capable of transcending the animal body. Yet in texts such as "The Mark of the Beast" we see that males also have a most precarious hold on human identity. One reason, to be sure, is the fact of homosexuality, already dismissed by sexology as an incompletely masculine and regressive state. When homoerotic desire is represented as an attack by abhuman monsters like the reptilian villain of Boothby's *The Curse of the Snake* (1902) or the slug-men in "*Glen Carrig*," this is again not unexpected, given the sociomedical conflation of homosexuality, degeneration, and animality.

Degenerate times require a heroic version of masculinity – the graceful athleticism of *She*'s Leo Vincey, the "stalwart manhood" of Arthur in *Dracula* (p. 152), *Night Land*'s chivalric and muscular narrator. But even the "normal" male subject, the man's man, is prone to breakdown. Attacked by the three vampire women, Jonathan lies passive and still and waits to be penetrated, "looking out under [his] eyelashes" almost girlishly (Stoker, *Dracula*, p. 42). Their inappropriately aggressive femininity requires as object an effeminized version of masculinity, as is true when the Beetle-woman's seduction turns Paul Lessingham, the "man of iron nerve," into a "fibreless, emasculated creature" (Marsh, *Beetle*, pp. 505, 635). Their subsequent nervous disorders – Jonathan's "brain fever," Lessingham's hysterical fits – mark them as degenerate types no less than the animalized, ambiguously sexed Mr. Hyde. But at the other end of the spectrum, masculinity that is too vigorous and too potent leads to degeneration of another, more savage sort. In "The Pale Ape" urgent male heterosexual desire is a brutalizing force, transforming the mild-mannered aristocrat Sir Philip Lister ("so perfect in gentleness, so shy, so staid!") into a savage beast covered with fur "an inch deep . . . and gross as the gorilla's."[20] The powerfully built Holly, nicknamed "Baboon," crushes two men to death with his long, simian arms: the brilliant Cambridge Fellow, "mad with rage," feels "that awful lust for slaughter which will creep into the hearts of the most civilised of us."[21] Victorian racial science described the non-European, in contrast to the civilized Englishman, as a semi-evolved barbarian, but in the imperial modernist Gothic it is the "pale ape," even more shockingly, who regresses into brutish animalism.

> Madness were easy to bear compared with truth like this.
>
> Stoker, *Dracula*, p. 173

Clearly abhumanness *spreads* in the modernist Gothic. It is not just socially problematic or marginalized individuals – feminists, "natives," homosexuals – who are liable to degeneration, devolution, and other bizarre transfigurations. All human subjects, it would seem, are potentially liminal, potentially abhuman.

The modernist Gothic negotiated a cultural moment within which traditional constructs of human identity were breaking down on all fronts. The new models that would replace them were not reassuring ones. Materialist science described a human subject thoroughly circumscribed within a grossly material body, rather than one capable of spiritual or intellectual transcendence of bodily identity. In late-Victorian psychology human subjectivity was fissured by the uncanny space of the unconscious, divided from and unknowable to itself and prone to a bewildering variety of nervous disorders.

The evolutionary sciences emphasized the changeful and chaotic nature, and the regressive tendencies, of the abominable human body. This was a profoundly difficult period of cultural transition particularly needy of what the Gothic can do. In his genre study *The Fantastic*, Tzvetan Todorov allows us to consider the Gothic's relation to widespread anxieties in a different way than that allowed by psychoanalytic criticism, and he does so by using the Gothic text as modernists did: to identify points of epistemological stress for its culture.

According to this account, the "fantastic is that hesitation experienced by a person who knows only the laws of nature, confronting an apparently supernatural event" (Todorov, *Fantastic*, p. 25). For instance, when Jonathan Harker sees Count Dracula crawling face-first down the castle wall, he cannot trust his own senses and fears that he is losing his mind. After the narrator of *"Glen Carrig"* encounters a slug-man for the first time, he is "all at a loss to know whether I had fallen asleep, or that I had indeed seen a devil" (Hodgson, *"House on the Borderland,"* p. 31). The fantastic text depicts the collision of two models of reality: the incursion of extranormal events, or seemingly extranormal events, into the everyday world. The extended moment of uncertainty, horror, anxiety, and dismay that results when the character or reader is unable to classify those events enables us to distinguish the fantastic from kindred genres like the fairy tale or science fiction, in which marvelous events are the norm. More importantly, the appearance of the symptom of convulsive uncertainty – the character's panicked inability to interpret the strange event – lets us know we have breached the knowledge systems of the text's culture, thus allowing us to determine where normal realities end and alternate or impossible realities begin for that culture. Human beings should not creep down walls like insects; beaked and tentacled humans should not swim up out of the Sargasso Sea.

Todorov argues that few texts can maintain the sensation of fearful hesitation that characterizes the fantastic for their duration: eventually the anomalous event is shown to be either explicable through natural causes or a genuine instance of the occult. The slug-men, however repulsive, are merely the products of evolution; Dracula, Jonathan Harker learns, is truly a supernatural monster. But what is notable in these modernist Gothic novels is how little closure such explanations provide. As we have seen, the psychiatrist Van Helsing still labors to understand Dracula within some scientific paradigm, whether provided by alienism, criminal anthropology, or chemistry. Hodgson's slug-men are called "weed-men," which marks them as natural products of their environment, the weed-filled Sargasso, but they are also called "devil-men," to denote their diabolical strangeness, and the narrator's nauseated horror of them only intensifies as they become more familiar to him. Moreover, the first-glimpsed "devil-man" reminds the narrator of the "great devil-fish" he has just seen clinging to the side of a derelict ship (Hodgson, *"Glen Carrig,"* in *"House on the Borderland,"* p. 30), and while Hodgson's fiction presents its giant cephalopods to great Gothic effect, they were proven monstrosities of natural history since mid-century, when zoologists identified the giant squid as a new species (as Jules Verne knew as well) and "marked [its] official transition . . . from the realm of fable into the scientific literature."[22] Aubrey populates his novels with all sorts of bizarre and terrible creatures; his overcharged language and suspenseful narration would indicate that these are Gothic monstrosities, but he then authenticates them whenever possible by footnoting scientific and travel literature. In *Queen of Atlantis* (1899), for instance, he interrupts a heated battle with a disgustingly oversized cuttle-fish ("The whole swaying balloon-like form was one mass of quivering rage") to footnote an 1897 *Chambers's Journal* article about a gigantic octopus corpse that washed up on the Florida coast. "Such a creature . . . is quite sufficient to account for the stories of great sea-serpents," his footnote concludes.[23]

Natural history describes real monsters. These monsters appear in aggravated form in the pages of the modernist Gothic, so that carnivorous plants like the Venus flytrap, newly classified by Victorian botanists, are exaggerated into anthropophagous trees in Aubrey's *The Devil-Tree of El Dorado* (1896) or Alice and Claude Askew's "Alymer Vance and the Vampire" (1914). But more importantly, natural history provides a mechanism for producing monsters. Theories of the evolution of species meant that any combination of morphic traits, any transmutation of bodily form, was possible. Since seemingly anomalous phenomena like giant cephalopods can be explained by natural processes like species' adaptation to environment, there is no reason that beaked and tentacled humans should *not* swim up out of the Sargasso Sea. The modernist Gothic thus stands in an opportunistic relation to the nineteenth-century sciences that while demolishing the idea of a stable human identity yet gave imaginative warrant to the richly loathsome variety of abhuman abominations that the Gothic went on to produce.

When Marsh's Beetle-woman shape-shifts from human to scarab, Robert Holt collapses in a "frenzy of unreasoning fear" and Paul Lessingham is reduced to gibbering hysteria. At the same time, the inventor Sydney Atherton, whose "attitude towards what is called the supernatural is an open one," feels only eager curiosity and hopes that he is witnessing "something new in scientific marvels" (Marsh, *Beetle*, pp. 450, 572, 542). Both types of reaction are appropriate, the text indicates: science has yet to finish quantifying and charting the strange potentialities of the natural world, but these potentialities are nonetheless horrific, and their containment within a scientific paradigm will not make them any less so. And yet, as Sydney's response makes clear, the spectacle of the evacuation of a fully human identity – the demonstration of the extreme plasticity of the human body – is fascinating as well as repulsive. Narrative energy, especially in the Gothic, is ever on the side of abomination. It should be clear that the modernist Gothic did not just manage cultural anxieties. It aggravated them, delineating the fluid and chaotic form of the modern abhuman subject with both hysterical nausea and speculative interest – all in a way that no realist genre ever could.

NOTES

1 See Nicholas Daly, *Modernism, Romance and the Fin de Siècle: Popular Fiction and British Culture, 1880–1914* (Cambridge: Cambridge University Press, 1999), pp. 12, 15.
2 M. R. James, *"Casting the Runes" and Other Ghost Stories* (Oxford: Oxford University Press, 1987), p. 94.
3 See Annette Kuhn, ed., *Alien Zone: Cultural Theory and Contemporary Science Fiction Cinema* (London: Verso, 1990), pp. 1–11.
4 See Kathleen Spencer, "Victorian Urban Gothic: the First Modern Fantastic Literature" in George E. Slusser and Eric S. Rabkin, eds., *Intersections: Fantasy and Science Fiction* (Carbondale: Southern Illinois University Press, 1987).
5 Arthur Machen, *The Three Imposters* (London: Everyman, 1995), p. 101.
6 Patrick Brantlinger, *Rule of Darkness: British Literature and Imperialism, 1830–1914* (Ithaca: Cornell University Press, 1988), chapter 8.
7 Charles Darwin, *The Origin of Species and The Descent of Man* (New York: Modern Library, n.d.), p. 911.
8 See Margot Norris, *Beasts of the Modern Imagination: Darwin, Nietzsche, Kafka, Ernst, and Lawrence* (Baltimore: Johns Hopkins University Press, 1986), chapter 2.
9 Machen, *Three Imposters*, p. 122.
10 See Daniel Pick, *Faces of Degeneration: a European Disorder, c. 1848–c. 1918* (Cambridge: Cambridge University Press, 1989).
11 H. G. Wells, *The Time Machine* (New York: Bantam, 1982), pp. 62, 71; Hodgson, *"House on the Borderland,"* pp. 328, 377.
12 Richard Marsh, *The Haunted Chair and Other Stories* (Ashcroft, BC: Ash-Tree Press, 1997), p. 245.
13 Elaine Showalter, *Sexual Anarchy: Gender and Culture at the Fin de Siècle* (Harmondsworth: Penguin, 1990), p. 112, emphasis in text.
14 Dick Donovan, *Tales of Terror* (London: Chatto and Windus, 1899), pp. 3–4.
15 Bram Stoker, *The Lair of the White Worm* (New York: Zebra, 1978), p. 116.
16 Janet Oppenheim, *"Shattered Nerves": Doctors, Patients, and Depression in Victorian England* (New York: Oxford University Press), pp. 146, 150.
17 H. Rider Haggard, *She* (Oxford: Oxford University Press, 1991), p. 256.
18 Frank Aubrey, *King of the Dead: a Weird Romance* (New York: Arno Press, 1978), pp. 142, 275, 281, 151, 205.

19 Marsh, *Haunted Chair*, p. 244.
20 M. P. Shiel, *The Pale Ape and Other Pulses* (London: T. Werner Laurie, n.d.), p. 21.
21 Haggard, *She*, p. 103.
22 Richard Ellis, *Monsters of the Sea* (New York: Doubleday, 1994), p. 127.
23 Frank Aubrey, *A Queen of Atlantis: a Romance of the Caribbean Sea* (New York: Arno Press, 1974), pp. 260–61.

II

MISHA KAVKA

The Gothic on screen

It may come as a surprise, in view of the generic force of the term *Gothic*, that there is no established genre called *Gothic cinema* or *Gothic film*. There are Gothic images and Gothic plots and Gothic characters and even Gothic styles within film, all useful to describe bits and pieces of films that usually fall into the broader category of *horror*, but there is no delimited or demonstrable genre specific to film called the Gothic. This is at least in part due to the fact that film, as a medium born with the twentieth century, is both a late-comer to and an avid, unashamed plagiarizer of earlier, literary forms of the Gothic. As such, the Gothic does not "belong" to film, and the film medium must content itself with providing a home for that catch-all category of terror and spookiness, the horror genre.

Nonetheless, if it is surprising that there is no such thing as Gothic cinema, that is because we perfectly well know the Gothic when we see it. There is, in fact, something peculiarly visual about the Gothic. As William Patrick Day has pointed out, the Gothic tantalizes us with fear, both as its subject and its effect; it does so, however, not primarily through characters or plots or even language, but through *spectacle* (Day, *Circles of Fear and Desire*, p. 63). The fearful effect of the Gothic, at least in its literary forms, depends on our ability to cast certain conventionalized images from the text onto the "screen" of our mind's eye. The Gothic is thus particularly suited to the cinema, trading as the latter does in images that affect the individual psyche, albeit in culturally legible terms. Indeed, this is both the strength and weakness of the Gothic on screen: its ability to capture the spectacular element of the Gothic effect and encode it in culturally recognizable – ultimately perhaps in all *too* recognizable – forms.

Given the overlap between the realm of spectacle and the (film) screen, if there has to date not been a genre called Gothic film, then we must strive to invent it. For Gothic film adds a specific dimension to earlier forms of the Gothic, one which could be said to provide, retrospectively of course, the connecting thread between eighteenth-century heroines in moldering castles,

Romantic wanderers and seekers after truth, nineteenth-century ghosts and bloodsuckers, and more contemporary alien presences from slashers to cyborgs. To this broad-ranging litany of figures, each of which has appeared in some form on screen, Gothic film brings a set of recognizable elements based in distinct *visual codes*. Such codes constitute the language, or the sign system, of Gothic film. The ruined castle or abandoned house on a hill made hazy by fog; the dark cemetery dotted with crosses and gnarled, bare branches; the heavy-built wooden doors that close without human aid; the high, arched or leaded windows that cast imprisoning shadows; the close-ups of mad, staring eyes (often above a cape drawn across the lower face); the towering, square body of a leaden-footed galvanic creation; even the passing of a black cloud across a full moon: these are the elements by which the historically mutable Gothic has become Gothic film. The visual codes so redolent of Gothic film make two things clear. On the one hand, we are the inheritors of a cultural legacy of the Gothic which is inseparable from the cinematic versions and visualizations made popular throughout the twentieth century. On the other hand, when the conventional themes of the literary Gothic are cast on screen, their discomfiting representation invariably draws its effect from the plasticity of *space*. Paradoxically, when the literary Gothic is transferred to a two-dimensional screen, the effect of fear is produced through the transformations, extensions, and misalignments of size and distance that are possible only in three-dimensional space. Gothic film thus reveals and reconstitutes an underlying link between fear and the manipulation of space around a human body.

This, of course, is insufficient as a definition of the Gothic as such, a definition which has been notoriously difficult to pin down. In fact, it may be as much as one can do to say that the Gothic is about fear, localized in the shape of something monstrous which electrifies the collective mind. But, in that case, how do we distinguish the Gothic from the catch-all film genre of horror? It is useful, perhaps, to specify that the Gothic is about paranoia, defined as a projection of the self on to the outside world, which is in turn read as hostile. Paranoia thus involves a blurring of boundaries between self and other, to the extent that the other becomes a version of the self returned, with interest, in the form of hostility. This blurring of boundaries depends precisely on the fear of a return, for something which has been expelled may well come back, half-expected, from the other side or the beyond. Julia Kristeva refers to this something as "the abject" in *Powers of Horror*, while Sigmund Freud has famously called it "the return of the repressed," a return of something which has always been there (in the unconscious) and whose sudden appearance calls up the feeling of the "uncanny," or the unfamiliar that is deeply familiar (see Freud, "Uncanny").

This notion of blurred boundaries, understood as the uncanny return of something which has been expelled or thrown off (*ab-ject*), may help to delimit the conventionalized themes or obsessions of the Gothic. For instance, the central figure of the Gothic, that creepy character who simultaneously draws our gaze and makes us avert our eyes, has traditionally been some form of the undead, the revenant, the corpse, or a patchwork of corpses brought back to life. As the Gothic so chillingly seeks to remind us, the boundary between life and death is not forever fixed; it may not be the one-way passage that we would like rationally to believe. A similar point can be made about history itself, specifically the boundary between past and present, for the Gothic is conventionally figured in terms of an earlier era. Whether arriving in our present out of the archaic past or haunting us from a previous generation, the Gothic is a "language for the peculiar unwillingness of the past to go away" (Sage and Smith, *Modern Gothic*, p. 4); it represents the incursions and invasions of a semi-imaginary past into the present. Moreover, a range of feminist and queer criticism has suggested that the Gothic must also be understood as a blurring of boundaries between the masculine and the feminine, where monstrosity is associated with the copying, mirroring, or incursion of one gender form onto or into the other. In *Frankenstein*, for instance, men undertake the female role of human reproduction; in *Dracula*, the vampire combines feminine with masculine sexual and emotional characteristics; elsewhere, as in the films *Cat People* (Tourneur, 1942) or *The Phantom of the Opera* (Julian, 1925), women see their own cultural position mirrored in the form and treatment of the monster.[1] Add to this unstable gender boundary the blurring of the sexual boundary, so that, as Eve Kosofsky Sedgwick claims about the end of *Frankenstein*, "the tableau . . . embodying primal human essence or originary truth [is] the tableau of two men chasing one another across a landscape" (Sedgwick, *Coherence of Gothic Conventions*, p. ix), and the distinction between homo- and heterosexuality is shown in the Gothic to be a site of paranoid defense, with the same blurred boundaries as those between the feminine and the masculine. We have thus come to understand the Gothic as a spectacle of the mutual interpenetration of categories that social and ideological institutions have long striven to keep separate.

Let us broadly say, then, that the Gothic captures, and to some extent makes available for catharsis, the fear associated with the unstable boundaries of our subjectivity, cast onto an imagined or imaginary past. To this end, Gothic film brings in the crucial element of plasticity of space, and thus expands, as well as seals for the future, the codes by which the Gothic comes to be expressed. Gothic film, however, even if we insist on its existence as a genre, cannot be circumscribed by a single period, a single figure, or a single set of images. Its potential, even within set visual codes, cannot be exhausted by even the most enthusiastic list of movies or directors or production companies. This is true in part because of the basic mutability of the Gothic, which has two sources. On the one hand, Gothic mutability derives from the limitations of representation, because it deals in those liminal regions of being, whether social or existential, which can be only fleetingly represented in words or images (as in the conventional complaint of Gothic literary characters that their horror is too deep for words, too radical for utterance). On the other hand, the Gothic is mutable because it is bound to the historical moment, constantly reworking the material of the past in terms of the cultural fears of the present. As cultural formations change, in terms of social, economic, and technological developments, so also do the fears they generate in the social imaginary. Thus, Bela Lugosi's version of Count Dracula (in Tod Browning's *Dracula*), appearing in 1931, resonates with an American interwar nervousness about its renewed relation to Europe after the long period of political isolationism in the second half of the nineteenth century. For us, however, Lugosi's Dracula has become absorbed into our own culture and serves as an icon of Gothic representation rather than as a figure caught between two worlds; he is thus more pleasurable than terrifying. The "stock" nature of such figures, in our time, indicates that the historical and cultural anxieties animating their visualization no longer hold for us. On the other hand, Gary Oldman's Count from *Bram Stoker's Dracula* (Coppola, 1992), when we first see him dragging a bloodied razor across his tongue, produces a much more uncanny effect, for his Dracula speaks to the anxieties and thrills associated with social transgressions that are recognizable to an early 1990s audience. The razor pulled across the tongue indicates our somewhat uncomfortable fascination in the 1990s with erotic piercing and cutting (as the pragmatic tongue is resignified by the razor as a site of perversion) while it simultaneously draws on the powerful fear of disease transmitted through blood in the era of HIV and AIDS.

The visual codes that constitute the sign system of Gothic film can thus be said not only to articulate paranoia about the blurring of subjective boundaries, but also to objectify this paranoia in historically specific forms. It is no coincidence that the era of "classic horror" stretches from the early 1930s to the mid-1940s, though its popularity begins to fade in the early 1940s. What these dates suggest is that, as with English Gothic novels in the 1790s, the classic monsters of the American horror film give imaginative – and hence to some degree pleasurable – shape to anxieties about the aggression of the outside world, which in this case were building up in the US throughout the 1930s and into the Second World War. Notably, once the United States entered the war and the enemy took on a more concrete, nationalized form, the monsters of Gothic cinema became increasingly superfluous as a means of representing this particular cultural anxiety. While this overview only represents a 15-year period, we can see that the Gothic must necessarily be a flexible genre, filled with different historical contents in different periods. Nonetheless, it would be mistaken to attempt to link a Gothic subgenre or film cycle to a single historical source. If the Gothic mode is about the blurring of boundaries between the outside and the inside, as is suggested by the psychological model of paranoia, then there can be no straightforward historical source "outside" the Gothic which is simply mirrored in its internal terms. The Gothic may indeed be materialized as a threat coming from without, but it always gives voice to anxieties from within – both within the subject and within the culture at large. Thus, no one-to-one correspondence between a historical event and a monstrous figure will exhaust the rich vein of Gothic representations. The Gothic is certainly grounded in historical conditions, which themselves give rise to changes in economic, technological, and cultural formations, but it also transcends specific historical moments by articulating the response to such changes in terms of anxieties about the social, sexual, and temporal borders of subjectivity. This explains in part why we easily recognize something called "the Gothic," even though it appears in ever different forms.

If a genre of Gothic film is to exist, it must be set off from other genres which share certain of its characteristics but lack what we intuitively consider to be the "Gothic" element. To work through this question of the limits of Gothic film, I will focus on three selected film clusters, each providing an influential and exemplary visualization of the Gothic: first, the classic horror period, entailing those films made in the 1930s and 1940s by Universal Studios, which usually take monsters from Gothic literature as their subject; second, the "female Gothic," involving a cycle of films from the 1940s and its interesting echoes in the early 1960s, which are stylistically linked to the *film noir*; and finally, the remakes of the stories of Edgar Allan Poe directed by Roger Corman in the early 1960s, in which Vincent Price first makes his appearance as the psychopathological hero of low-budget but highly effective horror films. Each of these clusters corresponds to a different historical moment and hence to a different set of cultural influences and anxieties. If the first, as I have suggested, should be read in terms of political and economic changes in the outside world, then the second, the "female Gothic," points to changes in the domestic space, particularly the social shifts and manifestations of desire related to postwar sexual politics. The third cluster of Corman films may be said to be the work of a single, isolated director rather than the result of cultural shifts, and yet this new psychopathological Gothic hero suggests that postwar anxieties about sexual politics, already visible in *film noir*, begin by the early 1960s to have a particularly destabilizing influence on the moral, psychical, and sexual certainty of earlier film representations of masculinity. Taking these three film clusters, I will work through the cinematic techniques that link space to psychology, while simultaneously creating a place for Gothic film where it has in fact historically been situated: between *film noir* and horror.

Monstrous space

The two undeniable classics of Hollywood Gothic cinema are Tod Browning's *Dracula* and James Whale's *Frankenstein*, both released in 1931 under the supervision of producer Carl Laemmle, Jr. These two films initiated Universal Studios' "golden age" of horror, and launched a series of films which did not surrender to the tedium of repetition (and falling audience profits) until the mid-1940s. Though the most classic version of *Dr. Jekyll and Mr. Hyde* (Mamoulian, 1931) was also released that year by Paramount, it is the imposing double presence of Bela Lugosi as the menacingly smooth-tongued Count Dracula and Boris Karloff as the oversized, semi-mechanistic stalker in a too-tight suit that became the cultural icons of Gothic film. While all three of these films are derived from literary classics (and, importantly, from stories already familiar to film audiences), *Dracula* and *Frankenstein* stand out as establishing a stranglehold on the immediate future of Gothic film. In the fifteen years following 1931 Universal released sequel after sequel to these films, extending the possibilities of the genre by adding more monsters (notably *The Mummy* [Freund, 1932] and *The Wolf Man* [Waggner, 1941]), by combining existent monsters (as in the forgettable *Frankenstein Meets the Wolfman* [1943]), and by retelling the same plot in a slightly different setting (as in *The Son of Frankenstein* [1939] and *The Ghost of Frankenstein* [1942]). The result was the codification of a set of techniques and characterizations that would cast its long shadow over all subsequent Gothic films, whether they were remakes, as in the British Hammer Horror series from 1957 to 1976, or parodies, as in Mel Brooks's *Young Frankenstein* (1974) or Dragoti's *Love at First Bite* (1979).

Shadows, in fact, are one of the crucial elements that the Universal series exploits for the visualization of the Gothic. Casting shadows is one way of manipulating space, either by taking something of human dimensions and recasting it in an extended, larger-than-life form that exerts menacing control, or by using shadows to create planes in space, so that the shadow serves as a metaphor for what lurks in another plane. This technique can be traced back to German expressionism, an aesthetic style developed in the late 1910s and 1920s by a group of filmmakers working in Germany whose names are still very familiar in film history: Fritz Lang, F. W. Murnau, Robert Wiene, Robert Siodmak, and Edgar Ulmer, to name a few. Derived from surrealistic theatrical staging, German expressionism is marked by phantasmagorical settings, unusual cinematography, and a thematic preoccupation with fate, evil, and madness. The stylistic techniques of German expressionism involve chiaroscuro lighting effects (that is, extreme distinction between light and dark), distorted backdrops, claustrophobic spaces, extreme camera angles, and shadows disproportionate to the objects that cast them, all techniques which serve to externalize a psychological (or psychopathological) crisis in the subjects on screen. This style becomes so closely connected with Gothic horror, as consolidated in the early Universal films, that the classic silent films of expressionism such as *The Cabinet of Dr. Caligari* (1919) and *Dr. Mabuse, the Gambler* (1922) are often listed as early horror films, though strictly this term only applies to *Nosferatu* (Murnau, 1922), the great vampire film of the silent era. The use of German expressionist techniques in the Gothic films of the 1930s, however, is no matter of coincidence or even indirect influence, for the late 1920s and early 1930s brought a raft of these German directors to America – directors such as Lang, Murnau, Siodmak, and Ulmer – where they exerted an immense influence on Hollywood filmmaking for the next two decades.

One of these émigrés was Karl Freund, a cameraman soon to become a director in his own right with *The Mummy*, who, as the cinematographer of Browning's *Dracula*, was responsible for the *mise-en-scène* and dramatic use of space in that film. The Transylvania sequence of *Dracula* opens with two shots which were to become tropes of Gothic cinema: the extreme long shot of shadowed castle ruins on top of a hill and the agonizingly slow opening of a coffin lid from which a claw-like hand menacingly protrudes. In each case in the 1931 *Dracula* the shot is redoubled for effect, with the castle appearing in long shot a second time from a different angle and the hand under the coffin lid repeated first with a female vampire and then, in an analogous position, with a skeleton. The theme of the Undead is thus keenly visualized: in the cellar of this dark, uninviting, ever-distanced castle, the lid of the coffin itself serves to mark the boundary between life and death, a boundary which is crossed by a hand pushing inexorably from within, coming as it were from the "other" side. In this film we are never allowed to mistake Dracula for something he is not, a member of the living; from the first, he and his female minions are introduced as the Undead, wordlessly, using only visual codes in a holdover of silent film techniques in the new era of sound.

The introduction of a human into this setting, the clerk Renfield, allows the audience a wary point of identification in a space that constantly expands and contracts and fragments into planes. The most striking image of *Dracula*, perhaps, is the scene in which Renfield enters the castle. Here Freund and Browning have constructed a colossal space, full of receding planes and tropes of Gothic architecture, a seeming tribute to that pre-Romantic etcher of vast ruins and dungeons, Giovanni Battista Piranesi (1720–78). In this cavernous hall Renfield is literally dwarfed, shot from above and behind so that he appears as a tiny figure at the bottom of the screen; this counterbalance of human insignificance and immense space is further reminiscent of the sublime landscapes of the eighteenth century. Our attention, like Renfield's, is drawn to the huge Gothic vaults and arches which become doubled as they recede into a distant plane. The only relief from this overpowering sense of space is provided by a cut to a close-up shot of the Gothic windows, where flapping bats framed by the narrow arches mark the boundaries of enclosure. The camera descends as Renfield backs in awe and confusion across the space, readjusting him to something like normal size, only for him to encounter, unawares, Count Dracula himself looking down from a stair landing. In the encoding of the Gothic memorably established by this sequence, the human is simultaneously dwarfed and enclosed by the space, which seems to press down on him, while the monstrous Undead controls the space through his superior positioning and his sly, smooth movement (of which *Bram Stoker's Dracula* later makes particularly good use [Coppola, 1992]). The 1931 vampire's spatial control, moreover, is exacerbated by the camera. When Renfield later swoons in front of French doors opening onto a dark terrace (another visual trope of Gothic film), the camera takes an active role in squashing the space, moving forward to Renfield's body as though it were mirroring the hungry advance of Dracula himself from the other side. Even more strikingly, in contrast to the long shots of Renfield, Dracula often appears in menacing close up, with a band of light across his staring eyes that make them seem to stand out from the screen. When he then goes to bite an unconscious victim, he leans further into the camera, filling the corner of the frame until he is so close as to be out of focus. In these close-ups he is larger than the screen space itself, seeming to extend out toward the audience and into the plane in front of the screen. Monsters, by definition, exceed spaces of enclosure – such as the screen itself – whereas humans are diminished and oppressed by Gothic space.

In Whale's *Frankenstein* humans are dwarfed by space, too, but in keeping with the theme of Promethean creation the colossal space here is that of Dr. Frankenstein's laboratory. The sequence which takes us to the heart of *Frankenstein* and all its sequels – the room in which a man in a lab coat and his lunatic assistant will animate a sewn-together body – begins with the visual signature of the Gothic: a long shot of a dark, ruined tower (with two windows lit for effect) set high on a crag in a rainstorm. The interior space of the laboratory appears curiously plastic through the combination of curved and angled walls and shadows which blur receding spaces. Add to this the terracing of the floor, and the entire space seems to shift and reform before the eyes. The disorienting effects of plastic space, and the tendency of the monster (whether Dracula or Frankenstein's creature) to traverse space in an uncomfortably inhuman way, are aligned in both films with the Gothic motif of the awakening of the dead or the inanimate thing. The hand of Dracula emerging from the side of his coffin becomes in *Frankenstein* the twitching fingers of the newly animated creature ("It's alive! It's alive!"). The sutured corpse of the latter film awakens from the dead following a display of primitive pyrotechnics, signaling a prescientific age of rationalist investigation into the epiphenomena of vitalism that still haunts modern scientific experimentation. The signature motif of the dread-filled awakening also animates the prolific zombie genre, from the Haitian walking dead of *White Zombie* (Halperin, 1932) to the Undead rising from the soil of graves in *The Plague of the Zombies* (1966) to George Romero's cannibalistic walking corpses in the only loosely Gothic *Night of the Living Dead* (1968). The question of whether such creatures are dead or alive, human or nonhuman – a line forever blurred by Frankenstein's experiment – reveals an ambiguity about the separation of existential spheres that is fundamental to the Gothic film.

The long-awaited appearance of the walking creature in *Frankenstein* completes a scene of revelation, and revenance, that began in the laboratory with the "unveiling" of the body on the gurney, surrounded by the Gothic paraphernalia of hanging ropes, chains and pulleys, and a thick wooden pillar which casts a shadow like a gallows. In place of the receding planes in *Dracula*, *Frankenstein* offers the romantic trope of an unveiling that does not fully reveal. When Dr. Frankenstein removes the sheet from the still creature's face, or rolls back a double layer of sheets from the body in readiness to animate it, what is revealed is another layer of veiling, a body wrapped in bandages like a corpse wrapped in a winding sheet. This is titillating, for it exposes the contours of the not-yet living body, but also disappointing, since one veil only gives way to another in the Gothic, just as one spatial plane recedes into the murkiness of another. Indeed, if planes are linked to shadows, as I have suggested, it is appropriate that what follows the creature's appearance on screen is an iconic use of shadow as metaphor, suggesting the permeable and uncertain boundary between the human and nonhuman. For as the creature steps forward to follow his creator's gestures toward a chair, he casts a disproportionately huge shadow on the wall, a shadow which both exceeds and precedes him as he moves toward the cowering Henry Frankenstein, who is being pushed to the edge of the frame. Inevitably, the shadow falls across the doctor, hand first, as though the creature were about to draw him into the darkness of death. Though the doctor will survive both *Frankenstein* and its sequel, *Bride of Frankenstein* (Whale, 1935), the meaning of the shadow is clear: this galvanically animated creature can only bring death to humans, who are so much smaller and less powerful than he.

The characterizations of the vampire and the Promethean monster of the 1930s were to become crucial elements of the Gothic visual code. We might even think of these characterizations themselves as a cultural technique, a mode in which the culture represents its animating fears to itself, developed out of more pragmatic techniques like costume, make-up, and prosthetics. In the silent German film *Nosferatu*, for instance, Count Orlock is not a smoothly mannered, menacingly attractive old-world aristocrat, but rather a feral, almost vermin-like creature with a smooth head, large pointed ears, and sharp front teeth. Browning's *Dracula*, by contrast, draws more directly on the characterization of the vampire in Bram Stoker's novel as an eastern European aristocrat, but even here the film version introduces a degree of social etiquette and charm – not to mention an opera cape that recalls Universal's silent *Phantom of the Opera* (Julian, 1925) – which draws on a received conception of old-world European aristocracy that is specifically American. The past and present are here refigured as the old and new world, with the unclean, ill-spoken immigrant reframed in more acceptable guise. This Count Dracula is a particular product of interwar American culture, a culture whose era of working-class European immigration is receding but which, through its involvement in the First World War, has been drawn back into Europe, only to find there its half-romanticized, half-feared visions of the old-world past. Though Dracula remains officially un-American, an immigrant from murky regions east of the tourist's Europe, once he is provided with a cape, a tuxedo, and an unlocatable European accent (as in the famous line "I...am...Drah-cu-la"), this image finds such resonance in the collective psyche that it becomes a signature in the vampiric subgenre of Gothic film.

The same holds true for the creature in *Frankenstein*. But whereas the characterization of Dracula draws on an imagined, displaced past, that of the Promethean monster looks forward to a technological era of the posthuman. With bolts in his neck, jointless limbs, and a heavy industrial walk, the monster of *Frankenstein* is an early cinematic draft of an android, an artificially constructed body that can be galvanized into a mimetic form of human life. But in the decades that follow this visual characterization of the creature in 1931, since technological advances do not in fact produce androids of the kind Dr. Frankenstein imagined, the Karloff image begins itself to work like a Gothic residue of the past. This is not just because the huge, square-headed body becomes synonymous with the early twentieth-century

Gothic, but also because the bolts on the creature's neck and his unbending knees represent for our technological age the experimental fantasies of a mechanical era that is already receding from memory. If we cannot remember it, we must (re)create it in order to situate our identities over against it: no wonder Lugosi's Dracula and Karloff's monster are so hard to kill off.

Monstrous sexuality

Despite the effectiveness of the star characterizations in *Dracula* and *Frankenstein*, the success of the Universal monster series was on the wane in the early 1940s. At this point another kind of Gothic film began to appear, which can be broadly categorized as the female Gothic of American cinema. Introduced by Hitchcock's 1940 film version of Daphne du Maurier's novel *Rebecca* (1938) – a story about a nameless new wife who struggles with the powerfully mythic presence of the former wife, now mysteriously dead – the female Gothic involves the haunting of a woman by another woman (usually a rival, a *Doppelgänger*, or a mother) and/or by her own projected sexual fears (see Palmer, *Lesbian Gothic*, p. 10). The films of the female Gothic thus posit a female protagonist who is simultaneously a victim and an investigator of a haunting that is caused by anxieties about transgressive sexuality. The haunting itself may be "real" or may be "simply" paranoid. What is important in these films, however, is that the line between the supernatural and the psychological remains permeable, with the result that phantoms must equally be read as psychological manifestations, while paranoid fears always suggest the possibility of uncanny materialization.

Even though actual ghosts may or may not exist in these films, one character that is crucial to the pattern of plot and theme is that of the house. Indeed, the domestic setting is such a fundamental element of the female Gothic that Norman Holland and Leona Sherman have distilled the Gothic formula to "the image of woman-plus-habitation" ("Gothic Possibilities," p. 279). Though this is surely too limiting a definition of the Gothic as such, it seems apt for the films of the female-centered Gothic, which combine the tropes of the nineteenth-century haunted house story with the style and themes of the 1940s/50s *film noir*. On the one hand, like the ghost story, the female Gothic is set in a house where a monstrous act or occupant (usually but not always female) is projected onto the monstrosity of the house itself. On the other hand, like the *film noir*, the female Gothic deals with the interrelated themes of investigation, paranoia, and (usually deviant) sexuality, though in place of the *film noir*'s setting in the malevolent city the female Gothic substitutes a domestic space made uncanny. The woman at the center of the female Gothic, then, stands at a crossroads between a constrained but respectable domestic normality and deviant, or excessive, sexuality. Her acts of investigation, coded as masculine, often threaten to drive her further into deviance, while her status as victim threatens to erase the possibility of domestic normality. She is, in line with the sexual politics of the 1940s through the early 1960s, caught between a rock and a hard place, and her survival in these films is by no means guaranteed.

While sharing a similar set of characteristics with *film noir* – the themes of investigation and sexuality, the tone and structure of paranoia, and visual techniques derived from German expressionism – the female Gothic can be differentiated from *noir* on at least three points. First and foremost, whereas the *noir* protagonist, and hence the subject of paranoia, is male, in the female Gothic paranoia is feminized. This means, on the one hand, as I have mentioned above, that the female protagonist tends to be both victim and investigator, as in the 1940s cycle of "paranoid woman's films" (e.g., *Rebecca* or Fritz Lang's *Secret Beyond the Door* [1948]) in which "a wife invariably fears that her husband is planning to kill her."[2] Add to this feminization of paranoia the scenario of the ghost story, or, more accurately, the possibility of fears being externalized as phantoms, and another twist comes into play: here the *femme fatale* of the *noir* cycle reappears in Gothic film as the double or alter ego of the female victim/investigator. Women, it turns out, are dangerous not only to each other but also to themselves, an insight which the female Gothic, seemingly at a loss to explain this possibility in terms other than those of uncanniness or monstrosity, casts into the zone of the supernatural. If the first point of difference refers to the gendering of paranoia, the second relates to its representation, for where *noir* expresses the paranoid blurring of boundaries in terms of symbolic doubles, usually between the investigator and the murderer, the female Gothic relies on mirrors and portraits to indicate that the conflation of woman and monster is a matter of psychological reflection, even identification, rather than simply of symbolism. Thus – and here is the third point of distinction – the Gothic is played out in the space of a wider law rather than the law of the everyday. Whereas *film noir* plots are set among representatives of and challengers to the law of the land, however ineffectual and corrupt it may be, the Gothic appeals to a more abstract, less visible law, imagined variously in terms of divine, psychological, or social law – that overarching system that demands our compliance with certain rules in exchange for our substantiation as subjects.

These distinctions can best be seen on film in *The Uninvited* (Allen, 1944), which combines the style and themes of *film noir* with the plot of a ghost story. Stylistically, this generic overlap becomes clear with the opening tones of a disembodied voice ("They call them the haunted shores") heard over images of waves pounding a barren shoreline. In true *noir* fashion, however, the disembodied voice (initially of the law) suddenly becomes the subjective voice of the narrator/male protagonist who sets up the entire narrative as a personal flashback. Though the fact of a central male narrator may seem to disqualify this film from the female Gothic, *The Uninvited* nonetheless compensates by providing an excess of female characters, actual and supernatural, who fill out the doubled positions of the female Gothic. The victim – the young Stella, whose grandfather refuses to allow her to go near the isolated, cliffside house in which she was born, apparently because there her mother had suffered a tragic, fatal fall into the sea – is a separate character from the female coinvestigator; the latter is the sister of the narrator, who falls in love with the abandoned house and insists that she and her brother buy it. The house, of course, turns out to be haunted, both by a woman's sobbing wails in the night and by the far gentler smell of mimosas, our first indication that female doubling in this film applies not only to the victim/investigator but also to ghosts.

The work of investigation, which always brings the party back to a house whose interior is shot in the *noir* style of single-point candles, flickering shadows, and eerie encounters on staircases, takes the form of figuring out which one of the female ghosts is the *femme fatale*: the much-mourned Mary, mother of Stella, or her husband's lover, a Spanish gypsy called Carmel. One of these ghosts keeps driving Stella literally to the cliff's edge, taunting her to take the plunge and fulfill her tragic generational legacy. The key to the investigation lies not in the tempting suggestion of Carmel's southern-blooded, adulterous sexuality, but rather in the use of a Gothic visual trope: a huge portrait of Mary in the keeping of the starkly masculine Miss Holloway, Mary's former nurse, who speaks to the painted image about a secret they share and calls her "my darling." The portrait suggests the doubling not of the mother and the daughter, as we might expect, but of the mother and her female "companion"; Mary's monstrosity is thus figured both in terms of an unspoken lesbian sexuality and in the final revelation that this mother is not in fact *the* mother, but a wifely stand-in who herself had "feared and refused motherhood." The sins of the mother, in this film, take a detour through homosexual and antiprocreative deviance before being visited on the daughter. In the film's resolution of this double haunting from the previous generation, Stella in fact turns out to be the daughter of Carmel, the kindly ghost whose presence is manifested by the smell of mimosas, while the *femme fatale* Mary, true to *noir* form, has been fatal to herself (being knocked into the sea during a struggle over the daughter with the good mother Carmel). The final shot of the film – which frames the daughter and the narrator's sister in the doorway of the cleansed house alongside their husbands-to-be – tells us that domestic procreative normality has been restored.

Such a happy, optimistic ending, however, is not always possible in the female Gothic, especially in those films where the element of transgressive sexuality has been internalized by the female victim/investigator and is projected outward as a fear of sex. This figure is the recognizable "frigid heroine" of the female Gothic, memorably exemplified in the first of the horror films Val Lewton produced in the 1940s, *Cat People* (Tourneur, 1942). In effect, *Cat People* offers an inversion, and a transsexing, of the vampire figure, for the heroine Irena Dubrovna comes from Serbia, specifically from a village with a terrible past of Satanism and witchcraft. In contrast to Dracula, however, Irena does not embrace the evil of her transgressive sexual nature but rather fears its capacity to turn her into a panther whenever she is whipped up into a jealous rage. She wants, in line with the war patriotism of the era, to become a good American. In the terms of the film, Irena is frigid, unable even to kiss her new American-as-apple-pie husband Ollie until she deals with "the evil within." In more metaphorical terms, however, it is clear from the amount of time Irena spends around the panther's cage in the zoo that the aggressive, *femme fatale* sexuality embodied by the panther (whom Irena hears from her apartment at night "scream like a woman") is as much a point of identification for Irena as of fear and self-hatred. In this version of the paranoid female Gothic the psychological becomes supernatural, with the sexual feelings which transgress the borders of "good" femininity projected outward in hostile form to take vengeance on those who have unwittingly caused them. For this lack of self-control Irena must die, sacrificing herself in the end to the panther in the zoo. What is striking about this film, however, is that it encodes an awareness of the constrictions of normative feminine sexuality while at the same time killing off its heroine for having transgressed these norms. By splitting the female protagonist into victim and *femme fatale*, into the wife and the panther, the film evokes our sympathy for the transgressively sexual woman, even as it allows this transgressive sexuality to break out of an old-world past to haunt and finally kill the would-be good American wife.

Cat People, which does not stage a haunted house as such, nonetheless suggests the same equivalence of house, woman, and supernatural monster as *The Uninvited*. For in *Cat People* much of the sexual tension felt by Irena is played out either on the dark, shadow-laden stairs leading up to her apartment or in the Gothically styled apartment itself. This connection between house, woman, and monstrosity can be seen even more clearly in *The Haunting* (Wise, 1963), based on Shirley Jackson's *The Haunting of Hill House* (1959). This film, though made in the 1960s, recalls the style and themes of the 1940s female Gothic, not least because its director served as an apprentice to Val Lewton's series of Gothic films with RKO. In

The Haunting, which again begins with a disembodied voiceover that re-solves into a subjective male narrator, the male protagonist Dr. Markway takes a back seat to the female victim/investigator, the highly sensitive Eleanor who has come to Hill House to escape the tawdry disputes of an empty life as the family spinster and caretaker of her mother. Assuming the role of one of four paranormal investigators, Eleanor is also the chosen victim of the monstrous house itself; not only does she say of the house, "it's alive," but the house selects her personally, as though *it* were her mother, by pro-ducing a chalked message on a wall: "Help, Eleanor, come home." By the end, Eleanor does "come home," delivering herself to the house by crashing her car at the exact spot on the estate where the first would-be mistress of the house, one of a line of women who had all died there, was upended in her carriage before reaching the door. In this way, Eleanor becomes the latest in a series of socially abjected, dead women (the childless second wife, the spinster daughter of the house, her isolated companion) whose unspent, or perhaps misspent, passion is displaced onto the monstrously animated house itself. In the closing scene a woman's voice intones over an image of the house, "we who walk here walk alone," thus eerily stressing the link between dead women, the house, and the supernatural.

What unites house, woman, and monster in these films is invariably the element of sexual deviation, for this, in effect, is what makes the woman monstrous; her sexuality becomes nonhuman, say catlike, because it lies be-yond the bounds of social sanction. As in *The Uninvited*, *The Haunting* suggests a strong overtone of lesbian sexuality, first in Eleanor's rather des-perate attempts to convince herself that she's interested in Dr. Markway, then in her inability to separate herself from the (dead) mother, and fi-nally in her charged relationship with fellow investigator Theodora, who becomes noticeably lesbian when she refers to her domestic life in terms of "we" but responds with an adamant "no" to the question of whether she is married.[3] This lesbian register of the Gothic, a feature of the genre at least since Coleridge's poem *Christabel* (1816), registers an anxiety about female desire, where the transgression of the boundary between hetero- and homo-sexuality provides one justification for the abjection of the nonprocreative, nondomestic woman into a homology with the haunted house.

Monstrous psychology

A further strong phase of the Hollywood Gothic, not unrelated to its female paranoid version, is the cycle of films directed by Roger Corman in the early 1960s as adaptations of the stories of Edgar Allen Poe. The cycle begins with *The House of Usher* (1960) and includes *The Pit and the Pendulum* (1961),

Tales of Terror (1961), *The Raven* (1963), *The Tomb of Ligeia* (1964), and *The Masque of the Red Death* (1964). All but the last two were scripted by Richard Matheson, who certainly understood the tropes of Poe's Gothic world, but the thread of greatest consistency throughout these films is provided by their star, Vincent Price, who, having appeared in *The House on Haunted Hill* (1959), went on to supersede the Corman–Poe cycle to become the principal representative of horror film in the 1960s and 1970s. Rather than making a particular characterization iconic, as can be said of Karloff's monster or Lugosi's Dracula, Price became synonymous with a new kind of Gothic protagonist: the introspective, pathological hero whose monstrosity lies within. In this sense, the Corman–Poe series can be seen as a successor to the female Gothic, which similarly figures the monstrosity of social transgression as an internal pathology made supernatural. In all of the Price films directed by Corman, the potent Gothic combination of traversable boundaries comes into play; the dead do not remain in their coffins, the past is encrypted in the present, and sexual uncertainty or transgression leads to monstrous deeds. Invariably, Price plays an aesthete of a frozen historical age, an aristocrat isolated from the external world and tied to his class by possession of – what else? – a grand labyrinthine house replete with towers, staircases, hidden passageways, and dungeons. The spatialization of the frustrated, repressed psyche could not be more clear, since in these films the house has no practical function (as one might say of Frankenstein's laboratory) other than to serve as the master's seat and hence, metaphorically, as the projection of his psyche. The master himself is the enervated, desexualized male paradoxically prone to murderous sexual rage, in keeping with Poe's particular set of Gothic obsessions.

The Pit and the Pendulum, though bearing little resemblance to Poe's 1839 tale, weaves together the psychological themes and spatial tropes of the Gothic while extending the system of visual codes already established by the earlier Undead series and the *noir* female Gothic cycle. It begins, of course, with the signature shot of a castle on a cliff in the distance, cross-cut with shots of waves pounding on the rocks below for good Gothic measure. In this house resides Don Medina, the Vincent Price character who oscillates between being a monster and a victim: a victim to his overblown grief for a dead wife, whom he fantasizes may have been buried alive, and also a monster who haunts the crypts of his house playing with the "toys" of his father's torture chamber. From the first, this film is set up as an investigation into the crypt, for the narrative follows the investigator, Francis Bonner, seeking information about the sudden death of his sister Elizabeth in the descending, primeval recesses of the house. Reminiscent of the receding spatial planes in *Dracula*, as well as Dante's truly medieval *Inferno*, the recesses here are divided into three successive areas of depth, each marked by an increasingly coarse, heavy gate and each representing a deeper space of (psychological) burial. These levels of space are linked to the underworld characters of the monstrous or Undead; behind the second gate Bonner discovers Don Medina, emerging from the torture chamber into a menacing close-up with a shadow cast across his maniacal eyes, and from behind the crypt wall on the deepest level Elizabeth herself will emerge, initially as no more than a bloody hand slowly protruding from beneath the coffin lid. The narrative climax of the film comes with these descending planes of space being traversed first by the living – Don Medina drawn down rough-hewn corridors and stone staircases by the sound of his wife calling his name – and then, in the opposite direction, by the Undead – the silhouetted figure of Elizabeth chasing a now horrified Don Medina back through the labyrinth. Don Medina fails to complete his ascent to the civilized world, however, and his fall down a spiral staircase coincides with his descent into madness. The plastic space of the Gothic is here in full affective play.

It is clear in this film that Gothic monstrosity belongs to two overlapping orders, namely the disinterred dead, in the form of Elizabeth arising from her coffin, and the disinterred past, in the form of Don Medina becoming the ghost of his sadistic father. This is all played out, however, at a psychological level that only wears the guise of the supernatural, for the walking "corpse" of Elizabeth turns out to be a living woman, fully kissable by Don Medina's best friend, the doctor. Medina Sr., the Inquisition torturer, in turn comes back not from the dead but from the deep psyche of a son haunted by having seen his father torture his mother to death for adultery. In this version of the uncanny return, the sins of the sadistic father, and of the adulterous mother who had been sleeping with her brother-in-law, are directly visited on the son in a riot of Gothic doubling. Medina's madness involves replaying, twice over, the sadistic murder by his father of his own brother: first in the "proper" form of the doctor, whom Medina misrecognizes as his mother's lover, and then in the redoubled form of the investigative brother, the next stand-in lover. Beneath the swaying pendulum Bonner thus bears the guilt of sexuality itself. When, in the end, domestic order is restored as the sister of Don Medina rescues the brother of Elizabeth, this occurs at the price of abjecting both monsters – Don Medina, the victim of internal monstrosity, and Elizabeth, the woman whose sexual transgression, it is no surprise, started the whole process. Of the two, Don Medina finds the quickest and most merciful death in the pit, while Elizabeth is punished in true Poe fashion by being buried alive. In this apotheosis of the Gothic, no boundaries remain impermeable; the dead who cross into life are simply acting out the demands of an invasive past which finds form in a generational and gender doubling that has, as its basis, an anxiety about sexuality itself, especially about a feminine sexuality that refuses social constraint.

Labyrinthine dungeons and walking corpses, torture chambers hidden beneath isolated mansions, innocent investigators at the mercy of murderous fiends: why insist on *The Pit and the Pendulum* belonging to a genre of Gothic film rather than to the more recognizable category of horror? I have at times used the two terms interchangeably, but it is worth thinking about the points of demarcation between the Gothic and horror, not least because we sense, at least intuitively, that there is some sort of difference. The question seems particularly pertinent in view of the more recent spate of seat-gripping, jump-out-of-your-skin films, the teenage slasher genre initiated by John Carpenter in *Halloween* (1978) and continued through Wes Craven's *Nightmare on Elm Street* and *Scream* series (the first begun in 1984 and the second in 1996). These films are now so generic as to be synonymous with "horror" at the turn of the last century. Could, however, these films also be called Gothic, or at least some of them? Peter Hutchings makes a convincing argument that *Halloween* and the *Nightmare on Elm Street* cycle should be read as bearing the distinctive mark of the Gothic mode, since the killers from both mark "a psychologically internalized transaction between the past and present," a transaction figured in the house as a metaphor for the teenage psyche.[4] This emphasis on permeable boundaries, both historical and spatial, sets the teenage slasher film apart, for Hutchings, from other serial killer thrillers of the 1980s and 1990s.

It strikes me, however, that though one can be quite specific about the iconography that the Gothic film shares with teenage slasher films, they are not always similar in effect. Both involve an investigator(s) who moves through dark, labyrinthine spaces – the domestic made uncanny, in other words – in order to generate paranoia in anticipation of a (possibly supernatural) monster who duly erupts on the scene. What the Gothic insists on, though, which is not always to be found in teenage slasher films, is a speaking from the "beyond" in the form of a figure that arrives from beyond the present, beyond the grave, or beyond the rational, material world. This is in effect what demarcates or delimits the Gothic on screen, for speaking from the beyond registers the paradoxical eruption of the unspeakable, or the unrepresentable, into the scene of representation. This is why, though the Gothic is first and foremost a spectacle, it can only be indicated through certain visual codes of the liminal (something just below or beyond a threshold) rather than being seen head-on. The medium of film is in a peculiarly advantageous position when it comes to the representation of liminality, for it can exploit both the cut-off points of visibility imposed by its frame as well as the manipulations that are possible in its composition of space. Film can thus be turned toward representing something that needs to retain a degree of the unrepresentable in order to be affective. This means, however, that in those instances where the paranoia once evoked by shadows or ghostly figures becomes the perfectly rational fear of a lunatic killer on the loose (whether Michael Myers at the end of *Halloween* or even the implacable, unstoppable Hannibal Lecter of Jonathan Demme's *The Silence of the Lambs* [1990]), we have moved from the Gothic into the realm of horror, into the dubious comfort of screaming at what we actually see. There is, in other words, a world of difference between not being able to see something that remains shadowed or off-screen (the Gothic), on the one hand, and being able to see something terrifying placed before our very eyes but from which we want to avert our gaze (horror), on the other. The horror genre, in contrast to the Gothic, demands that we see – not that we always answer the demand. In fact, we are not necessarily meant to, for a dialectic between seeing and not seeing is played out in horror cinema between the film and its viewers; the film shows us elements of something horrifying and we try not to see, or at least not to be caught out, unprepared to see.

In Gothic film, on the other hand, this same dialectic is at work, but it is part of the structure of visualization itself – the shadow-play of the Gothic. Rather than the horror film's challenge to the audience to open their eyes and see, the feared object of Gothic cinema is both held out and withheld through its codes of visual representation. As with the ghostly occupant of the eerie house or the corpse in the coffin, we strain to see, but the enticing scene is barred, shadowed, distanced or wrongly dimensioned. It is thus not just that we *do* not see, but precisely that we *cannot* see, which has metaphorical and affective import. In its aim to withhold from our gaze precisely what it appears to offer, Gothic film is always threatening to collapse the frame, befuddle the boundaries, question the stable norms of subjectivity; hence the elasticity of the form. Though this applies equally to the structure of the uncanny and to the Gothic at large, Gothic film adds its own media-specific element. For in Gothic film the dialectic between seeing and not seeing is visualized as a manipulation of space and frames that materializes the impossibility of representation actually grasping the thing "beyond." Whatever is dwarfed or shadowed or half-concealed is marked out as being something more than representation can fully encompass; it seems to be trailing a foot in the beyond even as it appears murkily on screen. The beyond is thus not strictly a thing but the very permeability of the shadow-thin boundary, an always existing "in-between state" potentially arousing paranoia. The Gothic operates as an *effect* of representation rather than as its *object*.

The success of the Gothic mode in cinematic history suggests that we conceptualize it as a genre that works within a particular function of representation. Rather than understanding film in this instance as a technical medium for representing an independent social, historical, or personal reality, film in the Gothic mode must be understood in the other sense of "medium," the sense given to us precisely by a literary history of ghost stories, séances, and paranormal activities. Gothic film should thus not be thought of as a medium of representation, but as a medium through which things are allowed to pass, from the past into the present, from death into life, from the beyond to here and back again. This understanding of film as a medium of passage suggests that it is a social technology for working through shared anxieties about the realm of the unrepresentable; indeed, film has proven to be the most effective social technology in the twentieth century for fielding the Gothic. Like a living medium who calls up spirits from the "other side," the film screen allows uncanny presences to "pass through" it in a way that sets our nerves pleasurably on edge. The effect of the Gothic is thus not quite that of horror, which is our response to having confronted something monstrous; rather, it bears witness to the permeability of boundaries, which is the point at which monstrosity begins to arise. In all the films under discussion something has come and gone, been glimpsed or sensed, without making a full appearance, yet it is bound through set visual codes to the effect of the beyond. Indeed, without its conventional, recognizable cinematic props, the Gothic could not work; it is precisely this iconography of the visual that serves as a medium, in a liminal way, for the presence of the otherworldly. As Vincent Price was fond of showing on the TV variety circuit in the 1970s, if you simply turn up the lights and snuff out the candles the Gothic element disappears, and, with it, the spine-tingling sense of something having arrived from the other side of representation. Of course, we would rather keep the lights down – and the projector running.[5]

NOTES

1 Linda Williams, "When the Woman Looks" in Barry Grant, ed., *The Dread of Difference: Gender and the Horror Film* (Austin: University of Texas Press, 1996), pp. 18–20.

2 Mary Ann Doane, *The Desire to Desire* (Bloomington: Indiana University Press, 1987), p. 123.

3 See Patricia White, "Female Spectator, Lesbian Specter: *The Haunting*" in *Inside/Out: Lesbian Theories, Gay Theories*, ed. Diana Fuss (New York: Routledge, 1991), pp. 142–72.

4 Peter Hutchings, "Tearing Your Soul Apart: Horror's New Monsters" in Victor Sage and Allan Lloyd Smith, eds., *Modern Gothic: a Reader* (Manchester: Manchester University Press, 1996), p. 99.

5 Many thanks to Martin Kavka and Johannes Binotto, whose video collections and film fanaticism made this chapter possible.

12

LIZABETH PARAVISINI-GEBERT

Colonial and postcolonial Gothic: the Caribbean

Land in a swamp, march through the woods, and in some inland post feel the savagery, the utter savagery, had closed round him – all that mysterious life of the wilderness that stirs in the forest, in the jungles, in the hearts of wild men.

Joseph Conrad, *Heart of Darkness*

The Gothic – as Walter Scott observed in his commentary on Horace Walpole's *The Castle of Otranto* – is above all the "art of exciting surprise and horror."[1] The genre's appeal to readers, in Scott's view, comes from its trying to reach "that secret and reserved feeling of love for the marvelous and supernatural which occupies a hidden corner in almost everyone's bosom." As it happens, this "literature of nightmare" (MacAndrew, *Gothic Tradition in Fiction*, p. 3) was, from its earliest history in England and Europe, fundamentally linked to colonial settings, characters, and realities as frequent embodiments of the forbidding and frightening. This mixed genre was still less than forty years old when Charlotte Smith – the eighteenth-century poet and novelist admired by so many in her time, including Jane Austen – set her novella "The Story of Henrietta" (1800) in the Blue Mountains of Jamaica, where the terrors of the heroine's situation are exacerbated by her atavistic fears of Jamaica's African-derived magicoreligious practice of Obeah and the possibility of sexual attack by black males.[2] By the 1790s Gothic writers were quick to realize that Britain's growing empire could prove a vast source of frightening "others" who would, as replacements for the villainous Italian antiheroes in Walpole or Radcliffe, bring freshness and variety to the genre. With the inclusion of the colonial, a new sort of darkness – of race, landscape, erotic desire and despair – enters the Gothic genre, and I here want to show and explain the consequences of that "invasion" throughout the nineteenth and twentieth centuries.

To begin with, the frightening colonial presence that we find in such English literary texts as Smith's "The Story of Henrietta," Maria Edgeworth's *Belinda* (1801) and "The Grateful Negro" (*Popular Tales*, 1804), or Thomas

Campbell's depiction of African barbarity in *The Pleasures of Hope* (1799) mirrors a growing fear in British society around 1800 of the consequences of the nation's exposure to colonial societies, nonwhite races, non-Christian belief systems, and the moral evils of slavery. The fear of miscegenation, with the attendant horror of interracial sexuality, enters public discourse at about the time Walpole began the Gothic novel. Edward Long, in *Candid Reflections . . . Upon the Negro Cause* (1772), voices English anxieties that stem from the fluctuations of colonial power, the need to foster and simultaneously control black physical strength, the ever-threatening possibility of slave rebellion, and the potential spread of anticolonial, antimonarchic ideologies in British-held territories in Africa, Asia, and the Caribbean. Note especially his description of the horrors of sexual miscegenation as an infectious illness:

> The lower class of women in England are remarkably fond of the blacks; for reasons too brutal to mention they would connect themselves with horses and asses if the laws permitted them. By these ladies they generally have a numerous brood. Thus, in the course of a few generations more the English blood will become . . . contaminated with this mixture . . . this alloy may spread so extensively as even to reach the middle, and then the higher orders of the people, till the whole nation resembles the *Portuguese* and the *Moriscos* in complexion of skin and baseness of mind. This is a venomous and dangerous ulcer, that threatens to spread its malignancy far and wide, until every family catches infection from it.[3]

Alan Richardson has therefore argued that the literary representation of Obeah in British fiction "illustrates the power of representation to generate, direct, or exorcise" such fears of racial boundary crossing, functioning, in this exorcism, rather like the cathartic practice of Obeah itself.[4] A similar argument can be made for the introduction of anxieties aroused by colonization into the very fabric of Gothic fiction at a time when proslavery forces and abolitionists in England were engaged in a fierce ideological struggle about labor and race. Indeed, a number of eighteenth-century Gothic novelists were directly involved in the slavery debate: William Beckford, author of *Vathek* (1786), had inherited a vast fortune accumulated by three generations of Jamaican sugar planters and actively represented the interests of West Indian slave owners in Parliament; Matthew Gregory Lewis, when writing *The Monk* (1796), was heir to several West Indian plantations dependent on slave labor. Indeed, he would eventually address his own notions of plantation society in his *Journal of a West India Proprietor* (1834), after having included black slave characters as supporting players in his biggest Gothic stage success, *The Castle Spectre* (1797). Gothic literature would be invoked as often to give voice to the fears awakened by colonial realities as it was used by abolitionists to dramatize the horrors and tortures of enslavement.

Howard L. Malchow has consequently argued, quite rightly, for a rereading of the nineteenth-century Gothic as responding to the "social and sexual, [but especially] racial, apprehensions of the literate middle and lower middle classes" in England (*Gothic Images*, pp. 4–5). Citing Mary Shelley's extensive knowledge of Bryan Edwards's proslavery history of the West Indies, he reads *Frankenstein* (1818) as echoing public anxieties about "other" races that were aroused by the Maroon rebellion in Jamaica in 1760 and the slave-led revolution in Haiti in the 1790s, ultimately claiming that Shelley's creature, colored partly black, is, among other things, "Frankenstein's Jamaican monster" (p. 191). Similarly, Maturin's *Melmoth the Wanderer* (1820), as Malchow renders it, uses its Spanish Gothic and East Indian settings to explore the problems of personal and national identity that had become so central to British culture as the extent of its colonial holdings increased. Malchow's analysis of British popular culture and cannibalism, which he links to allegations of sexual abuse of women by nonwhites, fear of miscegenation, and fascination with "perverse" practices such as sodomy, shows how myths that had originated in British folklore become racialized when seen through the prism of Gothic conventions and moved to a colonial setting. The genre often turned the colonial subject into the obscene cannibalistic personification of evil, through whom authors could bring revulsion and horror into the text, thereby mirroring political and social anxieties close to home.

The links between the colonial and the Gothic are particularly transparent in lesser-known, noncanonical works, where the textual devices are less successfully masked, as in the anonymous *Hamel, the Obeah Man* (1827).[5] This two-volume work, set in Jamaica, traces the career of Roland, a white preacher whose teachings about the equality of man and attempts to lead a slave rebellion are corrupted by his underlying desire to forcibly marry the daughter of a local planter. The novel, in its attempt to denounce Roland's unnatural desire to overthrow the legitimate social order represented by the plantation, turns him into a "villain of Gothic dimensions," whose "fevered mind twists increasingly towards violence as the tale progresses," culminating in "nightmare desperation."[6] A Eurocentric narrative haunted by the recent memory of the Haitian Revolution, it finds a hero in the black Obeah man, Hamel, who moves from enthusiastic revolutionary fervor to denunciation of the cause of revolutionary freedom. Hamel, a black man linked to his ancestral culture through his practice of Obeah, ultimately turns his back on "civilization" and sets out on a solitary journey to Guinea. In his ability to retreat to a mythical African homeland, Hamel is luckier than his mixed-race counterparts in this and similar texts, the "Gothic Unnaturals," as Malchow describes them, who stand in that contradictory space between "loyal subject and vengeful rebel," the tainted product of the undisciplined sexual passions of their white fathers" and the "savage inheritance of their non-white mothers,"[7] whose fate would be the subject of many a Gothic tale.

More particularly, though, the links between the literary production of terror and colonial literature are vital to the slave narrative and the abolitionist novel – particularly Mary Prince's *The History of Mary Prince* (Barbados, 1831), Juan Francisco Manzano's *Autobiography* (Cuba, 1840), and Gertrudis Gómez de Avellaneda's *Sab* (Cuba, 1841) – where Gothic conventions play a crucial role in unveiling the atrocities of the slave system. Prince's work, as is the case with many a slave narrative (see Winter, *Subjects of Slavery*), provides "a space for the safe rehearsal of pseudo-masochistic, erotic, and heroic fantasies" that bring it close to the titillating potential of some aspects of Gothic fiction.[8] The narrative's deeroticizing of Mary Prince's experiences through their insertion into the textual parameters of the sentimental novel, when coupled with the text's display of Mary's body as a site of torture – an "Otherness that seemed to make itself visible and willingly available for the reader's gaze"[9] – displays textual tensions that reverberate across the Gothic genre. Robin Winks sees these tensions as responsible for turning slave narratives into "the pious pornography of their day, replete with horrific tales of whippings, sexual assaults, and explicit brutality, presumably dehumanized and fit for Nice Nellies to read precisely because they dealt with black, not white man."[10] Similarly, in *Sab*, although a Romantic text with strong connections to the sentimental novel, Gómez de Avellaneda resorts to Gothic conventions, applied sparingly but effectively, to address the viciousness of the slave system and the radical nature of the black–white love triangle at the center of the plot. Manzano's narrative of his own experiences of physical and psychological trauma, with its focus on unveiling the brutalizing effects of slavery, opens with the primal experience of being entombed in a dark coal chute as punishment, and this fall becomes the metaphor of his life – "a fall from grace, a precipitous downward descent... into an invisible nonbeing."[11] As in Mary Prince's narrative, Manzano's emphasis throughout his text is on the inherent sadism of the slavery system, a cruelty projected from the individual slaveholder to the system itself, as we have seen previously in *Hamel, the Obeah Man*.

Hamel goes beyond Prince and Manzano's texts, however, in its exploration of the mysteries of Obeah. In this respect it typifies how some of the least understood cultural elements of colonial societies since the 1820s are appropriated into the Gothic, where they are used to reconfigure the standard tropes of the genre, either by the colonizer to be used in the ideological struggle against the colonial subject him/herself, or by the colonial in order to address the horrors of his/her own condition. The many Obeah men, "voodoo" priests, zombies, and sorcerers that people Gothic fiction, the many plots that revolve around the threat of mysterious practices associated with animal sacrifice, fetishes, and spells, all contribute to make of the colonized space the locus of horror necessary for the writing of Gothic literature.

The colonial space, however, is by its very nature a bifurcated, ambivalent space, where the familiar and unfamiliar mingle in an uneasy truce. Andrew McCann, in his analysis of Marcus Clarke's Australian Gothic novella, *The Mystery of Major Molineux* (1881), argues that "the Gothicizing of the settler-colony as a site of repression also anticipate[s] the dynamics of an analytical process in which the critic unearths the 'repressed' of colonization: collective guilt, the memory of violence and dispossession, and the struggle for mastery in which the insecurity of the settler-colony is revealed."[12] As in the myriad tales of *wazimamoto* (bloodsucking, vampire-derived firemen) that crop up throughout eastern and central Africa in the 1910s and 1920s – tales through which African men sought to address "the conflicts and problematics of the new economic social order" under a colonial regime growing increasingly more technological – vampires, zombies, and Obeah men have been uniquely positioned to represent the conflicts and ambiguities of colonial situations.[13]

Yet it is finally in Caribbean writing that a postcolonial dialogue with the Gothic plays out its tendencies most completely and suggestively. I therefore want to concentrate in what follows on the Caribbean as the premiere site of the colonial and postcolonial Gothic since the early nineteenth century. The Caribbean, it turns out, is a space that learned to "read" itself in literature through Gothic fiction. At first it appeared as the backdrop to terror, whether in travelogues, where it was depicted as the site of the mysterious and uncanny, or in histories that underscored the violent process that led to its colonization. But as the region's various literary traditions began to emerge during the final decades of the nineteenth century, Caribbean fictions – often through parody – mirrored the devices and generic conventions of their European models. The Caribbean Gothic has consequently entered into a complex interplay with its English and continental counterparts in a colonizer–colonized point-counterpoint whose foremost concern has finally become the very nature of colonialism itself.

The perception of the Caribbean as a site of terror dates back to the myriad tales of atrocities committed against white planters during the Tacky Rebellion in Jamaica in 1760 and three decades later in the gory and brutal slave rebellion that destroyed the colony of Saint Domingue in what is now Haiti. The Haitian Revolution, the foundational narrative of the Caribbean Gothic, as Joan Dayan has examined so perceptively in *Haiti, History and the Gods* (1997), becomes the obsessively retold master tale of the Caribbean's colonial terror. The birth of Caribbean literatures, particularly of the literatures of the Francophone and Anglophone Caribbean, is intrinsically connected to the exploration of the tensions and perversions of the political, economic, physical, and psychological bond between master and slave that, especially in Haiti, had culminated in widespread destruction and violence, rape, mutilation, and untold deaths.

Gothic literature – whether written in Britain or the Caribbean – in its attempt to address the violence of colonial conditions, has focused on this region's African-derived belief systems, chiefly Haitian Vodou, Jamaican Obeah, and Cuban Santería, as symbolic of the islands' threatening realities, of the brutality, bizarre sacrifices, cannibalism, and sexual aberrations that filled the imagination of authors and their audiences with lurid, terror-laden imagery. The Caribbean, as a colonial "dystopia of savagery and backwardness" replete with Obeah and Vodou practitioners, thus emerges in numerous texts published in the nineteenth and early twentieth centuries "as a tropical hellhole" plagued by superstition and witchcraft.[14]

In the Anglophone-Caribbean Gothic, the tradition most directly linked to British Gothic conventions, Obeah, as the African-derived religion most heavily represented in the slave population of the British West Indies, surfaces as the source of both uncanny magical practices and revolutionary fervor and violence. The term, given to a set of "hybrid" or "Creolized" beliefs dependent on "ritual incantation and the use of fetishes or charms,"[15] points to two very distinct categories of practice. The first involves "the casting of spells for various purposes, both good and evil: protecting oneself, property, family, or loved ones; harming real or perceived enemies; and bringing fortune in love, employment, personal or business pursuits"; the second incorporates "African-derived healing practices based on the application of knowledge of herbal and animal medicinal properties." Obeah thus conceived is not a religion as such but "a system of beliefs grounded in spirituality and the acknowledgment of the supernatural and involving aspects of witchcraft, sorcery, magic, spells, and healing."[16]

The practice of Obeah, seen by British colonial authorities as a threat to the stability of the plantation and the health of colonial institutions, had been outlawed in most Caribbean islands since the eighteenth century, after being perceived as one of the few means of retaliation open to the slave population. Obeah men, moreover, were seen as potential leaders who could use their influence over the slaves to incite them to rebellion, as had been the case in the Jamaican rebellion of 1760. "The influence of the Professors of that art," wrote the authors of the *Report to the Lords* of 1789, "was such as to induce many to enter into that rebellion on the assurance that they were invulnerable, and to render them so, the Obeah man gave them a powder with which to rub themselves."[17] Edward Long, after all, had already discussed the role of a "famous obeiah man or priest in the Tacky Rebellion in his *History of Jamaica*" (1774) – a work notorious for its virulent racism – and stated that among the "Coromantyns" (slaves shipped from the Gold Coast) the "*obeiah-men*" were the "chief oracles" behind conspiracies and would bind the conspirators with the "fetish or oath."[18] This link is a salient element in the history of the Haitian Revolution, which included the Vodou ceremony at Bois Caïman, at which the leaders of the rebellion finalized their plans for their attacks on whites. This episode remains a central moment even in Cuban writer Alejo Carpentier's novel *The Kingdom of this World* (1949), where it is related with many a Gothic flourish.

Obeah, then, as the primary conduit for an ideology of rebellion and for the communication of the knowledge of poisons, spells, and other subtle weapons to be used against the white population, is an ever-present element in Gothic texts produced in and about the West Indies. In West Indian literature it is most representatively portrayed in a classic text of early Jamaican literature: Herbert George De Lisser's *The White Witch of Rosehall* (1929). Based on the highly distorted legendary tales revolving around the much-maligned historical figure of Annie Palmer, mistress of the Rosehall plantation, this novel gathers all the familiar Gothic conventions into a systematic, yet ultimately limited, critique of British colonialism in the West Indies.

De Lisser seems particularly concerned here with deploying almost every conceivable Gothic convention for the purpose of showing how, throughout the years, Annie Palmer had evolved into a mosaic of all the evils that could attend whites in the "nasty dangerous tropics." The Palmer of legend, a young Irish girl born Annie May Patterson, had been orphaned at an early age and been raised by a "voodoo" priestess. This connection to Haiti, in De Lisser's text, serves to underscore the unnaturalness of her character and upbringing – she was "white, lovely, imperious, strong, fearless," and born with powers developed with the aid of friends well versed in old African magic – and to introduce a series of elements – necromancy, spirit possession, grave robbery, the role of the incubus, and the plantation house as haunted space – that have long been central to the Gothic genre. At age eighteen, Annie as a remarkably beautiful girl is believed to have used these skills to cast a spell on John Rose Palmer, master of Rosehall, to lure him into marriage, thereby bringing the threat of dispossession of the legitimate male plantation owner through the power of Obeah to the very core of this Gothic text. By her mid-twenties – such was her reputation for fearlessness and depravity – she had poisoned Palmer, thereby gaining control of the Rosehall plantation, strangled her second husband, adding his estates to her Rosehall holdings, stabbed her third husband to death, and taken numerous slave lovers whom she is reputed to have killed as she grew tired of them. De Lisser, borrowing from legend, focuses on Palmer's building of a balcony overlooking the courtyard of Rosehall, from which she would watch as she had slaves slashed to death, finding in the spectacle a source of titillation and sensual delight that becomes emblematic of her evil nature.

Palmer held control over her slaves and employees not only by bodily fear – "by dread of the whip and the iron chain" – but also by the threat of potent spiritual terrors, by the conviction she had instilled in them that she could summon fiends from hell at will and could beat down the resistance of any enemy through the secrets she had learned from her "voodoo" priestess nurse. This unnatural and unfeminine disregard for life, her un-British lack of respect for law and property, and her appropriation of the slaves' own tools for rebellion through her command of Obeah, all accounted for her unmatched wealth and might. Her position, however, tied as it was to planter hegemony, lasted only until the historical slave uprising of the 1831 Christmas holidays, when dozens of Jamaican planters were massacred. Among the first to die, at the age of twenty-nine, was Annie Palmer herself, killed by a "voodoo" priest whose magic had not been stronger than Annie's own and who sought revenge for the death of his granddaughter, murdered by the white witch. She had instilled such horror on the slaves of her plantation that they refused to bury her body, and a spell was cast on her tomb to keep her spirit at rest.

The White Witch of Rosehall blends the terror-producing aspect of Palmer's command of Obeah with the familiar Gothic convention of the pursued protagonist by focusing the plot on Palmer's murderous pursuit – through the deployment of her magical skills – of Millicent, an outspoken, free colored girl who becomes Annie's rival for the affections of Rutherford, a young English newcomer to Jamaica. In her pursuit of Rutherford and persecution of Millicent, Palmer embodies both the frightening succubus of Gothic fiction, bent on awakening sexual desire, and the Caribbean *soucouyant* who sucks Millicent's spirit out of her body until she becomes a soulless shell and dies.

At the very center of the plot of *The White Witch of Rosehall* we find a confrontation between Annie and Takoo, Millicent's grandfather, a former slave and Obeah man and as such the spiritual and political leader of the Rosehall slaves. Takoo, as a free man still constrained by the structures of slavery and the plantation, must measure his powers against those of Annie, a white woman, in their struggle for the life of his granddaughter, whose self-assurance in standing up to Annie Palmer as a rival for Rutherford's love stems from her confidence in her grandfather's position as a kind of sorcerer. Annie flaunts her superior skills as a witch in her dramatic defeat of Takoo, choosing to do so at the very moment that would have concluded his exorcism of the spell Annie had placed on Millicent. When Takoo can finally avenge his granddaughter – he strangles Annie Palmer to death during the slave uprising, in which he takes a leadership role – this revenge is only possible as a political act, as part of a revolt whose goal is to end the plantation system as they know it.

Over the years the legend of Annie Palmer, as preserved in *The White Witch of Rosehall* in all its Gothic qualities, has come to exemplify the morally corrupting influence of the plantation system, itself responsible for the creation of an environment where "only a vicious society could flourish." C. L. R. James, writing about the French planter society in Haiti, described it as a society of "open licentiousness" and "habitual ferocity," where the whites were accustomed to the indulgence of every wish. It was a society marked by the "degradation of human lives," where men sought "to overcome their abundant leisure and boredom with food, drink, dice, and black women," having long before 1789 "lost the simplicity of life and rude energy of those nameless who laid the foundation" of the Caribbean colonies.[19] The Annie Palmer of legend, a woman of voracious lust and uncontrollable brutality, embodies these negative "Creole" qualities of colonial and plantation rule.

The White Witch of Rosehall thus makes its Gothic antiheroine the supreme reflection of the colonial Jamaica that, as a slave colony, by its very nature incites corruption and sin. England, as the repository of strong and lasting moral values, is embodied by Rutherford, as principled and decent in his Englishness as Annie is debauched in her Creoleness, and who, as heir to his father's English and Caribbean estates, comes to Rosehall posing as a humble bookkeeper in order to learn plantation management from the bottom up. Seduced into a brief but intensely passionate affair with Annie Palmer, into whose seductive claws he falls resoundingly in his naive idealism, Rutherford must struggle to regain his moral strength and position himself as Millicent's protector in order to fight Annie Palmer's colonial reign of terror.

Ultimately, however, De Lisser's critique of plantation society fails to answer the very questions the novel poses about the nature of colonialism and slavery. Through the unfolding of the various interweaving plots of the novel, it becomes clear that De Lisser's critique of plantation life is too heavily dependent upon patriarchal sexual politics. The novel's focus on the evils of unbridled female power – a "corruption" by its very definition of the "natural" power hierarchies of the plantation – and its resolution, which by "taming" and destructing Annie's illegitimate power amid an aborted slave revolt allows the plantation system to remain essentially intact, leaves open (by means of Rutherford's departure from Jamaica never to return) the whole arguable issue of whether it is the plantation system or an excessive female power within it that is pernicious in the colonial environment. *The White Witch of Rosehall*, in the end, allows the Gothic excesses of its heroine's career to obscure the colonial evils that Gothic conventions served to expose so well in the text. In its corruption of Obeah, here reduced from its cultural and religious richness to trickery and charlatanism in the hands of a white witch, De Lisser finally diminishes the scope of his critique of plantation society.

In short, the traces of African religion and fragments of ancestral rituals that form "the kernel or core" of Caribbean cultures become in texts such as *The White Witch* the "mark of savagery" that justifies colonialism, while providing the required element for Gothic terror.[20] In other twentieth-century Caribbean Gothic literature, however, one can see this phenomenon operating most commonly in the titillating figure of the Haitian zombie itself, the prototypical Gothic bogeyman. Zombification, with the attendant horrors of necromancy, possession by evil spirits, and bloodsucking *soucouyants*, is the perfect target for sensation-seeking foreigners and readers of the Gothic.[21]

The mesmerizing figure of the zombie, the living/dead creature deprived of its soul and thus a Caribbean version of Frankenstein's monster, consequently dominate the region's writing throughout the twentieth century almost whenever it has any Gothic flavor at all. Zora Neale Hurston reveals a fascination with zombies to visitors and researchers such as herself in *Tell My Horse*.[22] Katherine Dunham, in her turn, seeks to define zombies in *Island Possessed* as either truly dead creatures brought back to life by black magic, "but by such a process that memory and will are gone and the resultant being is entirely subject to the will of the sorcerer who resuscitated [them], in the service of good or evil," or as persons given a potion of herbs brought from 'Nan Guinée by a bokor who "fall into a coma resembling death in every pathological sense" and are later disinterred by the bokor, "who administers an antidote and takes command of the traumatized victim[s]."[23] Zombies, Alfred Métraux argues, can be recognized "by their vague look, their dull almost glazed eyes, and above all by the nasality of their voice, a trait also characteristic of the 'Guédé,' the spirits of the dead...The zombi [thus] remains in that grey area separating life and death."[24]

Research into the ethnobiology and pharmacopoeia of zombification (of which Wade Davis's studies, *The Serpent and the Rainbow* and *Passage of*

Darkness, are perhaps the best-known examples[25]) has gone a long way to demystifying a phenomenon long believed to be solely the result of sorcery and black magic. Davis has demonstrated how zombification works as a form of "social sanction" administered in the service of Haitian secret societies – whose function is to protect "community resources, particularly land, as they define the power boundaries of the village" – so as to punish those who have violated its codes.[26] Disclosure by western researchers of the secrets and functions of zombification, however, has done very little to dispel the belief in Haiti that anyone whose death is the result of black magic may be claimed as a zombie.[27]

Zombification continues to be perceived in Haiti as a magical process by which the sorcerer seizes the victim's *ti bon ange* – the component of the soul where personality, character, and volition reside – leaving behind an empty vessel subject to the commands of the bokor. Such a notion has done even less to allay the dread induced by the prospect of zombification. The various western horror genres may have made of the zombie a terrorizing, murdering creature, as evident by the number of horror films that have made the zombie the most recognizable Caribbean contribution to the Gothic genre in film and literature. Haitians, on the other hand, do not fear any harm from zombies, yet they may live in fear of being zombified themselves. In Haitian culture, Maximilien Laroche has argued, death takes on "a menacing form in the character of the zombi...the legendary, mythic symbol of alienation...the image of a fearful destiny...which is at once collective and individual."[28] Zombification conjures up the Haitian experience of slavery, of the disassociation of man from his will, his reduction to a beast of burden at the will of a master. "It is not by chance that there exists in Haiti the myth of the zombi, that is, of the living-dead, the man whose mind and soul have been stolen and who has been left only the ability to work," René Depestre has argued. "The history of colonisation is the process of man's general zombification. It is also the quest for a revitalising salt capable of restoring to man the use of his imagination and his culture."[29]

The figure of the zombie enters the Gothic genre in full force in 1932, when, as Haitian resistance to American occupation intensified, American film audiences were treated to *White Zombie* (directed by Victor Halperin), a minor classic distinguished by its elaboration of two seminal elements in zombification: Bela Lugosi's portrayal of a Haitian "voodoo" sorcerer as a fiend who uses zombies as workers in his sugar fields (which links zombification to black labor in the colonial plantation) and the film's focus on the ensnaring of a young white woman, the eponymous "white zombie," by the sorcerer's evil magic (which resonates with eroticized Gothic notions of sorcerers as defiling fiends). The terrorized Haitian peasant, transformed into a terrorizing zombie lost in the depths of his own unspeakable horrors, literally comes to embody "a fate worse than death." Stories of zombification in the Haitian Gothic, it turns out, combine the critique of colonization that we have seen in Obeah-centered tales, the allegorical impulse manifest in the identification of slavery and colonization with zombification, and the threat of defilement of the heroine all as standard ingredients of the colonial Gothic.

If such legacies of the Haitian Revolution form the master-narrative for the Gothic representation of slave revolt in the Caribbean, the tale of Marie M. is the master-tale from which most Gothic accounts of zombification derive.[30] Called by Zora Neale Hurston "the most famous Zombie case of all Haiti," it is the story of the death in 1909 of a young upper-class woman from Port-au-Prince who died of loss of blood at the hands of her grandmother "and a prominent man." Buried with much pomp, Marie was nonetheless found five years later in a rural town, wild, unkempt, and demented. Her coffin was dug up, and in it was found the wedding dress in which she had been buried, but the remains proved to be those of a man. Métraux tells his own version, about a girl from Marbial, engaged to a young man she very much loved, who was "unwise enough to reject – rather sharply – the advances of a powerful *hungan*."[31] The spurned lover uttered numerous threats, and a few days later the girl was suddenly taken ill and died in the hospital at Jacmel. Some months after her burial, unconfirmed rumors spread of her having been seen in the company of the *houngan*, and a few years later, during the antisuperstition campaign, the *houngan* is said to have repented and returned the girl to her home, "where she lived for a long time without ever recovering her sanity." Arthur Holly, a Haitian doctor who claimed to have treated the young woman in question, offered his own version in *Les Daïmons du culte Voudo et Dra-Po* (1918): "The young daughter of our intimate friends was believed to be dead and was consequently buried. She was disinterred by a Vodou practitioner and recalled from her state of apparent death three days after the funeral. She is alive today and lives abroad."[32] C.-H. Dewisme, more recently, speaks of having found countless versions of the story: in some, as in Hurston's, she had been discovered by former classmates; in others, friends of her family on a hunting trip had come across her in a garden, eating with her hands "like a beast."[33] Found to have completely lost her mind, in several of these versions, she had been taken to the United States, where she was examined by the most famous neurologists and psychiatrists, who declared themselves powerless to help. In despair, her parents placed her in a convent in France, where she died many years later.

Jacques-Stephen Alexis, one of Haiti's foremost twentieth-century writers, consequently offers, in "Chronique d'un faux amour" ("Chronicle of a False Love," 1960), the first-person narrative of a young zombie confined to a convent in France, pining in her captivity and mourning her unfulfilled sensuality: "Here I have been for ten years awaiting my first night of love, the night that will awaken me and bring me back to daylight, the night that will wrench me from this uncertain and colorless hinterland where I vegetate, where my head rots between two realms" (p. 103, my translation). In Port-au-Prince she had been a beautiful, light-skinned, upper-class girl who had fallen in love with a mulatto young man of low birth but ample fortune. Taken on a visit to his adoptive father – a sorcerer and "former satrap general, and today a great lord of the plain, a grand feudal planter who cannot measure what he owns" (p. 135) – she falls victim to his soiling desire: "His gaze winds a forest of tangled-up lianas around me, a syrupy gaze that glides from my forehead to my nape, down my neck, my shoulders, running through my body like a cascade of ants with lecherous stings" (p. 137). Brimming with lust, he gives her the zombie poison to inhale in her wedding bouquet, and she collapses during her wedding ceremony, recovering her mobility when she is disinterred and the antidote is administered. Unable to escape her captor, she is condemned to live as a zombie, dressed in her white wedding dress embroidered in silver and her bride's veil, until the old man dies and she is sent to her convent in France. Alexis makes the most of the entrapment motif to convey the claustrophobic psychology of Gothic space in this tale, both through the imprisonment of his narrator in a convent and through her prior confinement in a coffin and subsequent captivity.

Fictional versions of the story of Marie M.'s zombification, such as Alexis's, posit sexual desire – the erotic – as a fundamental component of the zombified woman's tale, hinting at, although rarely addressing, the urge to transcend or subvert race and class barriers as one of the elements of the sorcerer's lust. The various accounts of Marie emphasize the girl's whiteness or light skin against the sorcerer's darkness; her wealth and position against his lack of social standing; and her buoyant, love-filled, wholesome desire against his sinister, debasing lust. This racial tension, this fear of miscegenation and interracial desire, has been an element of the Gothic since the earliest days of the genre. In a colonial setting, in an environment where racial differences have had profound social, political, and economic repercussions, they acquire greater meaning and significance, becoming yet another element through which the Gothic enters into the critique of colonialism.

The same elements reappear in René Depestre's *Hadriana dans tous mes rêves* (1988), a text that, through similar intertwinings of zombification and the erotic, returns to the exploration of the connections between zombification and a critique of colonization already evident in Alexis's text.[34] Set in Jacmel, Haiti, the story follows the apparent death, zombification, and carnivalesque wake of the beautiful, white Hadriana Siloé. This story of a young woman's zombification and eventful restoration to a "rightful" lover, however, is the point of departure for a somewhat problematic meditation on Haiti's history that is highly dependent on carnivalesque imagery. There are plenty of Gothic motifs in the text, but they appear in their parodic form, carnivalized and thereby distanced from their traditional connection to horror and evil.

The text opens with a Gothic transformation, that of Balthazar Granchiré, who is turned into an incubus as punishment for his sexual transgression with a sorcerer's *femme-jardin*; but his metamorphosis into a highly sexed butterfly, a sort of winged phallus that goes on to ravage unsuspecting young women as they sleep, has too much of the comic, despite its deeply rooted sexism, to produce horror. The same can be said of the text's description of the carnival figures that dance in ghostly abandon around the young woman's coffin as it rests in the town's main square. Using carnivalesque ghosts rather than horrific ghouls, more Halloweenesque than phantasmagoric figures, Depestre in this parade summons three centuries of Haitian history: Indian caciques, Elizabethan corsairs, barons and marquises of Louis XIV's court, black and mulatto officers of Napoleon's Grand Army, Pauline Bonaparte, Toussaint Louverture, Pétion, Christophe, and, discordantly, Stalin. But this carnivalesque celebration of death exploits the traditional classlessness of the carnival festival to deny the deeply rooted differences that divide Haitian people along class and race lines. In this indiscriminate parade, all historical figures, regardless of the nature of their historical role, the relative value of their deeds or misdeeds notwithstanding, are granted equal significance. The juxtaposition of the incongruous, irreconcilable images of the Haitian military, with their record of betrayal of the people, alongside the maroons who led the struggle for Haitian independence is characteristic of the profound contradictions in Depestre's representation of history in the text. These contradictions negate the conviction of the existence of iniquity and vice that gives to the colonial Gothic – as seen through the symbolic representation of the zombie – its potential for historical and social signification. Zombification moves from horror to a *jeu de masques*, a carnivalesque parody which reduces to a senseless game of disguises crucial aspects of Haiti's class and race divisions.

The carnivalesque aspects of the text notwithstanding, Depestre's novel still ponders the question of the Haitian people's collective zombification through their history of colonization, slavery, and dictatorship. The notion, within the context of this parodic postcolonial Gothic, debases the Haitian people to "the category of human cattle, malleable, pliable to one's will" (*Hadriana*, p. 128, my translation), denying the people's centuries-long history of struggle against natural calamities, dictatorship, and repression which, however unsuccessful, has been nonetheless real. In Depestre's presentation, however, the Haitian zombie emerges as the "biological fuel par excellence, what is left of Caliban after the loss of his identity, his life having been literally cut in two: the *gros bon ange* of muscular strength condemned to eternal forced labor; the *petit bon ange* of wisdom and light, of guilelessness and dreams, exiled forever into the first empty bottle found lying around" (p. 130). This depiction of the Haitian people as zombies negates any possibility of their transcending a history of colonialism, slavery, postcolonial poverty, and political repression since, as zombies, they are incapable of rebellion: "'Let's join our *gros bons anges* in a struggle for freedom': those are words one is not likely to hear from a zombi's mouth" (p. 131).

Depestre's hopelessness about the possibility of transcending the life–death symbiosis of the zombie-centered tale finds its counterargument in Pierre Clitandre's *La Cathédrale du mois d'août* (1980; *The Cathedral of the August Heat*, 1987), a text in which the Gothic elements parodied in Depestre's *Hadriana* reappear as vehicles for the reaffirmation not of the sorcery of the bokor but of the life-affirming and revolutionary qualities of Vodou itself. Although it focuses on John, a Haitian *tap-tap* (bus) driver, and his son Raphael, the novel is above all a metaphorical tale of a lost people's desperate struggle to recover their history and, with it, the source of precious water that can restore them to fertility and bounty. It celebrates hope and renewal through its emphasis on the carnivalesque and its faith in the regenerating and revolutionary power of Vodou.

Like Depestre's novel, *The Cathedral of the August Heat* is a hybrid text that blends the Gothic and the carnivalesque in its celebration and lamentation over the very materiality of the Haitian people's bodies. The hyperbolized, quasi-Rabelaisian grotesque images of the Haitian collective body are primarily olfactory: unbathed bodies smelling like ram goats, the abominable stench of rotting flesh, the nauseous smell of plague-ridden corpses, the stink of piss and decay, the smell of sweat, blood, and bruises. These images blend with Gothic, frightful images of the body as a mutilated, rotting corpse. The text abounds in images spawned from political terror: crushed hands, burnt bodies, cut-off penises, roasted testicles, sores, the blood that soaks and fertilizes the scorched earth. Death haunts the text, and the people are represented as subject to ever-threatening plagues, natural calamities, and repressive terror. The Gothic resonance of these images notwithstanding, death and the dead body are depicted as stages in the renewing of the ancestral body of the people, not as the limbo of zombification. The novel treats individual deaths not as signaling an irrevocable end but as natural and necessary phases in the cycle of life. Death ultimately asserts life, thus ensuring the indestructible immortality of the people.

Gothic resonances frame the second part of the tale most of all, once it is introduced by the *vèvè* (sacred symbol) for Petro, an invocation to the spirits of wrath and revolt. The Petro rites in Vodou, born of the rage against the evil fate suffered by Africans transported to the new world and the wrath against the brutality of displacement and enslavement,[35] fulfill a function in this text similar to that of the Gothicized Obeah of British fiction of the eighteenth and early nineteenth centuries: that of fomenting and sustaining the desire for revolt among slaves and exploited peasants. During the Haitian people's open revolt against the repressive authorities (Clitandre, *Cathédrale*, p. 123), the Petro *loas*, the gods of the Vodou pantheon born in the mountains, nurtured in secret, repositories of the moral strength and organization of the escaped slaves that led the Haitian Revolution, help Clitandre's people retrieve their lost history of struggle and revolt. Clitandre draws upon familiar Gothic conventions in describing the intimate communication between humans and *loas* that leads to "Another shouting for armed resistance against the great epidemic of repression" (p. 122, my translation), and in conveying the horror of the fierce wave of repression that follows the revolt of the trade unionists. Raphael, killed during the revolt, articulates the message of the Petro *loas* in the legacy of historical memory he leaves behind: "He had scraped it [into the old cannon] with the blade, as if he wanted to remove the rust of the Season of Neglect, as if to tell his father to keep his promise. That these brave ancestors who forged this free nation, floating like a bird on the blue Caribbean Sea, should not be forgotten" (p. 128).

Even more recently, Mayra Montero, in her short story "Corinne, muchacha amable" ("Corinne, Amiable Girl," 1991),[36] returns to the Gothic tropes carnivalized by Depestre and Clitandre, turning them inside out so as to expose their sexist, racist, and political underpinnings. Young Appolinaire Sanglier, "wallowing in the despair of his love like a victim of a blood spell," seeks the aid of Papa Lhomond, a *houngan* who knows "how to work the living dead," to turn light-skinned and yellow-eyed Corinne into his zombie wife (pp. 836–37). Corinne, the daughter of a white priest and a prostitute, is coveted for a beauty that owes much to her being partly white. But she is engaged to marry a politically active deaf-mute, aptly named Dessalines Corail, and is disdainful of the love-sick Appolinaire. Her zombification on the eve of her wedding will be as much a punishment for her disdain as the means of guaranteeing that, after her marriage to Appolinaire, "she will not become such a whore as her mother." Appolinaire dreams of her as she will be after she "returned from the blue well of the deceased, clean and submissive like God intended, with the pale gaze of those who never think, without that scowl of disgust she gave him every time he came near" (p. 836).

Here Montero is interested both in deploying the familiar Gothic conventions to lay bare the zombification of women as an act of power over them and in linking this issue to the larger one of the Haitian people's struggle against the Duvalier government, here represented by the dreaded Tonton Macoutes, the regime's feared militia. Set on the eve of an election, with Corinne's fiancé one of the most active workers on behalf of an anti-Duvalier local candidate, the story juxtaposes Corinne's determination to choose a husband freely against the people's struggle to elect a candidate committed to social justice. Both will be denied this right. Montero never dwells on the pathos of Corinne's situation, so there is no sentimentality wasted on describing the fate of the brave young girl who has dared to challenge Appolinaire's desire and the Tonton Macoute's wrath. Her individual fate is not Montero's central concern; it is depicted as bound to that of the Haitian people. As she lies in a deathlike stupor in her fresh grave, with Papa Lhomond and Appolinaire racing against time to dig her up before she suffocates, the people, her fiancé among them, are brutally attacked as they seek to exercise their democratic right to vote. The description of the massacre has too much of a connection to historical realities to be read as merely literary:

> Appolinaire slowed down. He noticed the half-severed necks and arms and concluded they had been killed by machete blows... When he turned the corner, without having the time to avoid it, he found himself facing a mob that was suddenly upon him, dragging him along little by little. Some men were sobbing loudly, their faces covered with blood and their clothes torn... He returned to his house near dawn, avoiding the soldiers piling up bodies on tarpaulin-covered trucks. ("Corinne, Amiable Girl," pp. 844–45, 846)

There is plenty of horror in descriptions such as this, but they slip away from the traditional Gothic almost as effectively as Depestre's carnivalesque images, moving the traditional motifs to a new realm of meaning.

The living dead remain a disquieting presence in "Corinne, Amiable Girl," another chapter in the narrative of the Haitian people's ongoing struggle for freedom from political and economic oppression. Montero denies the people's zombification through the very materiality of their butchered bodies, their "half-severed necks and arms." The dead bodies piled up anonymously on trucks and the still-living body of Corinne awaiting rescue into the half-life of zombiedom represent an unresolved historical quandary for which the zombie as metaphor can offer no deliverance.

Still, the Cuban-born Montero, a long-time resident of Puerto Rico, is, of all contemporary Caribbean writers, the most indebted to the Gothic tradition, which she has made her own, transforming the familiar conventions through her deep knowledge of Caribbean magicoreligious traditions and her concerns for social justice. Montero, as she did in "Corinne, Amiable Girl," appropriates the Gothic in *Del rojo de su sombra* (1992; *The Red of His Shadow*, 2001) to address the vicious and corrupt politics and African-derived religious beliefs that link the Dominican Republic and Haiti despite the enmity that has existed between the countries for centuries. In this, her most purely Gothic novel to date, she tells the disturbing tale of the contest of wills between the leaders of two Vodou societies – Mistress Zulé, an inexperienced but gifted priestess, and Similá Bolesseto, a notoriously violent and devious priest – and the disastrous impact they have on their religious communities, composed mostly of Haitians who have crossed the border into the Dominican Republic to cut sugar cane in slavery-like conditions. The world conjured up by Montero as a backdrop to this struggle is terrifying in its festering hatred, self-destructive greed, and sexual jealousy. The struggle, played out through the casting of spells meant to torture, maim, and kill, becomes more horrifying when the *loas*, those capricious Vodou gods, use the worshippers they possess during rituals as their puppets in bloody dramas of their own, with even more disastrous results.

In *Tú, la oscuridad* (1995; *In the Palm of Darkness*, 1999) Montero returns to the production of horror that served her so well in "Corinne, Amiable Girl" to tell the story of American herpetologist Victor Grigg, who, with the aid of his Haitian guide Thierry Adrien, is on a quest to find an elusive and dangerously threatened blood frog, extinct everywhere but on a dangerous, eerie mountain near Port-au-Prince. In the volatile and bloody setting of the Haitian mountains, controlled by violent thugs, by weaving together the stories and vastly different worldviews of her two protagonists, Montero uncovers a new haunting postcolonial space built upon the conflict between a scientific worldview and a more animistic one: the extinction of a species due to a collapsing environment; the troubled landscape of Haiti, peopled with zombies and other frightening, otherworldly creatures; political corruption and violence, senseless murder, sexual violence, and religious turmoil. In *Tú, la oscuridad*, as in "Corinne, Amiable Girl" and *Del rojo de su sombra*, Montero has reinvented the Caribbean Gothic, pushing the conventions of the genre from a critique of colonialism to an even wider engagement with social justice and political commitment.

Long before Montero, though, *I Walked with a Zombie*, a 1943 Hollywood film directed by Jacques Tourneur and loosely based on Charlotte Brontë's *Jane Eyre*, was the first of many cinematic rerenderings of British Gothic texts set against a Caribbean background. Its young protagonist, Betsy, a Canadian nurse, comes to the fictional island of San Sebastian to care for

Jessica, the wife of a plantation owner who has been transformed into a zombie by a "voodoo" curse and is now a soulless shell, weeping eerily at night, her will at the mercy of the drums beating unnervingly after every sunset. As in *Jane Eyre*, the young nurse falls in love with the master of the estate, and the romantic triangle is eventually dissolved through the death of the zombie, who is shown to have been an unfaithful wife. This movie – described by critics as an "enchanting film possessed of a subtlety at odds with the conventions of its genre and a beauty which might be described as otherworldly" – is also at odds with its genre in its "imposing respect" for the supernatural, its positive presentation of Vodou, and its "evocative link to unstated themes of the island's tragic racial history and the life–death symbiosis which governs the lives of the central characters."[37]

Although the movie strives to shed light on the island's history of colonial oppression through its representation of the realities of plantation life, it is visually dependent on the Gothic conventions that represent Vodou as that which is only half-comprehensible and half-frightening. The film's longest and most haunting scene offers a catalogue of Gothic motifs as it follows Betsy and Jessica through the rustling cane fields to a Vodou ceremony, a true voyage of penetration into a strange and foreboding world punctuated by the increasingly spellbinding beating of drums. The cinematography, which alternates between shades of black and white as it tracks the women's movements from light to shadow, outlines the image of their pale faces against that of the imposing figure of Carrefour, the black guardian of the crossroads, a zombie "who materializes with disquieting suddenness on their path."[38] At the ceremony itself, the eroticism of the drumming and frenzied dancing of the initiates menacingly frames Jessica's passive, semiconscious figure. Dressed in a robe reminiscent of that of a vestal virgin being offered for sacrifice, she steps into the vortex. The black bodies rustle past her as did the canes, their near-touch eroticized as emblematic of the forbidden, while her passivity makes her unable to forestall the taboo touch. Awakened by Jessica's attitude to the possibility of luring her back to the *hounfort*, the mulatto *houngan* and his subservient female acolytes, in subsequent evenings, attempt to summon her with the drums, aided by a blond "voodoo" doll before which he performs a highly eroticized dance characterized by jerky forward thrusts of the hips and groin. Earlier in the film the cinematographer has underscored the film's sexual imagery when he captures Betsy waking in the middle of the night to listen to the sound of Carrefour's shuffling footsteps. As she lies in bed, she is framed behind the ornate iron grille that protects her window, with Carrefour's phallic shadow standing threateningly against the wall that also holds a painting of a menacing, decaying Gothic fortress in the Udolpho tradition.

I Walked with a Zombie warrants attention in the present context because it is a thematic and visual reminder of how Gothic traditions rooted in British literature become relocated to a colonial setting. It shows how, in the Anglophone Caribbean (particularly in the work of those writers directly influenced by the novels of Emily and Charlotte Brontë), the Gothic tradition has come to provide a path to a fresh understanding of colonial conditions. The surprising number of Caribbean texts we can connect directly to *Jane Eyre* and *Wuthering Heights* – from Jean Rhys's *Wide Sargasso Sea* (1966), V. S. Naipaul's *Guerrillas* (1975), Michelle Cliff's *Abeng* (1984), and *No Telephone to Heaven* (1987), and Rosario Ferré's *Maldito amor* (1986; *Sweet Diamond Dust*, 1988) to Jamaica Kincaid's *The Autobiography of My Mother* (1996) – span forty years of Gothic literature in the Caribbean, proof of a continuing dialogue through which Caribbean writers seek to reformulate their connections to and severance from a European language and tradition.

In *Guerrillas*, for example (Naipaul's colonial rewriting of *Wuthering Heights*), the Trinidadian writer offers a version of the Gothic rooted in the conviction that the colonial system responsible for exploitation and terror in the Caribbean has left too deep a wound on the body and psyche of the colonized nation to allow for recovery. Naipaul's postcolonial Heathcliff, Jimmy Ahmed, a pseudovisionary touted as a black leader in London, returns to his colonized island home in order to form a farming commune and repeat slogans he himself knows to be pointless. He dreams of becoming a "hero," the embodiment of the fictional hero about whom he himself is writing a novel, the feared and respected protagonist of a ground-shaking revolt whose exploits would resound in the England he has left behind. His complex relationship with Roche, a former South African activist who has already written a book about his imprisonment and torture (thereby proving his heroism), and Jane, Roche's English girlfriend and Jimmy's would-be lover, mirrors in its turmoil and despair that of Heathcliff, Catherine, and Edgar Linton. In the bitterness of his Heathcliff-like sense of dispossession, Jimmy plans a revolt whose futility will only confirm the ultimate powerlessness and irrelevance of the resourceless islands of the Caribbean.

It should not be surprising that, in looking for British models with which to engage in an ideological/textual dialogue, Caribbean writes have found fertile ground in the works of the Brontë sisters. One motivation may be the vivid imagery and evocative environment of the Yorkshire moors as presented in *Wuthering Heights* (and to a lesser extent in *Jane Eyre*), an atmospheric richness capable of being recreated in the lush and threatening Caribbean landscape. These atmospheric correspondences are almost palpable in the Gothic renderings of the Caribbean natural environment that we find in West Indian novels set in Dominica, for example. Jean Rhys in *Wide Sargasso*

Sea – which uses actual characters from *Jane Eyre* as though it were a portion left out of the original novel – depicts the island's riotous vegetation and dramatic landscape with an intensity that prompts Rochester, who has married the Creole Antoinette (later known as Bertha), to equate it all with evil. Lally, the narrator of another Dominican classic, Phyllis Shand Allfrey's *The Orchid House* (1953), faced with the menacing power of the island's nature, ruefully concludes that it offers nothing but beauty and disease. Jamaica Kincaid, in *The Autobiography of My Mother*, conjures up the world of Dominica not to recreate it in its physical or social nuances but to inscribe in it a casual cruelty, to superimpose on it a world in which the ghosts of colonialism still haunt the relationships of contemporary men and women. In her depiction of Dominican nature Kincaid's narrator, Xuela, refuses to endow it with any semblance of positive meaning, stripping it of anything but cruelty and desolation.

Still, it is primarily in the haunting characters of Heathcliff and the mad Bertha Mason Rochester, both defeated "colonials" othered in their questionable racial provenance, swarthy and un-English, that Caribbean writers find their strongest foothold in the west European Gothic. The failed family romance of *Wuthering Heights*, the placid English domesticity temporarily shattered by the intrusion of foreign elemental passions, we must remember, lasts only as long as Heathcliff does. His obsessive haunting persists only until his death, when the marriage of the surviving heirs of Earnshaw and Linton restores an illusion of happiness and proper English complacence. In *Jane Eyre* too, where the death of the mad colonial wife is a prerequisite for the English heroine's happiness, the English Gothic introduces the colonial as a disturbing agent, a haunting presence, only to dispatch him/her when the time comes for happiness-ever-after.

Jimmy Ahmed, as a Caribbean Heathcliff, embodies Naipaul's profoundly pessimistic conviction that popular revolts such as the one his character is meant to lead are pointless gestures. Jimmy's Caribbean and Jane's England – as the text contends through its insistence on inscribing itself into the Gothic plot of *Wuthering Heights* – cannot escape what history (and literature) has made them: former colony and former imperial power, both societies mutilated and caught in cycles of exploitation. The revolt, when it finally comes, is a meaningless skirmish, and Jane's brutal murder – a hollow gesture – only underscores the islanders' incapacity for transcending the legacy of colonization. In *Guerrillas*, as Michael Neill has argued, "matching Naipaul's indignation at the destructive legacy of imperialism, [there] is a deepening despair at the seemingly irremediable confusion left in its wake. It implies, in its way, a critique of imperialism even more radical than [others]: for it wants us to contemplate the possibility of organic societies damaged beyond repair, of a world incapable, in any imaginable future, of putting itself together again."[39]

Jimmy, stranded in his colonial Thrushcross Grange, trapped in the structures of Brontë's text, is struggling for meaning in a society – and a text – that refuses to grant it. He wants to be feared, relevant, but from the opening pages of the book the text and its characters seem intent on depriving him of significance. "I don't think Jimmy sees himself as Heathcliff or anything like that," Roche explains to Jane, speaking of his having named the farming commune Thrushcross Grange, "[he] took a writing course, and it was one of the books he had to read. I think he just likes the name" (p. 2). Jimmy's plight, however, is that of being caught in the structures of someone else's plot – a sort of Heathcliff *manqué* – so much so that he is fated to a shoddier version of his model's Gothic purgatory of violence and passion. At the same time, his antiheroic trajectory, being more flagrantly social and political than that of Brontë's tormented hero, is played out on a larger canvas – that of the colonialism debate – and his ultimate defeat becomes a metaphor for colonial failure.

Naipaul's dialogue with *Wuthering Heights*, however, is primarily structural and symbolic. *Guerrillas* mirrors Brontë's text in its examination of the outsider as catalyst, and of his ultimate downfall as representative of colonial despair, but the author's vision of the Gothic in this text is not stylistic. Naipaul is less concerned with deploying the conventions and motifs of Gothic fiction as an aid to his narrative as he is with larger structures of meaning. Jamaica Kincaid, in her turn, deploys all the traditional elements of Gothic fiction in *The Autobiography of My Mother* in a more elaborate and systematic critique of postcolonial society. In Xuela, her female version of a Caribbean Heathcliff, she returns to the model of *Wuthering Heights*, a seminal text in her own formation as a writer, to inspire the passionate intensity and atmospheric power of her nightmarish vision of Caribbean history. Xuela, fierce and fearless, is a defiant figure endowed with remarkable prescience and farsightedness. Gifted with knowledge beyond reason, she, like Heathcliff, can hear the unhearable – the sounds of ghosts, spirits, and *djablesses* in the deep of the night – and understand the deep-seated cruelty of colonial and postcolonial relations. It is in her ability to detach herself from the passions surrounding her while paradoxically nurturing her own profound hatred that the character achieves her mirroring rapport with the passion-driven ruthlessness of her Brontëan prototype.

The world Kincaid creates as a setting for Xuela's tale is one where all ties of compassion and affection have been severed. Kincaid, as Cathleen Schine puts it, "intentionally simplifies the life around her main character, rendering it free of all everydayness, purifying it until it sparkles with hatred alone."[40] In one of the novel's earliest episodes, after Kincaid has established the bonds of casual cruelty that mark her relationships with others, the young Xuela falls in love with a pair of land turtles, the first things she admits to having truly loved. Yet she responds to what she perceives as their refusal to obey her commands by packing their necks with mud, forgetting them in the space where she has trapped them and killing them in the process. For all the narrator's references to the cruelty inherent in Dominican nature, the text underscores that cruelty is not the result of an indifferent nature but of an historical process that has led to widespread moral deformity.

In a society where the colonizers' historical narrative has silenced the vanquished's version of events, the basis on which a positive identity could be founded, the only defense against an absence of history, Kincaid argues, must be an articulation of the wounds of forced silence through an eloquent, deafening denunciation of the evils sustained in the name of colonial expansion. In *The Autobiography of My Mother* this narrative of symbolic denunciation is rendered through the interrelated Gothic themes of motherlessness, lovelessness, miscegenation, and the differences between the languages of the colonizer and the colonized. Kincaid, in conceiving this tale of a daughter of a Carib foundling who has died in childbirth and a man of mixed African and European race who is torn apart by his legacy, refuses to inscribe Xuela's tale in the world of romance, romance being "the refuge of the defeated" who need soothing tunes because their entire being is a wound. The Gothic is better suited as a vehicle for Kincaid's stance of denunciation, linked as it is to her literary model, Brontë's Heathcliff, and affording her a clarity of vision which Heathcliff would have envied.

The legacy of the Gothic in *The Autobiography of My Mother* can be glimpsed most clearly in the text's handling of dreams and the supernatural and in the various ways it articulates notions of evil linked to colonial realities. The mother whom Xuela has never met, for example, haunts the book as she haunts her daughter, appearing frozen in a recurring dream, descending a ladder, only the hem of her white dress visible. Xuela, after a tortuous abortion that leaves her in a nightmarish daze, embarks on a phantasmagoric voyage of possession along the periphery of her home island, Dominica, a journey which she describes as her claiming of her birthright of the villages, rivers, mountains, and people. The lengthy passage, rich in the incoherence and surrealism of dreams, allows her to see her father's face, in all its resemblance to the conquerors, as a map of the world that encompasses continents, volcanoes, mountain ranges, horizons that lead into "the thick blackness of nothing" (p. 91). The characters surrounding Xuela, liker her father, perform their particular versions of evil out of a bitterness and hatred rooted in their plight as colonized and exploited victims. Her father, divided from his own people by the very wealth he has accumulated through his emulation of the colonizers, leaves her as a baby in the care of his cruel and indifferent laundress; her stepmother attempts to kill her with a poisoned necklace. Her half-brother, weak and irresolute, dies from a debilitating parasitic worm, which fills his body with pus and emerges from his leg just as he dies. Her half-sister, an emotionally crippled, vengeful, envious, sad, and embittered woman, bears the crippling injuries she sustains after a freak accident as a mirror of her psychic scars. Moira, whose husband Xuela marries after her death, is a "waxy, ghostish," lifeless bigot who dies from her addiction to a hallucinatory tea made of local leaves provided by Xuela, which eventually turns her skin black and leads her to a painful, agonizing death.

The Gothic nuances of *The Autobiography of My Mother* allow Kincaid to compose with vivid hues a fictional world in which the colonizer and his mimics are validated at the expense of the colonized, a world in which those like Xuela, clear-sighted enough to understand the evil impact of the process – to grasp it visually from watching its Gothic signs on the bodies of the defeated – must assume the task of building a positive sense of self out of the remnants of colonial destruction. Xuela's narrative uses traditional Gothic imagery with striking effect to show what happens to those not visionary enough to reject collusion with a process that can only result in self-hatred and self-destruction. In her character's refusal to accept the colonizer's views of those like herself, Kincaid posits Xuela's obsessive, almost grotesque self-love as an alternative to self-loathing and the pernicious effects of assimilation. That she can accomplish this through a narrative steeped in the traditions of the Gothic attests to the genre's malleability and to the expressive richness it achieves in postcolonial adaptation.

Nowhere is this richness better displayed in a Caribbean text than in Jean Rhys's rewriting of *Jane Eyre*. *Wide Sargasso Sea* is the narrative of Antoinette Cosway, eventually the madwoman in the attic of Brontë's work. Rhys's exploration of Rochester's exploitative relationship with Antoinette, the West Indian heiress whom he marries for her fortune, depicts the cultural and economic clash between England and the West Indies and the tensions between colonizer and colonized through a thematic emphasis on Antoinette as victim and on the Gothic mansion, Rochester's Thornfield, as emblematic of patriarchal/colonial power. Nowhere has the Gothic mode crossed oceans more powerfully or in more of a sharp dialogue between the postcolonial and the English Gothic. *Wide Sargasso Sea* – a text remarkable for its evocation of landscape, its treatment of Obeah and the presence of colonial ghosts, its recasting of the haunted Mr. Rochester of *Jane Eyre* as a haunting Gothic villain, and its persecuted heroine – has consequently become a seminal West Indian text, spawning many secondary and tertiary links between itself, Brontë's text, and a younger generation of Caribbean writers.

The critical literature on Jean Rhys, the Brontës, and the Gothic tradition is extensive. Critics have found the ramifications of the relationship between these very different writers – particularly Rhys's challenge of such a canonical text as *Jane Eyre* in the service of redressing a "wrong" in the narrative of/about the colonial – an endlessly fascinating exercise.[41] It is of particular interest in our context because so much of what brings the two texts together – besides the obvious echoes of characters, places, and plot elements – is Rhys's masterful use of Gothic elements, from her use of landscape as a frightful, menacing backdrop through her appropriation of Thornfield Hall as a parallel space to the Caribbean plantation house to her sophisticated use of race and Obeah as sources of unease and terror. Rhys's play with intertextuality allows her to transcend definitions and categories, to reformulate forms – particularly that of the Gothic novel – and to open the way for a seemingly inexhaustible possibility of meanings. Rhys's "violation" of Brontë's text, it has been argued, results in the breaking of the integrity of *Jane Eyre*: the "mother text is maimed, and in essence, disarmed."[42] Yet Rhys can also be seen as forcing *Jane Eyre* "to be measured by a set of assumptions outside those of the master quest narrative."[43]

Rhys's opening of European texts to a new type of critical scrutiny – the very realization that the canon, particularly the ever-popular Gothic canon, can be interpolated, accosted, defied, and even disregarded – has made *Wide Sargasso Sea* a "mother text" in its turn, opening the way for some remarkable intertextual correspondences between it and other Caribbean texts. Of primary interest in these correspondences is the presence of the Gothic mode, even among writers – such as Rosario Ferré of Puerto Rico – working in literary traditions with little or no Gothic elements of their own.

In *Maldito amor* (*Sweet Diamond Dust*) in the 1980s, Ferré establishes a thematic link to Jean Rhys – and through her to Charlotte Brontë – that underscores the importance to her work of recognizing a female tradition, a separate Caribbean and women's canon in which she can establish herself as a writer. In *Sweet Diamond Dust*, as earlier in her short story "Pico Rico Mandorico," a rewriting of Christina Rossetti's "Goblin Market," Ferré pays homage to Rhys's pioneering literature, writing a tale which, although very much her own, resonates with echoes from *Wide Sargasso Sea*. Rhys and Ferré share thematic concerns over the decline of the planter class in the Caribbean and the exclusion of women from sources of power in patriarchal societies. Ferré approaches these dual concerns in her novel through the possibility of transferring ownership of the Diamond Dust sugar estate, and with it economic and social power, from an old high-bourgeois family to the mulatto nurse who has married the late heir. The problems of such a transfer manifest themselves vividly in the text through Ferré's highly Baroque prose and intricate, almost paranoid presentation of the intrigue, lies, misogyny, and manipulation that lead to the destruction of wills, deceitful renderings of history, and eventually murder, all played out against the backdrop of the ruin and bankruptcy brought on Puerto Rican sugar planters after the American invasion of 1898. What delights in this text is, above all, how well Ferré is able to incorporate into it, in ways quite Creolized and Hispanicized, a broad range of traditional Gothic elements that add texture and depth to her critique of Spanish colonialism and American neocolonialism. Her ambivalent exploration of her protagonist's potential madness, the mysterious circumstances of her husband's accident, the ambiguous nature of the presentation of erotic desire, the wariness that dominates relations across class, race, and gender, all serve to heighten suspense and awaken the multilayered insecurities and fears that link the text with Rhys and, through her, with centuries of Gothic texts. Gloria's setting the plantation on fire at the end of the text – an act that signals her refusal to participate as a woman and a mulatto in the corruption and exploitation of a postcolonial system – is also an act of identification with similarly placed Creoles of dubious racial and class heritages, as well as with Antoinette Cosway and, through her, Bertha Mason.[44]

This dialogue with the Gothic continues in present-day Caribbean writing, especially in writing by women. There is a passage in *No Telephone to Heaven* (1987), Michelle Cliff's tale of how Clare Savage, the protagonist of her earlier novel *Abeng* (1984), moves from a quest for spiritual integrity into revolutionary martyrdom, when Clare picks up a book at random, a copy of Charlotte Brontë's *Jane Eyre* brought from a second-hand bookstore. Her impulse to identify with Jane's plight – with "Jane. Small and pale. English" – is rejected in favor of an identification with Bertha –

Yes, Bertha was closer to the mark. Captive. Ragôut. Mixture. Confused. Jamaican. Caliban. Carib. Cannibal. Cimarron. All Bertha. All Clare.[45]

This catalogue of Bertha's possible signifiers – in a text where Gothic horrors are reproduced through the brutal futility of revolutionary struggle – testifies to the many ways in which the Caribbean and the colonial in general have entered into Gothic fiction as the frightful other, the defeated, the eerie, the disappeared, the dead, only to be transformed over the succeeding years. Clare's embracing of the marginal, her willingness to stand with Bertha in the midst of her own Gothic tale, is a powerful reminder of how the Gothic, especially in the Caribbean, has become a part of the language of the colonized, appropriated, reinvented, and in that way very much alive in worlds far beyond western Europe and the continental United States.

NOTES

1 *Sir Walter Scott on Novelists and Fiction*, ed. Ioan Williams (New York: Barnes, 1968), p. 87.
2 For a discussion of Charlotte Smith's "The Story of Henrietta" in the context of West Indian Obeah, see Alan Richardson, "Romantic Voodoo: Obeah and British Culture, 1787–1907" in *Sacred Possessions: Vodou, Santería, Obeah, and the Caribbean*, ed. Margarite Fernández Olmos and Lizabeth Paravisini-Gebert (New Brunswick, NJ: Rutgers University Press, 1997), pp. 171–94.
3 Edward Long, *Candid Reflections Upon the Judgment Lately Awarded by the Court of King's Bench, in Westminster-Hall, On What is Commonly Called the Negroe-Cause* (London: T. Lowden, 1772), p. 82.
4 Richardson, "Romantic Voodoo," p. 175.
5 *Hamel, the Obeah Man* (London: Hunt and Clarke, 1827).
6 Barbara Lalla, "Dungeons of the Soul: Frustrated Romanticism in Eighteenth- and Nineteenth-Century Literature of Jamaica," *MELUS* 21:3 (fall 1996): 10.
7 Cited from H. L. Malchow in Douglas A. Lorimer, "*Gothic Images of Race in Nineteenth-Century Britain* (Book Review)," *Victorian Studies* 41:4 (summer 1998): 681–84.
8 Mario Cesareo, "When the Subaltern Travels: Slave Narrative and Testimonial Erasure in the Contact Zone" in *Women at Sea: Travel Writing and the Margins of Caribbean Discourse*, ed. Lizabeth Paravisini-Gebert and Ivette Romero-Cesareo (New York: Palgrave, 2001), p. 110.
9 ibid., p. 111.
10 Cited in Frances Smith Foster, *Witnessing Slavery: the Development of Ante-Bellum Slave* (London: Greenwood Press, 1979), p. 45.
11 Miriam DeCosta-Willis, "Self and Society in the Afro-Cuban Slave Narrative," *Latin American Literary Review* 26:32 (1988): 9.
12 Andrew McCann, "Colonial Gothic: Morbid Anatomy, Commodification and Critique in Marcus Clarke's *The Mystery of Major Molineux*," *Australian Literary Studies* 19:4 (October 2000): 399.
13 Louise White, "Cars Out of Place: Vampires, Technology, and Labor in East and Central Africa," *Representations* 43 (summer 1993): 41.
14 James Ferguson, "*Haiti, History and the Gods* (Book Review)," *Race and Class* 38 (1997): 94.
15 See Richardson, "Romantic Voodoo," p. 173.
16 Karla Frye, "Obeah and Hybrid Identities in Elizabeth Nunez Harrell's *When Rocks Dance*" in Fernández Olmos and Paravisini-Gebert, *Sacred Possessions*, p. 98.
17 *Report to the Lords of the Committee of the Council Appointed for the Consideration of All Matters Relating to Trade and Foreign Plantation* (London, 1789).
18 Edward Long, *The History of Jamaica*, 3 vols. (London: T. Lowndes, 1774), II, 451–52, 473.
19 C. L. R. James, *The Black Jacobins* (New York: Vintage Books, 1963), p. 27.

20 See Joan Dayan, "Erzulie: a Women's History of Haiti" in *Postcolonial Subjects: Francophone Women Writers*, ed. Mary Jean Matthews Green (Minneapolis: University of Minnesota Press, 1996).

21 Harry A. Franck, *Roaming Through the West Indies* (New York: Century Co., 1920), p. 164.

22 Zora Neale Hurston, *Tell My Horse: Voodoo and Life in Haiti and Jamaica* (New York: Harper and Row, 1990), p. 179.

23 Katherine Dunham, *Island Possessed* (Chicago: University of Chicago Press, 1969), pp. 184–85.

24 Alfred Métraux, *Voodoo in Haiti*, trans. Hugo Charteris (New York: Schocken, 1959), pp. 250–51.

25 Wade Davis, *The Serpent and the Rainbow* (New York: Warner Books, 1985) and *Passage of Darkness: the Ethnobiology of the Haitian Zombie* (Chapel Hill: University of North Carolina Press, 1988).

26 See Davis, *Passage of Darkness*, pp. 8–10. See also Bernard Diederich, "On the Nature of Zombi Existence," *Caribbean Review* 12 (1983): 14–17, 43–46.

27 Davis's anthropological work, supported by scholarship and science, itself fell victim to Hollywood's craving for sensationalism where zombies are concerned. The film based on his book *The Serpent and the Rainbow* (1988; Universal; directed by Wes Craven, produced by David Ladd and Doug Claybourne) is replete with evil voodoo sorcerers, sexual torture, and cries of "Don't let them bury me. I'm not dead!"

28 Maximilien Laroche, "The Myth of the Zombi" in *Exile and Tradition: Studies in African and Caribbean Literature*, ed. Rowland Smith (London: Longman, 1976), p. 47.

29 René Depestre, *Change*, Violence II, 9 (Paris: Seuil, 1971): 20.

30 For a detailed account of the story of Marie M. and its many fictional retellings, see Lizabeth Paravisini-Gebert's "Women Possessed: Exoticism and Eroticism in the Representation of Woman as Zombie" in *Sacred Possessions*, ed. Fernández Olmos and Paravisini-Gebert, pp. 37–58.

31 Métraux, *Voodoo in Haiti*, p. 284.

32 *Les Daïmons du culte Voudo et Dra-Po* (Port-au-Prince: n.p., 1918).

33 C.-H. Dewisme, *Les Zombis ou le secret des morts-vivants* (Paris: Edition Bernard Grasset, 1957), pp. 146–47.

34 For a longer, more detailed discussion of Depestre's novel see my "Authors Playin' Mas': Carnival and the Carnivalesque in the Contemporary Caribbean Novel" in *History of Caribbean Literatures*, ed. A. James Arnold, volume III (Philadelphia: John Benjamins, 1997), pp. 215–236.

35 Maya Deren, *Divine Horsemen: The Living Gods of Haiti* (Kingston, NY: McPherson, 1970), p. 62.

36 Montero originally published "Corinne, muchacha amable" in *Cuentos para ahuyentar el turismo*, ed. Vitalina Alfonso and Emilio Jorge Rodríguez (Havana: Arte y Literatura, 1991), pp. 285–306. My translation is cited here from the journal *Callaloo* in 1994 and is reprinted as "Corinne, Amiable Girl" in *Remaking a Lost Harmony: Short Stories from the Hispanic Caribbean*, ed. Margarite Fernández Olmos and Lizabeth Paravisini-Gebert (Fredonia, NY: White Pine Press, 1995). References in the main text are to the *Callaloo* version.

37 Blake Lucas, "*I Walked with a Zombie*" in *Magill's Survey of Cinema: English Language Films*, 2nd series, volume III, ed. Frank N. Magill (Englewood Cliffs, NJ: Salem Press, 1981), p. 1094.

38 ibid., p. 1096.

39 Michael Neill, "*Guerrillas* and Gangs: Frantz Fanon and V. S. Naipaul," *Ariel* 13:4 (1982): 54–55.

40 Cathleen Schine, "A World as Cruel as Job's," *New York Times Book Review*, 4 (February 1996): 7.

41 Salient studies include Anthony E. Luengo's "*Wide Sargasso Sea* and the Gothic Mode," *World Literature Written in English* 15 (1976): 229–45; Joyce Carol Oates's "Romance and Anti-Romance from Brontë's *Jane Eyre* to Rhys's *Wide Sargasso Sea*," *Virginia Quarterly Review* 61 (1985): 44–58; and Dennis Potter's "Of Heroines and Victims: Jean Rhys and Jane Eyre," *Massachusetts Review* 17 (1976): 540–52. For an excellent overview of Rhys's career as a Caribbean writer, see Elaine Savory, *Jean Rhys* (Cambridge: Cambridge University Press, 1999).

42 Ellen G. Friedman, "Breaking the Master Narrative: Jean Rhys's *Wide Sargasso Sea*" in *Breaking the Sequence: Women's Experimental Fiction*, ed. Ellen G. Friedman and Miriam Fuchs (Princeton: Princeton University Press, 1989), p. 122.

43 ibid., p. 124.

44 For a detailed examination of the ending of *Sweet Diamond Dust* as related to *Wide Sargasso Sea*, see Ricardo Gutiérrez Mouat's "La 'Loca del desván' y otros intertextos de *Maldito amor*," *MLN* 109 (1994): 283–306.

45 Michelle Cliff, *No Telephone to Heaven* (New York: Vintage Books, 1989), p. 116.

13

STEVEN BRUHM

The contemporary Gothic:
why we need it

My title suggests a rather straightforward enterprise: I want to account
for the enormous popularity of the Gothic – both novels and films – since
the Second World War. However, the title proposes more questions than it
answers. First, what exactly counts as "the contemporary Gothic"? Since
its inception in 1764, with Horace Walpole's *The Castle of Otranto*, the
Gothic has always played with chronology, looking back to moments in an
imaginary history, pining for a social stability that never existed, mourning
a chivalry that belonged more to the fairy tale than to reality. And contemporary Gothic does not break with this tradition: Stephen King's *IT*
(1987) and Anne Rice's vampire narratives (begun in the 1970s) weave in
and out of the distant past in order to comment on the state of contemporary
American culture, while other narratives foreground their reliance on prior,
historically distant narratives. Peter Straub's *Julia* (1975), Doris Lessing's
The Fifth Child (1988), and John Wyndham's *The Midwich Cuckoos* (film
version: *The Village of the Damned* [1960]) all feed off *The Turn of the
Screw* (1898) by Henry James, itself arguably a revision of Jean-Jacques
Rousseau's *Emile* (1762), a treatise on the education of two children at a
country house. And as many contributors to this volume demonstrate, the
central concerns of the classical Gothic are not that different from those of
the contemporary Gothic: the dynamics of family, the limits of rationality
and passion, the definition of statehood and citizenship, the cultural effects
of technology. How, then, might we define a contemporary Gothic? For to
think about the contemporary Gothic is to look into a triptych of mirrors
in which images of the origin continually recede in a disappearing arc. We
search for a genesis but find only ghostly manifestations.

Nor is the idea of origin the only problem here, for there is also the problem embedded in my title: why we need the contemporary Gothic. Certainly
its popularity cannot be disputed – films like *Rosemary's Baby* (1968), *The
Exorcist* (1973), and *The Silence of the Lambs* (1991) take home Oscars, and
Stephen King habitually tops the best-seller lists – but why are we driven to

consume these fictions? Is this craving something structural or social? Does it stem from our desire to see the political tyrant bested or the weak, deformed, or unfortunate (as in Shirley Jackson's *The Lottery* [1949]) scapegoated in a ritual purgation of blood? The Gothic has always been a barometer of the anxieties plaguing a certain culture at a particular moment in history, but what is the relationship between these general social trends and particular individual psyche? When the children of *Nightmare on Elm Street* (1984) conjure Freddy Kruger in their dreams, are they expressing a personal night-mare about what lies beneath their consciousnesses, a social nightmare about how America treats its dispossessed, or some amorphous combination of the two? For that matter, do we need to see each child's Freddy Kruger as the same Freddy Kruger? The "we" who needs the Gothic is by no means a uni-fied, homogeneous group. I do not necessarily need the same things you do. I do not necessarily take the same things from a Gothic narrative as do the others who have bought the book or the theatre ticket. Like the question of origin I addressed above, the basis of need and desire is not only a theme in Gothic narratives but a theoretical quandary for the spectators and readers who consume those narratives.

We can best address the question of audience need by placing the con-temporary Gothic within a number of current anxieties – the ones we need it both to arouse and assuage. One of these anxieties, taken up by Stephen King is his nonfictional *Danse Macabre* (1982), is political and historical. He discusses at length the degree to which the Second World War, the Cold War, and the space race gave rise to particular kinds of horror in the 1940s and 1950s. Central to this horror is the fear of foreign otherness and monstrous invasion. We need only consider Ira Levin's *The Boys from Brazil* (1976), William Peter Blatty's *The Exorcist* (1971), or Stephen King's *The Tommyknockers* (1988) to see the connection between national purity and the fear of foreign invasion, be it from Germany, the Middle East, or outer space. Another anxiety, not unrelated to the first, is the technological explo-sion in the second half of the twentieth century. Advances in weaponry – both military and medical – have rendered our culture vulnerable to almost total destruction (as in Boris Sagal's *The Omega Man* [1971] or King's *Firestarter* [1980] and *The Stand* [1978]) or have helped us conceive of superhuman beings unable to be destroyed (the cyborgs and animate machines of *2001: a Space Odyssey* [1968], the *Terminator* series [1984, 1991], or *Dark City* [1998]). Third, the rise of feminism, gay liberation, and African-American civil rights in the 1960s has assaulted the ideological supremacy of traditional values where straight white males ostensibly control the public sphere. In the midst of this onslaught comes a further blow to Euro-American culture: the heightened attack against Christian ideology and hierarchy as that which should "naturally" define values and ethics in culture. The Satanism of *Rosemary's Baby*, the continued cult worship of the Dracula figure in all his manifestations, and the popularity of anti-Christ figures from Damien Thorne of *The Omen* (novel, 1976; film, 1976) to Marilyn Manson all attest to the powerful threat (and attraction) posed by our culture's increasing secularity. And regardless of whether one loathes the anti-Christian figure in these narratives or cheers him on, one cannot help but be impressed by the degree to which this "attack of the Gothic" has infiltrated our culture and fractured any ideologically "natural" state of personal or social well-being.

The Gothic texts and films I have already mentioned circle around a particular nexus: the problem of assimilating these social anxieties (which I will momentarily discuss in terms of "trauma") into a personal narrative that in some way connects the Gothic protagonist to the reader or spectator. What becomes most marked in the contemporary Gothic – and what distinguishes it from its ancestors – is the protagonists' and the viewers' compulsive return to certain fixations, obsessions, and blockages.[1] Consequently, the Gothic can be readily analyzed through the rhetoric of psychoanalysis, for many the twentieth century's supreme interpreter of human compulsions and repressions. In both theory and clinical practice, psychoanalysis is primarily attributed to the work of Sigmund Freud, for whom the Gothic was a rich source of imagery and through whom the Gothic continues to be analyzed today.[2] Psychoanalysis provides us with a language for understanding the conflicted psyche of the patient whose life story (or "history") is characterized by neurotic disturbances and epistemological blank spots. More often than not, such psychoanalytic accounts are intensely Gothic: "The Uncanny" (1919) and "A Seventeenth-Century Demonological Neurosis" (1922),[3] along with a number of Freud's case studies, make the figure of the tyrannical father central to the protagonists' Gothic experiences, as does Matthew Lewis's *The Monk* (1796) or Stoker's *Dracula* (1897); "On Narcissism: an Introduction" (1914) and *Group Psychology and the Analysis of the Ego* (1921) offer us purchase on the person in society looking for acceptance while at the same time remaining abject and individualized, a central problem in Gothic novels; and the phantasms generated by the Wolf Man or Dr. Schreber, like those experienced by the grieving subject in *Mourning and Melancholia*, cannot be dissociated from the Gothic ghost, the revenant who embodies and projects the subject's psychic state.

But perhaps what is most central to the Gothic – be it classical or contemporary – is the very process of psychic life that for Freud defines the human condition. While the id finds its narrative expression in the insatiable drives of the desiring organism (Dean Koontz's Bruno in *Whispers* [1981], the mutant child in the film *It's Alive* [1974]), the superego takes monstrous form in the ultrarational, cultured figures of Hannibal Lecter, Damien Thorne, or Anne Rice's blood-drinking literati. The battle for supremacy between the ravenous id and the controlling superego translates in myriad ways into the conflicts of the Gothic. Indeed, what makes the contemporary Gothic contemporary, I hope to show, is not merely the way Freudian dynamics underlie Gothic narratives (for this, uncannily, is also the condition of classical eighteenth-century Gothic), but how contemporary Gothic texts and films are intensely *aware* of this Freudian rhetoric and self-consciously *about* the longings and fears it describes. In other words, what makes the contemporary Gothic contemporary is that the Freudian machinery is more than a tool for discussing narrative; it is in large part the subject matter of the narrative itself. A major theme of the Gothic has always been interior life, as in the paranoid Gothic of William Godwin's *Caleb Williams* (1794) or James Hogg's *The Private Memoirs and Confessions of a Justified Sinner* (1824), but the rise of psychoanalysis in the twentieth century has afforded Gothic writers a very particular configuration of this internal life. To the degree that the contemporary Gothic subject is the psychoanalytic subject (and vice versa), she/he becomes a/the field on which national, racial, and gender anxieties *configured like Freudian drives* get played out and symbolized over and over again.

The unconscious, Freud postulates, is born from the moment the child first encounters a prohibition or law against satisfying desires. In Freud's work, the most important desire is that of the (male) child to have uninterrupted access to his mother. The Oedipus complex arises, Freud suggests, when the boy wants to continue to use his mother as an uninterrupted source of pleasure and nourishment as well as the provider of the physical tactility that will ensure this safety. The father interrupts this infantile desire – what Freud calls "primary narcissism" – by prohibiting the child's continued desire for the mother. In the interests of fashioning the child's masculinity and his individuality, the father forces him to submit to the patriarchal law of finding his own other-sexed partner, thereby leaving the mother to return her affections to the father rather than lavishing them on the son. But, true to the Freudian schema, the child's desires for the mother, and his attendant aggression, hatred, and fear of the father, do not disappear. They are put away in a space where they are no longer socially visible (lest the child appear "queer"[4]) but where they structure the developing personality and help control what that child will come to desire, both socially and sexually. This is the key point to a Freudian understanding of the Gothic in general: as human beings, we are not free agents operating out of conscious will and self-knowledge. Rather, when our fantasies, dreams, and fears take on a nightmarish quality, it is because the unconscious is telling us what we *really* want. And what we really want are those desires and objects that have been forbidden.

What makes the contemporary Gothic particularly contemporary in both its themes and reception, however, is that these unconscious desires center on the problem of a lost object, the most overriding basis of *our* need for the Gothic and almost everything else. That loss is usually material (parents, money, property, freedom to move around, a lover, or family member), but the materiality of that loss always has a psychological and symbolic dimension to it. When the Freudian father pries the son away from the mother and her breast, he is seen by the child to introduce a sense of *loss*, an absence that will then drive the child to try to fill the empty space that prohibition creates. In the psychoanalytic Gothic, we intensely desire the object that has been lost, or another object, person, or practice that might take its place, but we are aware at some level that this object carries with it the threat of punishment: the anger of the father, the breaking of the law, castration. When the desire for an object butts up against the prohibition against the fulfilling of that desire, the result is the contemporary human subject. Simply put, we *are* what we have become in response to the threat of violence from anything like the figure of the father. Furthermore, the mode in which the late modern subject most enacts this scene of prohibition – and the mode in which we as audience take it up – is the Gothic, itself a narrative of prohibitions, transgressions, and the processes of identity construction that occur within such tensions. Let us, then, consider first the themes of the contemporary Gothic before speculating on why we as an audience take it up with such relish.

Oedipal battles between parent and child are not new in the Gothic, to be sure; *Frankenstein* (1818) is just one progenitor of novels such as *The Exorcist, Pet Sematary* (1983) or *Interview with the Vampire* (1976). Even so, a novel such as Stephen King's *The Shining* (1977) offers an especially textbook case of the oedipal conflict. The oedipal family – a trinity of daddy, mommy, child – is trapped in a remote hotel where the caretaker goes mad and tries to kill the son he thinks is a traitor to him. While the horror story of cabin fever is clear, Stephen King is too consciously Freudian to allow the plot to stay there: "Freud says that the subconscious never speaks to us in a literal language," his protagonist Jack Torrance tells wife Wendy, "Only in symbols" (p. 264). Chief among these symbols is their son Danny's ability to read minds and to glimpse the future (a talent the novel calls "shining"). This ability is, among other things, a way of looking into his parents' minds to see what they are thinking. In fact, this very act of looking corresponds to a famous Freudian moment called "the primal scene." In Freud's case study of the Wolf Man (1918), he postulated that his patient had seen his parents having sex *a tergo*, so that both parents' genitals were visible. The father was deemed to have a penetrating and violently aggressive penis while the mother had lost her penis (the male child being unable to imagine that not all people have a penis as he does) to the violating father.

In both Freud and *The Shining*, this hypothesis gives the primal scene a special Gothic undertone. For the boy-child, it is a primary threat: the father has the penis and can remove someone else's. For Danny Torrance, in particular, it shrouds shining – that is, sexual knowing – in a pall of disgust, transgression, and prohibition. Likening his talent for shining to "peeking into [his parents'] bedroom and watching while they're doing the thing that makes babies" (p. 83),[5] Danny also reads his father's mind to determine the level of paternal hatred toward him and his mother. In this primal shining, there is more than one lost object: mother and son lose phallic power *vis-à-vis* the father, and the family loses the bond that was supposed to keep them safe and close. It is small wonder, then, that when Danny begins to explore the Overlook Hotel and discovers/hallucinates its horrible ghosts – such as the dead woman in the bathtub – he does so out of a desire to heal the family: "Danny stepped into the bathroom and walked toward the tub dreamily, as if propelled from outside himself, as if . . . he would perhaps see something nice when he pulled the curtain back, something Daddy had forgotten or Mommy had lost, something that would make them both happy" (p. 217). Danny's desire to look – perhaps like ours, as desirous voyeurs of the Gothic – is ultimately the desire to find that which has been lost, that which will unify an otherwise fragmented subjectivity. And in Freud, as in King, it is the lost object (the penis) that constitutes the identity of the male: "normal" boys rigorously imitate masculine identity precisely because they fear the father will rob them of the marker of masculine entitlement, the penis, if they do not. Danny's, then, is a remarkably *contemporary* problem: whereas the original *Frankenstein* at least believed in the possibility of real fatherhood, real domesticity, and a real self, Danny is forced to operate in a psychological sphere where some crucial aspect of the self is always lost and must always be sought, but can never provide the happiness for which it is desired.

The contemporary Gothic, in other words, reveals the domestic scene in a world after Freud and the degree to which that domestic scene is predicated on loss. The ideology of family continues to circulate with as much atmospheric pressure as it did in the novels of Ann Radcliffe or Mary Shelley, but with a difference: whereas financial greed, religious tyranny, and incestuous privation interrupt the smooth workings of the eighteenth-century family (only to exhort the importance of the family as a concept), the contemporary Gothic registers the (Freudian) impossibility of familial harmony, an impossibility built into the domestic psyche as much as it is into domestic materiality. For in such a novel as *The Shining*, everybody hates a parent and presumably the *wrong* parent. Wendy hates her mother and loves her father (as is the case with Susan Norton in *'Salem's Lot* [1975]); Jack hated his mother but respected his abusive father; and even Danny, whose suffering at the hands of his father we have just noted, "loved his mother but was his father's boy" (King, *Shining*, p. 54). So why this bond with the tyrannical father? Why is the mother, Wendy, reduced to a walking talking breast to whom Danny can periodically run for solace (rocking, cooing, the singing of lullabies) but who holds little other value in Danny's emotion economy? Why this change from the classical Gothic, where the male child also hated the tyrannical father but without the same psychological complications?

The reason is Freud. In the contemporary psychological schema, we desire not only the lost object but the approval of the tyrant who took that object from us. Freud's *Totem and Taboo* (1913) maps the path by which the rebel sons become their hated father by consuming his body after they have killed him. In order to kill the father and thus establish their own autonomy, they first have to assume the father's strength beforehand, a psychological incorporation of the father/tyrant that will later be ritualized in the consuming of his body and later cannibalistic rituals like it, ranging from the Holy Eucharist to Gothic vampirism. *The Shining*, similarly, documents Danny's vacillation between child and man, or between parental appendage and autonomous adult. Here he vacillates between being the child who fears the father figure and being a father figure himself: both Jack and Danny are male figures responsible for taking care of Wendy; both Jack and Danny shine; and both Jack and Danny are caretakers of a hotel, although in the end it is Danny who will excel over Jack by remembering what his father forgot (how to take care of the boiler). This becoming-father, then, is an act both of homage and of transgression: the son adores the father to the degree that he must kill him in order to *become* him. King and the contemporary Gothic thus write into the family romance Oscar Wilde's quite modern realization that we kill the thing we love. Horror, mutilation, and loss thus become more than shock effect; they constitute the very aesthetic that structures the human psyche in the twentieth century, connecting the Freudian vision of the human mind generally to the dynamics of Gothic villainy and victimization.

Indeed, such ambivalence between the abusive parent and the desiring child is not limited to father–son dynamics. Although father and son constitute the usual scenario in Freud's phallically centered thinking, the Gothic provides equal opportunity for the monstrous mother as well. Famous girl stories in this vein include that of Carrie White and her mother in King's *Carrie* (1974) or Eleanor in Shirley Jackson's *The Haunting of Hill House* (1959); boy-centered versions appear in Norman Bates's relation to his mummified mummy in Hitchcock's *Psycho* (1960, based on the 1959 novel by Robert

Bloch) and the castrating mother of Daniel Mann's *Willard* (1972).[6] A number of forces conspire to frame this contemporary mother. A narrative such as *The Exorcist*, for example, at least momentarily blames a child's demonic possession on her mother's feminism: Chris McNeil has left her husband, she supports herself and her daughter Regan through her successful acting career, and she has abandoned the usual religious and social codes of feminine propriety. For this she is punished, as a demon enters the body of her (maternally neglected) child. Moreover, Blatty's antifeminism resonates with another theory of the monstrous maternal, that of psychoanalyst Julia Kristeva. According to Kristeva, paternal prohibition is not the only reason the child must achieve distance from the mother. The child must "abject" the mother – discard or jettison the primal connection to her, deem her dangerous and suffocating – if she/he is to gain any autonomous subjectivity whatsoever. That thrown-off mother, at least in the child's fantasy, continually lures and seduces the child back to the primary bond where she/he is completely taken care of; in response, the child must demonize and reject her in order "to constitute [it]self and [its] culture" (Kristeva, *Powers of Horror*, p. 2).[7] And because that act of abjecting "is a violent, clumsy breaking away, with the constant risk of falling back into under the sway of a power as securing as it is stifling" (ibid., p. 13), the mother is continually reinvented as monstrous but in a way the child incorporates as much as she/he abjects. Regan McNeil comes to embody Chris's sexual knowledge, her foul language, and her refusal to adhere to conventional social codes governing women; Carrie White *becomes* the murderous, vindictive mother/God she hates. We come then not to be mere victims of the lost object – the mother – but active agents in the expulsion of that mother. We are creatures of conflicted desires, locked in an uncanny push-me-pull-you that propels us toward the very objects we fear and to fear the very objects toward which we are propelled. We must bond with our parents, but not too much; we must distance ourselves from our parents, but not too much.

That the persecuted subject should escape persecution either by returning to the maternal breast or by becoming the parent she/he fears marks a problem in that subject's personal history, a problem central to the contemporary Gothic. According to Freud, the obsessive return to the nurturing, safe mother is a *regression*, one that arrests the individual's psychological development. But taking the path forward toward adulthood by no means guarantees a happy growth or linear progress. Adults such as Jack Torrance of *The Shining*, Thad Beaumont of *The Dark Half* (1989), Clarice Starling from Thomas Harris's *The Silence of the Lambs* (1988), or Hannibal Lecter in Harris's sequel *Hannibal* (1999) are all to a great extent determined by the familial relations they experienced in childhood. At the level of the parental, Jack Torrance remains subject to his father's abusive control (he *becomes* his father), while Carrie White adopts the brutal, punishing, destructive power of her mother – although it might be more accurate to say that Carrie becomes Margaret's punitive angry God, new England's cosmic Father. And as Gothic children threaten the role of the parent by consuming or incorporating that parent's power, we find in them intellects that soar beyond what children are supposed to have. See, for example, the children of *Village of the Damned*, whose intellects far surpass those of adults, a condition we also find in Regan McNeil of *The Exorcist* or Gage Creed and Timmy Baterman of King's *Pet Sematary* (1983). Our domestic lives are supposed to be governed by a logic of chronology – older and wiser parents care for and instruct their innocent and vulnerable offspring – but not in the Gothic. Psychological subject positions shift and float, rearranging and destabilizing the roles assumed to belong to each person in the domestic arrangement.

This disruption of domestic history is ultimately based on a fluidity in the Gothic protagonist's personal history; contemporary Gothic characters often utterly confuse their childhood experiences with their adult lives. This confusion results from the unconscious as Freud described it, a repository of prohibited desires, aggressions, and painful or terrifying experiences. As these psychological experiences mesh with the sense of loss that accompanies them (loss of parent, loss of security, loss of ego or stable sense of self), they set up echoes of childhood in the subject's later life. What was repressed thus returns to haunt our heroes with the vivid immediacy of the original moment. And it is this moment of return, seminally theorized by Freud in *Totem and Taboo*, that highlights the key difference between the contemporary Gothic and its classical predecessors' understanding of personal and social history. In the late eighteenth-century Gothic of Ann Radcliffe or Matthew Lewis, moments from the historical past (often appearing as spectral figures) haunt the heroes in order to proclaim some misdeed regarding property or domestic relations. It is often the project of those novels to expose ancient tyrannies, to foil the characters perpetuating them, and to return property and persons to their divinely ordained spheres. In so doing, the classical Gothic returns its society to a logic of historical progression. The contemporary Gothic, conversely, cannot sustain such a program, precisely because of its characters' psychological complications. With the ravages of the unconscious continually interrupting one's perception of the world, the protagonist of the contemporary Gothic often experiences history as mixed up, reversed, and caught in a simultaneity of past-present-future.[8] History has made a promise – that one will grow from a fragile, vulnerable child to an autonomous, rational adult – but it is unable to keep that promise in the twentieth century. It can only offer a future that is already suspended between present and past. While the Gothic may ostensibly plot the movement of chronological time, it really devastates any sense of linear progression that we might use to put together our "personal history."

Especially when viewed through the lens of psychoanalysis, then, the contemporary Gothic markedly registers a crisis in personal history: in the world depicted in such works, one is forced simultaneously to mourn the lost object (a parent, God, social order, lasting fulfillment through knowledge or sexual pleasure) and to *become* the object lost through identification or imitation. This history of repetition, I would argue, constitutes a sense of *trauma*, and it is finally through trauma that we can best understand the contemporary Gothic and why we crave it. Speaking of the Gothic as analogous to trauma, or even as the product and enactment of trauma, makes sense for a number of reasons. First, the Gothic itself is a narrative of trauma. Its protagonists usually experience some horrifying event that profoundly affects them, destroying (at least temporarily) the norms that structure their lives and identities. Images of haunting, destruction and death, obsessive return to the shattering moment, forgetfulness or unwanted epiphany ("you will remember what your father forgot," Tony tells Danny Torrance [King, *Shining*, p. 420]) all define a Gothic aesthetic that is quite close to Cathy Caruth's definition of trauma and its corollary, post-traumatic stress disorder (PTSD):

> there is a response, sometimes delayed, to an overwhelming event or events, which takes the form of repeated, intrusive hallucinations, dreams, thoughts or behaviors stemming from the event, along with numbing that may have begun during or after the experience, and possibly also increased arousal to (and avoidance of) stimuli recalling the event . . . [T]he event is not assimilated or experienced fully at the time, but only belatedly, in its repeated *possession* of the one who experiences it.[9]

Caruth has in mind survivors of Auschwitz and Vietnam, but her descriptions also remind us of a number of protagonists of the contemporary Gothic. Peter Straub's fictions habitually portray men (although *Julia* is an exception) who have endured some invasion, violation, or uncanny experience in younger life and have never comprehended the full effects of that experience. Sears James in *Ghost Story* (1979), the narrator of "The Juniper Tree" in *Houses Without Doors* (1991), and Tim Underhill in *Koko* (1988) and *The Throat* (1994) all return to earlier experiences and only gradually "assimilate" them, if at all.

Gothic horrors in these texts are the distortions, hallucinations, and nightmares that proceed from these experiences. Memories of that moment flash before the Gothic hero's eyes only to be inaccessible minutes later: when

Dr. Louis Creed of *Pet Sematary* loses his first patient at his new job, his mind immediately "seemed to be wrapping those few moments in a protective film – sculpting, changing, disconnecting" (p. 77). Similarly, as he prepares to disinter his dead child Gage, Louis "realized he could not remember what his son had looked like... He could see [Gage's features] but he could not integrate them into a coherent whole" (p. 334). The child-woman Claudia of *Interview with the Vampire* lives fully as a vampire but cannot recall the moment that made her one (unlike Lestat and Louis, who remember everything). *The Exorcist*'s Regan has experienced the "numbing" that characterizes the subject during trauma – Regan "herself" is inaccessible to herself, her mother, the doctors, and priests – and she remembers nothing of her experience after the exorcism. Time and again the contemporary Gothic presents us with traumatized heroes who have lost the very psychic structures that allow them access to their own experiences. As I have been suggesting, such narratives emphasize a lost object, that object being the self. Individual autonomy, unity of soul and ego, and personal investment in will and self-reliance have all been shattered by the forces of the social and the ravages of the unconscious upon the ego in contemporary existence. The self is shattered into pieces, the "many" rather than the "one" that defines a character like Regan McNeil, who now is "no *one*" (p. 325, emphasis added), but rather "quite a little group," a "stunning little multitude" (p. 245).

That loss of wholeness, that destruction of the thing in favor of many things, so obsesses Gothic fiction in the later twentieth century that many such narratives are about the impossibility of narrative. Jack Torrance's writer's block (which Stanley Kubrick changes in his 1980 film to an obsessive repetition of the cliché "all work and no play makes Jack a dull boy") is not unlike Catharine Holly's inability to tell the story of Sebastian in Tennessee Williams's southern Gothic play, *Suddenly Last Summer* (1958, adapted as a film in 1959). Eleanor in *The Haunting of Hill House* is unable to narrate the death of her mother, and so the story is told only fleetingly in the words appearing on the walls of the mansion. King's *Pet Sematary* opens with a list of books written by people who have done important things in the world and follows with a list of people who attended the corpses of those famous authors but who have not written books or told their stories themselves. King concludes: "*Death is a mystery, and burial is a secret.*" Trauma collapses the ability to render experience in a narrative, as recent studies of concentration camp prisoners and child sexual abuse survivors are making very clear. Trauma destroys what Pierre Janet calls "narrative memory," the ability to apply principles of coherence and analytical understanding to one's life events.[10] Indeed, *Pet Sematary* implicitly compares the temporality of trauma (a forgetting that is interrupted by unwilled remembering) with the experience of a child learning a language: "babies make *all* the sounds the human voice box is capable of...They lose the capability as they learn English, and Louis wondered now (and not for the first time) if childhood was not more a period of forgetting than of learning" (p. 221). What Louis as adult will then come to "re-member" (his dead son Gage returned from the grave) is pretty horrific, but lest my analogy seem far-fetched, *The Exorcist* makes the same move and much more clearly. "Cryptomnesia: buried recollections of words and data" that Regan may have learned in early childhood come "to the surface with almost photographic fidelity" (p. 268), and by now no one needs to be reminded of what kind of verbal spectacle Regan makes of herself.

All of this together fashions a contemporary Gothic phenomenon. Words, the building blocks of stories, rise and fall in consciousness, constituting horrifying returns and traumatic suggestions. The very act of storytelling itself has the resonance of multiple traumas that we, like Louis Creed at the graveside, cannot integrate into a coherent whole. What gets left in this blank space where our narratives cannot be is, paradoxically, a massive production of other Gothic narratives. In the process of trauma shattering us from one into a "stunning little multitude," we are forced to confront our demons, our worst fears about the agents and influences that might control and create us.

It is here, too, that we can see the link between the domestic anxieties we have been discussing and more far-flung social anxieties. The Gothic mother who must be abjected and the authoritative tyrannical father who must be overthrown are, according to psychoanalysis, parts of one's self that must be feared because they define the self at the same time as they take one's self-definition outside, to an other and perhaps to many outside versions of that other. The volatile status of otherness, it is true, has come to haunt the Gothic mode since the eighteenth century. But in the contemporary moment, that otherness is often framed by a psychoanalytic model of the psyche that includes a larger social vision full of phobias and prejudices about many types of "others." Gothic plots such as *Ghost Story* or *The Hand That Rocks the Cradle* (1992) connect their *femmes fatales* to motherhood in general, meshing the need for abjection with a larger cultural misogyny and fear of too-powerful women. Same-sex bonding between men, which, as Eve Kosofsky Sedgwick argues, is the glue that cements capitalist relations in the west,[11] finds its Gothic counterpart in the homosexual panic of King's Jack Torrance, Robert Bloch's Norman Bates, or Peter Straub's Peter Barnes.[12] And in our contemporary imagination, where homosexuality is also pedophilia in the eyes of many, narratives from King's *'Salem's Lot*, King and Peter Straub's *The Talisman* (1984) to Straub's "The Juniper

Tree" and "Bunny Is Good Bread" (in *Magic Terror* [2000]) do more than tell a horror story about children's victimization at the hands of a monster; they project the Gothic terror of our culture's contemporary cult of child-worship.[13] Why else would Louis Creed, looking at his sexually arousing wife, think that "she looked amazingly like [their daughter] Ellie...and Gage" (King, *Pet Sematary*, p. 187)? Then, too, can we read the racist representation of vampires as Mexican immigrants in John Carpenter's 1998 film *Vampires* without seeing it as an up-to-date version of the fear of eastern Europeans in Stoker's *Dracula*, which additionally indicates the fear of the unknown, "foreign" parts of ourselves, be they sexual or "spiritual"? Or might we see in the gypsy who curses Billy Halleck in Richard Bachman's *Thinner* (1984), or in Dr. Rabbitfoot in Straub's *Ghost Story*, the fear of the "magical" animism, where internal thought can suddenly become external object or action, a process which to Freud constitutes the infantile thinking we never completely forget?[14] In the spaces left by many kinds of trauma, we rush in to supply all kinds of stories. We generate an industry of narrative fantasies that merge all too nicely with other social prejudices, and we do all of this to convince ourselves that the horror of consciousness is not ours, that it really comes from the outside.

Yet we have done so, in the end, without much psychological success. The Gothic continually confronts us with real, historical traumas that we in the west have created but that also continue to control how we think about ourselves as a nation (be it "America," "Canada," "Great Britain," or some other country). Ira Levin's *The Boys From Brazil* directly invokes the Jewish Holocaust, while *Carrie* at least briefly nods to the war in Vietnam, as if her personal trauma were somehow linked to America's great social trauma of that time. Whatever metonymic affiliations Carrie might have with Vietnam, in fact, it makes her telekinetic power analogous to the nuclear bomb, thus providing us with some of the same Cold War anxieties we see in *Village of the Damned* and Margaret Atwood's *The Handmaid's Tale* (1985). *Pet Sematary* may be about the personal trauma of losing a child, but it is also about American colonization. The Micmac burial ground that lies beyond the pet cemetery exerts a malignant and ancient spiritual influence over the environs of Ludlow, Maine; the Wendigo who presides over this burial ground is the amoral nature god who returns to reclaim what Christianity has taken from the natives. Hence the parody of resurrection: what returns from the grave is not the Christ-child but a murderous demon, an aboriginal trickster figure who, in the Gothic imagination, has been transmogrified into a knife-wielding killer. Each of these social and national traumas was caused by human agency, yet they have rendered humans unable to tell any kind of complete story about them. Thus the Gothic renders them in fits and starts, ghostly appearances and far-fetched fantasies, all attempting to reveal traumatic contradictions of the collective past that cannot be spoken.

In short, it seems that we are caught in what Freud would call a repetition-compulsion, where we are compelled to consume the same stories (with minor variations), experience the same traumatic jolts, behold the same devastating sights. So, to return to the questions I asked at the beginning of this chapter, why are we so drawn to the Gothic? Who is this "we" that are craving it? We find ourselves compelled to accept more than one answer. Clearly, there is some kind of comfort associated with repetition, but what kind of theory explains that comfort? Walter Benjamin might suggest that such horror narratives confirm for us that we are spectators, safely distanced onlookers whose integrity is guaranteed by the dissolution of another. As Benjamin puts it, "What draws the reader to the novel is the hope of warming his shivering life with a death he reads about,"[15] and the compulsive repetition of this hand-warming gives us the necessary assurance that the victim is not us. But the very seductiveness of Gothic fiction makes such a claim to being outside it impossible to sustain. We seem to want these fictions from the inside out; we crave them not for their distance but for their immediacy, for they make our hearts race, our blood pressure rise, our breathing become shallow and quick, and our stomachs roll. Like the traumatized subject, we physically roil when faced with a parade of uncontrollable and horrifying images that are strangely familiar, as uncanny as they are abject. We crave these "stimuli," to use Caruth's word, and we feel possessed by them. Indeed, as an individual reader or viewer, I may not *be* traumatized at the moment of reading, but I certainly join with the Gothic mode in *feeling like one who is traumatized*. Father Merrin of *The Exorcist* says of horror's agent, "I think the demon's target is not the possessed; it is us...the observers...every person in this house" (p. 369). So if the priests of *The Exorcist* can perform an exorcism on Regan, we need to consider that Gothic fiction in general can perform some kind of exorcism on us, the observers in this highly oedipal and traumatized house.

Perhaps the repetition compulsions underlying trauma can provide us with some insight. While both the Gothic and trauma are characterized by the inability to comprehend fully one's experience and to filter that experience through what Pierre Janet has called "narrative memory," they suggest more than the horrors of ineffability. Caruth argues that "trauma can make possible survival" by actually capitalizing on the distance one takes from the traumatic experience. We have already seen King's Louis Creed respond to disaster by partially removing himself from the anxiety-inducing scene: a "protective film" disconnects him from the moment. Caruth provides an interesting take on this phenomenon. "[T]hrough the different modes therapeutic, literary, and pedagogical encounter," she says, trauma is not experienced as a mere repression or defense, but as a temporal delay that carries the individual beyond the shock of the first moment. The trauma is a repeated suffering of the event, but it is also a continual leaving of its site ... To listen to the crisis of a trauma ... is not only to listen for the event, but to hear in the testimony the survivor's departure from it; the challenge of the therapeutic listener, in other words, is *how to listen to departure.*[16]

One thinks here of Louis in Rice's *Interview with the Vampire,* as he is compelled to tell the whole story of his life with Lestat as a means of displacing it into history and into a story that the listening boy eagerly wants to hear. According to Robert Jay Lifton, the subject shattered by trauma "struggles to put together the pieces, so to speak, of the psyche, and to balance the need to reconstitute oneself with the capacity to take in the experience."[17] But as we know, to repeat is to visit the same place but with a difference: in repetition, we relive an event but the intervening distance of time and space means that the repetition cannot be perfect or authentic, that it can only produce the original experience differently. Moreover, repetition with a difference must usually be performed through literature and fiction. When Lifton was researching his 1986 book *The Nazi Doctors,* he found himself having nightmares that *he* was an Auschwitz prisoner. At some level, he endured the horror of the traumatized survivor, in that both he and the survivor had a distanced presence to the "real" experience. Narrative, not corporeal presence, engaged him in a shattering moment through which, as Elie Wiesel told him, he could only begin to write about the Holocaust. Lifton was lured into his research in much the same way Rice's interviewer is seduced – and in fact wants to live out – Louis's narrative account of vampirism. Says Lifton, "it's being a survivor by proxy, and the proxy's important" (p. 145).

Surviving by proxy: Lifton's phrase begins to explain why we crave the Gothic. We crave it because we *need* it. We need it because the twentieth century has so forcefully taken away from us that which we once thought constituted us – a coherent psyche, a social order to which we can pledge allegiance in good faith, a sense of justice in the universe – and that wrenching withdrawal, that traumatic experience, is vividly dramatized in the Gothic. We do not seek out one Gothic experience, read one novel, or see one movie, we hunt down many. We do not tell one story, we tell many, even as all of them are knitted together by those familiar, comforting, yet harrowing Gothic conventions. For our traumas, like Regan McNeil's demons, are legion: the tyranny of the lawgiving father, the necessity of abjecting the mother, the loss of history and a sense of pre-formed identity, and the shattering of faith in a world that can permit the Holocaust and genocide or reconstruct us as cyborgs or clone each of us into another self (the deepest anxiety in Cronenberg's *Dead Ringers* [1988]). What better venue can there be for working through our always vague sense of these traumas than a malleable form of fiction-making that cannot really grasp all its own foundations – indeed, that beholds fragments of them always receding into a distant past – just as we feel about ourselves in the west as we watch older ways of grounding our "natures" dissipate and disappear?

As we confront this underlying terror of our times, after all, the Gothic provides us a guarantee of life even in the face of so much death. Who is more alive than Regan when she is hurling a priest across the room? Who is more alive than Carrie when she is incinerating her graduating class? Who is more alive than I when I am thoroughly gripped by a horror story that actually changes my physiological condition as I read or watch? But the pleasantly terrifying thing may be that this life, this consciousness of being alive, is constantly shadowed by previous and imminent breakage and dissolution. Contemporary life constantly reminds us that we are moving toward death, or at least obsolescence, and that life we must continually strive to hold together. Paradoxically, we need the consistent consciousness of death provided by the Gothic in order to understand and want that life. This realization brings us back to the quandaries with which this chapter began: the problem of delimiting and thus anchoring both the "Gothic" and the "contemporary Gothic." But now we see why those problems still bedevil us. The Gothic's basic investment in ravaging history and fragmenting the past meshes with our own investments now as we attempt to reinvent history as a way of healing the perpetual loss in modern existence. "We" do this, moreover, as a western civilization shattered by personal and social traumas, yet "we" do not exist except as a collection of individual psyches whose personal histories are inflected by social history but not completely determined by it. We want *our* life and *our* death, and in that vacillation between wanting life and capitulating to destruction, we keep needing the Gothic to give shape to our contradiction. By now we have become like an Anne Rice vampire or a Stephen King family man: we crave presence, we crave departure, we *crave*.[18]

NOTES

1 This pattern becomes especially apparent in the course of King's *Danse Macabre* and Skal's *The Monster Show*.

2 For a more complete discussion of Freud's relation to the construction of the Gothic, and vice versa, see Fred Botting, "The Gothic Production of the Unconscious" in Glennis Byron and David Punter, eds., *Spectral Readings: Towards a Gothic Geography* (London: Macmillan, 1999), pp. 11–36.

3 In addition to the works by Freud in the guide to further reading below, see the following: "From the History of an Infantile Neurosis (The 'Wolf Man')" (1914)

in *The Standard Edition of the Complete Psychological Works of Sigmund Freud*, ed. and trans. James Strachey (London: Hogarth, 1955–61), XVII, 1–122; "Group Psychology and an Analysis of the Ego" (1921) in *Standard Edition*, XVIII, 67–143; "Mourning and Melancholia" (1915), trans. Joan Rivière, in *Standard Edition*, XIV, 237–58; "On Narcissism: an Introduction" (1915) trans. C. M. Baines, in *Standard Edition*, XIV, 67–102; "Psychoanalytic Notes on an Auto-biographical Account of a Case of Paranoia (Dementia Paranoides) (Schreber)" (1910) in *Standard Edition*, XII, 1–82; and "A Seventeenth-Century Demonological Neurosis" (1922), trans. E. Glover, in *Standard Edition*, XIX, 67–105.

4 In my use of the term *queer* here, I am thinking specifically of the Freudian explanation for male homosexuality. In his essay "On Narcissism: an Introduction" Freud theorizes that the proto-homosexual male child refuses to break the connection with the mother in time to develop "normal" relations. The result, Freud suggests, is that the child takes up the identity or subject-position of the mother and seeks a love object whom he can love the way his mother loved him. In this sense, Freud sees male homosexual desire as "narcissistic," in that the homosexual supposedly seeks himself in a love object.

5 For other textual connections between shining and various forms of the primal scene, see Stephen King, *The Shining* (Harmondsworth: Penguin, 1977), pp. 201, 297, and 303.

6 The mother, however, need not be a castrating bitch in order to produce a Gothic effect. Sometimes the horror is "caused" by her strong sense of love that becomes overindulgence. See for example Robert Aldrich's film *Whatever Happened to Baby Jane?* (1962) or Mervyn LeRoy's *The Bad Seed* (1956).

7 For a more complete analysis of maternal rejection and its relation to the Gothic, see Steven Bruhm, "The Gothic in a Culture of Narcissism" in *Reflecting Narcissus: a Queer Aesthetic* (Minneapolis: University of Minnesota Press, 2001), pp. 144–73.

8 This "history" is perhaps best allegorized in Danny Torrance's imaginary friend Tony. With hair like Danny's mother and a facial structure like his father, Tony is "the Daniel Anthony Torrance that would someday be – . . . a halfling caught between father and son, a ghost of both, a fusion" (King, *Shining*, p. 420). He seems to suggest a history that is not one, a future tense that is completely infected by the past.

9 Cathy Caruth, "Trauma and Experience: Introduction" in *Trauma: Explorations in Memory*, ed. Cathy Caruth (Baltimore: Johns Hopkins University Press, 1995).

10 For a discussion of Janet's thought, see Bessel A. van der Kolk and Onno van der Hart, "The Intrusive Past: the Flexibility of Memory and the Engraving of Trauma" in *Trauma*, ed. Caruth, pp. 158–82. For more on the problem of storytelling and trauma, see Elaine Scarry, *The Body in Pain: the Making and Unmaking of the World* (Oxford: Oxford University Press, 1985).

11 See Eve Sedgwick, *Between Men: English Literature and Male Homosocial Desire* (New York: Columbia University Press, 1985), especially chapters 5 and 6, for a powerful treatment of the homosocial bond in the Gothic.

12 For a more complete discussion of Gothic misogyny and contemporary homosexual panic, see Bruhm, "Gothic in a Culture of Narcissism."

13 The most intelligent books to date on child-worship and its manifestations in contemporary culture are both by James Kincaid – *Child-Loving: the Erotic Child*

and Victorian Culture (New York: Routledge, 1992) and *Erotic Innocence: the Culture Of Child Molesting* (Durham, NC: Duke University Press, 1998).

14 See chapters 2 and 3 of Freud, *Totem and Taboo*, for his explanation of animism and totemism, as well as their relation to the demonic.

15 Walter Benjamin, *Illuminations*, trans. Harry Zohn (New York: Schocken Books, 1969), p. 101. In Steven Bruhm, *Gothic Bodies: the Politics of Pain in Romantic Fiction* (Philadelphia: University of Pennsylvania Press, 1994) I make a similar argument about the late eighteenth-century Gothic and its functions within the discourse of sentimentality and moral sense philosophy.

16 Caruth, "Trauma and Experience," p. 10.

17 Caruth, "An Interview with Robert Jay Lifton" in *Trauma*, p. 137.

18 I want to thank the Social Sciences and Humanities Research Council of Canada for financial assistance in the preparation of this chapter.

14

FRED BOTTING

Aftergothic: consumption, machines, and black holes

Doom with a view

A hand appears, clutching an automatic pistol. Walls of gray and slimy concrete provide the gloomy surroundings. The flickering half-light of low ceilings, dark corridors, and sliding steel doors offer little orientation as the handgun begins to negotiate the uninviting dungeon. Outside, a bleak, rocky landscape is visible. So, too, the harsh walls of the desolate bunker fortress, labyrinth, and prison. Suddenly, a shadowy movement is glimpsed through the pale glow of dials and lamps. A shot. The assailant, a barely human figure in fatigues and body armor, lumbers from a dark alcove, preparing to fire again. The pistol reacts, kicking slightly in the hand. It kicks again. The attacker recoils and falls, a bloody mess on the floor. More shapes lurch from the darkness. The pistol responds, its semicrazed fire continuing until all the mutant soldiers are splattered corpses. Welcome to *Doom*.

There is something strangely familiar about this popular computer game. Its labyrinths, ghostly figures, and monstrous mutants evoke primitive fears and instinctual responses; its violent shocks and graphic images set the pulse racing; its repetitive structure sacrifices imaginative narrative involvement for more immediate sensational pleasures. Computer games owe a debt to horror cinema: *Silent Hill* evokes tension through dark, obscure settings, its player/wanderer suddenly shocked by "blood-curdling monsters"; *Resident Evil* takes scenes directly from George Romero's 1978 cult horror movie, *Dawn of the Dead.*[1] A longer look at the generic history of Gothic fiction reveals further parallels in form and effect. Horace Walpole, discussing his new style of romance in 1765, argued that it leaves "the powers of fancy at liberty to expatiate through boundless realms of invention, and thence creating more interesting situations" (Walpole, *Castle of Otranto*, pp. 7–8). The "first-person shooter" genre, in which a hand holding a gun offers an illusion of on-screen involvement, similarly draws the player into the virtual world. For John Romero, *Doom*'s creator, the blurring of fantasy and reality is crucial in the production of emotional effects rather than meanings: "when the monster jumps out, real adrenaline roars through your body."[2] A world of ghosts and monsters is rendered palpable. However, where superstitious credulity and imaginative identification are required to realize fictions emotionally, computer games perform the work of visualization themselves, while continuing to play with patterns of anticipation, expectation, and uncertainty drawn from the basic Gothic plot set out in *The Castle of Otranto*.

Virtual environments are designed to evoke horror and terror. The foggy world of *Silent Hill* obscures visibility and clouds the player in apprehension; the labyrinths, gloom, and postindustrial ruins of *Doom* produce the tense atmosphere of pursuit and disorientation. While these environments stimulate visceral emotions, games also generate loftier feelings: the "breathtaking environments" of *Tomb Raider* are "awe-inspiring spaces," "cathedrals of fire."[3] The artificial sublimity of computer-generated worlds are comparable to eighteenth-century aesthetic notions, in which a sense of the sublime occurs in an encounter with an immensity the mind cannot comprehend, a natural and divine power found in the sovereign shape of rugged, mountainous landscapes. First overwhelmed by the spectacle, the viewer is then elevated by the sense of grandeur. Self-possession is lost then regained on another, imaginative, level. Though terror, in Edmund Burke's mid-eighteenth-century aesthetics, invigorates an elevated idea of selfhood and the sacred, its energy comes from a baser, bodily source: "a sort of delightful horror, a sort of tranquillity tinged with terror; which as it belongs to self-preservation is one of the strongest of all the passions" (Burke, *Enquiry*, in Clery and Miles, *Gothic Documents*, p. 121). Self-preservation, moreover, is one of the more "instinctual" emotions central to the enjoyment of games, an "appreciation of dynamic properties hard-wired into the species – it's essential for survival."[4]

The sublime has economic and cultural dimensions underlying its popularity as an aesthetic technique. A mode of appropriating luxurious, wasteful expenditure (associated, in bourgeois commercial culture, with the excesses of feudal aristocracy), it manifests a significant change in ideas of self and nature, the former becoming increasingly individualistic, the latter being invested with powers at once increasingly measurable by empirical science and elusively spiritual in Romanticism. In the natural images, architectural ruins, and courtly customs frequently employed in a Gothic sublime, the past is appropriated and expelled in an attempt to separate a civilized, rational eighteenth century from its barbaric and feudal forbears. Remnants of the past – ruins, superstitions, passions – are attributes of an earlier epoch superseded by modern practices and qualities. Gothic figures thus mark turning

points in cultural historical progress, points at which feudalism is apprehended and dismissed as a ruined past in a movement toward a more enlightened future. The momentum of change, however, carries with it anxieties:
has the barbaric past really been surpassed? Have primitive energies and passions really been overcome? Gothic figures come to represent these anxieties
and give them fearful form as monsters, ghosts, and demons whose return
terrifies bourgeois normality and undermines ordered notions of civilized
humanity and rational progress.

Here the power of science to guarantee a comfortable future is brought
into question. From *Frankenstein* onwards scientific discovery is as much a
threat as it is a promise. In H. G. Wells's *The Island of Dr. Moreau* (1896)
the biologist's attempt to accelerate evolution according to Darwinian principles only causes rapid regression to bestial states and unleashes a reversion
to savagery and a host of horrible hybrid creatures. The hi-tech worlds of
computer games – linking instinctual energies and powerful machines (rather
than natural or supernatural forces) – participate in this narrative of ruin.
The future is anxiously perceived as another place of destruction and decay,
as ruined as the Gothic past. Social and corporeal disintegration awaits in
postindustrial devastation, in genetic experimentation, in alien and mutant
forms of life and death.

Supernatural demons, natural forces (passion, guilt, sexuality), and most
recently technological powers have successively assumed a predominant role
in Gothic representations of cultural anxieties. The latter fear brings out
an uncanny element latent in the process: "there is no difference between
occult and technological media."[5] For Terry Castle, discussing the popularity of phantasmagoria and magic lanterns in the late eighteenth century, the
magical materialization of ghostly images caused thought to become "phantasmagorical," and so the mind found itself "supernaturalized" at the same
time as rational science discovered a technical language and instrumentation
to represent mental operations (Castle, *Female Thermometer*, pp. 141–62).
Human identity and society, it seems, are continually subject to transformation and redefinition by representational and mechanical technologies.
The manufacture of automata, for instance, participates in the development and disturbances shaping individuals in the course of the eighteenth
century: "the mechanical doll" provides "a metaphor of, and counterpoint
to, the autonomous subjectivity."[6] Machines double human functions and
identity so that it becomes difficult to tell them apart. Cinema, too, not
only materializes these disturbing doubles, it makes them move across a
screen as figures for the cinematic apparatus itself: "in *Golem*, in *The Other*,
in *The Cabinet of Dr. Caligari*, in *The Student of Prague* – everywhere
doppelgängers appear as metaphors for the screen and its aesthetic."[7] The

magical, ghostly movement of cinema images has recently been surpassed by new computer technologies. Dataglove and digital bodysuit disclose the "industrial production of a personality split, an instantaneous cloning of living man, the technological recreation of one of our most ancient myths: the myth of the *double*, of an electro-ergonomic double whose presence is spectral."[8] The movement of virtual images not only dispossesses the body of its shadows so that identity becomes no more than a phantasmic electronic flickering. The polygons composing computer graphics also assume an almost spiritual life of their own: "now the polygons have become animated, literally, given a soul. A machine soul."[9] Spirits and selves entwine on the spectral screens to manifest uncanny disturbances in which past, present, and future collapse.

Gothic representations are a product of cultural anxieties about the nature of human identity, the stability of cultural formations, and processes of change. As a result the representations are influenced by the cultures that produce them: evil is located in the past or the future, whether it be aristocratic excess for an eighteenth-century bourgeoisie *or* genetic experimentation for a late twentieth-century consumer culture. However, Gothic styles, while concerning themselves with disturbing, duplicitous powers of representation and simulation, inevitably remain effects of the representational techniques. They retain a double function in simultaneously assuaging and intensifying the anxieties with which they engage. Hence the persistence of Gothic throughout the 200-year period associated with modernity.

The similarity and differences of Gothic images and effects in the contemporary world can be seen in critical reactions to fiction and computer games. For one contemporary critic, games are "a degenerate spectacle awash in the flood of information-images," internalizing "current and archaic phantasms of pleasure, violence and control through simple narratives, crude moralizing filters and forms of self-identification."[10] The vocabulary reiterates eighteenth-century criticism of Gothic fiction. Short-circuiting judgment and discrimination through excessive stimulation of emotional energies, romances were accused of hindering learning, character development, and moral understanding. According to such critics of that era, a base kind of identification is activated: "the love we mostly meet with, in such *Circulating Library* books, is devoid of *passion*; has more of *sensation*, than *sentiment*, in it. More *desire*, than *wish*. Were brutes gifted with speech and reason, they would express their *instinct*, in the very stile of modern Novelists."[11] Fiction horrifies the discriminating critic with the specter of a regression to uncivilized (animal or infantile) appetites and immoral behavior. Similarly, the psychological and social effects of game-playing concern critics today. As with the idle indulgence in fanciful romances that irritated so many eighteenth-century critics, game-playing, it is argued, wastes too much time, energy, and resources. Through repeated exposure to sensation and violence, social values and other beings are rendered inconsequential. Rational discrimination, too, is set aside. The moral panic about computer games is reflected in the panic induced by them: *Doom* develops from Atari video games like *Battlezone* and *Missile Command*, the latter a "panic-inducing arcade game... which initially grew out of a military simulation to see how many nuclear warheads a human radar operator could track before overload set in."[12] Rational faculties are overwhelmed by the bombardment of images, sense is overstimulated by sensory excitation, and self-consciousness sacrificed to unreflecting immersion in the flow of the game.

The recurrence of such critical opinions suggests that culture is again in decline, its social and parental order apparently threatened by pleasures that make no concession to reason, intellect, or morality. In these accounts, specters of loss underline the absence of good, civilized, and rational cultural values. The possibility of decline and the fears evoked by so many negative features also provide the occasion for the assertion of the characteristics that are lacking. The antithetical, countercultural features of Gothic representation serve as the inverted image of acceptable qualities, threats to be expunged like dark stains on the shining mirror of enlightened modernity. Their destruction allows for the projection and restoration of missing human factors: the stain is cleaned up or cast out so that reason, morality, and good sense prevail.

However, at a time when human qualities are considered less and less central to systems of postindustrial production or social reproduction, the restorative cultural functions of Gothic negativity are less easily identified and the effulgence of terrifying figures less readily contained. Gothic fictions once provided the dark mirror in which modern culture recognized higher values and returned readers to normality, family order, and paternal authority in a social context in which rational judgment, useful production, and empirical reality established the dominant framework for everyday life. Now machines dominate exchanges of messages and circulations of images to replace human abilities and faculties, thereby rendering rational judgment and morality redundant. In the context of a movement from a modernity associated with rational production to a *post*modernity linked to accelerated technological consumption, Gothic images and horrors seem less able to restore boundaries by allowing the projection of a missing unifying (and paternal) figure. No single framework stabilizes social meanings and identities. Once the dark underside of modernity, Gothic horror now outlines the darkness of the postmodern condition. Critical judgments invoking paternal authority become more strident and less credible, and the possibility of restoring order is increasingly enveloped in an unending and repetitious series of computer simulations.

Paternal figures and the rise of Gothic fiction

Gothic fiction is bound up with the function of the paternal metaphor. Since Walpole, Gothic has emerged as an effect of and an engagement with a crisis in the legitimacy and authority of the structured circulation of social exchanges and meanings over which the father figure presides. More precisely, the usual subject of Gothic fiction can be defined as the transgression of the paternal metaphor. Transgression, however, is not simply a celebratory breaking of laws and taboos considered unjust or repressive, nor is it a straightforward liberation from rules and conventions binding individuals within strict frameworks of duty or normative identity. Michel Foucault outlines the complex "play" that relates transgression and limits: there is no transgression without a prior limit. But the reverse also pertains: "limit and transgression depend on each other for whatever density of being they possess; a limit could not exist if it were absolutely uncrossable and, reciprocally, transgression would be pointless if it merely crossed a limit composed of illusions and shadows." Transgression gives the limit its power, while the latter serves to mark out a zone of attraction providing transgression with its force. Hence "transgression carries the limit right to the limit of its being," forcing "the limit to face the fact of its imminent disappearance, to find itself in what it excludes."[13] In the absence of absolute boundaries, the play of limit and transgression establishes the divisions, differences, and oppositions structuring social and subjective existence.

The key figure is the father, who "is the one who protects when, in his proclamation of Law, he links spaces, rules, and language within a single and major experience."[14] Foucault's rendering of a psychoanalytic account of the father stresses the role of division and decision central to structures of language and experience. The paternal figure polices the boundaries of legitimacy, thereby constituting meaning, behavior, and identity. In Jacques Lacan's terms the paternal figure or metaphor in western culture determines the symbolic function of language: the father's name is given to the child, positioning him or her from birth in a structured set of relationships defining social and sexual identity and directing subsequent development by establishing "a form into which the subject is inserted at the level of his being."[15] The paternal metaphor is formal and not substantial in its operations: different figures can assume its function (God, father, teacher, priest, etc.) in acts of "imposture."[16] The symbolic structure depends on the identification of those positioned within it and is underpinned, not by any positive content, but by a fundamental absence, gap, or lost object providing a locus of projection and subjective fantasy. The primary signifier – the phallus – is therefore "a ghost."[17]

From its beginnings, Gothic fiction takes the form of a family romance in which paternal figures assume a variety of guises: tyrants, murderers, rapacious villains, ghostly revenants. Prince Manfred in *The Castle of Otranto* encompasses nearly all these roles, as well as underlining his villainy with incestuous ambitions. Ann Radcliffe's villains, though glossed with diabolical energy, are less extreme and more materialistic: Montoni in *Udolpho* has an eye on Emily's inheritance; Montalt, the fratricidal uncle (and suspected father) of Adeline in *The Romance of the Forest*, has only the satisfaction of his own selfish interests at heart. Matthew Lewis's villainous monk, Ambrosio, conceals his violent passions behind a veil of vanity and pious respectability, but he is also "an orphan" who "enacts the mandates of the oedipal struggle through the most lofty of surrogates, the parental arms of the Catholic church. In his ambitious virtue, he supplants all other 'Fathers,' and nothing less than the Madonna excites his lust."[18] Ambrosio's desire manifests the most exorbitant of paternal identifications. In a different way, Victor Frankenstein exhibits ambition on an equally fantastic scale. In mastering the secrets of nature and assuming the ability to create life from death, he aspires to the most divine of paternal roles: "a new species would bless me as its creator and source; many happy and excellent natures would owe their being to me. No father could claim the gratitude of his child so completely as I should deserve theirs"(Shelley, *Frankenstein*, p. 54).

Later in the nineteenth century a diabolically evil father appears in *Dracula*: bloodlust and sovereign command of natural and supernatural forces make the Count an archaic father of the primal horde, beyond law and free to indulge his inhuman and irreligious desires. In Stoker's homosocial late Victorian setting, masculinity and virility are in crisis. In the twentieth century the paternal metaphor still remains at stake. The queer undercurrent of Stephen King's *The Shining* (1977), less consumed with Victorian anxieties, restores the paternal figure in the relationship between men.[19] As a genre, nonetheless, Gothic fiction seems to threaten paternal order: Robertson's *An Essay on Education* (1798) makes the common case that fiction leads young readers astray in an "abjuration of all parental authority" (De Bolla, *Discourse of the Sublime*, p. 272). A reviewer of *The Monk* offers a similar cautionary judgment: "in full conviction that we are performing a duty, we declare it to be our opinion, that the Monk is a romance, which if a parent saw in the hands of a son or daughter, he might reasonably turn pale."[20] Fiction relates seductive transgressions *and* perpetuates them on a social scale.

There are few families in Gothic fiction, a telling absence which suggests that the importance of the family lies as much in a symbolic dimension as in actual existence. Mothers are long dead, fathers rarely stay the course. Parentless children are left to roam the wild and gloomy landscapes without protection or property and often without the secure sense of themselves that comes with a proper name and position. So it is for Adeline as she flees through the woods in Radcliffe's 1791 *Romance of the Forest*. So, too, for Emily, imprisoned in Udolpho. She has, moreover, failed to observe her father's dying wishes and begun to suspect his honor and the legitimacy of her own family origins. Her doubts impeach paternal authority and provide the occasion for terrible speculations. Similarly, the whole narrative of Regina Maria Roche's *Clermont* turns on suspected paternal guilt: the motherless heroine has a living, guilty father deprived of name, social position, and economic entitlement. Orphans, or children dispossessed of inheritance and due identity, like the heroine of Eleanor Sleath's *The Orphan of the Rhine*, become emblematic figures of the revolutionary decade, cast adrift in a world bereft of social and familial security. The threats to paternal order disclose an underlying instability, an absence, at the heart of any social or symbolic structure.

The absence of a stable paternal order provides room for the projection of both ideal and terrifying figures of authority and power. In Gothic fiction, fatherly authority is assumed by rapacious aristocrats, ambitious monks, and impassioned bandits more often than benevolent role models. These substitute fathers indicate the familial, religious, and social institutions threatened by moral and paternal decline. Figures of transgression thus mark out the dangers of crossing symbolic boundaries and call for their restoration. *Dracula*, for instance, closes with the birth of a son to the Harkers; a novel full of good and bad parental substitutes finally renders paternity actual, thereby restoring an order whose existence was only made possible negatively, imagined throughout as the antithesis to vampiric transgression. The ending of *Udolpho*, for all its emphasis on a providentially ordered cosmos where virtue is rewarded and vice is punished, presents the matrimonial celebrations as enchantments and fairy tales (Radcliffe, *Mysteries of Udolpho*, p. 671; see Castle, *Female Thermometer*, p. 122). Order has been restored on a symbolic level through marriage, but the conclusion remains as fantastic as the terrors dominating the novel. Nothing real, then, is recovered: a fairy-tale, but acceptable, form of reality is projected in place of its imagined and nightmarish opposite.

The movement between opposites charts the eighteenth-century transition from feudal to bourgeois modes of social organization. Gothic fiction articulates the symbolic dimensions of the shift from a feudal economy based on land ownership, patrilinear property rights, and aristocratic rule and privilege on the one hand to a bourgeois economy maintained through commercial contracts, mobile, monetary wealth, and the production and exchange of commodities on the other. The provenance of Horace Walpole's own country house offers a good example of this shift:

> The house at Strawberry Hill was acquired from the proprietor of a London toyshop, and the happy coincidence was not lost on the new owner as he systematically transformed the building into what we call today a "theme park" treatment of aristocratic ascendancy. As the feudal origins of the aristocratic order were turned into the plaything of a whimsical hobbyist, its present legitimacy was symbolically diminished.
>
> (Clery, *Rise of Supernatural Fiction*, p. 76)

As commercial power comes to dominate social organization, the remnants of feudalism are decoratively reconstructed in an idle aesthetic fashion. Lost, they are recovered in another form, subject to a different arrangement of economic practices, given a new meaning as the phantasmic opposite and heritage past of the eighteenth-century present. This past, moreover, is simulated. Just as the origin of his "Gothic Story" is fabricated, so, too, is Walpole's Gothic mansion.[21]

Divested of economic and political power, the aristocracy is imagined as the antithesis of bourgeois values of sobriety, merit, and industriousness. Its luxuriously wasteful indulgences are considered decorative and idle ways of spending time and money in a commercial culture where rational production, moral regulation, and useful activity are now predominant. The association between Gothic styles and aristocratic excess, though giving aristocracy a dark and dangerous allure (it is no accident that Dracula is a count), nonetheless places both forms in a position subordinate to emerging bourgeois values. However, as global economic practices change in the twentieth century and industrial production cedes to postindustrial consumption in western societies, excess, waste, and useless activities come to the fore and transform the significance of the Gothic genre. As a result, it begins to shed its older negative associations and assumes a defining role within an anxious and uncertain postmodern culture.

Gothic times: horror today

"We live in Gothic times," commented Angela Carter, in an account of the way that genres once consigned to cultural margins have begun to prevail over their canonized counterparts.[22] Gothic figures and fictions now circulate with greater visibility to manifest the absence of strict, prohibitive

mechanisms or a strong, exclusionary force. Where the restoration of symbolic, normative boundaries was celebrated in the violent climaxes to older
tales of terror, monstrous figures are now less often terrifying objects of an-
imosity expelled in the return to social and symbolic equilibrium. Instead,
they retain a fascinating, attractive appeal: no longer objects of hate or fear,
monstrous others become sites of identification, sympathy, desire, and self-
recognition. Excluded figures once represented as malevolent, disturbed, or
deviant monsters are rendered more humane while the systems that exclude
them assume terrifying, persecutory, and inhuman shapes. The reversal, with
its residual Romantic identification with outcast and rebel, alongside its feeling for liberation and individual freedom, makes transgression a positive act
and diffuses the negative charge of spectral paternal prohibition. Transgression becomes just another permitted social activity.

In her late twentieth-century fiction, Carter powerfully, and often critically, demonstrates the reversal of values and identifications that occurs via
the Gothic genre. Otherness takes center stage: sexual transgression, dark
desire, and fantastic deviance wonderfully subvert the restrictive orders of
reason, utility, and paternal morality. An energy of rebellion and liberation
associated with the political and sexual movements of the 1960s challenges
aesthetic conventions and social taboos. The pastiche Gothic of "The Bloody
Chamber," for example, plays with conventional elements of fear and desire
in its gloomy castle, tremulous heroine, and rapacious vampire. But it ends on
a parodic note: the heroine is saved from the clutches of undeath by a knight
in shining armor, yet the appropriate fairy-tale form is undone when the
visor is lifted and the face of the mother revealed. A feminine figure replaces
the father or his heroic male substitute, a future or would-be son-in-law, but
the reversal of hierarchy does not institute a new regime of the mother as
an inverted replica of the old order. In turning over expectations and conventions, "The Bloody Chamber" exposes the artifice of social and symbolic
meanings and refuses any preservation of credulity at a fictional level, significantly disrupting the credibility of the ideological framework in which
any tale is given meaning. Here the Gothic coincides with postmodernism's
"incredulity towards metanarratives."[23] Figures of authority are rendered
suspect. With its ghostly power demystified, the space of a single credible,
paternal figure is left vacant, to be filled with a host of fleeting specters of
delegitimized (governmental, conspiratorial, military, corporate, criminal, or
alien) power.

In Gothic times margins may become the norm and occupy a more central
cultural place. Consequently, that center is now characterized by a dispersal,
emptied of both core and apex. The Gothic times of the present, then,
though linked to a world of innumerable real and imagined terrors and

horrors, do not simply signify a new dark, barbaric age or a life spent in fear. Anxiety floats freely, reflecting and thus ghosting the high-speed circulation of information and commodities. To live in Gothic times at present means that Gothic loses its older intensity, shedding some of the allure of darkness, danger, and mystery. A matter of style, life-choice, even personal taste, Gothic currently exists in domains of fashion and entertainment as one genre among many: normalized and commodified, it has a whiff of the delicatessen in its taste for blood, its macabre topics lightly spiced by camp and kitsch. A report on a recent World Dracula Congress in Romania sketches the diversity of tones, meanings, and lifestyles associated with the genre. Ingrid Pitt, a former horror film star for Hammer Studios in England who continues to make a living out of the vampire entertainment industry, finds the facilities primitive: the toilets are "bloody disgusting and the paper's scratchy as hell." While the superficial celluloid attractions of vampirism remain good for business, there is certainly no wholehearted indulgence in a life of degradation and defilement. "Other horrors" beset the Dracula Congress delegates: Arlene Russo, an editor of a vampire magazine, "is shocked at eastern Europe's lack of vegetarian food, and at having to walk back from the restaurant through an unlit pine forest after midnight." These are rather anachronistic complaints to level at an event celebrating a nocturnal bloodsucker. A man in search of ancestral connections to the original Vlad the Impaler in central Europe, a German forensic scientist studying New York's vampire youth and their regular dietary predilection for each other's blood, a researcher into "psychic vampirism": all these were among the participants.[24] Screen image, social practice, and psychic therapy congregate at a convention embracing academics, fans, and tourists.

Vampires have become commodities. Dracula attained Dell comic book superhero status in 1962 and, more comically in the 1980s, turned into the children's cartoon character "Count Duckula,"[25] as well as "the Count" in public television's *Sesame Street*. Vampires saturate contemporary culture and provide a normative image of the latter-day consumer. Poppy Z. Brite's *Lost Souls* (1993) shows America populated by "vampire teens" who "leave their soulless broken homes" to seek "other black-garbed, hollow-eyed, amoral, abandoned teens," vampirism defined "by wish and by fashion in our world."[26] Since the 1970s Anne Rice's vampires have existed in a world of luxurious consumption, wasted images of desire beyond an end of history left to be spent in perpetual spending. The assimilation culminates in Hollywood: "with [popular actor Tom] Cruise playing Lestat . . . the vampire has ceased to be unrecognizable. Once a menace to the conclaves of average America, he was now an honorary resident."[27] Vampires offer mirrors of contemporary identity and sympathetic identification. They assume a strangely human, if not more than human, form. Rice's Lestat fantastically absorbs a range of posthuman possibilities as a liminal figure "nicely" exemplifying "a style of cyborg existence, capturing the pain and complexity of attempting to adapt to a society, a lifestyle, a language, a culture, our epistemology, even in Lestat's case a species, that is not one's own."[28] The vampire becomes a metaphor of current associations between machines, bodies, and patterns of consumption. In itself, it exists on the borders between life and death, between human, animal, and supernatural identities: she/he is a figure of transgression disturbing boundaries between inside and outside, home and foreignness. But what the vampire does is also crucial: consuming bodies, it transforms beings, contaminating them with its own appetites and desires. Marx's use of the vampire metaphor to depict the way that human life is turned into dead labor to feed the insatiable machine of capitalist production provides the economic coordinates of a horrifying transformation become the norm of late twentieth-century existence.[29] As production cedes to consumption, all bodies are changed from being simply the victims or the wage slaves of vampiric capitalism to its willing participants. They assume its voracious identity as their own: "Marx's gluttonous capitalist rat has been transformed into an army of consuming mall-rats"(Rob Latham, "Consuming Youth," in Gordon and Hollinger, *Blood Read*, p. 131).

Changes in patterns of consumption are linked, through Gothic figures, to new methods of reproduction and genetic manipulation that literally threaten paternal formations. While Frankenstein and Dracula have always been associated with science and technology,[30] "vampires, aliens, and feminist heroics, all represent anxieties about an unauthorized reproduction that challenges proper (i.e., paternal) reproductive order and human aegis": the threat involves "a patriarchal order that has allied itself with the very technology whose system has already spelled its transmogrification."[31] Like the vampire, once the shadowy support of a paternal order, technology monstrously undoes the system which designed it: Sadie Plant's "cyberfeminism" observes that the digital matrix which was "the culmination of his machinic erections" also surpasses male power, so that "man confronts the system he built for his own protection and finds it is female and dangerous."[32] Computer and genetic codes allow everything from identity to bodies to be rewritten according to a different, supplementary logic. If the future is vampiric, it is also female and machine-like. Noting the "viral loss of determinacy" of a culture given over to the flows of transsexuality, transeconomics, transaesthetics, Jean Baudrillard has charted the body's changing significance from being a metaphor for the soul or sex to being "no longer a metaphor for anything at all, merely the locus of metastasis, of the machine-like connections between all its processes, of an endless programming devoid of any symbolic organization or overarching purpose."[33] Cloning materializes the viral revision of reproduction according to a matrix in which digital and biological code combine to erase "natural" human creation underpinning symbolic structure: "No more mother, no more father: just a matrix." Today difference is sucked into a "hell of the same."[34] We are indeed in Gothic times.

Questions of woman, reproduction, and cloning are foregrounded in the *Alien* series of feature films, which began with *Alien* itself (Ridley Scott, 1979). Maternal bodies are presented as sites of abjection, places where numerous cultural fears are thrown off and dissolve together.[35] The excess represented by the deadly female alien is counterposed with hubris of the "Company" that wishes to control and exploit her power. In between, the single crew member to survive, Ripley, must defy both and be stalked through the dark labyrinths of the mining ship. As the heroine becomes more like the alien mother throughout the series, the feminine position moves away from conventional, hysterical responses to terror and assumes a defiant posture in the face of death. At the same time, the fight with the monstrous mother in the second film, *Aliens* (1986), never diminishes the proximity of otherness. By *Alien 3* (1992), Ripley is revealed to be carrying the embryo of a female alien: she has become a breeder of all that she most fears, pregnant with a monster whose offspring will threaten humanity with extinction. This does not, however, end her resolve. The climax of *Alien 3* again pits Ripley against aliens and the corporate machine. Unable to save herself without condemning humanity, she makes the ultimate gesture, throwing herself into an industrial furnace as the young alien bursts through her ribcage. Her self-sacrifice, in Christ-like pose as she falls back into the flames, stages a sovereign confrontation with her own death and supposedly seals the fate of the alien while apparently ending this whole sequence of films.

In a technological medium obsessed by technical innovation, however, the death of the heroine and only link between the films is a small obstacle to be overcome. The device to reanimate the heroine and bring the film's story back from the dead is also incorporated as the principal theme and locus of anxiety: genetic experimentation enables the cloning of a new Ripley and a new alien at a stroke. In *Alien Resurrection* (Jeunet, 1997), the technical innovations move well beyond the opposition between human and alien that were tenuously preserved in the three preceding films. No longer is a feminized humanity fighting to preserve its life and identity against the threats of an overwhelming alien and a cruel and inhuman system interested in exploiting resources, bodies, and species for profit. The monstrosity of the military/scientific complex is instead made plain from the start. The curved lens of the film's opening shows the results of failed genetic experiments in extreme close-up: pulsating repellent hybrids composed of human eyes, alien teeth, scissored jaws, and stretched pallid skin preserved in jars. No humanity is in evidence: Ripley, with the number 8 tatooed on her arm, remains expendable, a "meat by-product" to be put down or exhibited, like "1–7" before her. Stasis-bound survivors of another spaceship are used as hosts for further alien reproduction. The cavernous labyrinth of the military vessel is a breeding-ground of mutants and a museum of scientific atrocities, a floating island of Dr. Moreau and, like *Doom*, an arena of violence and pursuit.

With the military machine able to supplant human reproductive processes and write its own code, all pretensions to humanity are discarded: its mastery of the biological matrix and breeding of aliens makes it the counterpart of the alien mother that it always held up as its ultimate prize. Cross-breeding extinguishes humanity and, for all the attempts to erase difference, recycles it: the replication of sameness introduces internal deviations and mutations that short-circuit successful cloning and subsequent training so that even number 8 manifests a resistance to the system that created her. But her resistance is not that of an heroic humanity or a suffering, abjected femininity become sovereign. Though she looks like a woman, Ripley is far from human: any feeling and compassion she exhibits, attributes usually signifying humanity, are reserved for androids and aliens. Call, the young female android intent on saving the world by destroying the host body of alien propagation, manifests the most intense human feelings. But, as Ripley notes on discovering she is a "robot," "I should have known – no human being is that humane." An android designed by machines has been programmed to care. With the programming comes a sense of exclusion and self-hate: "I'm disgusting," Call comments. The alien queen is also changed by genetic mutation and hybridization: her "gift" from Ripley is a human reproductive system and the pain that comes with it. Her child renounces his alien origins, crushing her skull in his jaws, before turning to Ripley – his grandmother – for maternal affection. Abandoned, the child longingly pursues her, until it is sucked into fragments through a small hole in a depressurized escape craft. This climax refuses straightforwardly explosive models of legitimate expulsion and arouses confused emotions. At the end, after a maternal hug, Ripley sends her hideous grandchild to his death, an act drawn out by the anguish in the alien's human eyes and Ripley's own mouthing of the words "I'm sorry."

Pain, compassion, suffering and a "posthumane" identification with the other add a new twist to the alien series. The "resurrection" that follows the climactic "crucifixion" of *Alien 3* discloses relationships more complicated than a symbolic human triumph over death: humanity has virtually disappeared in the course of four films. Neither a transcendent order nor a sacred mythology is reinvoked as a model for human relations. An alien has saved the Earth, but the salvation is not triumphant. As Ripley and Call look out at the Earth, which they see for the first time, the sunset or sunrise evokes emotions of wonder: "it's beautiful." Significantly, the Earth, not its population, is admired. "You did it, you saved the world," Call comments, "What happens now?" "I don't know, I'm a stranger here myself," replies Ripley. The return to Earth apparently involves a new colonization inspired by the odd pairing of femin-alien and femin-android, both capable of feeling for another. A strange posthumanity emerges in this feminine-identified compassion. Genetically hybrid, their sense of strangeness and alienation, from themselves as much as others, enables uncertain but deeply affective identifications: what matters is not what one is, but how one identifies.

From female abjection and otherness, from corporeal destruction and rebirth, a new subject appears to be resurrected, with an ethical, compassionate spirit, at the end of the *Alien* series. On the basis of feminine associations and identifications, it seems, the final film presents the possibility of a new understanding of otherness: the alien, once providing a monstrous threat enabling the expulsion of internal anxieties caused by a collapsing symbolic order, has come closer to home. The place of otherness gives way to a generalized sense of strangeness consuming all beings in uncertain identifications. Hybrid figures are turned away from seeking a stable, unified identity and look, through pain and compassion, toward less structured networks. Ripley and Call do not know what happens next. But *Alien Resurrection* refuses to locate the sacred excess of the cruel machine in the rediscovery of an ineffable femininity associated with childbirth, love, and pain. There is no clear shift from representations of abjection to sacralized images of suffering, no recuperation of a messianic maternity as the model of a new, or resurrected, global order. The uncertain position with which the film closes can be summed up in the ambivalence of the word "*post*human": humanity has been left behind, but the future cannot be defined except in terms of the human features that have been negated.

The intensities of emotion emanating from identifications with otherness, however, are still tied to the preservation of the image, the maintenance of imaginary feminine figures despite all knowledge of their nonhuman composition. Toned, dark-haired, and beautiful in black leatherette, both Call and Ripley survive and continue to look good. Perhaps there is nothing more important in a film produced by an entertainment industry where looking good is the overriding imperative: personal trainers, dietitians, and cosmetic surgeons are all conscripted to ensure that the body be enhanced beyond decay and death, be reborn as pure image, as undying simulation. These functionaries are dedicated to the vision machines whose operations parallel the work of digital and genetic coding to reproduce sameness. There is no transcendence or traditional resurrection, only the uncanny circulation of cinematic simulations. Uncertain of what to do, strangers to themselves, the woman-alien and female android fill the screen but wait, unsure, for the next episode in the *Alien* series.

Alien Resurrection, though returning to Earth, does not reawaken human values. Its concern with images, technology, and sensational effects focuses instead on a realm of simulations and visual surfaces unconcerned with notions of reality and humanity. These ideas, so important in the development of modern culture, now seem redundant, evacuated of significance by a form of scientific progress which is no longer interested in materially benefiting human life or furthering human communities. The present rush to invest in, patent, and market the results of genetic research acknowledges the predominance of such overt commercial concerns. The lack of credulity given to the metanarratives of modernity, science, and democratic government is paralleled by the increasingly nonhuman economic interests pursued by technoscience and corporate bureaucracy: "excellence," "performance enhancement," "profit," and technical "optimization" are today's buzzwords of efficiency. Communities disintegrate, families break up, bodies are surgically altered: the bonds and bases of human culture are unraveled. The gap between human formations and the machines of production, exchange, and innovation widens and nothing seems to articulate the divide except the rapid generation of more and more simulations. This gap is not covered over by the technological production of images and simulations. It remains visible as a source of anxiety, a black hole of horror which no single figure can fill. No one monster, it seems, functions as an object of terror capable of giving form and focus to anxiety and thus to shore up symbolic boundaries. As a result, there are no limits to what commerce can exploit in these techno-Gothic times.

The holes marking the divisions between and failures of human institutions are not simply visible marks of cultural fragmentation in the face of global commercial reconfiguration. The world of simulations also transforms inner life. The modern subject defined in terms of individual, familial, and national identity as a morally responsible, rationally self-conscious, and economically productive being is no longer a central figure. Instead, as a consumer of goods and services, she/he is determined by what she/he buys: identity is externalized as an effect of images, consumer objects, and the lifestyles they conjure up. Integral identity is hollowed out and filled by the rapid, repetitious transmission of images. Speed is crucial: allowing no time for thought or reflection, it encourages only immediate, affective responses to stimulation. Just as the body is redesigned in the interests of performance, so the mind is remade as a better processor of information and consumer of images. Computer games, with their images of terror, exemplify the transformation. The subjective hollow corresponds to another empty space, a dark no-place pulsing with pixels. Mental images and screen images criss-cross a void subtending the vast network of machines defining the information age. The information and images circulating in and around nothing depend on an incessant flickering of light and darkness. All the pleasures, sensations, and excitements of simulation are thus underpinned by an emptiness, a lack of content, substance, resolution, or meaning. Despite the instantaneous gratifications of virtual life, anxiety continues to circulate freely. Nothing stops the incessant flickering or fills the black hole forming the subjective and cultural center of this curiously Gothicized postmodern existence.

Love in a void ("it's so good")

Unlike the earlier *Alien* films, the fourth is dominated by United Systems Military and "not some greedy corporation." Corporate or military organizations are standard models of power in future fictions and, significantly, the institutions most involved in technological development. The cyborg emerges from military research; the Internet was preceded by Darpanet.[36] Early video games were used as army training simulations; *Doom* was redesigned to train US Marines in the art of "one-shot kills" and described by a military expert as a "how-to manual for killing without a conscience."[37] Morality is replaced by murderous efficiency, reason by reaction time, knowledge by technique. A new subject is produced in video games. It exhibits "hyperkinetic attunements of perception and reflex reminiscent of the preternatural sensory-motor apparatus of Anne Rice's vampires" and is associated with teenagers "as stupefied as the zombies shambling through George Romero's [1978] classic film of mall life, *Dawn of the Dead*"(Rob Latham in Gordon and Hollinger, *Blood Read*, p. 138). The model of the individual promoted in the nineteenth century as the apex of culture and the ideal around which social cohesion established itself in cultural and ideological terms, is redundant. Highly efficient operators, skilled technicians, experts in a limited field, are the required products of vocational training.[38] The adepts in video gaming are new trainees in this commercial and performative ethos. *Dawn of the Dead*, set in a shopping mall populated by zombies, locates fear in a culture given over to consumption, divested of reason, agency, or self-control, and characterized by zombies and automata whose self-possession and desires have been consumed by pleasure and terror. These days, parents need not be concerned about where their children are "but what they are."[39]

Freedom and choice become a nightmare; invested in commodities, freedom is consumed (even used up) as soon as it is enacted. The subject bombarded by images and commodities no longer knows the object of desire: "the new media deprive the subject radically of a knowledge of what he wants: they address a constantly malleable subject who has constantly to be told what he wants – that is, the very evacuation of a choice to be made performatively creates the need for an object of choice" (Žižek, *Plague of Fantasies*, p. 153). Gothic times present a double bind: invited to choose, the subject is overwhelmed by the choices available; with the subject unable to choose, the matter of choice becomes all the more pressing. The deregulation of subjective desire and the confrontation with an insurmountably sublime excess of choice signals a shift toward "postmodern capitalism." The collapse of distinctions between useful production and wasteful consumption means there is no regulative figure or ideal other than accelerated circuits of production, consumption and expenditure. Nothing, it seems, escapes capitalist economy and its flows: all that is "sacred" or "transcendent," everything apparently heterogeneous to its operations, "including desire" notes Jean-Joseph Goux, are dropped into its "magnetic field."[40]

In the eighteenth century excessive consumption was repeatedly subject to censure. The indulgence of appetite and sensation at the expense of rational judgment, idle and useless employment of one's time and immoral gratifications of pleasure: all this constituted economic grounds for the condemnation cast on older Gothic characters and fictions by paternal figures of power. In contrast, the postmodern economy enjoins consumption beyond measures of rationality, morality, or utility: if the phantasmagoria of the late eighteenth century were invented "at precisely that moment when traditional credulity had begun to give way, more or less definitively, to the arguments of scientific rationalism" (Castle, *Female Thermometer*, p. 162), then the combination of rapid technological advances and performative economic imperatives have since accelerated circulation and expenditure so that excess has become the norm. The imperatives are now work harder, longer, faster, and spend more – more quickly, more extravagantly, more wastefully. Economy thus turns on desire, on the "metaphysical uncertainty regarding the object of human desire."[41] Pac-Man, the game figure consuming its way through a screen maze while avoiding lethal ghostly blobs, is the image of consumer desire, wanting "to feel whole," although "no conceivable quantity of dots is enough." Consumption cannot end: it "is doomed forever to metaphysical emptiness."[42] And endless desiring.

The intense pleasures of gaming and consuming absorb self-consciousness in flows. "Flow," for Anne Friedberg, is "the fluid subjectivity of the spectator-shopper" who "potentially allows for the performative enactment of labile identities under the aegis of the commodity's transformative power" (Latham in Gordon and Hollinger, *Blood Read*, p. 133). The consumer enjoys the same process, "purifying and expelling the unreconcilable and heterogeneous semiotic flows dumped on the person from the body of capital."[43] Late capitalism's "flow of desire" (and goods, images, information) extinguishes the possibility of a sacred, final Meaning: "flow involves the transcendence of meaningful units by a system whose only meaning is the fact of its global non-meaning." Incoherence and excess are not negative by-products of this system, but constitutive elements. The "incoherence" of cultural productions actively encourages the loss of agency, reason and will, "an invitation for individuals to exceed previous boundaries, to be in excess of an analytical, literally conservative control of productivity." Capital's flows encourage "excessive expenditure," promoting "a desire that is not sublimated or organized within the frame of an oedipalized family."[44]

Technology enhances the effects of incoherence on the consuming subject. For Paul Virilio, vision machines "would make derangement of the senses a permanent state."[45] Media overstimulation serves to "evacuate all judgement, any system of rational evaluation": "proper training of the younger generation is already ensured through the success of video games exclusively based on the virtuality of disappearance and elimination – reflex games that can induce total loss of consciousness in photosensitive subjects similar to the orgasmic effects of epilepsy."[46] Overstimulation shocks consciousness with its limit, emptying it out. Beneath the saturation of images lies a void: "why do we stand amazed before the assumed properties of the black holes of outer space? Aren't all our puncta of observation and all our quanta of action simply black holes of scientific thought? These are the black dots of a line wherein begin and end our rational representations."[47] At the limit of reason and science, black holes also form an absence incomprehensible yet basic to any system of understanding:

if forgetting is indispensable to the projectivity of imagination and the propagation of thought, the point is a point of reference of geometric projectivity only to the extent that it is a gap or lack, an absence of dimension, a black hole. As an obscurity, the point is as necessary to the revelation of physical appearances as the darkroom is to the objective appearances in photography and cinematographic photogram.[48]

Dark puncta constitute the possibility of imagination, thought, and projection. Concurrently they are also a locus of dissolution, a space of loss and mystery in which all meanings are consumed, all thought loses itself, all sense evaporates, and all boundaries collapse.

The black hole opened by the decline of the paternal figure and the loss of belief in metanarratives marks out a final limit and then substitutes a plunge into limitlessness, an ultimate meaning as meaninglessness. This is the black hole of postmodern culture and the ultimate horror of postmodern Gothic. Nothing escapes from a black hole, not even light. In 1796 a French mathematician – Pierre Simon, the Marquis de Laplace – proposed the possibility of "dark bodies," objects with so great a gravitational force that light would not be able to free itself from the pull. Since then, speculation, science, and fiction have developed the hypothesis with concepts of "escape velocity" and "event horizon": when a star contracts everything is trapped inside, unable to break the boundary – the event horizon – of the black hole where the speed of light is the velocity required to move beyond the gravitational pull. At the surface of the black hole, Newton's laws do not operate. Nothing is visible inside the perimeter of the event horizon and, as the star shrinks, it virtually disappears from the universe. In cultural terms, such a powerful consuming void forms the ultimate figure: postmodernity's impending collapse of all laws and distinctions. The light of enlightened modernity no longer has the speed to overcome the dead weight of its own history or advance in glorious progress. It is pulled back to the black hole of its uncertain, postmodern present and recycles Gothic images in an attempt to give form to anxiety and horror.

The neo-Gothic film *Event Horizon* (Anderson, 1997) situates itself at this point. Set in the near future, this tale of technological hubris looks back to a range of Gothic features and plots to give form to a horror emanating from beyond the universe. The story is straightforward: a spaceship, the *Event Horizon*, powered by a revolutionary "gravity drive," has reappeared in the solar system after being mysteriously lost seven years earlier on its maiden voyage. A rescue ship, the *Lewis and Clark*, is dispatched to investigate, with the inventor of the new drive, Dr. Weir, on board. He explains that the "gravity drive" was designed to generate an artificial black hole, folding space and erasing time and distance. At the same time, he claims to have no idea where the *Event Horizon* has been. Other mysteries surround the ship: an enigmatic last message initially understood as "save me" and, too late, recognized as "save yourselves"; video recordings that show the crew engaged in an orgy of violence and mutilation; and numerous spectral appearances. On board the deserted ship, described Gothically as a "tomb," events begin to move beyond the bounds of reason. Scanners are saturated with unspecific bioreadings, rescuers behold their own hallucinations realized before them, corpses come alive to bleed or burn again. The "gravity drive" seems to operate under its own volition. An incredible explanation is offered: the *Event Horizon* is alive, animated by a malevolent force intent on imprisoning the new arrivals. While the rescue crew vainly try to repair their own damaged ship, the scientist becomes possessed by his creation and sabotages their escape efforts. He has discovered that the ship's drive has torn a hole in the universe and crossed into a realm of pure chaos and evil, a dimension beyond the imagination and all human coherence.

A haunted house in space, an animated machine with diabolical powers feeding off the lives it torments, the *Event Horizon* is presented as a Gothic emanation of the abyss. Dr. Weir plays the Frankensteinian scientist who, having implemented a discovery that abolishes spatial and temporal boundaries and opens the universe to human control, finds the truth of his fantasy in actualized nightmare. The machine designed to master the heavens materializes an unimaginable hell, and hell lies within as much as without. The narrative plays upon the guilt and fear of its protagonists: Weir is haunted by the suicide of his wife, who appears repeatedly, her eyeless sockets manifestations of the soul he has lost in his work; the captain of the *Lewis and Clark* is pursued by memories of a crewman he had to leave in a fire. The images are animated by the ship; it seems to know the most intimate of secrets and the most private of fears. One crewman, pushed to attempt suicide by the ship, observes that it activates "the dark inside one from the other place." The black hole within individuals corresponds to the rent in the fabric of the universe.

As the "gravity drive" prepares to plunge everyone into the hell beyond the black hole, the captain sacrifices himself to save the surviving few by separating the engineering section from the rest of the ship. The survivors drift off, to be rescued seventy-two days later by another rescue ship, with all of them still in shock, still possessed by the horror they encountered. The drifting hulk and the second rescue manifest the problems the film has with ending: no climactic explosion destroys the evil thing which disappears into the unknown dimension from whence it came, no final expenditure declares an heroic and satisfying triumph. The possibility of any pleasurable *frisson* of terror is refused by the pervasive horror attendant on the last-ditch escape from the pull of the void. Despite the religious tones emphasized in the scientific realization of hell, no sacred structure erects itself in the face of ultimate dissolution. Nor is there any suggestion that the dangerously Promethean ambitions of human science can be arrested or inner demons overcome. Aroused from stasis, a survivor can only scream.

Suspended in space and not free of the horror, the world of this film, like postmodern Gothic generally, closes in the shadow of the black hole, unable to see beyond the event horizon. Though it pulls away from the void, there is, it seems, nowhere else to go but back again. It does not have the escape velocity to conjure up an idea of transcendence or an imaginable and inhabitable future. Images of a realized hell (an orgy of mutual violence, bodies ripped apart to a soundtrack of screams) turn the technological fulfillment of a temporally and spatially boundless fantasy into an eternity of excruciating pain, human degradation, and suffering. The black hole artificially created in the future returns upon the holes of the present and vacantly replays once religious and Gothic images from the past. The collapse of all distinctions between space and time, near and far, actual and imaginary, the limitless domain of pain, subjective and corporeal dissolution represented by the hell of the film: all this also signifies the realm of deregulated freedoms and choices of the present turned upside down. This formless space of violent consuming reflects the freedom to consume in our times as a void in which subjects are anxious, uncertain, subject to simulations and flows beyond human knowledge and control.

A sense of cultural exhaustion haunts the present. An inhuman future is shrouded in old Gothic trappings emptied of any strong charge; past images and forms are worn too thin to veil the gaping hole of objectless anxiety. Gothic fiction, which served as earlier modernity's black hole and has served up a range of objects and figures crystalizing anxiety into fear, has become too familiar after two centuries of repetitive mutation and seems incapable of shocking anew. Inured to Gothic shocks and terrors, contemporary culture recycles its images in the hope of finding a charge intense enough to stave off the black hole within and without, the one opened up by postmodernist fragmentation and plurality. Gothic figures, once giving form to the anxieties surrounding the transition from aristocratic to bourgeois culture, now disclose only the formlessness, the consuming void, underlying the flickering thrills of contemporary western simulations. Since they seem unable to envisage a future that is not finally cloaked in darkness, the only projections to be made offer us a weary and ominously doom-laden view.

NOTES

1 Steven Poole, *Trigger Happy: the Inner Life of Videogames* (London: Fourth Estate, 2000), p. 79.
2 Paul Keegan, "In the Line of Fire," *Guardian: G2* (1 June 1999): 2.
3 Poole, *Trigger Happy*, pp. 236–37.
4 ibid., p. 63.
5 Friedrich Kittler, *Discourse Networks 1800/1900*, trans. M. Metteer with C. Cullens (Stanford: Stanford University Press, 1990), p. 229.
6 Mladen Dolar, "La femme-machine," *New Formations* 23 (1994): 46.
7 Kittler, *Discourse Networks*, pp. 246–47.
8 Paul Virilio, *Open Sky*, trans. J. Rose (London: Verso, 1997), pp. 39–40.
9 Poole, *Trigger Happy*, p. 140.

10 Adrian MacKenzie, "Losing Time at the PlayStation: Realtime Individuation and the *Whatever Body*," *Cultural Values* 4 (2000): 257.
11 Richard Griffiths, "Novels" (1772) in Ioan Williams (ed.), *Novel and Romance, 1700–1800* (London: Routledge, 1970), p. 277.
12 Poole, *Trigger Happy*, p. 50.
13 Michel Foucault, *Language, Counter-Memory, Practice*, trans. D. F. Bouchard and S. Simon (Oxford: Blackwell, 1977), p. 34.
14 ibid., pp. 81–82.
15 Jacques Lacan, *The Psychoses: the Seminar of Jacques Lacan, Book III (1955–56)*, trans. R. Grigg (London: Routledge, 1993), p. 179.
16 Jacques Lacan, *Ecrits*, trans. A. Sheridan (London: Tavistock, 1977), pp. 310–11.
17 Jacques Lacan, "Desire and the Interpretation of Desire in *Hamlet*," *Yale French Studies* 55/56 (1977): 50.
18 Michelle Masse, "Psychoanalysis and the Gothic," in David Punter, *A Companion to the Gothic* (Oxford: Blackwell, 2000), pp. 236–37.
19 Steven Bruhm, "Picture this: Stephen King's Queer Gothic" in David Punter, ed., *A Companion to the Gothic* (Oxford: Blackwell, 2000), p. 278.
20 Review of *The Monk, Critical Review*, 2nd series, 19 (1797): 197.
21 See Jerrold E. Hogle, "The Ghost of the Counterfeit in the Genesis of the Gothic" in Allan Lloyd Smith and Victor Sage, eds., *Gothick Origins and Innovations* (Amsterdam: Rodopi, 1994), pp. 23–33.
22 Angela Carter, *Fireworks* (London: Quartet, 1974), p. 122. See also Beate Neumeier, "Postmodern Gothic: Angela Carter's Writing," in Victor Sage and Allan Lloyd Smith, eds., *Modern Gothic: a Reader* (Manchester: Manchester University Press, 1996), pp. 141–51.
23 Jean-François Lyotard, *The Postmodern Condition*, trans. G. Bennington and B. Massumi (Manchester: Manchester University Press, 1984), p. xxiv.
24 Kate Connolly, "Dracula Reclaimed," *Guardian: G2* (30 May 2000): 4.
25 Judith Roof, *Reproductions of Reproduction: Imaging Symbolic Change* (London: Routledge, 1996), p. 169.
26 Jan Gordon, "Sharper than a Serpent's Tooth: the Vampire in Search of its Mother," in Jan Gordon and Veronica Hollinger, eds., *Blood Read: the Vampire as Metaphor in Contemporary Culture* (Philadelphia: University of Pennsylvania Press, 1997), pp. 45–55.
27 Sandra Tomc, "Dieting and Damnation: Anne Rice's *Interview with the Vampire*," in Gordon and Hollinger, *Blood Read*, pp. 95–114.
28 Allucquere Rosanne Stone, *The War of Desire and Technology at the Close of the Mechanical Age* (Cambridge, MA: MIT Press, 1995), p. 178.
29 Karl Marx, *Capital*, trans. B. Fowkes (Harmondsworth: Penguin, 1976), I, 343.
30 Friedrich Kittler, "Romanticism – Psychoanalysis – Film: a Short History," in J. Johnston (ed.), *Literature Media Information* (The Netherlands: G and B Arts International, 1997), pp. 85–100.
31 Roof in *Reproductions of Reproduction*, pp. 10, 149.
32 Sadie Plant, "On the Matrix: Cyberfeminist Simulations," in R. Shields, ed., *Cultures of the Internet: Virtual Spaces, Real Histories, Living Bodies* (London: Sage, 1996), p. 183.
33 Jean Baudrillard, *The Transparency of Evil*, trans. J. Benedict (London: Verso, 1993), p. 7.

34 ibid., pp. 115, 113.
35 Barbara Creed, "Horror and the Monstrous-Feminine: an Imaginary Abjection" in J. Donald, ed., *Fantasy and Cinema* (London: BFI Publishing, 1989), pp. 63–89.
36 Chris Hables Gray, ed., *The Cyborg Handbook* (London: Routledge, 1995).
37 Keegan, "In the Line of Fire," p. 2.
38 Lyotard, *The Postmodern Condition*, p. 48.
39 Peter Buse, "Nintendo and Telos: Will You Ever Reach the End?," *Cultural Critique* (fall 1996): 164. See also Tania Modleski, "The Terror of Pleasure: the Contemporary Horror Film and Postmodern Theory" in Tania Modleski, ed., *Studies in Entertainment: Critical Approaches to Mass Culture* (Bloomington: Indiana University Press, 1986), pp. 155–66.
40 Jean-Joseph Goux, *Symbolic Economies: After Marx and Freud*, trans. J. C. Gage (Ithaca: Cornell University Press, 1990), p. 202.
41 Jean-Joseph Goux, "General Economics and Postmodern Capitalism," *Yale French Studies* 78 (1990): 211.
42 Poole, *Trigger Happy*, pp. 192–93.
43 Rhonda Lieberman, "Shopping Disorders" in Brian Massumi, ed., *The Politics of Everyday Fear* (Minneapolis: University of Minnesota Press, 1993), pp. 246–47.
44 Dana Polan, "Brief Encounters: Mass Culture and the Evacuation of Sense" in Modleski, *Studies in Entertainment*, pp. 179, 183, 178.
45 Paul Virilio, *The Aesthetics of Disappearance*, trans. P. Beitchman (New York: Semiotext[e], 1991), p. 92.
46 Paul Virilio, *The Art of the Motor*, trans. J. Rose (Minneapolis: University of Minnesota Press, 1995), p. 74.
47 Paul Virilio, *The Lost Dimension* (New York: Semiotext[e], 1991), p. 67.
48 ibid., pp. 103–04.

Major Gothic texts

Alexis, Jacques-Stephen. "Chronique d'un faux amour" in *Romancero aux étoiles*. Paris: Gallimard, 1960.

Austen, Jane. *Northanger Abbey* (1818), ed. Marilyn Butler. Harmondsworth: Penguin, 1995.

Beckford, William. *Vathek* (1786), the two French editions with translation by Samuel Henley and introduction by Robert J. Gemmett. Delmar, NY: Scholars' Facsimiles, 1972.

Blatty, William Peter. *The Exorcist*. Toronto: Bantam, 1971.

Bloch, Robert. *Psycho*. New York: Tom Doherty Associates, 1959.

Brontë, Charlotte. *Jane Eyre* (1847), ed. Ian Jack and Margaret Smith. Oxford: Oxford University Press, 1969.

Brontë, Charlotte. *Villette* (1853), ed. Herbert Rosengarten and Margaret Smith. Oxford: Oxford University Press, 1984.

Brontë, Emily. *Wuthering Heights* (1847), ed. Hilda Marsden and Ian Jack. Oxford: Oxford University Press, 1976.

Brown, Charles Brockden. *Edgar Huntly or, Memoirs of a Sleep-Walker* (1799), ed. Norman Grabo. Harmondsworth: Penguin, 1988.

Brown, Charles Brockden. *Wieland, or the Transformation, and Memoirs of Carwin the Biloquist* (1798), ed. Jay Fliegelman. Harmondsworth: Penguin, 1991.

Burke, Edmund. *A Philosophical Enquiry into the Origin of our Ideas of the Sublime and Beautiful* (1757), ed. Adam Phillips. World's Classics. Oxford: Oxford University Press, 1990.

Carter, Angela. *The Bloody Chamber*. London: Victor Gollancz, 1979.

Clitandre, Pierre. *La Cathédrale du mois d'août*. Port-au-Prince, Haiti: Fardin, 1980.

Collins, Wilkie. *The Woman in White* (1860), ed. John Sutherland. Oxford: Oxford University Press, 1998.

Dacre, Charlotte. *Zofloya, or The Moor* (1805), ed. Adriana Craciun. Petersburgh, Ontario: Broadview Press, 1997.

Depestre, René. *Hadriana dans tous mes rêves*. Paris: Gallimard, 1988.

De Lisser, Herbert George. *The White Witch of Rosehall* (1929), 3rd edn. London: E. Benn, 1958.

Dickens, Charles. *Little Dorrit* (1855–57), ed. Harvey Peter Sucksmith. Oxford: Clarendon, 1978.

Dinesen, Isak (Karen Blixen). *Seven Gothic Tales* (1934). New York: Random House, 1962.

Faulkner, William. *Absalom! Absalom!: The Corrected Text* (1936). New York: Random House/Vintage, 1986.

Faulkner, William. *Light in August* (1932), introduction by Cleanth Brooks. New York: Random House/Modern Library, 1968.

Gilman, Charlotte Perkins. "The Yellow Wallpaper" (1892) in *The Charlotte Perkins Gilman Reader*, ed. Ann J. Lane. New York: Random House/Pantheon, 1980.

Godwin, William. *Caleb Williams* (1794), ed. David McCracken. Oxford: Oxford University Press, 1970.

Harris, Thomas. *The Silence of the Lambs*. New York: St. Martin's Press, 1988.

Hawthorne, Nathaniel. *Novels*, ed. Millicent Bell. New York: Library of America, 1983.

Hodgson, William Hope. *"The House on the Borderland" and Other Novels*. Soule City, WI: Arkham House, 1946.

Jackson, Shirley. *The Haunting of Hill House* (1959). Harmondsworth: Penguin, 1984.

James, Henry. *The Turn of the Screw* (1898), ed. Peter G. Beidler. Case Studies in Contemporary Criticism. Boston: St. Martin's/Bedford, 1995.

Kincaid, Jamaica. *The Autobiography of My Mother*. New York: Farrar, Strauss, and Giroux, 1996.

King, Stephen. *Carrie*. New York: Doubleday, 1974.

King, Stephen. *Misery*. Scarborough, Ontario: New American Library, 1988.

King, Stephen. *Pet Sematary*. Harmondsworth: Penguin, 1983.

King, Stephen. *'Salem's Lot*. New York: Doubleday, 1975.

King, Stephen. *The Shining*. Harmondsworth: Penguin, 1977.

Kipling, Rudyard. "The Mark of the Beast" (1890) in *Life's Handicap*. Harmondsworth: Penguin, 1989.

Le Fanu, Joseph Sheridan. *Best Ghost Stories of J. S. Le Fanu*, ed. E. F. Bleiler. New York: Dover, 1964.

Le Fanu, Joseph Sheridan. *Uncle Silas* (1864), ed. W. J. McCormack. Oxford: Oxford University Press, 1981.

Lee, Sophia. *The Recess* (1783–85), introduced by Devendra P. Varma. 3 vols. New York: Arno, 1972.

Levin, Ira. *Rosemary's Baby* (1967). New York: Dell, 1968.

Lewis, Matthew G. *The Monk* (1796), ed. Howard Anderson. Rev. edn. Oxford: Oxford University Press, 1997.

Machen, Arthur. *The House of Souls*. New York: Alfred A. Knopf, 1922.

Machen, Arthur. *Tales of Horror and the Supernatural*. New York: Alfred A. Knopf, 1948.

Marsh, Richard. *The Beetle* (1897), in *Victorian Villainies*, ed. Graham and Hugh Greene. New York: Viking, 1984.

Maturin, Charles Robert. *Melmoth the Wanderer* (1820), ed. Douglas Grant. Rev. edn, introduced by Chris Baldick. Oxford: Oxford University Press, 1989.

Melville, Herman. *Pierre or, The Ambiguities* (1852), ed. Henry A. Murray, introduced by Lawrence Thompson. New York: New American Library, 1964.

Montero, Mayra. "Corinne, Amiable Girl" (1991), trans. Lizabeth Paravinisi-Gebert, *Callaloo* 17:3 (summer 1994): 836–46.

Montero, Mayra. *In the Palm of Darkness* (1995), trans. Edith Grossman. New York: Harper Flamingo, 1999.

Montero, Mayra. *The Red of his Shadow* (1992), trans. Edith Grossman. New York: Ecco Press, 2001.

Morrison, Toni. *Beloved* (1987). Harmondsworth and New York: Penguin/Plume, 1988.

Naipaul, V. S. *Guerrillas* (1975). New York: Random House/Vintage, 1980.

Poe, Edgar Allan. *Poetry and Tales*, ed. Patrick F. Quinn. New York: Library of America, 1984.

Polidori, John William. *The Vampyre* and *Ernestus, Bechthold; or The Modern Oedipus* (1819), ed. D. L. Macdonald and Kathleen Scherf. Toronto: University of Toronto Press, 1994.

Radcliffe, Ann. *The Italian* (1797), ed. Robert Miles. Harmondsworth: Penguin, 2000.

Radcliffe, Ann. *The Mysteries of Udolpho* (1794), ed. Bonamy Dobrée and Frederick Garber. Oxford: Oxford University Press, 1980.

Radcliffe, Ann. *The Romance of the Forest* (1791), ed. Chloe Chard. Oxford: Oxford University Press, 1986.

Reeve, Clara. *The Old English Baron* (1778), ed. James Trainer. Oxford: Oxford University Press, 1967.

Rhys, Jean. *Wide Sargasso Sea* (1966). New York: Norton, 1982.

Rice, Anne. *Interview with the Vampire*. New York: Ballantine, 1976.

Scott, Walter. *The Antiquary* (1816), ed. David Hewett. Edinburgh: Edinburgh University Press, 1995.

Scott, Walter. *The Bride of Lammermoor* (1819), introduced by W. M. Parker. Everyman's Library. London: Dent, 1976.

Seltzer, David. *The Omen*. New York: Signet, 1976.

Shelley, Mary Wollstonecraft. *Frankenstein or The Modern Prometheus: The 1818 Text*, ed. James Rieger. Phoenix edition. Chicago: University of Chicago Press, 1982.

Stevenson, Robert Louis. *Dr. Jekyll and Mr. Hyde* (1886), introduced by Vladimir Nabokov. Harmondsworth and New York: Penguin/Signet, 1987.

Stoker, Bram. *Dracula* (1897), ed. Nina Auerbach and David J. Skal. Norton Critical edition. New York: Norton, 1997.

Straub, Peter. *Ghost Story*. London: Jonathan Cape, 1979.

Straub, Peter. *Houses Without Doors*. Harmondsworth: Penguin, 1991.

Updike, John. *The Witches of Eastwick* (1984). Harmondsworth: Penguin, 1985.

Walpole, Horace. *The Castle of Otranto: a Gothic Story* (1764–65), ed. W. S. Lewis and E. J. Clery. Rev. edn. Oxford: Oxford University Press, 1996.

Wells, H. G. *The Island of Dr. Moreau* (1896). New York: Signet, 1988.

Wilde, Oscar. *The Picture of Dorian Gray* (1891), ed. Isobel Murray. Oxford: Oxford University Press, 1974.

Wolf, Leonard (comp., ed., and trans.) *The Essential Phantom of the Opera, including the Complete Novel by Gaston Leroux* (1910). Harmondsworth and New York: Penguin/Plume, 1996.

Important collections of Gothic writing

Baldick, Chris (ed.) *The Oxford Book of Gothic Tales*. Oxford: Oxford University Press, 1992.

Clery, E. J., and Robert Miles (eds.) *Gothic Documents: a Sourcebook, 1700–1820*. Manchester: Manchester University Press, 2000.

Cox, Jeffrey N. (ed.) *Seven Gothic Dramas, 1789–1825*. Columbus: Ohio State University Press, 1992.

Crow, Charles (ed.) *American Gothic: an Anthology, 1787–1916*. Oxford: Blackwell, 1999.

Dickens, Charles, and others. *The Haunted House* (1859). Windsor: Netka, 1998.

Franceschina, John (ed.) *Sisters of Gore: Seven Gothic Melodramas by British Women, 1790–1843*. New York: Garland, 1997.

Hale, Terry (ed. and trans.) *The Dedalus Book of French Horror: The Nineteenth Century*. Cambridge: Dedalus, 1998.

Kessler, Joan C. (ed. and trans.) *Demons of the Night: Tales of the Fantastic, Madness, and the Supernatural from Nineteenth-Century France*. Chicago: University of Chicago Press, 1995.

Morrow, Bradford, and Patrick McGrath (eds.) *The New Gothic: a Collection of Contemporary Gothic Fiction*. New York: Random House, 1991.

Major studies of the Gothic

Aiken, Susan Hardy. "Gothic Typographies" in *Isak Dinesen and the Engendering of Narrative*. Chicago: University of Chicago Press, 1990. 67–83.

Auerbach, Nina. *Our Vampires, Ourselves*. Chicago: University of Chicago Press, 1995.

Backscheider, Paula. "Gothic Drama and National Crisis" in *Spectacular Politics: Theatrical Power and Mass Culture in Early Modern England*. Baltimore: Johns Hopkins University Press, 1993. 149–233.

Becker, Susanne. *Gothic Forms of Feminine Fictions*. Manchester: Manchester University Press, 1999.

Birkhead, Edith. *The Tale of Terror: a Study of Gothic Romance*. London: Constable, 1921.

Botting, Fred. *Gothic*. Critical Idioms. London: Routledge, 1996.

Botting, Fred. *Sex, Machines, and Navels: Fiction, Fantasy, and History in the Future Present*. Manchester: Manchester University Press, 1999.

Brantlinger, Patrick. *The Reading Lesson: the Threat of Mass Literacy in Nineteenth-Century British Fiction*. Bloomington: Indiana University Press, 1998.

Brown, Marshall. "A Philosophical View of the Gothic Novel." *Studies in Romanticism* 26 (1987): 275–301.

Bruhm, Steven. *Gothic Bodies: the Politics of Pain in Romantic Fiction*. Philadelphia: University of Pennsylvania Press, 1994.

Bruhm, Steven. "The Gothic in a Culture of Narcissism" in *Reflecting Narcissus: a Queer Aesthetic*. Minneapolis: University of Minnesota Press, 2001. 144–73.

Carroll, Noël. *The Philosophy of Horror, or Paradoxes of the Heart*. New York: Routledge, 1990.

Castle, Terry. *The Female Thermometer: Eighteenth-Century Culture and the Invention of the Uncanny*. Oxford: Oxford University Press, 1995.

Cavaliero, Glen. *The Supernatural and English Fiction*. Oxford: Oxford University Press, 1995.

Clemens, Valdine. *The Return of the Repressed: Gothic Horror from* The Castle of Otranto *to* Alien. Albany: State University of New York Press, 1999.

Clery, E. J. *The Rise of Supernatural Fiction, 1762–1800*. Cambridge Studies in Romanticism. Cambridge: Cambridge University Press, 1995.

Day, William Patrick. *In the Circles of Fear and Desire: a Study of Gothic Fantasy*. Chicago: University of Chicago Press, 1985.

De Bolla, Peter. *The Discourse of the Sublime: Readings in History, Aesthetics, and the Subject*. Oxford: Blackwell, 1989.

DeLamotte, Eugenia C. *Perils of the Night: a Feminist Study of Nineteenth-Century Gothic*. Oxford: Oxford University Press, 1990.

Edmundson, Mark. *Nightmare on Main Street: Angels, Sadomasochism, and the Culture of Gothic*. Cambridge, MA: Harvard University Press, 1997.

Ellis, Kate Ferguson. *The Contested Castle: Gothic Novels and the Subversion of Domestic Ideology*. Urbana: University of Illinois Press, 1989.

Evans, Bertrand. *Gothic Drama from Walpole to Shelley*. University of California Publications in English, 18. Berkeley: University of California Press, 1947.

Fiedler, Leslie. "Charles Brockden Brown and the Invention of the American Gothic" in *Love and Death in the American Novel*. Rev. edn. New York: Dell, 1966. 126–61.

Frankl, Paul. *The Gothic: Literary Sources and Interpretations Through Eight Centuries*. Princeton: Princeton University Press, 1960.

Freud, Sigmund. *Totem and Taboo* (1913) in *The Standard Edition of the Complete Psychological Works of Sigmund Freud*, trans. James Strachey. London: Hogarth, 1955. XIII, 1–162.

Freud, Sigmund. "The Uncanny" (1919) in *Collected Papers*, ed. and trans. Joan Riviere et al. New York: Basic Books, 1959. IV, 368–407.

Gamer, Michael. *Romanticism and the Gothic: Genre, Reception, and Canon Formation*. Cambridge Studies in Romanticism. Cambridge: Cambridge University Press, 2000.

Geary, Robert. *The Supernatural in Gothic Fiction: Horror, Belief, and Literary Change*. Lewiston, NY: Edwin Mellon, 1992.

Gelder, Ken. *Reading the Vampire*. London: Routledge, 1994.

Gilbert, Sandra, and Susan Gubar. *The Madwoman in the Attic: The Woman Writer and the Nineteenth-Century Literary Imagination*. New Haven: Yale University Press, 1979.

Goddu, Teresa A. *Gothic America: Narrative, History, and the Nation*. New York: Columbia University Press, 1997.

Hadley, Michael. *The Undiscovered Genre: a Search for the German Gothic Novel*. Berne: Peter Lang, 1977.

Haggerty, George E. *Gothic Fiction/Gothic Form*. University Park: Pennsylvania State University Press, 1989.

Haggerty, George E. "Literature and Homosexuality in the Late Eighteenth Century: Walpole, Beckford, and Lewis." *Studies in the Novel* 18 (1986): 341–52.

Halberstam, Judith. *Skin Shows: Gothic Horror and the Technology of Monsters.* Durham, NC: Duke University Press, 1995.

Heilman, Robert B. "Charlotte Brontë's New Gothic" in *From Jane Austen to Joseph Conrad,* ed. R. C. Rathburn and Martin Steinman. Minneapolis: University of Minnesota Press, 1958. 118–32.

Heller, Tamar. *Dead Secrets: Wilkie Collins and the Female Gothic.* New Haven: Yale University Press, 1992.

Heller, Terry. *The Delights of Terror: an Aesthetics of the Tale of Terror.* Urbana: University of Illinois Press, 1987.

Hendershot, Cyndy. *The Animal Within: Masculinity and the Gothic.* Ann Arbor: University of Michigan Press, 1998.

Henderson, Andrea. "'An Embarrassing Subject': Use Value and Exchange Value in Early Gothic Characterization" in *At the Limits of Romanticism: Essays in Cultural, Feminist, and Materialist Criticism,* ed. Mary A. Favret and Nicola J. Watson. Bloomington: Indiana University Press, 1994. 225–45.

Hoeveler, Diane Long. *Gothic Feminism: the Professionalization of Gender from Charlotte Smith to the Brontës.* University Park: Pennsylvania State University Press, 1988.

Hogle, Jerrold E. "*Frankenstein* as Neo-Gothic: From the Ghost of the Counterfeit to The Monster of Abjection" in *Romanticism, History, and the Possibilities of Genre,* ed. Tilottama Rajan and Julia Wright. Cambridge: Cambridge University Press, 1998. 176–210.

Hogle, Jerrold E. "The Struggle for a Dichotomy: Abjection in Jekyll and his Interpreters" in *Dr. Jekyll and Mr. Hyde After One Hundred Years,* ed. William Veeder and Gordon Hirsch. Chicago: University of Chicago Press, 1988. 161–207.

Hogle, Jerrold E. *The Undergrounds of* The Phantom of the Opera: *Sublimation and the Gothic in Leroux's Novel and its Progeny.* New York: St. Martin's Press/Palgrave, 2002.

Holland, Norman N., and Leona F. Sherman. "Gothic Possibilities." *New Literary History* 8 (1977): 279–94.

Howard, Jacqueline. *Reading Gothic Fiction: a Bakhtinian Approach.* Oxford: Clarendon Press, 1994.

Howells, Coral Ann. *Love, Mystery, and Misery: Feeling in Gothic Fiction.* University of London: Athlone Press, 1978.

Hughes, Winifred. *The Maniac in the Cellar: Sensation Novels of the 1860s.* Princeton: Princeton University Press, 1980.

Hume, Robert D. "Gothic Versus Romantic: a Revaluation of the Gothic Novel." *PMLA* 84 (1969): 282–90.

Hurley, Kelly. *The Gothic Body: Sexuality, Materialism, and Degeneration at the Fin de Siècle.* Cambridge Studies in Nineteenth-Century Literature and Culture. Cambridge: Cambridge University Press, 1996.

Jackson, Rosemary. *Fantasy: the Literature of Subversion.* London: Methuen, 1981.

Kahane, Claire. "The Gothic Mirror" in *The (M)other Tongue: Essays in Feminist Psychoanalytic Interpretation,* ed. Shirley Nelson Garner, Kahane, and Madelon Sprengnether. Ithaca, NY: Cornell University Press, 1985. 334–51.

Kelly, Gary. "Romantic Fiction" in *The Cambridge Companion to British Romanticism,* ed. Stuart Curran. Cambridge: Cambridge University Press, 1993. 196–215.

Kiely, Robert. *The Romantic Novel in England*. Cambridge, MA: Harvard University Press, 1972.

Kilgour, Maggie. *The Rise of the Gothic Novel*. London: Routledge, 1995.

King, Stephen. *Stephen King's Danse Macabre*. New York: Everest House, 1982.

Kliger, Samuel. *The Goths in England: a Study in Seventeenth- and Eighteenth-Century Thought*. Cambridge, MA: Harvard University Press, 1952.

Kristeva, Julia. *Powers of Horror: an Essay on Abjection* (1980), trans. Leon S. Roudiez. New York: Columbia University Press, 1982.

Lévy, Maurice. *Le Roman "Gothique" Anglais, 1764–1824*. Toulouse: Association des Publications de la Faculté des Lettres et Sciences Humaines, 1968.

Lovecraft, H. P. *Supernatural Horror in Literature*. New York: Dover, 1973.

MacAndrew, Elizabeth. *The Gothic Tradition in Fiction*. New York: Columbia University Press, 1979.

Madoff, Mark. "The Useful Myth of Gothic Ancestry." *Studies in Eighteenth-Century Culture* 8 (1979): 337–50.

Malchow, H. L. *Gothic Images of Race in Nineteenth-Century Britain*. Stanford, CA: Stanford University Press, 1996.

Massé, Michelle A. *In the Name of Love: Women, Masochism, and the Gothic*. Ithaca, NY: Cornell University Press, 1992.

Mighall, Robert. *A Geography of Victorian Gothic Fiction: Mapping History's Nightmare*. Oxford: Oxford University Press, 1999.

Milbank, Alison. *Daughters of the House: Modes of the Gothic in Victorian Fiction*. London: Macmillan, 1992.

Miles, Robert. *Ann Radcliffe: The Great Enchantress*. Manchester: Manchester University Press, 1995.

Miles, Robert. *Gothic Writing, 1750–1820: a Genealogy*. London: Routledge, 1993.

Mishra, Vijay. *The Gothic Sublime*. Albany: State University of New York Press, 1994.

Monleon, Jose B. *A Specter is Haunting Europe: a Sociological Approach to the Fantastic*. Princeton: Princeton University Press, 1990.

Moretti, Franco. "Dialectic of Fear" in *Signs Taken for Wonders: Essays in the Sociology of Literary Forms*, trans. Susan Fischer et al. London: Verso, 1983. 83–108.

Navarette, Susan J. *The Shape of Fear: Horror and the Fin de Siècle Culture of Decadence*. Lexington: University Press of Kentucky, 1998.

Palmer, Pauline. *Lesbian Gothic: Transgressive Fictions*. London: Cassell, 1999.

Paulson, Ronald. "Gothic Fiction and the French Revolution." *ELH* 48 (1981): 532–54.

Pirie, David. *A Heritage of Horror: the English Gothic Cinema, 1946–1972*. London: Gordon Frasier, 1973.

Platzner, Robert. "Gothic Versus Romantic: a Rejoinder." *PMLA* 86 (1971): 266–74.

Prawer, S. S. *Caligari's Children: the Film as Tale of Terror*. Oxford: Oxford University Press, 1980.

Punter, David. *The Literature of Terror: a History of Gothic Fictions from 1765 to the Present Day*. Second edn. 2 vols. London: Longman, 1996.

Radway, Janice A. *Reading the Romance: Women, Patriarchy, and Popular Literature*. Chapel Hill: University of North Carolina Press, 1984.

Railo, Eino. *The Haunted Castle: a Study of the Elements of English Romanticism*. London: Dutton, 1927.

Ringe, Donald A. *American Gothic: Imagination and Reason in Nineteenth-Century Fiction*. Lexington: University Press of Kentucky, 1982.

Sage, Victor. *Horror Fiction in the Protestant Tradition*. London: Macmillan, 1988.

Schmitt, Cannon. *Alien Nation: Nineteenth-Century Gothic Fictions and English Nationality*. Philadelphia: University of Pennsylvania Press, 1997.

Sedgwick, Eve Kosofsky. *Between Men: English Literature and Male Homosocial Desire*. New York: Columbia University Press, 1985.

Sedgwick, Eve Kosofsky. *The Coherence of Gothic Conventions* (1980). New York: Methuen, 1986.

Skal, David J. *The Monster Show: a Cultural History of Horror*. New York: Norton, 1993.

Spencer, Kathleen. "Purity and Danger: *Dracula*, the Urban Gothic, and the Late Victorian Degeneracy Crisis." *ELH* 59 (1992): 179–225.

Stuart, Roxana. *Stage Blood: Vampires of the Nineteenth-Century Stage*. Bowling Green, OH: Pennsylvania State University Press, 1994.

Summers, Montague. *The Gothic Quest: a History of the Gothic Novel*. London: Fortune Press, 1938.

Todorov, Tzvetan. *The Fantastic: a Structural Approach to a Literary Genre* (1971), trans. Richard Howard. Cleveland: Press of Case Western Reserve University, 1973.

Tompkins, J. M. S. *The Popular Novel in England, 1770–1800*. London: Constable, 1932.

Tropp, Martin. *Images of Fear: How Horror Stories Helped Shape Modern American Culture, 1818–1919*. Jefferson, NC: McFarland, 1990.

Twitchell, James B. *Dreadful Pleasures: an Anatomy of Modern Horror*. Oxford: Oxford University Press, 1985.

Varma, Devendra P. *The Gothic Flame: Being a History of the Gothic Novel in England*. London: Arthur Barker, 1957.

Watt, James. *Contesting the Gothic: Fiction, Genre, and Cultural Conflict, 1764–1832*. Cambridge Studies in Romanticism. Cambridge: Cambridge University Press, 1999.

Wiesenfarth, Joseph. *Gothic Manners and the Classic English Novel*. Madison: University of Wisconsin Press, 1988.

Williams, Anne. *Art of Darkness: a Poetics of Gothic*. Chicago: University of Chicago Press, 1995.

Wilt, Judith. *Ghosts of the Gothic: Austen, Eliot, and Lawrence*. Princeton: Princeton University Press, 1980.

Winter, Kari J. *Subjects of Slavery, Agents of Change: Women and Power in Gothic Novels and Slave Narratives, 1790–1865*. Athens: University of Georgia Press, 1992.

Wolstenholme, Susan. *Gothic (Re)visions: Writing Women as Readers*. Albany: State University of New York Press, 1993.

Wood, Robin. "An Introduction to the American Horror Film." *American Nightmare: Essays on the Horror Film*, ed. Andrew Britton et al. Toronto: Festival of Festivals, 1979. 7–28.

Žižek, Slavoj. *A Plague of Fantasies*. London: Verso, 1997.

Important collections of criticism on the Gothic

Bloom, Clive (ed.) *Gothic Horror: a Reader's Guide from Poe to King and Beyond*. New York: St. Martin's Press, 1998.

Botting, Fred (ed.) *The Gothic*. English Association *Essays and Studies*. Cambridge: Boydell and Brewer, 2001.

Byron, Glennis, and David Punter (eds.) *Spectral Readings: Towards a Gothic Geography*. London: Macmillan, 1999.

Fleenor, Julianne E. (ed.) *The Female Gothic*. Montreal: Eden Press, 1983.

Gordon, Jan, and Veronica Hollinger (eds.) *Blood Read: the Vampire as Metaphor in Contemporary Culture*. Philadelphia: University of Pennsylvania Press, 1997.

Graham, Kenneth W. (ed.) *Gothic Fictions: Prohibition/Transgression*. New York: AMS Press, 1989.

Grant, Barry Keith (ed.) *The Dread of Difference: Gender and the Horror Film*. Austin: University of Texas Press, 1996.

Hoeveler, Diane Long, and Tamar Heller (eds.) *Approaches to Teaching Gothic Fiction: the British and American Traditions*. New York: Modern Language Association, 2002.

Horner, Avril (ed.) *European Gothic: a Spirited Exchange, 1760–1960*. Manchester: Manchester University Press, 2002.

Magistrale, Tony, and Michael A. Morrison (eds.) *A Dark Night's Dreaming: Contemporary American Horror Fiction*. Columbia: University of South Carolina Press, 1996.

Martin, Robert K., and Eric Savoy (eds.) *American Gothic: New Interventions in a National Narrative*. Iowa City: University of Iowa Press, 1998.

Miles, Robert, and William Hughes (eds.) *Gothic Studies*. Journal of the International Gothic Association. 1:1 (1999–).

Mulvey-Roberts, Marie (ed.) *The Handbook to Gothic Literature*. London: Macmillan, 1998.

Punter, David (ed.) *A Companion to the Gothic*. Blackwell Companions to Literature and Culture. Oxford: Blackwell, 2000.

Riquelme, John Paul (ed.) *Gothic and Modernism*. Special issue of *Modern Fiction Studies* 46 (2000): 585–799.

Sage, Victor (ed.) *The Gothic Novel: a Casebook*. London: Longman, 1990.

Sage, Victor, and Allan Lloyd Smith (eds.) *Modern Gothic: a Reader*. Manchester: Manchester University Press, 1996.

Smith, Allan Lloyd, and Victor Sage (eds.) *Gothick Origins and Innovations*. Amsterdam: Rodopi, 1994.

Sullivan, Jack (ed.) *The Penguin Encyclopedia of Horror and the Supernatural*. Harmondsworth: Penguin, 1986.

Thompson, G. R. (ed.) *The Gothic Imagination: Essays in Dark Romanticism*. Olympia: Washington State University Press, 1974.

Wolf, Leonard. *Horror: a Connoisseur's Guide to Literature and Film*. New York: Facts on File, 1989.

Bibliographies on the Gothic

Barron, Neil (ed.) *Horror Literature: a Reader's Guide*. New York: Garland, 1990.
Fisher, Benjamin F., IV. *The Gothic's Gothic: Study Aids to the Tale of Terror*. New York: Garland, 1987.
Frank, Frederick S. *The First Gothics: a Critical Guide to the English Gothic Novel*. New York: Garland, 1987.
Frank, Frederick S. *Gothic Fiction: a Masterlist of Criticism and Research*. Westport, CT: Meckler, 1987.
Frank, Frederick S. *Guide to the Gothic: an Annotated Bibliography of Criticism*. Metuchen, NJ: Scarecrow Press, 1984.
Frank, Frederick S. *Guide to the Gothic II: an Annotated Bibliography of Criticism, 1983–1993*. Lanham, MD: Scarecrow Press, 1995.
Frank, Frederick S. *Through the Pale Door: a Guide to and Through the American Gothic*. Westport, CT: Greenwood Press, 1990.
Garside, Peter, James Raven, and Rainer Showerling (eds.) *The English Novel 1770–1829: a Bibliographical Guide*. 2 vols. Oxford: Oxford University Press, 2000.
McNutt, D. J. *The Eighteenth-Century Gothic Novel: an Annotated Bibliography of Criticism and Selected Texts*. Folkestone: Dawson, 1975.
Raven, James. "The Novel Comes of Age" in Garside et al. (eds.), *English Novel*, I, 15–121.
Spector, Robert D. *The English Gothic: a Bibliographic Guide to Writers from Horace Walpole to Mary Shelley*. Westport, CT: Greenwood Press, 1984.
Tracy, Ann B. *The Gothic Novel, 1790–1830: Plot Summaries and Index to Motifs*. Lexington: University Press of Kentucky, 1981.

FILMOGRAPHY

Allen, Lewis, Dir. *The Uninvited* (1944). Paramount. Prod. Charles Brackett.
Anderson, Paul, Dir. *Event Horizon* (1997). Paramount. Prods. Lawrence Gordon et al.
Browning, Tod, Dir. *Dracula* (1931). Universal. Prod. Carl Laemmle, Jr.
Castle, William, Dir. *House on Haunted Hill* (1958). Columbia. Prod. Castle.
Coppola, Francis Ford, Dir. *Bram Stoker's Dracula* (1992). Columbia. Prod. Fredric S. Fuchs.
Corman, Roger, Dir. *The House of Usher* (1960). American International. Prod. Corman.
Corman, Roger, Dir. *The Masque of the Red Death* (1964). American International. Prod. Corman.
Corman, Roger, Dir. *The Pit and the Pendulum* (1961). American International. Prod. Corman.
Fisher, Terence, Dir. *The Curse of Frankenstein* (1957). Hammer. Prod. Anthony Hinds.
Fisher, Terence, Dir. *Dracula* (a.k.a. *Horror of Dracula*) (1958). Hammer. Prod. Anthony Hinds.
Freund, Karl, Dir. *The Mummy* (1932). Universal. Prod. Carl Laemmle, Jr.
Friedkin, William, Dir. *The Exorcist* (1973). Warner Bros. Prod. William Peter Blatty.
Halperin, Victor, Dir. *White Zombie* (1932). United Artists. Prod. Edward Halperin.
Hillyer, Lambert, Dir. *Dracula's Daughter* (1932). Universal. Prods. Carl Laemmle, Jr. and E. M. Asher.
Hitchcock, Alfred, Dir. *Psycho* (1960). Paramount/Universal. Prod. Hitchcock.
Hitchcock, Alfred, Dir. *Rebecca* (1940). United Artists. Prod. David O. Selznick.
Jeunet, Jean-Pierre, Dir. *Alien Resurrection* (1997). 20th-Century Fox. Prods. Gordon Carroll et al.
Julian, Rupert, Dir. *The Phantom of the Opera* (1925). Universal. Prod. Carl Laemmle.
Lang, Fritz, Dir. *Secret Beyond the Door* (1948). Universal. Prod. Lang.
Lee, Rowland V., Dir. *Son of Frankenstein* (1939). Universal. Prod. Rowland V. Lee.
Lynch, David, Dir. *Blue Velvet* (1986). DeLaurentiis Entertainment Group. Prod. Lynch.
Mamoulian, Reuben, Dir. *Dr. Jekyll and Mr. Hyde* (1931). Paramount. Prod. Mamoulian.
Murnau, F. W. Dir. *Nosferatu* (1922). Prods. Albin Grau and Enrico Dieckmann.

Polanski, Roman, Dir. *Rosemary's Baby* (1968). Paramount. Prod. William Castle.

Romero, George, Dir. *Dawn of the Dead* (1978). Laurel Group. Prod. Richard P. Rubinstein.

Scott, Ridley. Dir. *Alien* (1979). 20th-Century Fox. Prods. Gordon Carroll et al.

Siodmak, Robert, Dir. *The Spiral Staircase* (1946). RKO. Prod. Dore Schary.

Tourneur, Jacques, Dir. *Cat People* (1942). RKO. Prod. Val Lewton.

Tourneur, Jacques, Dir. *Out of the Past* (a.k.a. *Build My Gallows High*) (1947). RKO. Prod. Warren Duff.

Tourneur, Jacques, Dir. *I Walked with a Zombie* (1943). RKO. Prod. Val Lewton.

Waggner, George, Dir. *The Wolf Man* (1941). Universal. Prod. Waggner.

Whale, James, Dir. *Bride of Frankenstein* (1935). Universal. Prod. Carl Laemmle, Jr.

Whale, James, Dir. *Frankenstein* (1931). Universal. Prod. Laemmle, Jr.

Whale, James, Dir. *The Old Dark House* (1932). Universal. Prod. Laemmle, Jr.

Wilder, Billy, Dir. *Sunset Boulevard* (1950). Paramount. Prod. Charles Brackett.

Wise, Robert, and Gunther von Fritsch, Dirs. *The Curse of the Cat People* (1944). RKO. Prod. Val Lewton.

Wise, Robert, Dir. *The Haunting* (1963). MGM. Prod. Wise.

INDEX

abhuman, 190, 192–3, 195–7, 198, 202
abjection, 7–8, 9, 10, 16–17, 170–1,
    174, 181, 185, 210–11, 223, 225,
    266, 289, 291
Abraham, Nicolas, 174
Addison, Joseph, 27–8
Aikin, Anna Laetitia and John
    Miscellaneous Pieces in Prose, 31–2
    "Pleasure Derived from Objects of
    Terror, On The," 32, 42, 43
    "Sir Bertrand," 32, 42
Ainsworth, William Harrison, 148,
    149, 158
    Guy Fawkes, 146
    Lancashire Witches, The, 146
    Tower of London, The, 146–7
    Windsor Castle, 146–7
Alexis, Jacques-Stephen
    "Chronique d'un faux amour," 240–1
Alien Resurrection (Jeunet, 1997 film),
    12, 289–92, 293
Aliens (1986 film), 12, 289
Alien 3 (1992 film), 12, 289
Allfrey, Phyllis Shand
    Orchid House, The, 249
Amadis de Gaul, 22
Amours de Charlot et Toinette, Les, 75
Anderson, Paul
    Event Horizon (1997 film), 296–298
Andrews, Miles Peter
    Enchanted Castle, The, 126
Anti-Jacobin, 55–6, 138
antiquarianism, 27, 29–30, 99, 100,
    108, 109, 113, 118–19, 147–8
Apparition, The, 45

Arabian Nights, 34, 35
Aristotle, 25
    Poetics, 22
Arasse, Daniel, 73
Askew, Alice and Claude
    "Alymer Vance and the Vampire,"
    205
Atwood, Margaret
    Handmaid's Tale, The, 271
Aubrey, Frank, 190
    Devil-Tree of El Dorado, The, 205
    King of the Dead, 201
    Queen of Atlantis, 205
Austen, Jane, 229
    Northanger Abbey, 52, 57–8, 59, 132

Babeof, François Emile, 78
Bachman, Richard
    Thinner, 271
Backscheider, Paula, 130
Badcock, Samuel, 36
Baldick, Chris
    Gothic Tales, 203, 205–6
Baillie, Joanna, 31
    Ethwald I, 94
    Ethwald II, 94
    Monfort, De, 127, 140
    Orra, 140
    Plays on the Passions, 59
Balzac, Honoré de
    Peau de Chagrin, La, 79
Banks, Iain, 107
Banville, John, 107
Barclay, John
    Argensis, 33